MO⬤N

_B_

D0396253

COASTAL OREGON

UPDATED BY JUDY JEWELL & BILL McRAE

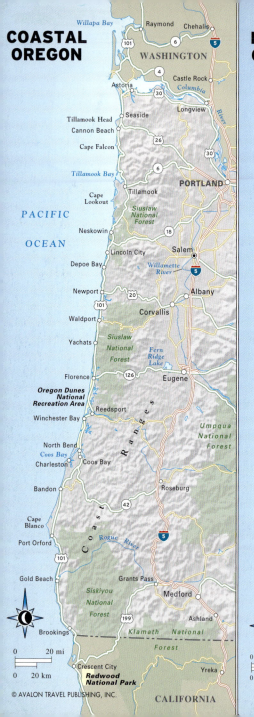

COASTAL OREGON

Willapa Bay
Raymond
Chehalis
WASHINGTON
Castle Rock
Columbia
Longview
Astoria
Seaside
Tillamook Head
Cannon Beach
Cape Falcon
Tillamook Bay
Cape Lookout
Tillamook
Siuslaw National Forest
PORTLAND
Neskowin
Salem
Lincoln City
Depoe Bay
Willamette River
Newport
Albany
Waldport
Corvallis
Yachats
Siuslaw National Forest
Fern Ridge Lake
Florence
Eugene
Oregon Dunes National Recreation Area
Reedsport
Winchester Bay
Umpqua National Forest
North Bend
Coos Bay
Charleston
Coos Bay
Bandon
Roseburg
Cape Blanco
Rogue River
Port Orford
Coast Ranges
Gold Beach
Grants Pass
Siskiyou National Forest
Medford
Ashland
Brookings
Klamath National Forest
Crescent City
Redwood National Park
Yreka
CALIFORNIA

PACIFIC OCEAN

0   20 mi
0   20 km

© AVALON TRAVEL PUBLISHING, INC.

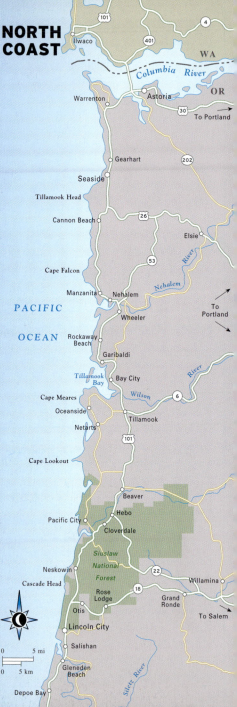

NORTH COAST

Ilwaco
Columbia River
WA
Warrenton
Astoria
OR
To Portland
Gearhart
Seaside
Tillamook Head
Cannon Beach
Elsie
Cape Falcon
Nehalem River
Manzanita
Nehalem
Wheeler
To Portland
Rockaway Beach
Garibaldi
Bay City
Tillamook Bay
Wilson River
Cape Meares
Oceanside
Tillamook
Netarts
Cape Lookout
Beaver
Hebo
Pacific City
Cloverdale
Siuslaw National Forest
Neskowin
Willamina
Cascade Head
Rose Lodge
Grand Ronde
Otis
To Salem
Lincoln City
Salishan
Gleneden Beach
Siletz River
Depoe Bay

PACIFIC OCEAN

0   5 mi
0   5 km

CENTRAL COAST

PACIFIC OCEAN

Neskowin
22
Siuslaw National Forest
Otis
18
Rose Lodge
Lincoln City
Salishan
Gleneden Beach
Depoe Bay
229
Cape Foulweather
Siletz
Logsden
Yaquina Head
Agate Beach
Newport
Toledo
Eddyville
20
To Corvallis
Siletz River

101
Waldport
Tidewater
To Corvallis
34
Alsea River
Cape Perpetua
Yachats
Siuslaw National Forest
Minerva
Swisshome
36
To Eugene
126
Florence
Siuslaw R.

Oregon Dunes National Recreation Area
101
Siltcoos Lake
Sulphur Springs
Tahkenitch Lake
Smith River
Gardiner
Reedsport
Winchester Bay
38
Scottsburg
Umpqua River
Eel Lake

0   5 mi
0   5 km

SOUTH COAST

Reedsport
Winchester Bay
To Florence
38
Eel Lake
N. Tenmile Lake
Lakeside
Tenmile Lake

Oregon Dunes National Recreation Area
101

PACIFIC OCEAN

Allegany
North Bend
Charleston
Coos Bay
Coos Bay
S. Fork Coos River
Cape Arago
Sumner
Coquille
425
Dora
Coquille Point
Norway
Bandon
Myrtle Point
42
Bridge
To Roseburg
South Fork Coquille River
101
Langlois
Denmark
Powers
Cape Blanco
Sixes
Port Orford
Siskiyou National Forest
Rogue River
Ophir
Agness
Illinois River
Wedderburn
Gold Beach
101
Rogue River
Carpenterville
Chetco River
Klamath Mountains
Siskiyou National Forest
Brookings
Harbor

0   5 mi
0   5 km

DISCOVER COASTAL OREGON

Oregon's 360 miles of Pacific coastline are the state's greatest tourist assets: a rugged mixture of forest, mountain, beach, bay, and river all fronting the tempestuous waves of the Pacific. In few other places is the meeting of land and sea so dramatic and beautiful as along this stretch of land and water from the mouth of the Columbia River to the redwood forests at the California border. Here, at the far western skirt of the continent, nature has found an expansive stage on which to act out the full range of its varied and ceaseless dramas, from the microcosm of a tidepool to the ferocious storms that make first landfall here, walloping the headlands and beaches with their full might. Like a series of postcards, rocky headlands rise high above the ocean, dropping away to the pounding waves in cliffs hundreds of feet high. Lone fingers of rock poke through sandy beaches and march out far into the surging waves. Seals, sea lions, puffins,

The graceful Siuslaw River bridge is a Florence landmark.

© PAUL LEVY

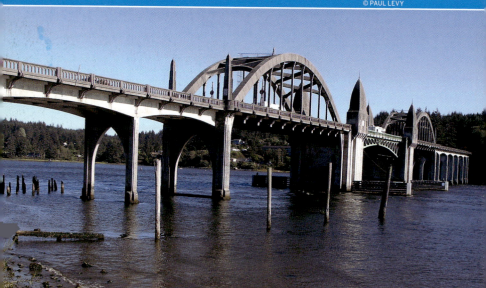

and innumerable shorebirds make their watery home in this marine wilderness. The Oregon coast is one of those blessed corners of the earth where you come upon fresh scenes of wonder at every turn.

The visitor here can find as intense a solitude as he or she might desire, in company of only the mewing seabirds, and experience firsthand why residents refer to this coast as The Edge. The comforts of civilization and human company are close by in an inviting string of towns and villages, each with its own character and charms, from the resurgent Victorian hospitality of Astoria to the family-friendly resort attractions of Seaside; from the understated sophistication of Cannon Beach or the hardworking fishing harbor of Newport to the New Age warmth of Bandon.

Although part of a seamless whole, sharing a common shoreline and linked by an unbroken scenic highway, each part of the coast

formal gardens at Shore Acres State Park

© MICHAEL MCCLURE

possesses a distinct regional flavor and allure that has attracted visitors for centuries.

In the north – journey's end for Lewis and Clark – steep headlands break up wide, sandy beaches, extending to the state's far northwestern tip at the mouth of the Columbia River. The northern Oregon coast is the most developed and heavily populated part of the coast, which is no surprise considering this region is just 1.5 hours from the Portland metro area, making it perfect for second homes and weekend getaways. However, ample state parks make it easy to escape from the crowds. Clumped up near the northern edge of the coast, historic Astoria, fun-loving Seaside, and artsy Cannon Beach are all within a short drive of one another, but are remarkably different in character. But don't think it's just one town after another here – huge areas of the coast are set aside as state parks, and there are ample opportunities to hike and camp.

The central coast is anchored at its northern end by sprawling Lincoln City (and its attendant lovely wide beaches) and is centered around Newport, the largest city in the area, with charming older

the Heceta Head Lighthouse on the Oregon coast

© PAUL LEVY

neighborhoods and several very good restaurants. At the southern end of the region, Florence and Reedsport are great bases for visits to the astounding Oregon Dunes, which form an otherworldly sand-scape dotted with lakes and bisected by broad, lazy estuaries.

The south coast feels far from everything, a landscape of mountains cloaked by dense evergreen forest, parting to reveal wild rivers and black-sand beaches punctuated with dramatic rock formations. Here the largest city is Coos Bay, joined by the adjacent North Bend. West of this mostly drab metropolis are wild and beautiful natural areas, including Cape Arago and the fascinating estuarine area at South Slough. Bandon is an almost perfect counterpoint to Coos Bay – small, cozy, and full of tourists (many there for the world-class golf courses at Bandon Dunes). The southernmost part of Oregon's coastline may well be its most scenic, especially the stretch between Gold Beach and Brookings.

Don't neglect the opportunity to get outdoors and experience firsthand the full range of recreation available here. Cycling the Oregon Coast Bike Route is a rite of passage for many bicycle tourists from around the world, and the Oregon Coast Trail provides hikers

face to face: watching the waves by Face Rock, Bandon

© STEFANO BONI

many opportunities to explore the coastline. The bays and estuaries are tempting destinations for kayakers, as they provide a watery backdrop for excellent marine bird- and wildlife-viewing. Diminished wild salmon runs have limited some coastal sportfishing expeditions, but the catch is still good for halibut, tuna, and bottom fish. And when fishing boats from Newport, Depoe Bay, Garibaldi, and Astoria aren't seeking finned prey, they offer whale-watching trips. Surfing the chill waters of the north Pacific is a relatively new sport to Oregon, but it's caught on big time.

Considering the scenic splendor of the Oregon coast, it may seem odd that it remains largely unblemished by upscale tourist infrastructure. In part, this is due to a far-sighted state government, which in the 1910s set aside as public land the entire length of Oregon's Pacific coastline. In addition, many miles are preserved as state parks – Oregon has nearly 50 state parks along the Pacific. In remarkable ways, the Oregon coast belongs to the people – or rather, it's a place of meeting where human visitors can encounter the creatures of the sea and forest and the mighty forces of nature.

Low tides near Cape Perpetua expose intertidal starfish.

© BILL MCRAE

Contents

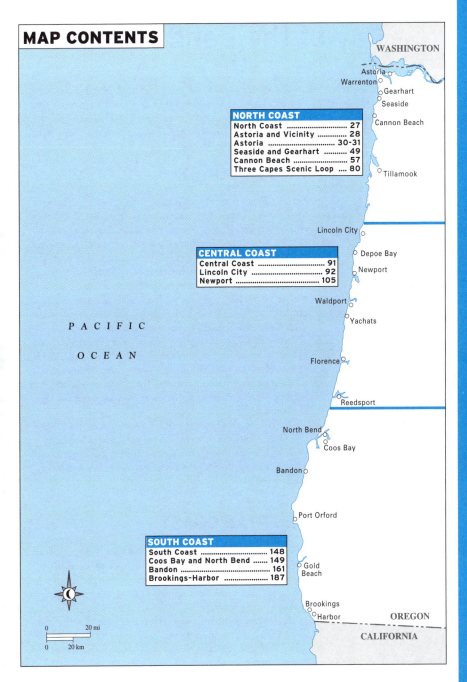

MAP CONTENTS

WASHINGTON

Astoria
Warrenton
Gearhart
Seaside
Cannon Beach

Tillamook

Lincoln City

Depoe Bay

Newport

Waldport

Yachats

Florence

Reedsport

North Bend

Coos Bay

Bandon

Port Orford

Gold Beach

Brookings

Harbor

OREGON

CALIFORNIA

PACIFIC

OCEAN

0   20 mi

0   20 km

11

The Lay of the Land

U.S. 101 hugs the Oregon coastline from Astoria, at the mouth of the Columbia River, to Brookings at the California border. This long and winding road links the entire Oregon coast, and many travelers will elect to follow this road the length of the coastline. However, there are subtle differences between the northern, central, and southern coasts, and travelers on a tight schedule may wish to concentrate their visit on a single region.

NORTH COAST

At the northern extremity of Oregon, historic Astoria is filled with Victorian-era homes, fine museums, historic sites, and a slacker charm that befits an aging seaport. Seaside and Cannon Beach are just seven miles apart in distance, but light years apart in attitude and atmosphere. Cannon Beach is artsy, elite, and perhaps the most attractive of Oregon's coastal towns. On the other hand, Seaside—with its bumper cars, fudge shops, video game arcades, throngs of children, and concrete Promenade along the beach—can often seem more like a high-energy, out-of-control circus. What they share, though, are miles and miles of sandy beaches.

Alongside Tillamook Bay, the working port of Garibaldi hosts one of the coast's busiest commercial fishing fleets, making this an excellent spot for sportfishing charters. The Tillamook area is famed for its dairies (as a whiff of the air will attest), and free tours of the huge Tillamook Cheese Factory are a popular family diversion.

The Three Capes Scenic Loop links three coastal promontories: Cape Meares provides impressive vistas with a handsomely squat lighthouse; Cape Lookout is a hikers' destination, and Cape Kiwanda provides the backdrop for surfers and beachcombers at Pacific City.

CENTRAL COAST

Lincoln City is an attenuated beach town with little in the way of quaint charm, but an abundance of inexpensive hotel rooms. The actual beachfront is very pleasant, though for drivers on U.S. 101 this seven-mile-long strip mall of a town is synonymous with congestion.

The Westin Salishan Lodge, seven miles south of Lincoln City, is the coast's premier resort. In addition to the noted 18-hole golf course, the lodge restaurant is recognized as one of the best in Oregon.

Past Depoe Bay, a tiny, rock-lined harbor noted for whale-watching boat tours, is the region's largest city, Newport, which offers stellar beaches, an active fishing harbor, good seafood restaurants, and the Oregon Coast Aquarium.

South of Yachats, the peaks of the Coast Range edge to the ocean's verge. This section of rugged coast, which includes the Cape Perpetua Scenic Area, contains a series of dramatic lava formations, tidepools, and the famous Sea Lion Caves, a natural sea grotto filled with roaring sea lions.

South of Florence, with its charming old harbor, is the Oregon Dunes National Recreation Area, the largest expanse of coastal sand dunes in the United States. The dunes front the Pacific Ocean but undulate east as much as three miles to meet coastal forests, with a succession of curious ecosystems in between.

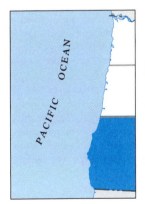

SOUTH COAST

The village of Bandon is the quintessential Oregon beach town, part artist colony, part New Age retreat, and part rough-edged logging center. Somehow it works, especially when seen against the backdrop of the spectacular beaches just south of town. Just north of town is Bandon Dunes Golf Club, one of the state's most renowned.

South of Bandon to the California border, the coastline grows more rugged. This stretch of the Oregon coast remains relatively pristine and is far from large population centers.

Port Orford sits in a dramatic location, with Humbug Mountain rising south of the town. Just to the north is Cape Blanco, the most westerly point in the continental United States, with the oldest and tallest operational lighthouse in Oregon.

At Gold Beach, the Rogue River enters the Pacific and from here jetboats leave on a variety of daylong Rogue River tours.

Four state parks protect much of the seacoast between Gold Beach and Brookings. Cliffs drop hundreds of feet into the surf, and steep hiking trails lead down to tiny, beautiful beaches huddled at the base of rocky canyons. Marching far out to sea are strings of tiny island chains, home to shore birds and braying sea lions. Grey whales edge close to this rugged coastline during their yearly migrations.

Planning Your Trip

Coastal Oregon boasts an ideal mix of recreational, cultural, and relaxation opportunities, in a natural setting as pleasing to the senses as any in the world. However, considering the scenic splendor of the Oregon coast, it may seem odd that it remains largely undeveloped by tourist infrastructure that this stirring seascape might have engendered elsewhere. Because Oregon has always been a rather poor rural state, few people had the money to build or frequent flashy developments of the sort common elsewhere. This means that food and lodging along much of the coast is decidedly casual, almost offhand. However, the scenery is fantastic and a number of small towns offer comfortable, unfussy hotels, resorts, and restaurants to welcome the traveler.

The Oregon coast is a popular destination with something for everyone, from families looking for a safe and inexpensive vacation, spring-breakers blowing off steam, couples seeking a romantic weekend away from the routine, hard-core hikers and surfers, to RV-driving retirees summering in a cooler clime. With all these people heading to the coast—often on the same weekend—a little forward planning can make all the difference.

If you are exploring the Oregon Coast by automobile, don't let its 360-mile length fool you into thinking you can drive it in a single day. The road is very slow, due to twisting grades and leisurely traffic. With a moderate number of stops for sightseeing, you should plan—at the very least—on three days to drive the entire Oregon Coast along U.S. 101. As you'll see below, we think you should allocate 10 days to see all the top sights and experience the glories of this marvelous coastline.

WHEN TO GO

Unless you're a died-in-the-wool rain-loving Northwesterner, you'll most likely want to visit the Oregon coast during the summer, when there's a far better chance of sunshine. Even then, it's best to bring a fleece jacket, for fog can put a real chill on things, and a windbreaker for the gale-force gusts that locals call "the breeze." It's also best to bring rain gear—we somewhat superstitiously consider it to be insurance against a summertime storm. But don't be surprised if a mid- to late-summer trip sees you wearing little more than shorts, a T-shirt, flip-flops, and sunscreen.

From late fall through spring, the hardcore storm watchers come to the coast to feel the blustery bite of rain pelting their faces as they walk the beaches. It can be really thrilling to stay in a beachfront motel or cottage (paying a fraction of the summertime rates) and watch the storm clouds roll in. And the big secret is that there can be absolutely beautiful weather in between storms when sun breaks through and temperatures are generally much milder than in other parts of the state.

Another reason to visit in December or late March (roughly Christmastime or spring break) is to see whales migrating between their winter homes off Baja California and their summertime grounds near Alaska. Look for "Whale Watching Spoken Here" signs to find good vantage points.

Seasons

The height of summer—July until Labor Day—is the peak time to visit the Oregon coast. Summer weather is mostly sunny, temperatures are moderate, and beach towns erupt with festivals and musical events. As you might expect, hotels, campgrounds, and restaurants can fill up fast. Reserve rooms as early as you can, particularly if you're hoping to stay at some of the coast's newer and more upscale hotels.

Also remember that the Oregon coast, even in August, doesn't guarantee a laze-by-the-beach, swim-in-the-surf kind of vacation. When high pressure builds in interior Oregon—for instance, when Portland and the Willamette Valley have prolonged periods with temperatures over 90°F—then cool marine air is pulled in off the Pacific and obscures the coast, resulting in the same kind of chilly summer fogs common to San Francisco. Another consideration for people who aren't locked into summer holidays by children with school schedules is the sheer mass of people that descend onto the coast in summer, particularly during August. Coast roads can be absolutely jammed, and beaches, particularly in northern towns like Seaside, Cannon Beach, and Lincoln City, can have their own human traffic issues.

Finally, newcomers to the region at any time of year should know that the icy temperatures of the coastal waters (as low as 40–45°F) make the beaches more valued for beachcombing than for swimming. Even in the hottest days of summer, water temperature doesn't exceed 62°F, and hypothermia is an ever-present danger that sometimes kills.

Keep in mind that the coast isn't just for summer anymore. Increasingly, it's becoming a year-round destination. Sunny and warm weather usually lasts well into October, making early fall an excellent time to visit, particularly for people without school-age children. When winter weather arrives—usually in November, lasting through February—another kind of visitor arrives at the coast to enjoy what some euphemistically call the storm-watching season. The warm-weather crowds are long gone, beaches are deserted, seafood is at its prime, and prices at most lodgings drop to very attractive rates.

Spring starts in March and lasts through June, when weather is unpredictable. Brilliant sunny days are followed by lashing storms.

Spring temperatures along the coast are often higher than those in the interior valleys, and seaside gardens and coastal forests respond with a glorious display of early spring growth and blossoms. Bear in mind that spring school holidays are staggered throughout the Northwest during mid-March and early April; hotels can be surprisingly busy during what should be an off-season.

WHAT TO TAKE

Oregon is notoriously casual, and it's hard to underdress here. Even the finest restaurants demand no more than clean jeans and a nice shirt. That said, if it's more your style to dress up, you won't be out of place in the larger towns or resort hotels.

Even in the summer, evenings and mornings will be cool, so bring a sweater and a jacket. At any time of year, it's a good idea to pack rain gear, although you probably won't need it in the summer. In the fall, winter, and spring, it is essential, if you plan to do much hiking or biking, to bring breathable waterproof gear, and rain pants are a vital part of the outfit. A rain hat is a better item to pack than an umbrella—coastal winds will make short work of the average umbrella.

If you're camping along the beach, it's best to have a warm sleeping bag, a fleece jacket, a tent with a rain fly, and a ground cloth. Aside from that, let your packing list be determined by your own inclinations.

Be sure to bring binoculars and a wildlife guidebook, as you're likely to see marinelife, and it will make your trip a richer experience if you're able to easily view and identify birds and marine mammals. The coast offers innumerable opportunities to watch birdlife; pinnipeds, particularly sea lions and seals, as well as gray whales, are commonly sighted.

Explore Coastal Oregon

COASTAL HIGHWAY ROAD TRIP

For many travelers, following the coastal highway U.S. 101 along the rugged Oregon coast is a trip of a lifetime. Although the coast route counts just 360 miles, don't try to rush this trip or squeeze it into anything less than three days. Twisting roads, heavy traffic, and jaw-dropping vistas are sure to slow you down, so start out by planning flexibility into your schedule.

If you're not lucky enough to have time for a trip spanning the entire coast and need to sample just a section of the coast, it's easy to use the I-5 freeway corridor (roughly 60 to 80 miles inland) as a quick north or south arterial, cutting over to the coast near to your destination.

So feel free to tinker with this strict north–south itinerary. If you are flying in and out of Portland, it may make sense to leapfrog your way down the coast, catching the intervening towns on your way back north.

Day 1

From Portland, drive northwest to **Astoria,** a city full of history and spunky do-it-yourself charm. Visit the **Columbia River Maritime Museum** to learn about the area's maritime past, and check out the city's many art galleries to sense its more contemporary currents. Walk the hilly streets behind downtown to view resplendent Victorian homes. Spend the night at the Cannery Pier Hotel beneath the over-four-mile-long Astoria-Megler Bridge, which spans the mighty Columbia.

Day 2

Drive south, stopping by the replica **Fort Clatsop National Memorial,** which served as Lewis and Clark's winter home in 1805 and 1806. If the day is fair, drive to **Fort Stevens State Park** to stroll along the shore, or simply continue to **Cannon Beach,** with its dramatic beach dominated by sea stacks. Stroll through the town's attractive and maze-like downtown shopping district, and stay at the Stephanie Inn.

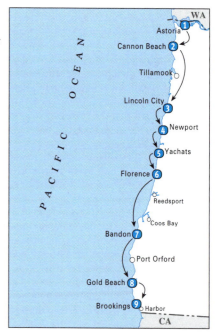

Day 3

From Cannon Beach, drop through the lush temperate rainforest in **Oswald West State Park,** stopping on the flanks of Neahkahnie Mountain, atop 700-foot cliffs, to admire the views of the Pacific and the Nehalem River Bay. Stop for lunch in the commercial fishing village **Garibaldi,** with some of the freshest and tastiest fish and chips you're likely to eat. In Tillamook, stop at the unique **Tillamook**

Air Museum, housed in a former World War II blimp hangar, to view a collection of historic planes. The hangar itself is worth the admission. Continue south to **Lincoln City** via U.S. 101, staying at the Star Fish Manor.

Day 4

From Lincoln City continue south to **Depoe Bay,** worth a stop to admire the pocket harbor, then take Otter Crest scenic loop, cresting at the Cape Foulweather vista. You'll reach **Newport** before lunch, which is lucky because you'll want to have two meals' worth of eating to explore the good food here. Spend the afternoon at the **Oregon Coast Aquarium** and the night at the Elizabeth Street Inn.

Day 5

This is a short day of driving, because you'll want to save time to hike. Proceed south to **Yachats,** one of the coast's most charming towns and gateway to **Cape Perpetua,** a wonderful natural area where mountains meet the sea and acres of tidepools rise above the surf. Meanwhile, you've reserved rooms at the very comfortable Overleaf Lodge, and all that hiking along Cape Perpetua has you hungry for dinner at one of Yachat's excellent restaurants.

Day 6

Florence is set alongside the Siuslaw River, and its riverside Old Town will briefly steal your attention away from the ocean. It's a good base for exploring the **Oregon Dunes,** which start just south of town and rise up to 500 feet tall. Hike through this striking habitat, or go for the thrills of a dune buggy ride or sandboarding. Spend the night in Florence.

Day 7

Although **Coos Bay** doesn't beckon the average traveler, it is the gateway to some astoundingly beautiful headlands and beaches just west. Don't miss blustery Cape Arago and the gardens of Shore Acres State Park. Head south along Seven Devils Road and spend the night in **Bandon.** With its Old Town, beaches, and golfing at internationally touted Bandon Dunes Golf Resort, this town demands attention. Bandon is laid back and easy to explore on foot, with more good restaurants than you'd expect.

Day 8

It's tempting to shrug off Gold Beach's jetboat tours up the mighty **Rogue River** as hokey tourist schlock, but these rides are actually pretty great, with good commentary and the chance to see bald eagles and other wildlife.

Day 9

Between Gold Beach and Brookings, the coastline is at its finest, with many pullouts offering paths down to secluded rocky beaches. Be prepared with a sweatshirt and a windbreaker and spend an afternoon exploring this stretch. In **Brookings,** it's important to stop for a walk and some bird-watching at Harris Beach State Park, but also get off the coastal strip and explore the Chetco River. Afred A. Loeb State Park has good river access and a path through myrtle and redwood trees.

Day 10

If you're heading back to the I-5 corridor after your tour of the coast, consider dropping down to Crescent City, California, and heading inland on U.S. 199. This highway, which you pick up 22 miles south of the state border, passes through the northern edge of the California redwoods on its way to I-5 at Grants Pass, Oregon.

AN OUTDOOR ENTHUSIAST'S PARADISE

Visitors to coastal Oregon are often astounded at the large number and high quality of the state parks here. Indeed, there are nearly 80 state parks—19 with campgrounds—easily accessible from U.S. 101 in Oregon. In addition, where national forest land reaches out to the coast, there are Forest Service campgrounds. Parks are located at all of the coast's most beautiful places, making access easy and affordable.

North Coast

A dramatic start to a tour of the coast's parks begins at the point where the Columbia River enters the Pacific, at the northern edge of the huge **Fort Stevens State Park.** Miles of bike and hiking trails lead past abandoned gunneries (this was originally a Civil War military station); along the beach, the skeletal remains of the *Peter Iredale* shipwreck is a focal point. The campground here is the state's largest—stay here if you want showers and a kid-friendly atmosphere; for more solitude, head south and inland a bit to camp at **Saddle Mountain State Park,** located at the base of a fantastic hiking trail.

Get up early and drive south past Cannon Beach to **Oswald West State Park,** a small hike-in campground nestled in an old-growth forest with trails to Short Sand Beach, Cape Falcon, and Neahkahnie Mountain. If you aren't able to score a site here, or would rather just be on the safe side and reserve ahead, plan to spend the night at Nehalem Bay State Park, a short beach walk from the lovely little town of Manzanita.

Head south to Tillamook and pick up the Three Capes Loop. The state park at **Cape Lookout** will be your bedding-down place, but take time to explore the parks at Cape Meares (bring the binoculars and look for puffins on the rocks here) and Oceanside. South of Cape Lookout, visit **Cape Kiwanda** to climb up on the bluff and run down the sand dunes.

Central Coast

As you pass through the more developed areas of Lincoln City, Depoe Bay, and Newport, be sure to stop at some of the day-use parks along

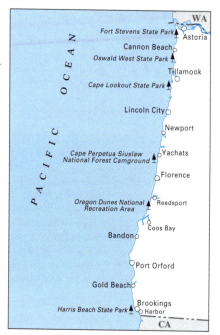

the way. **Boiler Bay,** a mile north of Depoe Bay, is a great place to explore tidepools and ponder the power of the surf, and **Yaquina Head,** at the north end of Newport, is good for a couple of hours of exploration. For the night, stay at the **Siuslaw National Forest** campground at Cape Perpetua.

After hiking the trails and exploring the tidepools at Cape Perpetua, continue south to the **Oregon Dunes.** Here you'll have your choice between a number of Forest Service campgrounds between Florence and Reedsport, including those at the Waxmyrtle and Carter and Taylor Dunes trails, and a couple of state park spots (Tugman and Umpqua Lighthouse) south of Reedsport.

South Coast

Head to the western edge of the continental United States and pitch your tent at **Cape Blanco.** Along with the trails around the cape and down to the beach, be sure to visit the historic lighthouse.

Take your time on the trip south from Cape Blanco. Here, in the stretch between Gold Beach and Brookings, are the many roadside pull-outs along the 12 miles of **Samuel H. Boardman State Park.** Drop in for a walk along Whaleshead or Lone Ranch Beaches, or hike the Oregon Coast Trail between a couple of coves. At the north end of Brookings, **Harris Beach State Park** is a bustling campground near another lovely beach.

RIDING THE PACIFIC WAVES

Surfing is increasingly popular in Oregon, but it can be a little confusing to know where to go, especially if you're a novice. Spend a week dropping in on the following spots, selected with a special nod to places where a beginner can show up without feeling too out of place. Don't skimp on the wetsuit accessories—a hood and booties are often the key to staying comfortable.

Before setting out on this surf vacation, invest in or rent a good wetsuit; that, along with strong swimming skills, will go a long way toward making this a fun trip rather than an ordeal. Surf shops in Seaside, Cannon Beach, Lincoln City, Depoe Bay, and Newport and a sporting-goods store in Brookings can supply rental gear. Surf with a buddy, and be aware that sharks do occasionally show up at surf spots. A good website, www.oregonsurf.com, has some tips and links to forecasting sites and webcams.

Cannon Beach Area

Start off with a class. Oregon Surf Adventures and Northwest Women's Surf Camps both offer friendly, supportive instructors and fun programs.

If you're lucky, you'll score a walk-in spot at Oswald West, and spend the day practicing at Oz West's **Short Sands Beach.** More advanced surfers may want to check out the cove at **Indian Beach,** at the foot of Ecola State Park; this beach is also popular with surf kayakers. Seaside can be fiercely locals-only and is not recommended for beginners.

Lincoln City to Newport

Another spot for surfers who know what they're doing is the **Road's End State Recreation Area** beach at the very north end of Lincoln City. Stop here for a while, or continue south to the somewhat protected beach at **Otter Rock,** a few miles south of Depoe Bay. Otter Rock is quite popular, and a good place for beginners. Spend the night down in Newport, where Beverly Beach campground, just north of town, is a large campground that takes reservations.

In Newport, you can try **Agate Beach** (the parking is right next to the tall Best Western hotel) or head south of town to South Beach State Park.

Florence to Charleston

Pack up and head south, perhaps with a stop at Florence's South Jetty, to Charleston, where you can check out the waves at **Bastendorff Beach County Park.** There's also a nice campground at Bastendorff, as well as the large Sunset Beach State Park campground a few miles away. (Sunset Beach itself is mostly a swimming beach.)

Floras Lake

Head south through Bandon to the little town of Langlois, and turn in toward the ocean and Floras Lake, where you'll break it up with a day of windsurfing at Floras Lake. Lessons and equipment rentals are easy to come by here, and the wind is almost always ripping.

Port Orford to Brookings

It may be time to head back north, dropping in on your new favorite surf spots. But if you're headed all the way down the coast, pull off the highway at Port Orford to see if the surf is up at **Battle Rock Beach.** Otherwise, aim for **Sporthaven Beach** on the Brookings jetty south of the Chetco River, a popular all-levels surf beach.

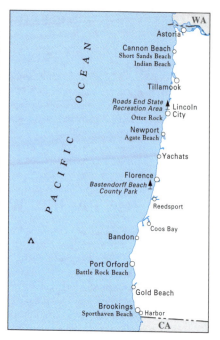

COZY SEASIDE INNS

Oregon doesn't have many big resorts along the coast—instead, it features many smaller bed-and-breakfasts and inns. This travel itinerary highlights the top spots for a cozy and comfortable stay at smaller and typically Oregon-style lodgings.

Astoria

Astoria's **Hotel Elliott** isn't really an inn—in fact, when it was built in the 1920s, it was the classiest place to stay in Astoria. And, after a more than $4 million makeover in 2003, it still is. This historic hotel with lovingly refurbished rooms will get a coast trip off to a great start.

Nehalem Bay

After nosing in and out of coastal harbors, you may wish that you had brought your boat along. Why bother: At Nehalem's **Ripple Run Resort,** you can settle in for the night on

floating but moored boats, including a tugboat and a choice of barges, in a quiet spot along the Nehalem River.

Depoe Bay

The Channel House in Depoe Bay offers that perfect contrast of luxury and primitive environment. Watch the surging tides colliding with the rocky shore and fishing boats negotiating the narrow harbor from the comfort of your outdoor whirlpool tub.

Newport

History and literature intersect at the **Sylvia**

Beach Hotel in Newport, a one-of-a-kind historic hotel cum B&B where all the rooms are decorated in literary themes. The Edgar Allan Poe room, anyone?

Yachats

There are few more charming locales than the parklike setting at Yachats' **Shamrock Lodgettes.** While you have a choice of vintage cabins or modern motel rooms, of course you want the 1930s-era log cabins, complete with stone fireplace and snug kitchen. From your cabin, it's a short two-minute stroll to the beach, without having to cross a busy highway. These cabins are places to create great family memories.

Bandon

Bandon's **Sea Star Guesthouse** is right in Old Town, just across from the waterfront. Although there are more elegant places to stay in Bandon (for instance, any of the accommodations at the Bandon Dunes Golf Resort), this is the place that'll make you feel like you're part of the heartbeat of this charming town. Even budget travelers can afford the hostel rooms here.

Port Orford

Drop into a meditative calm at **Wildspring Guest Habitat,** perched above the Pacific Ocean in Port Orford. Everything here is designed to lead you to a state of serenity, whether it's the labyrinth walk, the exquisite hot tub, the meditation alcoves, or the hammock outside your cabin.

Gold Beach

Upriver from Gold Beach, **Tu Tu Tun Resort** is the only full-out resort on the south coast, and it's a wonderful place to feel pampered in a thoroughly Oregonian kind of way. But another good bet along the lower Rogue is the **Rogue River Lodge,** an erstwhile budget motel that's been totally remodeled into comfy riverside suites.

Brookings

Down in Brookings, there are a couple of fine B&Bs. If you want to be near the ocean, stay at the **South Coast Inn,** an elegant Bernard Maybeck–designed house; if you'd rather be up the Chetco River, near the Kalmiopsis Wilderness Area, surrounded by lavender gardens, the **Chetco River Inn** is the best bet.

FORAGING THE COAST

Fishing, crabbing, clamming, and mussel-gathering isn't just fun, it's what's for dinner. There's plenty for foragers to eat along the Oregon coast, if you know where to look for it.

All crabbers and clam-diggers need a shellfish license, available pretty much any place that rents crab traps ($6.50 resident, $16.50 out of state, $9 for a three-day nonresident license).

Clamming is best during a "minus" tide, when more beach is exposed. Equipment consists of a shovel, a bucket, and—ideally—rubber boots. It's also helpful to have a dowel or stick to use as a probe and clam-marker. Look for the clam holes, and dig toward the ocean side.

Pay attention to the signs at the entrance to the beach—they may be telling you about health precautions. Occasionally shellfish toxins mandate the closure of certain areas. These higher levels of bacteria and toxins are most likely to occur during the summer, and they are carefully monitored by the Oregon Department of Agriculture: check www.oregon.gov/ODA/FSD/shellfish_status.shtml for details.

Astoria

The mother of all salmon rivers is the Columbia. While Astoria was once one of the world's top fishing ports, precipitous declines in salmon runs have spelled doom for its once abundant salmon packaging plants. However, there is **seasonal sportfishing** for most salmon runs, and tuna, halibut and bottom fish harvesting is strong; plenty of **charter fishing** operations are ready to take you out to where the big ones are biting.

Garibaldi

Garibaldi is a scrappy little fishing village on Tillamook Bay, where you'll have no trouble joining a charter boat heading out for whatever's in season. **Crabbing** is also a high point, as are **local oysters,** found at the Pacific Oyster processing plant at nearby Bay City, where you can forego foraging and just buy and eat your fish or seafood while watching shuckers battle against a mountain of bivalves.

Newport

Oregon's second-largest **fishing fleet** departs from Newport, and the bayfront here is a wonderful spot to plan a fishing or **whale-watching** trip. Right in the midst of barking seals and the smells of fishing boats, you can also score some of the freshest fish and seafood you'll ever find in numerous harborside restaurants.

Cape Perpetua

Northwesterners didn't catch on to mussels until recently, and it's still news to many locals that the black-shelled bivalves that coat the rocks and tidepools here are good eating. Harvesting **wild mussels** along the rugged Cape Perpetua shores is easy, though be sure to watch for signs, particularly in hot summer weather, which alert shellfish gatherers of toxic algae blooms and dangerous levels of bacteria. Bring a pot, a bottle of white wine, and some garlic. Light a campfire, and you've got a meal.

Winchester Bay

Just south of Reedsport, the tiny town of Winchester Bay is almost entirely given over to fishing. Along with a busy commercial fishing port, there are many charter operators here who will take you out to the ocean for **salmon, halibut, tuna, or bottom fish.** Even if you aren't fishing, a meal at one of the dockside restaurants here will allow you to eat close to the source.

Charleston

Charleston is so thoroughly pervaded with seafood that even the angler's grudging spouse will get caught up in the excitement. Don't like fishing charters, or want to forage on the cheap? No problem... get to **crabbing and clamming** instead. Local shops here rent gear; crab right off the pier, and clam on the beaches at Charleston or on Coos Bay's North Spit.

Bandon

In Bandon, stop by the bait store at the Old

Town docks to pick up some crab traps, then go toss them over the side of the dock. Hang around and check the traps every so often—if you bring in a haul and don't want to fuss with the cooking and cleaning, just head back to the bait store and have them prepare the **crabs** for you.

Rogue River

Anglers will want to stay a couple of days in Gold Beach, either in town or up the Rogue River, famous for its salmon and steelhead runs. **Spring Chinook salmon, fall king salmon, silver salmon, summer and winter steelhead**—all these runs are of legendary proportion. It's best to go with a guide in a boat, and just about every local you'll meet is a guide.

Chetco River

Although it's not as well known as the Rogue, the Chetco River upstream from Brookings is also good for late fall and winter salmon and steelhead fishing. Mostly, though, Brookings is a good place to take a charter out into the ocean to fish for **salmon and bottom fish.**

NORTH COAST

The north coast, from the mouth of the Columbia River south to Lincoln City, is little more than an hour's drive from the Portland metro area, and the region is the most popular of Oregon's Pacific shoreline. Still, apart from the weekend crush at Cannon Beach and Seaside, there's more than enough elbowroom for everyone along this enchanting and varied coast.

Overlooking the Columbia River as it flows into Pacific, the former shipping and canning center of Astoria is fast rediscovering its own potential, with a lively arts scene, adventurous cuisine, and brightly painted Victorian homes hosting overnighters for bed and breakfast. Its long-idle waterfront is growing busy again with tourist attractions—most notably the wonderful Columbia River Maritime Museum, one of the best in the west.

West of Astoria, at Oregon's far northwestern tip, where the mighty Columbia River meets the Pacific, visitors to Fort Stevens State Park can inspect the skeleton of a century-old shipwreck, as well as a military fort active from the Civil War to World War II—as well as revel in miles of sandy beaches. Fort Clatsop National Memorial (now part of Lewis and Clark National Park) includes a re-creation of the Corps of Discovery's winter 1805–1806 quarters—a must-stop for Lewis and Clark buffs.

Cannon Beach and Seaside are two extremely popular resort towns that are polar opposites of one another. Cannon Beach, an understated enclave of tastefully weathered cedar-shingled architecture, is chockablock with art galleries, boutiques, and upscale lodgings and restaurants. Seaside is Oregon's quintessential fam-

© BILL MCRAE

HIGHLIGHTS

[(Columbia River Maritime Museum:
One of Oregon's top museums, it tells the story
of seafaring on the Columbia River (page 31).

[(Flavel House Museum: An astounding
mansion from Astoria's Victorian heyday, the
museum is filled with antiques and amazing
woodwork (page 33).

[(Fort Clatsop National Memorial: This
replica of Lewis and Clark's 1805–1806 winter
camp offers a fascinating glimpse into frontier life (page 34).

[(Haystack Rock: The highlight of Cannon
Beach, this soaring sea stack is home to thousands of seabirds (page 57).

[(Saddle Mountain State Park: This
knobby mountain rises high above the northern coast, with a hiking trail leading through
unusual plantlife on the way to an eye-popping
vista (page 60).

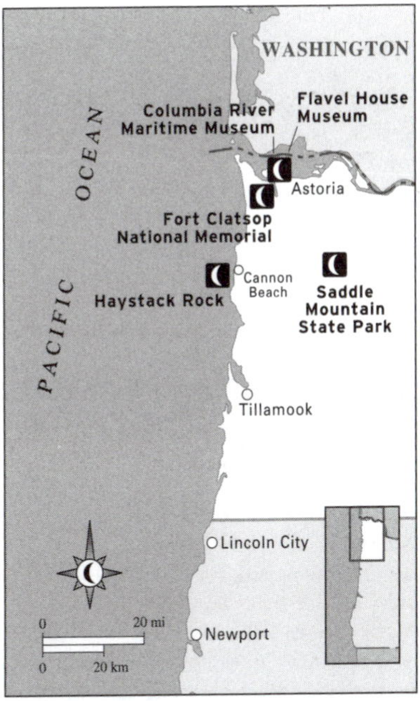

WASHINGTON

Columbia River
Maritime Museum

Flavel House
Museum

OCEAN

Astoria

Fort Clatsop
National Memorial

Haystack Rock

Cannon
Beach

Saddle
Mountain
State Park

PACIFIC

Tillamook

Lincoln City

0   20 mi

0   20 km

Newport

LOOK FOR [(TO FIND RECOMMENDED SIGHTS,
ACTIVITIES, DINING, AND LODGING.

ily-friendly beach resort, with a long boardwalk, candy and gift shops, and noisy game arcades.

Just south, Oswald West State Park is a gem protecting old-growth forest and hand-some little pocket beaches, as well as, some believe, a Spanish pirate treasure buried on Neahkahnie Mountain. Beyond Neahkahnie's cliff-top viewpoints along U.S. 101, the Ne-halem Bay area attracts anglers, crabbers, and kayakers, as well as discriminating diners who come from far and wide to enjoy surprisingly sophisticated cuisine.

Tillamook County is home to more cows than people and is synonymous with delicious dairy products—cheese and ice cream in par-ticular. It's no surprise that Tillamook's biggest visitor attraction is cheese-related. More than

a million people a year come to the Tillamook Cheese Factory to tour the cheese-making op-erations and sample the excellent results. The Tillamook Air Museum is another popular diversion, housing an outstanding collection of vintage and modern aircraft in gargantuan Hangar B, the largest wooden structure in the world. Tillamook Bay, fed by five rivers, yields great harvests of oysters and crab, while the active Garibaldi charter fleet targets salmon, halibut, and tuna in the offshore waters.

South of Tillamook, the Coast Highway wends inland through its lush pastureland to Neskowin. It's a pleasant enough stretch, but the Three Capes Scenic Loop, a 35-mile sce-nic coastal detour, is a more attractive if time-consuming option. The spectacular views and bird-watching from Capes Meares and Lookout introduce the attraction of this beautiful drive. At Pacific City, at the southern end of the Three Capes Loop, commercial anglers launch their dories right off the sandy beach and through the surf in the lee of Cape Kiwanda and mammoth Haystack Rock—a sight not seen anywhere else on the West Coast. Just north of Lincoln City, Cascade Head beckons hikers to explore its rare prairie headlands ecosystem.

PLANNING YOUR TIME

In general, the North Coast is a destination for two types of trips: those that focus on coastal towns with the beach a backdrop to relaxed dining, shopping, golfing, museum visiting, and simply hanging-out, or those that celebrate outdoorsy recreation such as camping, hiking, boating, biking, and fishing. Of course, these aren't either/or choices, and many people combine a coastal hike with a bit of gallery hopping and boutique shopping. However, it's good to keep in mind when planning a trip to the North Coast that state parks and national forests offer many opportunities for outdoor adventure—even in rain and winter you can enjoy a hike or explore tidepools.

Astoria and Vicinity

The mouth of the mighty Columbia River, with its abundance of natural resources, was long a traditional meeting place for the Native American tribes of this region. Early European explorers and settlers found the river and its bays to be propitious as a trading and fishing center. These features continue to lure travelers seeking prime recreational opportunities to this historic seaport community.

Astoria is the oldest permanent U.S. settlement west of the Rockies, and its glory days are preserved by museums, historical exhibits, and pastel-colored Victorian homes weathered by the sea air. Hollywood has chosen Astoria's picturesque neighborhoods to simulate an idealized all-American town on close to a dozen occasions.

Such idealization often creates the expectation of a Williamsburg of the West, where the portrayal of history and heritage is a focal point of the local identity. The reality of modern-day Astoria, however, is more accurately captured in a locally popular bumper sticker that defiantly proclaims, "We Ain't Quaint!" Instead, Astoria is a real city, warts and all. The preserved pioneer past and attractive Victorian homes may soften the rough edges of a once-bustling port that has seen better days, but not enough to let anyone mistake blue-collar Astoria for an ersatz tourist town. The decommissioning of the U.S. Naval station after World War II, the decline in the logging and fishing industries, and the closure of several dozen canneries on the waterfront have had lasting effects on this town of 10,000 people. Empty storefronts here tell the story of a resource-based economy bruised by progress, but there's plenty of pluck left in this old dowager, and her best years may be yet to come.

Astoria hath many charms: Historic buildings downtown are undergoing restoration, cruise ships are calling, fine restaurants are multiplying, a lively music and arts scene is

© BILL MCRAE

The Astoria-Megler Bridge is 4.1 miles long.

thriving, and there's new life along the waterfront, anchored by the excellent Columbia River Maritime Museum.

Orientation

The waters surrounding Astoria define the town as much as the steep hills it's built on. Along its northern side, the mighty Columbia, four miles wide, is a mega-highway carrying a steady flow of traffic, from small pleasure boats to massive cargo ships a quarter mile long. Soaring high over the river is an engineering marvel that's impossible to miss from most locations in town. At just over four miles long, the Astoria-Megler Bridge, completed in 1966, is the longest bridge in Oregon and the longest bridge of its type (cantilever through truss) in the world. On Astoria's south side, the Young's River, flowing down from the Coast Range, broadens into Young's Bay, separating Astoria from its neighbor Warrenton (pop. 4,000) to the west.

A few miles to the northwest, the Columbia River finally meets the Pacific, 1,243 miles from its headwaters in British Columbia. Where the tremendous outflow (average 118 million gallons per minute) of the River of the West encounters the ocean tides, conditions can be treacherous, and the sometimes-monstrous waves around the bar have claimed more than 2,000 vessels over the years. This river mouth could well be the biggest widow-maker on the high seas, earning it the title Graveyard of the Pacific. Lewis and Clark referred to it as "that seven-shouldered horror" in a journal entry from the winter of 1805–1806.

Any visitor to Astoria should consider crossing the Astoria-Megler Bridge to visit the extreme southwest corner of Washington State. Here the sands and soil carried by the Columbia create a 20-mile long sand spit called the Long Beach Peninsula. Some of the West Coast's most succulent oysters grow in Willapa Bay, the body of water created by this finger of sand. Historic beach communities plus numerous Lewis and Clark sites also reward the visitor to this charming enclave (see sidebar *The Long Beach Peninsula*).

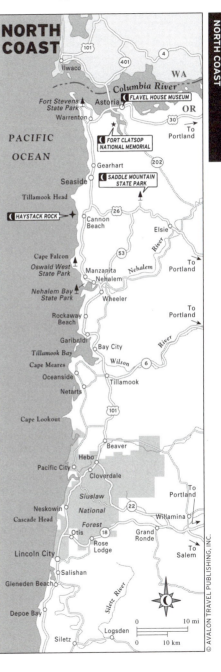

© AVALON TRAVEL PUBLISHING, INC.

NORTH COAST

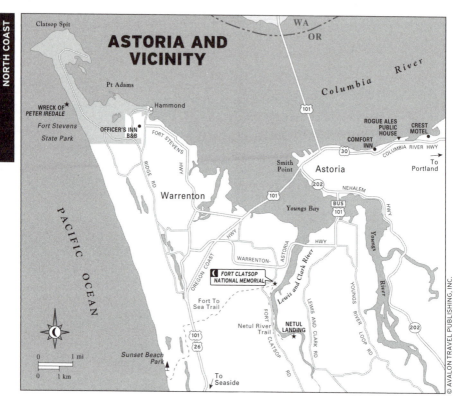

ASTORIA AND VICINITY

Clatsop Spit

Pt Adams

WRECK OF PETER IREDALE

Fort Stevens State Park

Hammond

OFFICER'S INN B&B

FORT STEVENS HWY

RIDGE RD

PACIFIC OCEAN

Warrenton

WA
OR

Columbia River

101

ROGUE ALES PUBLIC HOUSE

COMFORT INN

CREST MOTEL

COLUMBIA RIVER HWY

30

Smith Point

Astoria

To Portland

202

NEHALEM

BUS 101

101

Youngs Bay

HWY

WARRENTON-ASTORIA HWY

OREGON COAST HWY

Lewis and Clark River

LEWIS AND CLARK RD

Youngs River

YOUNGS RIVER LOOP RD

202

FORT CLATSOP NATIONAL MEMORIAL

Fort To Sea Trail

Netul River Trail

NETUL LANDING

FORT CLATSOP RD

101

26

Sunset Beach Park

To Seaside

0   1 mi
0   1 km

© AVALON TRAVEL PUBLISHING, INC.

HISTORY

The Clatsop Indians, a Chinook-speaking tribe, lived in this area for thousands of years before Astoria's written history began. When Lewis and Clark arrived in 1805, the Clatsops numbered about 400 people, living in three villages on the south side of the Columbia River, but began a steady decline soon after contact with whites.

The region was first chronicled by Don Bruno de Heceta, a Spanish explorer who sailed near the Columbia's mouth in August 1775. He named it the Bay of the Assumption of Our Lady, but the strong current prevented his ship from entering. American presence on the Columbia began with Captain Robert Gray's discovery of the river in May 1792, which he christened after his fur-trading ship, *Columbia Rediviva*.

Thereafter, Lewis and Clark's famous expe-

dition of 1803–1806, with its winter encampment at Fort Clatsop, south of present-day Astoria, helped incorporate the Pacific Northwest as part of a new nation. In 1811, John Jacob Astor's agents built Fort Astoria on a hillside in what would eventually grow into Astoria—the first American settlement west of the Rockies. Despite temporary occupation by the British between 1813 and 1818, the fort and a shaky American presence were able to hold on until settlers came to farm the region during the Oregon Trail era of the 1840s. During the Civil War, Fort Stevens was built to guard against a Confederate naval incursion.

From that time until the 1900s, the dominant immigrants to the Astoria area were Scandinavian. Commerce grew with the export of lumber and foodstuffs to gold rush–era San

Francisco and the Far East. Salmon canneries became the mainstay of Astoria's economy during the 1870s, helping it grow into Oregon's second-largest city—and a notorious shanghaiing port. Over the ensuing decades, logging, fishing, and shipbuilding coaxed the population up to 20,000 by World War II.

Some believe that the port city might have grown to rival San Francisco or Seattle had it not been for the setback of a devastating fire in 1922. In the early morning hours of December 8, a pool hall on Commercial Street caught fire, and the flames spread rapidly among the wooden buildings, many supported on wooden pilings, of Astoria's business district. By daybreak, more than 200 businesses in a 32-block area had been reduced to smoldering heaps. The downtown was rebuilt in the ensuing years, largely in brick and stone, but the devastation changed the fate of Astoria.

Near the end of World War II, a Japanese submarine's shelling of Fort Stevens made it the only fortification on American soil to have sustained an attack in a world war. After the war, the region's fortunes ebbed and flowed with its resource-based economy. In an attempt to supplement that economy with tourism, the State Highway Division began constructing the Astoria-Megler Bridge in 1962 to connect Oregon and Washington. When it opened in 1966, the bridge provided the final link in 1,625-mile-long U.S. 101.

Unfortunately, preserving Astoria's glory days could not make up for the closing of the canneries and the decline of logging and fishing. The modern era has been characterized by a steady cultivation of tourism dollars, resulting in the thoughtful development of the waterfront, including the two-mile River Walk and plans for a conference center at the port. Astoria is becoming an increasingly popular port-of-call for cruise ships, with more than a dozen visiting per year. Whether or not Astoria's ship ever comes in, let's hope the unpretentious charm of this hillside city-by-the-sea will not be lost in the process.

SIGHTS
Astoria Column
The best introduction to Astoria and envi-

rons is undoubtedly the 360-degree panorama from atop the 125-foot-tall Astoria Column on Coxcomb Hill, the highest point in town. Patterned after the Trajan Column in Rome, the reinforced-concrete tower was built in 1926 as a joint project of the Great Northern Railroad and the descendants of John Jacob Astor to commemorate the westward sweep of discovery and migration. The graffito frieze spiraling up the exterior illustrates Robert Gray's 1792 discovery of the Columbia River, the establishment of American claims to the Northwest Territory, the arrival of the Great Northern Railway, and other scenes of Northwest history. The vista from the surrounding hilltop park is impressive enough, but for the ultimate experience, the climb up 164 steps to the tower's top is worth the effort.

Before ascending, get oriented with the annotated bronze relief map in front of the column, which notes the distances and directions to landmarks near and far. From this vantage point, you can see across the rooftops of the town, the Astoria Bridge, giant freighters gliding up and down the Columbia, and a long sweep of the Washington shore. To the northwest are the Columbia Bar and Cape Disappointment. On clear days, look northeast to Mount St. Helens and to Mount Hood on the far eastern horizon. Looking over Young's Bay south and west of Astoria, the Clatsop Plains extend to Tillamook Head and Saddle Mountain.

Get to the Astoria Column from downtown by following 16th Street south (uphill) to Jerome Avenue. Turn west (right) one block and continue up 15th Street to the park entrance on Coxcomb Drive. Open dawn–dusk daily; call 503/325-2963 for further info. A $1 parking fee is requested at the visitors center.

Walking Tour
After getting a bird's-eye view from Coxcomb Hill, you might want to take a closer look at Astoria on foot. The town is home to dozens of beautifully restored 19th-century and early-20th-century houses. A walking tour of many of them is laid out in a brochure available for $3 at the Heritage Museum (1618 Exchange St.) and other businesses. You can also book

a guided tour through **Historical Tours of Astoria** (612 Florence Ave., 503/325-3005, raegoforth@charter.net).

If you want to forgo the purchase and let the architectural scenery do the talking, here's a suggested route: From the Flavel House Museum, at 8th Street and Duane Street, start walking south on 8th Street and turn left on Franklin Avenue. Continue east to 11th Street, then detour south one block on 11th Street to Grand Avenue, east on Grand, north on 12th Street, and back to Franklin, continuing your eastward trek. Walk to 17th Street, then south again to Grand, double back on Grand two blocks to 15th Street, then walk north on 15th to Exchange Street and east on Exchange to 17th, where you'll be just two blocks from the Columbia River Maritime Museum. The route takes you past 74 historical buildings and sites.

On the Waterfront

While most of Astoria's waterfront is lined with warehouses, industry, and docks, the **6th Street Riverpark** and River Walk will get you front-row views of the river. The park is a local favorite to watch ships from the sheltered observation platform and to fish for Columbia River salmon. Placards around the park display information about the Lewis and Clark Expedition and the area's Chinook natives.

Walk east from Pier 6, past the fish-packing plants, for an interesting if malodorous and noisy (thanks to the sea lions) perspective on what is still a working commercial fishing port. The 11th Street Pier has been developed with a restaurant and shops, and the 14th Street Pier and 17th Street Dock are two other convenient access points for watching cargo ships, sea lions, and fishing boats.

The **River Walk** provides riverside passage for pedestrians and cyclists along a three-mile stretch between the Port of Astoria and the community of Alderbrook. Eventually, the path will extend another two miles eastward to Tongue Point, and west past the Port of Astoria to Smith Point.

An excellent way to cover some of the same

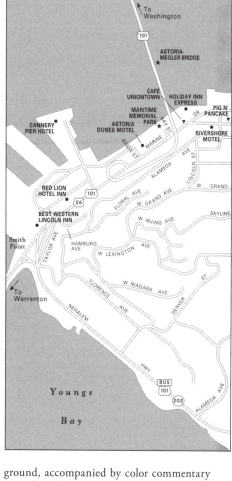

ground, accompanied by color commentary on sights and local history, is by taking a 40-minute ride on Old Number 300, the **Astoria Riverfront Trolley** (503/325-6311), which runs on Astoria's original train tracks alongside the River Walk as far east as the East Mooring Basin. The lovingly restored 1913 trolley originally served San Antonio and later ran between Portland and Lake Oswego in the 1980s. Old Number 300 runs daily during the summer 3 P.M.–9 P.M. Mon.–Thurs., noon–9 P.M. Fri.–Sun. Off-season, it operates weekends only, until dark. During heavy rains, the antique

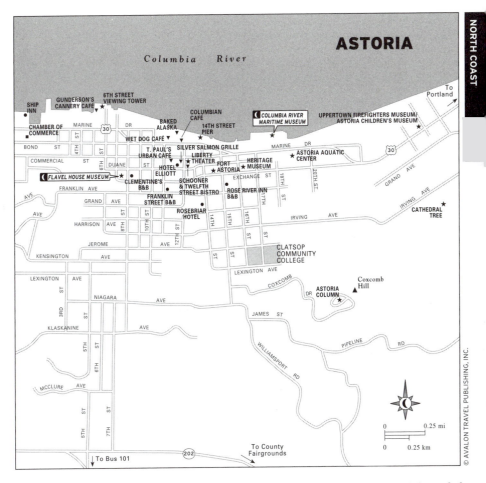

Columbia River

ASTORIA

To Portland

© AVALON TRAVEL PUBLISHING, INC.

trolley may stay put in its newly constructed barn. It costs $1 to ride the trolley as long as you stay onboard; the $2 all-day fare lets you get on and off as often as you like.

Columbia River Maritime Museum

On the waterfront a few blocks east of downtown Astoria, the Columbia River Maritime Museum (1792 Marine Dr., 503/325-2323, www.crmm.org, open 9:30 A.M.–5 P.M. daily but closed Thanksgiving and Christmas, adults $8, seniors $7, children ages 6–17 $4,

and under six free) is hard to miss. The roof of the 44,000-square-foot museum simulates the curvature of cresting waves, and the gigantic 25,000-pound anchor out front is also hard to ignore. What's inside more than matches this eye-catching facade. The museum's recent $5 million expansion features an award-winning film about the region's maritime history and includes displays on the Coast Guard, salmon fishing, tugboats, and canneries of Astoria. Floor-to-ceiling windows in the Great Hall allow visitors to watch the river traffic in comfort.

River pilots guide huge freighters across the Columbia River bar and upstream past Astoria.

Times when tribal canoes plied the Columbia, Lewis and Clark camped on its shores, and dramatic shipwrecks occurred on its bar are recounted with scale models, exquisitely detailed miniatures of ships, paintings, and artifacts. The most dramatic exhibit is of a 44-foot U.S. Coast Guard motor lifeboat, poised precariously on a wave in a life-size re-creation of a rescue on the Columbia River Bar. The chance to walk the bridge of a World War II destroyer, steer a tugboat, or tie a cleat hitch and other useful knots adds a hands-on aspect to the experience. Local lighthouses, the evolution of boat design, and harpoons are the focus of other exhibits here. There are also some artifacts from the *Peter Iredale* and other ships that have met their ends on the Oregon coast. Scrimshaw, fishing and cannery memorabilia, a small watercolor of the harbor by a crewmember on Robert Gray's 1792 voyage of discovery, and sea charts dating as far back as 1587 also highlight your visit.

Your ticket also lets you board the 128-foot Lightship *Columbia,* now permanently berthed alongside the museum building. This vessel served as a floating lighthouse, marking the entrance to the mouth of the river and helping many ships navigate the dangerous waters. After almost three decades of service it was replaced in 1979 by an unstaffed 42-foot-high navigational buoy. The gift shop has a great collection of books on Astoria's history and other maritime topics.

Uppertown Firefighters Museum and Astoria Children's Museum

Sharing space in a historic redbrick building (formerly the North Pacific Brewery, built in 1896) are two museums that will especially appeal to kids (2968 Marine Dr., open 11 A.M.–2 P.M. Wed.–Fri., 10 A.M.–3 P.M. Sat., $3 admission to both museums).

The Uppertown Firefighters Museum (503/325-2203) displays an extensive collection of firefighting equipment from 1873 to 1963. Featured are hand-pulled, horse-drawn, and motorized fire engines, including a 1912 American LaFrance fire truck, a Stutz fire en-

THE LONG BEACH PENINSULA

If you've come as far as Astoria, at the edge of the continent and at the mouth of the Columbia River, you should consider crossing the soaring Astoria-Megler Bridge to explore sights on the Columbia's northern shore. There are both scenic and historical reasons to visit this remote corner of Washington State. The new Lewis and Clark National and State Historical Parks aggregation includes a number of sites just across from Astoria in Washington, notably **Cape Disappointment State Park,** with a newly expanded Lewis and Clark Interpretive Center.

The **Long Beach Peninsula,** the thin sand spit just north of the mouth of the Columbia River, claims to have the world's longest beach. And with 28 unbroken miles of it, the boast has to be taken seriously. Like Seaside in Oregon, beach resorts at Seaview and Long Beach have a long pedigree, dating from the 1880s, when Portland families journeyed down the Columbia River by steamboat to summer at the coast. The bay side of the Long Beach sand spit creates **Willapa Bay,** known to oyster-lovers around the country for the excellent bivalves that grow in this shallow inlet, which is fed by six rivers. Most of Willapa Bay is protected as a national wildlife refuge, and it's an excellent bird-watching site. **Oysterville,** a tiny village along the bay, stands largely unchanged since the 1880s, and the entire town has been placed on the National Register of Historic Places. The very tip of the peninsula is preserved as 807-acre **Leadbetter Point State Park,** with informal hiking trails along both sandy beaches and the reedy bay.

Perhaps the best reason to cross the Columbia is to eat. Restaurants here have big reputations, including the **Shoalwater Restaurant** in Seaview (360/642-4142), housed in an 1896 stagecoach inn, and **The Ark** in Nahcotta (360/665-4133), which was praised by local boy James Beard and which has long enjoyed the reputation as one of the top restaurants in the Pacific Northwest.

gine, and a 1946 Mack fire truck. The photos and information about the devastating fires of 1893 and 1922 are fascinating.

The Astoria Children's Museum (503/325-8669) provides hands-on activities and other fun and educational programs for kids. Permanent exhibits include a child-sized grocery store and an active toddler area. Additional special activities are scheduled during school breaks and summer vacation.

Heritage Museum and Research Library

The Clatsop County Historical Society operates the Heritage Museum (1618 Exchange St., 503/325-2203, open 10 A.M.–5 P.M. daily May–Sept., $4 adults, $2.50 seniors, $2 children 6–12). Housed in the handsome neoclassical building that was originally Astoria's city hall, it has several galleries filled with antiquities, tools, vintage photographs, and archives chronicling various aspects of life in Clatsop County. The museum's new centerpiece exhibit concentrates on the culture of the local Clatsop and Chinook tribes, from before European contact to the present day. Other exhibits highlight the natural history, geology, early immigrants and settlers in the region, the development of commerce in such enterprises as fishing, fish packing, logging, and lumber. The research library has recently expanded and is open to the public.

Fort Astoria

In a tiny park at the corner of 15th and Exchange streets, a reproduction of a rough-hewn log blockhouse and mural commemorate the spot where Astoria began, when John J. Astor's fur traders originally constructed a small fort in 1811. It's worth a quick stop for buffs of early Northwest history.

◖ Flavel House Museum

Captain George Flavel, Astoria's first millionaire, amassed a fortune in the mid-19th century through his Columbia Bar piloting monopoly and later expanded his empire through shipping, banking, and real estate. Between 1884 and 1886, he had a home built in the center of Astoria, now the Flavel House Museum (441 8th St., 503/325-2203, open 10 A.M.– 5 P.M. daily May–Sept. and 11 A.M.–4 P.M. Oct.–April, $5 adults, $4 seniors/students, $2 children ages 6–17, five and younger free) overlooking the Columbia River, where he retired with his wife and two daughters. From its fourth-story cupola, Flavel could watch the comings and goings of his sailing fleet. Although the captain died in 1893, members of the family lived in the house until 1933. The amazing story of the Flavel family was depicted in colorful detail by Calvin Trillin in a February 1993 issue of the *New Yorker*.

When the Clatsop County Historical Society assumed stewardship in 1951, the mansion was slated for demolition, to be paved over as a parking lot for the adjacent courthouse. Fortunately, thanks to the efforts of the historical society and many volunteers, the house still stands today, at the corner of 8th Street and Duane Street. The splendidly extravagant Queen Anne mansion reflects the rich style and elegance of the late Victorian era and the lives of Astoria's most prominent family. Known locally as "the house with the red roof," it has withstood more than a century of storms off the Columbia River estuary.

The property encompasses a full city block. With its intricate woodwork inside and out, period furnishings, and art, along with its extravagantly rendered gables, cornices, and porches, the Flavel House ranks with the Carson Mansion in Eureka, California, as a Victorian showplace. The 14-foot ceilings, Persian rugs, and an array of imported tiles are upstaged only by the fireplaces framed in exotic hardwoods in every room. The recently restored Carriage House is now an orientation center for visitors, with exhibits, an interpretive video, and museum store.

Lewis and Clark National Wildlife Refuge

Six miles east of Astoria in the Burnside area is the **Twilight Creek Eagle Sanctuary.** To get there, drive east on U.S. 30 and turn left at Burnside. Another left a half mile later you to the viewing platform, which overlooks the 35,000 acres of mudflats, tidal marshes, and islands (which Lewis and Clark called "Seal Islands") of the Lewis and Clark National Wildlife Refuge. Bald eagles live here year-round, with 30–35 active nest sites. The area provides wintering and resting habitat for waterfowl (including an estimated 1,000 tundra swans in winter), shorebirds, and songbirds. Beavers, raccoons, weasels, mink, muskrats, and river otters live on the islands; harbor seals and California sea lions feed in the rich estuary waters and use the sandbars and mudflats as haul-out sites at low tides.

◖ Fort Clatsop National Memorial

On November 7, 1805, after a journey of nearly 19 months and 4,000 miles, the Lewis and Clark expedition thought they had at last reached their destination, the Pacific Ocean. "Ocian in View! O! the joy," wrote William Clark in his journal. Alas, they were close, but from the Washington side of the Columbia River they had mistaken its broad mouth for the sea itself. Hindered by waves and foul weather, it would take nearly another week before they actually beheld the Pacific. They explored farther west, to Cape Disappointment, and spent 10 uncomfortable days exposed to the elements on the north shore of the Columbia, then decided to move south for a more suitable location to pass the coming winter.

They chose a thickly forested rise alongside the Netul River (now the Lewis and Clark River), a few miles south of present-day Astoria, for their campsite. There the Corps of Discovery quickly set about felling trees and building two parallel rows of cabins, joined by a gated palisade. The finished compound measured about 50 feet square. The party of 33 people, including one African American, a Native American woman, and her baby, moved into the seven small rooms on Christmas Eve and named their stockade Fort Clatsop for the nearby tribe.

The winter of 1805–1806 was one of the worst

on record—cold, wet, rainy, and generally miserable. Of the 106 days spent at the site, it rained on all but 12. The January 18, 1806, journal entry of expedition member Private Joseph Whitehouse was typical of the comments recorded during the stay: "It rained hard all last night, & still continued the same this morning. It continued Raining during the whole of this day."

While at Fort Clatsop, the men stored up meat and other supplies, sewed moccasins and new garments, and traded with local tribes, all the while coping with the constant damp, illness and injuries, and merciless plagues of fleas. As soon as the weather permitted, on March 23, 1806, they finally departed on their homeward journey to St. Louis.

Within a few years, the elements had erased all traces of Fort Clatsop, and its exact location was lost. In 1955, local history buffs took their best guess and built a replica of the fort, based on the notes and sketches of Captain Clark. In 1999, an anthropologist discovered a 148-year-old map identifying the location of Lewis and Clark's winter encampment, and as it turns out the reproduction is sited very close to the original. In 2005, this replica of Fort Clatsop burned, and a new replica, built mostly by volunteers using period tools, was reopened in 2006. This new Fort Clatsop is more authentic than the previous replica to the actual fort that housed the intrepid Corps of Discovery.

Today, in addition to the log replica of the fort, a well-equipped visitors center, museum, and other attractions make Fort Clatsop National Memorial a must stop for

LEWIS AND CLARK NATIONAL PARK

On November 2, 2004, President George W. Bush signed a bill into law to create the 59th national park in the United States. The Lewis and Clark National and State Historical Parks honor explorers Meriwether Lewis and William Clark, whose journey in 1804–1806 paved the way for the American settlement of the West. The park focuses on the sites at the mouth of the Columbia River, where the Corps of Discovery spent the famously wet winter of 1805.

The park is somewhat unusual in that it is essentially a rebranding of current National Park facilities and a federalization of current state parks. The new park includes a dozen sites linked to Lewis and Clark exploration, campsites, and lore. One of these, **Fort Clatsop National Memorial,** south of Astoria and where the Corps actually spent the winter, was already operated by the National Park Service, while **Cape Disappointment State Park** (formerly Fort Canby State Park), on the Washington side of the Columbia, remains a Washington state park but will be managed by the national park entity.

Besides these two existing facilities, units of the new national park include the **Fort to Sea Trail,** a path linking Fort Clatsop to the Pacific; **Clarks Dismal Nitch,** a notoriously wet campsite near the Washington base of the Astoria-Megler Bridge; **Station Camp,** another improvident campsite for the Corps; the **Salt Works** in Seaside, where the Corps boiled seawater to make salt; **Netal Landing,** the canoe launch area used by Lewis and Clark near Fort Clatsop; and a **memorial to Thomas Jefferson** yet to be constructed on the grounds of Cape Disappointment State Park.

The new national park also encompasses the existing **Fort Columbia State Park** in Washington, which preserves a turn-of-the-20th-century military encampment, and **Fort Stevens, Sunset Beach,** and **Ecola state parks** in Oregon.

The national park designation changes little for these once disparate sites, at least in the near future. Fort Clatsop has been expanded to 1,500 acres, and the **Lewis and Clark Interpretive Center** at Fort Disappointment State Park was revamped. Visitors will mostly notice new and consistent signage throughout the park units, and a lot more docents. Living history re-enactors promise to bring to life the famous, often very wet events that took place here over 200 years ago.

anyone interested in this pivotal chapter of American history. The expedition's story is nicely narrated here with displays, artifacts, slides, and films, but the summertime "living history" reenactments are the main reason to come. Paths lead through the grove of old-growth Sitka spruce, with interpretive placards identifying native plants. A short walk from the fort leads to the riverside, where dugout canoes are modeled on those used by the corps while in this area. In addition, the new six-mile **Fort to Sea Trail** follows the general route blazed by Capt. Clark from the fort through dunes and fields to the Pacific at Sunset Beach. The Corps used the trail to explore the coastline and while camping at the beach when extracting salt from seawater.

The winter of 1805–1806 put a premium on wilderness survival skills, some of which are exhibited here by rangers in costume. You can see the tanning of hides, making of buckskin clothing and moccasins, and the molding of tallow candles and lead bullets. In addition, visitors may occasionally participate in the construction of a dugout canoe or try their luck at starting a fire by striking flint on steel. For a taste of what Lewis and Clark and their party experienced here, a visit on a cold, wet, wintry day, when every branch and leaf is dripping with rain, is an opportunity to better appreciate their fortitude.

This 1,500-acre park sits six miles southwest of Astoria and three miles east of U.S. 101 on the Lewis and Clark River. To get there from Astoria, take Marine Drive and head west across Young's Bay to Warrenton. On the other side of the bay look for signs for the Fort Clatsop turnoff. Then turn left off the Coast Highway and follow the direction markers to Fort Clatsop National Memorial (92343 Fort Clatsop Rd., Astoria 97103, 503/861-2471, www.nps.gov/focl, open 9 A.M.–6 P.M. daily Memorial Day–Labor Day, until 5 P.M. the rest of the year, $5 adults, $2.50 children 16 and under, off-season discounts).

Fort Stevens State Park

Ten miles west of Astoria, at the far north-west corner of the state, this Civil War–era outpost was one of three military installations (the others were Forts Canby and Columbia in Washington) built to safeguard the mouth of the Columbia River. Established shortly before the Confederates surrendered on April 9, 1865, Fort Stevens served for 84 years, until just after the end of World War II. Today, the remaining fortifications and other buildings are preserved along with 3,700 acres of woodland, lakes, wetlands, miles of sand beaches, and three miles of Columbia River frontage.

The fort's creation was not the only outgrowth of the Civil War on the West Coast. The year before, President Abraham Lincoln had founded the city of Port Angeles, Washington, for "lighthouse purposes." Given the subsequent creation of Fort Stevens shortly thereafter, it's a logical assumption that "lighthouse purposes" also meant watching out for Confederate ships and the British, whom the Union feared would ally with the South. The remote northwest Oregon coast may seem a world away from the bloody battles of the Civil War, until you consider that the last shots of the conflict were fired even farther away, in the Bering Strait. On June 5, 1865, the *Shenandoah* attacked a fleet of Yankee whalers, because the Confederate skipper was unaware of the Appomattox treaty, which had ended the war two months before.

Though Fort Stevens did not see action in the Civil War, it sustained an attack in a later conflict. On June 21, 1942, a Japanese submarine fired 17 shells on the gun emplacements at Battery Russell, making it the only U.S. fortification in the 48 states to be bombed by a foreign power since the War of 1812. No damage was incurred, and the Army didn't return fire. Shortly after World War II, the fort was deactivated and the armaments were removed.

Today, the site features a memorial rose garden, a Military Museum with old photos, weapons exhibits, and maps, as well as seven different batteries (fortifications) and other structures left over from almost a century of service. Climbing to the commander's station for a scenic view of the Columbia River and

THE *PETER IREDALE*

exploring the wreck of the *Peter Iredale*, Fort Stevens State Park

One of the best known of the hundreds of ships wrecked on the Oregon coast over the centuries is the British schooner *Peter Iredale*. This 278-foot four-master, fashioned of steel plates on an iron frame, was built in Liverpool in 1890 and came to its untimely end on the beach south of Clatsop Spit on October 25, 1906. En route from Mexico to pick up a load of wheat on the Columbia River, the vessel ran aground during high seas and a northwesterly squall. All hands were rescued and, with little damage to the hull, hopes initially ran high that the ship could be towed back to sea and salvaged. That effort proved fruitless, and eventually the ship was written off as a total loss. Today, nearly a century later, the remains of her rusting skeleton protruding from the sands of Fort Stevens State Park are a familiar sight to most who have traveled the north coast. Signs within Fort Stevens State Park lead the way to a parking area close to the wreck.

South Jetty are popular visitor activities. The massive gun batteries, built of weathered gray concrete and rusting iron, eerily silent amid the thick woodlands, also invite exploration; small children should be closely supervised, as there are steep stairways, high ledges, and other hazards.

During the summer months, guided tours of the underground Battery Mishler ($2) and a narrated tour of the fort's 37 acres on a two-ton U.S. Army truck ($2.50) are also available. The summer programs include Civil War reenactments and archaeological digs; consult the visitors center for schedules.

Nine miles of bike trails and six miles of hiking trails link the historic area to the rest of the park and provide access to Battery Russell and the 1906 wreck of the British schooner *Peter*

Iredale. You can also bike to the campground one mile south of the Military Museum.

Parking is available at four lots about a mile apart from one another at the foot of the dunes. The beach runs north to the Columbia River, where excellent surf fishing, bird-watching, and a view of the mouth of the river await. South of the campground (east of the *Peter Iredale*) there's a self-guided nature trail around part of the two-mile shoreline of **Coffenbury Lake.** The lake also has two swimming beaches with bathhouses and fishing for trout and perch.

To get there from U.S. 101, drive west on Harbor Street through Warrenton on Hwy. 104 (Ft. Stevens Highway) to the suburb of Hammond, and follow the signs to **Fort Stevens Historic Area and Military Museum** (503/861-1671 or 800/551-6949). The fort's hours are 10 A.M.–6 P.M. daily Memorial Day–Labor Day, and 10 A.M.–4 P.M. Wednesday–Sunday the rest of the year. Except for the tours, museum admission is free. There is a $3 parking fee within the park, which is covered by the Oregon Coast Annual Pass and Oregon Coast 5-Day Pass.

Fort Stevens State Park is one of the most popular campgrounds in Northwest Oregon; for details, see *Camping* under *Sports and Recreation* in this section. Note that from mid-June through Labor Day a shuttle bus service links Fort Stevens campground with Fort Clatsop and the Fort to Sea Trailhead at Sunset Beach.

SPORTS AND RECREATION
Fishing Charters
More than any other industry, commercial fishing has dominated Astoria throughout its history. Salmon canneries lined the waterfront at the turn of the century. Albacore and longline shark fishing put dinner on the table in the 1930s and 1940s. In the modern era, commercial fishing has turned to sole, rockfish, flounder, and other bottom fish. If it's not enough to watch these commercial operations from the dock, try joining a charter.

Tiki Charters (503/325-7818, www.tiki charters.com) will take you out for salmon and sturgeon. Trips depart from the West Moor-

ing Basin in Astoria. River tours are also available. Given the retail price of fresh salmon, you could theoretically pay for a charter trip by landing a single fish. **Gale Force Guides** (Warrenton, 503/861-1494) takes sport anglers fishing for salmon in either salt- or freshwater, depending on the season. On your own, go after trout, bass, catfish, steelhead, and sturgeon in freshwater lakes, streams, and rivers. Lingcod, rockfish, surfperch, or other bottom fish can be pursued at sea, off jetties, or along ocean beaches.

Hiking
An in-town hike that's not too strenuous begins at 28th Street and Irving, meandering up the hill to the Astoria Column. If you drive to the trailhead, park along 28th. It's about a one-mile walk to the top. En route is the **Cathedral Tree,** an old-growth fir with a sort of Gothic arch formed at its roots.

The **Oregon Coast Trail** starts (or ends) at Clatsop Spit, at the north end of Fort Stevens State Park. The most northerly stretch extends south along the beach for 14 miles to Gearhart. It's a flat, easy walk, and your journey could well be highlighted by a sighting of the endangered silver-spot butterfly. The species frequents just six sites, including four in Oregon; Clatsop County is one of them. The endangered status of the creature protects it by law and has stopped developers from building resorts on coastal meadows and dunes north of Gearhart. Look for a small orange butterfly with silvery spots on the undersides of its wings.

You also might encounter cars on the beach. This section of shoreline is, inexplicably, the longest stretch of coastline open to motor vehicles in Oregon. Call the State Parks and Recreation Division (800/551-6949) for an up-to-date report on trail conditions before starting out.

Fort Stevens State Park has nine miles of hiking trails, through woods, wetlands, and dunes. One popular hike here is the two-mile loop around **Coffenbury Lake.**

In 2005, as part of the expansion of Lewis and Clark National Park, the **Fort to Sea Trail** was created to link Fort Clatsop to the Pacific. The 6.5-mile trail follows the route through forest, fields, and dunes that the Corps traveled as they explored and traded along the Pacific coast.

The Fort To Sea Trail starts from the visitors center at Fort Clatsop. The first two miles involve a gentle climb to the Clatsop Ridge, where on a clear day you can see through the trees to the Pacific Ocean. The ridge makes a fine destination for a short half-day hike. To hike the length of the trail, continue down the ridge through deep woods and forested pastures dotted with small lakes. The trail passes by a tunnel underneath U.S. 101 and then through dunes to the Sunset Beach/Fort to Sea Trail parking lot. From there, a one-mile path leads to the beach.

Unless you plan to return along the trail—which makes for a long day's hike—you'll need to arrange a pickup. Consider hopping on the Fort Clatsop/Fort Stevens/Sunset Beach shuttle bus operated by **Sunset Empire Transit District** (503/776-6406, www.ride-thebus.org). The shuttle operates once hourly 9:45 A.M.–4:45 P.M. Monday–Saturday from mid-June through Labor Day. This bus connects with local buses to Astoria and Seaside.

Camping
Families flock to **Fort Stevens State Park** (800/452-5687 for reservations, open year-round). With 253 tent sites, 343 RV sites, and a special area for walk-in campers and bicyclists, the campground is the largest in the state park system. With the park's amenities and other attractions, this is the perfect base camp from which to take advantage of the region. Just be sure to avoid spring break (around March 23–29) if you wish to be spared the rites of spring enacted here by Oregon teenagers. Reservations are accepted here, and a $17–22 fee is charged. Yurts can be had for $29, and hiker-biker sites for $4.

Across the road from the state park, **Astoria Warrenton Seaside KOA** (1100 NW Ridge Rd., Hammond 97121, 503/861-2606 or 800/562-8506) has 310 sites, with 54 cabins. Summer rates (Apr.–Sept.) are $25.95–33.95

for basic tent sites, $39.95–49.95 for deluxe RV sites with all the hookups; one-room cabins (sleep five) run $45.95–55.95 or two-room cabins (sleep six) run $55.95–65.95. Prices drop about 10 percent the rest of the year. Amenities include an indoor pool and hot tub, game room, miniature golf, and bike rentals.

Kayaking
Columbia River Kayaking, based out of Skamokawa, Washington (P.O. Box 52, Skamokawa 98647, 360/849-4016, www.columbiariverkayaking.com) offers guided day and multi-day kayak trips along the lower Columbia River. One popular half-day excursion explores Young's Bay and the area around Lewis and Clark's 1806 lodgings at Fort Clatsop ($75 per person). Kayak rentals are available from **Pacific Wave** (2021 U.S. 101, Warrenton, 503/861-0866), a water sports company that also rents surf and boogie boards and related equipment.

The Astoria Aquatic Center
The Astoria Aquatic Center (20th and Marine Dr., 503/325-7027, open 5:30 A.M.–8 P.M. Mon.–Thurs., 5:30 A.M.–7 P.M. Fri., noon–7 P.M. Sat., noon–4 P.M. Sun., $4.50 adult, $3.50 children 2–17, and $10.50 family) houses four pools, including a 100-foot water slide with a 20-foot drop and lazy river current; a six-lane, 25-yard lap pool; adult hydro spa pool; kiddies' wading pool; locker rooms; and a variety of fitness equipment. Pool hours are subject to change and may be extended during summer months.

ENTERTAINMENT
For the lowdown on all the happenings in and around Astoria, get your hands on a copy of *Hipfish,* Astoria's spirited monthly tabloid distributed free all over town.

Nightlife
As befits a vintage fishing port, Astoria has lots of old bars and watering holes. As tribute to Astoria's scrappy spirit, explore some of the city's classic bars. The **Portway** (422 West Marine

ASTORIA GOES TO THE MOVIES

In recent decades, the Victorian homes and ocean view in Astoria's hillside neighborhoods and the surrounding maritime settings have provided the backdrop for such fanciful modern sagas as *Free Willy I* and *II*, *Kindergarten Cop*, *Teenage Mutant Ninja Turtles III*, *Short Circuit*, *Come See the Paradise*, and *The Goonies*. The last movie, a cult favorite shot in 1985, concerns a gang of local kids hunting for pirate's treasure; happy memories of the movie continue to attract a steady stream of visitors looking for the locations used in the film. More recently, films shot in Astoria have gravitated toward horror, including *The Ring Two* and *Cthulhu*, a film based on the horror novels of H. P. Lovecraft. A guide to movie locations is available at the Oregon Welcome Center in Astoria, the Heritage Museum, Flavel House Museum, and the Warrenton Visitors Center.

Dr., 503/325-2651) is the oldest bar in the oldest American settlement west of the Rockies. Though the present building dates from 1923, it's loaded with character and characters. On the eastern edge of Astoria, the slightly disreputable-looking **Desdemona Club** (2997 Marine Dr., 503/325-8540) is in fact a friendly *Cheers*-type pub that welcomes strangers with pool tables and good food. **Phyllis & Bob's Labor Temple Café & Bar** (939 Duane St., 503/325-0801) is the oldest communal union hall in the Northwest and not to be missed. The clientele is a mix of longtime union activists, twenty-something artists from Cocktail Nation, and rowdy young sailors, making for some interesting dynamics.

Both of Astoria's brewpubs are friendly places to start a conversation or quietly muse on the world. **Rogue Ales Public House** (100 39th St., 503/325-5964) is on a former cannery pier thrust out into the Columbia, while

the **Wet Dog Cafe** (144 11th St.) overlooks the river and features live music on weekends.

Other top choices for live music include **Café Uniontown** (218 W. Marine Dr., 503/325-4775) and the **Voodoo Room** (1102 Marine Dr., 503/325-2233, www.columbianvoodoo.com).

Astor Street Opry Company

Astoria's long-running *Shanghaied in Astoria*, based on the town's dubious distinction as a notorious shanghai port during the late 1800s, is a good old-fashioned melodrama. Chase scenes, bar fights, and a liberal sprinkling of Scandinavian jokes will have you laughing, in between applauding the hero and booing the villain. Performed with gusto by the Astor Street Opry Company, the show has been going on for two decades. It shows Thurs.– Sat. evenings mid-July–mid-September in the converted **Old Finnish Meat Market building** (279 W. Marine Dr., 503/325-6104). Tickets are $12–16 adults, with discounts for seniors and students.

Liberty Theater

The handsome Liberty Theater (503/325-5922, www.liberty-theater.org), whose colonnaded facades along Commercial and 12th Streets converge at the corner box office, is a vibrant symbol of Astoria's ongoing rejuvenation. The ornate Mediterranean-style building in the heart of downtown began its life in 1925 as a venue for silent films, vaudeville acts, and lectures. The theater continued as a first-run movie house, but after decades of neglect this grande dame was showing her age badly, and it looked as though the Liberty would eventually meet the sad wrecking-ball fate of so many fine old movie palaces. Happily, though, a nonprofit organization undertook efforts to restore the theater to its original elegance and equip it to be a state-of-the-art performing arts center. Work is ongoing, but the Liberty currently hosts concerts, recitals, theater, and other events; check the website for scheduled concerts and programs.

River Theater

This local cultural treasure is located underneath the Astoria Bridge. Every May since 1998, the nonprofit River Theater (230 W. Marine Dr., 503/325-7487, www.rivertheater .com) stages a new edition of its original "Simple Salmon" sketch comedy series. Part writing competition, part theatrical production, the cast acts out sketches submitted by the public, and the audience votes for their favorites. During the rest of the year, open mic readings, dinner theater, live community-radio (KMUN) broadcasts, and plays from Shakespeare to Ionesco fill out the changing bill of fare. In addition, the River hosts an impressively eclectic lineup of local and touring musicians, covering most of the bases with Celtic, bluegrass, folk, blues, and jazz, with pop, punk, rock, and gospel tossed in for good measure. Check its website or *Hipfish* for scheduled events.

Movies

Adjacent to the Columbian Cafe, the **Columbian Theatre** (corner of 11th St. and Marine Dr., 503/325-3516) screens the big movies you may have missed a month before in their first run. Dine on beer, wine, pizza, and other munchies while you watch. Shows nightly at 7 P.M., $3 general admission, $2 seniors and kids.

Astoria Gateway Cinema (1875 Marine Dr., 503/338-6575) is a modern movie multiplex, showing the usual stuff, where you can pass an afternoon trying to forget the interminable winter rains here.

Bookstores

Several bookstores in town invite serious browsing, buying, and intellectual stimulation. **Lucy's Books** (348 12th St., 503/325-4210) is a small but big-hearted locally owned bookshop with an emphasis on Northwest regional subjects. Owner Laura Snyder hosts readings by local and visiting writers, and she publishes an entertaining quarterly newsletter and book reviews. On the next block, **Godfather's Books and Espresso** (1108 Commercial St., 503/325-8143) sells a mix of new and used books and has a case of excellent antique maps and prints depicting the Columbia River and

north coast. The espresso bar is a good place to dry out on a rainy afternoon and catch up on local gossip. **Kneedeep in Books** (1052 Commercial St., 503/325-9722) specializes in used books and remainders, as well as new books.

EVENTS
Fisher Poets Gathering

Modeled after Elko, Nevada's popular Cowboy Poets Gathering, the Fisher Poets Gathering provides a forum in which men and women involved in the fishing and other maritime industries share their poems, stories, songs, and artwork in a convivial seaport setting. Inaugurated in 1998, the annual February event draws writers and artists from up and down the Pacific coast and farther afield for readings, art shows, concerts, book-signings, workshops, films, silent auction, and other activities at pubs, galleries, theaters, and other venues around town. Participation isn't limited to fisherfolk but extends to anyone with a connection to maritime activity, and themes range from the rigors (and humor) of life on the water to environmental issues. Admission is by donation ($5) at the ticket booth of the Columbian Theater (11th St. and Marine Dr.). For more details and full schedule, check the Clatsop Community College website (www.clatsopcollege.com/fisherpoets).

Astoria-Warrenton Crab and Seafood Festival

The Astoria-Warrenton Crab and Seafood Festival (503/325-6311 or 800/875-6807), held the last weekend in April at the Clatsop County Fairgrounds, is a hugely popular event that brings in crowds from miles around. Scores of booths feature a cornucopia of seafood and other eats, regional beers and Oregon wines, and arts and crafts. Activities include continuous entertainment, crab races, a petting zoo, and kids' activities. A traditional crab dinner caps off the evening. Admission is $5–7 for adults, $3 for those over 62 and $1 for kids 12 and under. Hours are 4–9 P.M. Friday, 10 A.M.– 8 P.M. Saturday, and 11 A.M.–4 P.M. Sunday. To get to the fairgrounds from Astoria, take Highway 202

4.5 miles to Walluski Loop Road and watch for signs. Parking is limited at the fairgrounds. Frequent shuttle service takes folks between the fairgrounds, Park & Ride lots, the Port of Astoria, and local hotels and campgrounds.

Scandinavian Midsummer Festival

The legacy of the thousands of Scandinavians who arrived to work in area mills and canneries in the late 19th and early 20th centuries is still strong in Astoria, with public steam baths, *lutefisk, smrrebrod* platters, and church services in Finnish. Today, the biggest event in town is the Scandinavian Midsummer Festival (503/325-6311, www.astoriascanfest.com), which usually takes place the third weekend of June, Friday through Sunday. Local Danes, Finns, Icelanders, Norwegians, and Swedes come together to celebrate their heritage. Costumed participants dance around a flowered midsummer pole (a fertility rite), burn a bonfire to destroy evil spirits, and have tugs-of-war pitting Scandinavian nationalities against each other. Food, dancing, crafts, and a parade bring the whole town out to the Clatsop County Fairgrounds on Walluski Loop Road just off Highway 202. Admission is $6 for adults and $2 for children over six.

Astoria Regatta Week

A tradition since 1894, Astoria Regatta Week is considered the Pacific Northwest's longest-running festival. Held on the waterfront in early August, the five-day event kicks off with the regatta queen's coronation and reception. Attractions include live entertainment, a grand land parade, historic home tours, ship tours and boat rides, sailboat and dragon boat races, a classic car show, a salmon barbecue, arts and crafts, food booths, a beer garden, and a twilight boat parade. For details and schedule, contact the Astoria Regatta Association (P.O. Box 24, Astoria 97103, www.astoriaregatta.org).

Silver Salmon Celebration

If you miss the spring crab festival, get a second shot in mid-October at the Silver Salmon Celebration, held at the foot of Basin Street, near Astoria's West End Mooring Basin. Get fresh salmon right off the boat and enjoy seafood delicacies, beer and wine-tasting, arts and crafts, live music, and lots of activities for little ones. For more information, contact the Astoria-Warrenton Area Chamber of Commerce (503/325-6311).

SHOPPING

From Mother's Day to early October, follow local tradition and stroll leisurely up and down 12th Street, between Marine Drive and Duane Street, where vendors offer farm-fresh produce, crafts, and specialty foods. **Astoria's Sunday Market** is held 10 A.M.–3 P.M. each Sunday.

A local store worth noting is **Finnware** (1116 Commercial St., 503/325-5720) which stocks Scandinavian crystal and glassware, jewelry, books, and kitchen tools. This is a store that takes its Finnish roots seriously.

Art Galleries

Astoria has a well-deserved reputation as a art center, with many downtown storefronts now serving as art galleries. Not to miss is **Valley Bronze Gallery** (1198 Commercial St., 503/325-3076), a showcase for the premier art foundry in the Pacific Northwest. Although the casting is performed in Joseph, Oregon, this gallery offers a wide selection of the bronze, silver, and stainless steel statuary produced by the foundry. Next door is **RiverSea Gallery** (1160 Commercial St., 503/325-1270), with a large and varied selection of work by local painters, glass artists, jewelry makers, and fine craftspeople. For a more quixotic art scene, go to **Lunar Boy Gallery** (1133 Commercial St., 503/325-1566), dedicated to animation art, cartooning, and objects best described as simultaneously weird and cool.

Local Foods

Josephson's Smokehouse (106 Marine Dr., 503/325-2190, www.josephsons.com) was established in 1920 in a false-front clapboard building near the waterfront. Josephson's is Oregon's most esteemed purveyor of gourmet smoked fish, producing Scandinavian cold-smoked salmon without dyes or preservatives. Josephson's caters to mail-order clientele and fine restaurants. You can buy direct here at a cheaper (but not cheap) price than the mail-order rates. Pickled salmon, salmon jerky, sturgeon caviar, crab, oysters, and a variety of alder-smoked and canned fish are also sold here. On typically foggy days here in midwinter, there's nothing finer than a cup of Josephson's very thick clam chowder.

To shop the daily catch, which can include Dungeness crab, wild salmon, halibut, albacore tuna, and rock fish, go to **Uniontown Fish Market and Deli** (229 W. Marine Dr., 503/325-9592), which can package fresh fish for shipping or to take on a plane.

ACCOMMODATIONS

With its wealth of large, elegant Victorian homes, it's not surprising that Astoria has more B&Bs than any other town on the Oregon coast. The historic former homes of merchants, politicians, sea captains, and salmon canners number among them. In addition, a classic downtown hotel has been completely spiffed and renovated, offering very comfortable rooms with vintage elegance. Several new hotels take advantage of wonderful riverfront views.

You'll also find about a dozen motels to choose from in and around Astoria, most of them located along U.S. 30, otherwise known as Marine Drive, in the northwest section of town. Most are fairly similar and don't have the charm that the town's B&Bs offer, but they're generally a bit less expensive and are reasonably close to downtown.

The prices noted in the text are for high season (summer). Rates fall by as much as half off-season.

$50-100

Astoria has several motels that offer basic but clean rooms. Except on summer weekends, the following should have rooms available without reservations. On the eastern edge of Astoria, the **Crest Motel** (5366 Leif Erickson Dr./U.S. 30, 503/325-3141 or 800/421-3141,

doubles $62–84, depending on views) offers cliffside river views, a coin-operated laundry, and a whirlpool set in a gazebo overlooking the river. Two blocks from the West Mooring Basin and its charter docks, the **Astoria Dunes Motel** (288 W. Marine Dr., 503/325-7111 or 800/441-3319, doubles from $75) has 58 rooms, an indoor heated pool and whirlpool tub, and king- and queen-size beds. About a half mile east of the Astoria-Megler Bridge, the **Rivershore Motel** (59 W. Marine Dr., 503/325-2921, doubles from $59) has 43 rooms with coffeemakers, microwaves, refrigerators, and Internet access. Some rooms include kitchens.

For something more elegant (and away from busy Marine Drive) consider staying at one of Astoria's grand B&Bs. Built as a private Georgian-style residence in 1902, then converted to use as a convent in the 1950s, the elegant **Rosebriar Hotel** (636 14th St., 503/325-7427 or 800/482-0224, www.rosebriar.net, doubles $75–275) was renovated into a small, comfortable hotel in the early 1990s. Set on a quiet neighborhood street a few blocks uphill from the Maritime Museum, the large bowfront windows of the parlor/lobby and many of the upstairs rooms command a sweeping view of the town and river below. Original woodwork, tastefully understated decor and furnishings, private bathrooms, and cordial service make a stay here quite pleasant. Discounts offered for three-night stays; call or check the website for packages and other specials. A full breakfast is also included. The recently opened Captain's Suite includes a kitchenette, large master bath, soaking tub overlooking the Columbia, and a sitting room with fireplace. The 1885 carriage-house cottage adjacent to the main hotel has its own kitchen, plus fireplace, whirlpool tub, and private patio. The Rosebriar is one of Astoria's most popular lodgings, so it's a good idea to reserve at least two weeks in advance during summer.

A block east of the Rosebriar Hotel, the **Rose River Inn B&B** (1510 Franklin Ave., 503/325-7175, www.roseriverinn.com, doubles from $90), offers two river-view suites and two guest rooms in a large, cheerfully painted Victorian, decorated with European antiques and art and surrounded by a neatly tended garden. Each room includes a clawfoot tub, and the River Suite also has a Finnish sauna.

Franklin Street Bed and Breakfast (1140 Franklin St., 503/325-4314, www.franklin-st-station-bb.com, doubles from $80) is a grand, four-story Victorian built in 1900. Six rooms and suites, five with private bath and queen beds, accommodate up to 14 guests. The view from the fourth-floor Starlight Suite is unmatched, and there's even a telescope for up-close ship spotting. The Hide-Away Suite has its own kitchen, dining area, living room, and private entry. Rich woodwork and local art are appreciated extras. It's within easy walking distance of downtown. A minimum two-night stay is required on weekends, and 10-day advance reservations have become necessary due to the popularity of this place.

Clementine's Bed and Breakfast (847 Exchange St., 800/521-6801, www.clementines-bb.com, doubles from $90), a handsome two-story home built in the Italianate style in 1888, stands in good company across the street from the Flavel House and is itself on Astoria's Historic Homes Walking Tour. From the gardens around the house come the fresh flowers that accent the guest rooms and common areas, as do the herbs that spice the delicious gourmet breakfasts. There are five rooms in the main house, all with feather beds and private baths; upper-story rooms have private balconies with river views.

In addition to these guest rooms, two spacious, sunny suites are available in the Moose Temple Lodge, adjacent to the main house, for $150–155. Built in 1850, this is the oldest extant building in Astoria; it was the Moose Temple from 1900 to 1940 and later served as a Mormon church. Renovated with skylights, wood floors, fireplaces, small kitchens, and several beds, these are ideal for families or groups. Pets are welcome. September–May, Clementine's offers packages combining

cooking classes with one- or two-night stays. Courses include bread- and pastry-making and theme classes such as A Weekend in Provence. Clementine's requires a two-night minimum stay on weekends mid-May–mid-Oct. and on holiday weekends. Single-night stays are fine the rest of the year, and discounts are available off-season.

A 10-minute drive west of Astoria, adjacent to the Fort Stevens Historic Area in quiet Hammond, the **Officer's Inn Bed-and-Breakfast** (540 Russell Pl., Hammond, 503/861-2524 or 800/377-2524, www.officersinn.net, $79–99) was built in 1905 and formerly housed Army officers and their families before the fort was decommissioned. A broad porch running the full length of the building overlooks the fort's original parade grounds. The 8,000-square-foot inn offers eight guest units, all with private baths and king- or queen-size beds; two-bedroom family suites each have a queen-size bed and two double beds.

$100-150

The new **Comfort Suites** (3420 Leif Erickson Dr./U.S. 30, 503/325-2000, doubles from $119) has river-view rooms with microwave, fridge, and free HBO; continental breakfast is served 6–10 A.M. Facilities include a heated pool, spa, sauna, exercise room, and laundry. You can't top the views at the new **Holiday Inn Express Hotel & Suites** (204 W. Marine Dr., 503/325-6222 or 888/898-6222, www.astoriahie.com, doubles from $149), directly under the Astoria-Megler Bridge. Guest rooms have a refrigerator, microwave, coffeemaker, high-speed Internet connection, TV, and DVD player. Facilities include indoor pool, breakfast bar, business center, and exercise room. Pets are welcome.

The sprawling **Red Lion Inn** (400 Industry St., 503/325-7373 or 800/RED-LION, doubles from $115) is located right at the Mooring Basin Marina, just off Marine Drive. Motel units seem a bit worse for wear, but it's right on the river, and view rooms have a front-row balcony seat on the passing ship traffic.

$150-200

At the west end of town, the **Best Western Lincoln Inn** (555 Hamburg St., 503/325-2205 or 800/621-0641, doubles from $157) has 73 rooms in a five-story structure overlooking Young's Bay. Facilities include indoor pool, sauna, hot tubs, and laundry.

After a $4.3 million, two-year renovation, the **❰ Hotel Elliott** (357 12th St., 877/378-1924, www.hotelelliott.com, doubles from $169) reinvented itself in 2003 as a tiny boutique hotel in the heart of downtown Astoria. The Elliott first opened in 1924, and its current incarnation preserved much of the original charm of its Craftsman-era details, including the mahogany-clad lobby, handcrafted cabinetry, wood and marble fireplaces, and stone floors in all bathrooms, plus such 21st-century modern conveniences as high-speed Internet access and big-screen TVs. The Elliott has five lovely suites (from $275 nightly) plus the five-room Presidential Suite ($650) with access to a rooftop garden. An original banner painted across the hotel's north side proudly proclaims Hotel Elliott—Wonderful Beds. The new Elliott has made a point of living up to this claim, with goose-down pillows, luxurious 440-thread-count Egyptian cotton sheets, featherbeds, and top-of-the-line mattresses to ensure a memorable slumber.

❰ Cannery Pier Hotel (10 Basin St., 503/325-4996 or 888/325-4996, www.cannerypierhotel.com, doubles from $159) is a newly built luxury hotel on the former site of a historic cannery, jutting 600 feet out into the Columbia below the Astoria-Megler bridge. The opulently furnished rooms have dramatic views, even from the shower; all rooms have balconies, fireplaces, and beautiful hardwood floors. Complimentary continental breakfast is included in the rates, as are hors d'oeuvres and wine in the afternoon. There's also a day spa in the hotel, plus a Finnish sauna, fitness room, and hot tub.

FOOD

Over the past several years, Astoria has developed a reputation for excellent dining at fair prices, with a number of restaurants standing out for their creative and consistently delicious fare. Espresso fans will also be pleased to know that there are no fewer than 20 outlets in town, with hole-in-the-wall cafés seemingly down every side street. Part of the fun is finding them. In addition to the restaurants and cafés listed below, you'll find do-it-yourself options at Astoria's Sunday Market and Josephson's Smokehouse (see *Shopping* in this section).

Casual Fare

As widely appreciated as it is small, the **❰ Columbian Cafe** (1114 Marine Dr., 503/325-2233, open for breakfast and lunch daily, for dinner Wed.–Sat., main courses $11–24) is where the meatless '60s collides with cutting-edge Northwest cuisine. The good selection of pasta entrées, crepes, and fresh catch of the day specials are all expertly prepared and moderately priced. The chef here is also famous for Uriah's St. Diablo jelly, which comes in garlic, jalapeño, and red-pepper flavors. These jellies are available here and sold throughout the state. You may also enjoy the free-flowing political repartee with the staff and regulars in this cramped (several booths and a lunch counter) but friendly place. Breakfast is a highlight here. If this is your first time to the Columbian Cafe, don't let the tiny, slightly seedy-looking venue put you off. Just barge in and take a seat—the servers will make you feel comfortable and the rest is all culinary pleasure.

A state travel magazine once named the **Ship Inn** (1 2nd St., 503/325-0033, main courses $6–14) the best pub in Oregon, and another regional publication gave it a thumbs-up for its seafood and business lunches. Despite its unprepossessing exterior, the Ship is popular with locals and visitors who appreciate good fish and chips, cheese plates, Cornish pasties, and other English specialties such as steak-and-kidney pie and bangers and mash, as well as imported brews. A welcoming fire, great waterfront views, and live music, including jazz and bluegrass, also provide conviviality here.

"Eat well, laugh often, and love much" is the motto that neatly sums up the vibe at the easygoing **T. Paul's Urban Cafe** (1119 Commercial St., 503/338-5133, open for lunch and dinner daily in summer, closed Sun. Oct.–June). The menu of hip diner food with fresh Northwest twists includes towering turkey sandwiches, bay shrimp ceviche, Caribbean jerk quesadillas, prawn pasta, and clam chowder. Coffee drinks, beer, and wine are served.

A good choice for families with kids, the Astoria outlet of **Pig 'N Pancake** (146 W. Bond St., 503/325-3144, open for three meals daily) of this small north-coast chain (others are in Seaside and Cannon Beach) excels at big, filling breakfasts at reasonable prices. The specialty is homemade pancakes and waffles, available in a dozen variations, including potato pancakes, Swedish (thin, crispy pancakes with lingonberries), pecan-filled, and, of course, pigs in a blanket.

Brewpubs

Astoria's first brewpub, the **Wet Dog Cafe** (144 11th St., 503/325-6975, open for lunch and dinner Mon.–Sat., main courses $6–14) is home to the Astoria Brewing Company, maker of eight handcrafted microbrews, ranging from the golden Pacific Pale Ale to the full-bodied Sow Your Wild Oatmeal Stout. There's also a full bar and live music Thursday through Saturday nights. The café is housed in a cavernous remodeled former waterfront warehouse, with good views out the big windows. Food is good, basic pub grub: fish and chips, burgers, pizza, sandwiches, and salads, with all-you-can-eat ribs on Friday.

The **Rogue Ales Public House** (100 39th St., 503/325-5964, open for lunch and dinner daily, main courses $9–13) is east of downtown in the new Hanthorn Pier development. The pub is set inside a wood plank structure atop a former cannery pier and offers excellent ales plus burgers, pizza, and sandwiches.

Northwest Cuisine

In the days when transportation here was mostly by water, Astoria's neighborhoods developed unique personalities. One of these was Uniontown, located west of the present downtown, where Scandinavian fishermen and longshoremen hung out near the fish-processing plants. Underneath the Astoria Bridge in this waterfront district, **Cafe Uniontown** (218 W. Marine Dr., 503/323-8708, open for dinner Tues.–Sun., main courses $12–22) boasts an upscale menu with such seasonal offerings as raspberry hazelnut chicken breast; oven-roasted lobster tail; portobello, ricotta, and garlic ravioli; and bacon-wrapped filet mignon. Live music on Tuesday through Saturday nights. Check out the 1907-vintage bar in the restaurant's lounge.

For one of Astoria's more notable restaurants, try **Silver Salmon Grille** (1185 Commercial St., 503/338-6640, open for lunch and dinner daily, main courses $15–24) for fine dining in an atmosphere that's somewhat formal but not starchy. Attractive murals of the eponymous fish adorn the walls inside and out, and salmon takes pride of place on the dinner menu as well, in a variety of preparations that are fresh and cooked to a T. Pasta dishes, additional seafood items such as razor clams, and several meat choices such as London broil, pork, and chicken, fill out the extensive menu. A selection of Northwest microbrews and a wine list favoring Oregon and French vintages nicely complements the main courses.

In a century-old converted cannery building on Pier 6, **Gunderson's Cannery Cafe** (1 6th St., 503/325-8642, open for lunch and dinner Mon.–Sat., for brunch Sun., main courses $9.50–25) seats you as close to the waterfront as you can get without a boat. This 13-table restaurant serves up an innovative bill of fare that's popular with locals and knowledgeable out-of-towners. Whether you have crab cakes in red pepper pesto or pecan-crusted halibut, leave room for the desserts you'll pass in the display case at the entrance. The lunch menu features a halibut burger, generous Caesar salads, pizzas on homemade focaccia crust, and what many consider to be Astoria's best clam chowder.

At the end of 12th St., overlooking the Columbia, **Baked Alaska** (1 12th St., 503/325-7414, open for lunch and dinner daily, main courses $18–24) features local seafood in Northwest cuisine preparations. Featured dishes include Alaska-style campfire wild salmon with amber ale barbecue sauce, coffee-dusted albacore tuna with balsamic ginger glaze, and a selection of hand-cut steaks and baby back ribs. Views rival the food, particularly in summer when there's deck seating.

Located across from Hotel Elliott and just behind the renovated Liberty Theater, the **Schooner and Twelfth Street Bistro** (360 12th St., 503/325-7882, open for lunch and dinner daily, main courses $10–22) is in the space of a former tavern (the cool neon is about all that's left). The urban swank dining room is a good spot for steak, pasta, and seafood. The adjacent bar has a hip martini-sipping crowd at night and offers live music on Friday and Saturday evenings.

For Astoria's top Italian food, go to **Fulio's Pastaria** (1149 Commercial St., 503/325-9001, open for lunch and dinner daily, main courses $8–17) with excellent pasta, Tuscan-style steaks, and a good wine list in a lively and convivial dining room.

INFORMATION AND SERVICES
Visitor Information
The **Astoria Chamber of Commerce** (111 W. Marine Dr., P.O. Box 176, Astoria 97103, 503/325-6311 or 800/875-6807, www.oldoregon.com, open 8 A.M.–6 P.M. daily in summer, 9 A.M.–5 P.M. Mon.–Fri. Oct.–Apr.) operates the Oregon Welcome Center at its offices, providing a plethora of brochures and maps for visitors to Astoria and other destinations on the north Oregon coast and southwest Washington. They will send you a free guidebook with plenty of handy information.

Car Rentals
Astoria has the greatest number of car rental agencies on the coast—two. Try **Hertz** (1492 Duane St., 503/325-7700) or **Enterprise Rent-A-Car** (644 W. Marine Dr., 503/325-6500).

Newspapers and Radio
With 10,000 people, Astoria is the largest city and the media hub of the north coast. The local newspaper, the *Daily Astorian,* is sold around town and is worth a look if only to get the editorial slant of Steve Forrester. This former Washington correspondent's witty commentary on local, regional, and national events pulls no punches. The *North Coast Times Eagle* is a political activist monthly that holds forth on coastal issues. It's sold around town and in Powell's Bookstore in Portland. The free monthly *Hipfish* is a publication in the great tradition of the alternative press of the 1960s. Whether you agree with its take on regional politics or not, the thoughtful, lively articles and complete entertainment listings will enhance your visit to the North Coast.

Throughout the north coast, **KMUN** (91.9 FM Astoria and Seaside, 89.5 in Cannon Beach) is a public radio station with especially diverse community-based programming. Folk, classical, jazz, and rock music, public affairs, radio drama, literature readings, children's bedtime stories, and National Public Radio news will keep your dial glued to this frequency.

Other Services
The **Astoria Post Office** is located in the Federal Building at 750 Commercial Street. The **library** (458 10th St., 503/325-7323) is open Tuesday–Sunday.

Clean Services Coin Laundry (823 W. Marine Dr., 503/325-2027) will help you deal with any mud you might have accumulated on your clothes from walking around Fort Clatsop trails after a rainstorm.

Other useful numbers include the **county sheriff** (503/225-2061), the **Coast Guard** (2285 Airport Rd., Warrenton, 503/861-6220), and **Columbia Memorial Hospital** (2111 Exchange St., Astoria, 503/325-4321).

The local **Bank of America** (977 Commercial St.) in Astoria houses an ATM. In Warrenton, head to **Costco** (180 SE Neptune Ave.) for access to an ATM.

GETTING THERE AND AROUND

Amtrak Thruway Motorcoach Service runs daily between the north coast and Portland Union Station. Board the coach in Astoria at the Welcome Center (111 W. Marine Dr.). Departure from Astoria is at 8 A.M.; arrival in Portland, 10:15 A.M. Depart Portland at 6 P.M.; arrive in Astoria at 8:15 P.M. The bus stops upon request at Seaside, Warrenton, and Gearhart. For information and reservations, call 800/USA-RAIL or check the Amtrak website (www.amtrak.com).

Getting around Astoria can have its pitfalls for the unsuspecting. Potentially troublesome for visitors are the steep hills and the city's layout of seemingly random one-way streets. Holidays and summer weekends bring heavy traffic along U.S. 30, a.k.a. Leif Erickson Drive (east end of town) and Marine Drive (center and west), Astoria's major traffic artery. In light of this, you might consider the following alternatives.

For visitors willing to let go of their cars for a while, the Sunset Empire Transportation District, better known as **The Bus** (503/861-RIDE or 503/861-7433 or 800/776-6406, www.ride thebus.org), provides reasonably frequent transportation around Astoria and along the coast from Warrenton (including the campgrounds at Fort Stevens State Park and Fort Clatsop) to Cannon Beach. Most routes are served every 40–60 minutes, Monday–Saturday.

Seaside and Gearhart

Seaside is Oregon's quintessential, and oldest, family beach resort. The beach is long and flat, sheltered by a scenic headland, with lifeguards on duty during the summer months, beachside playground equipment, and a boardwalk winding through the dunes. Ice cream parlors, game arcades, eateries, and gift shops crowd shoulder to shoulder along the main drag, Broadway. The aromas of cotton candy and french fries lend a heady incense to the salt air, and the clatter of bumper cars and other amusements can induce sensory overload. Atlantic City it's not—thank goodness—but on a crowded summer day the town evokes the feeling of a carnival midway by the sea. During spring break, when Northwest high school and college students arrive, the town's population of 6,200 can quadruple almost overnight.

South of town, the presence of clammers and waders in the shallows, and surfers negotiating the swells, also recalls the liveliness of a southern California or Atlantic shorefront instead of the remote peacefulness of many Oregon beaches. East Coast visitors often liken Cannon Beach to Provincetown, and Seaside to Coney Island—prior to their declines as destination resorts. Neighboring Gearhart, a mainly residential community (pop. 995) just to the north, has a few lodgings away from the bustle of Seaside, as well as a venerable 18-hole golf course.

Located along the Necanicum River, in the shadow of majestic Tillamook Head, Seaside has attracted tourists since the early 1870s, when transportation magnate Ben Holladay sensed the potential of a resort hotel near the water. But better transportation was needed to get customers to the place. At that time, the way to get to Seaside was first by boat from Portland down the Columbia River to Skipanon (now Warrenton), and from there by carriage south to Seaside. To speed the connection, Holladay later constructed a railroad line from Skipanon to Seaside.

To escape Portland's summer heat, families in the late 19th century would make the boat and railroad journey to spend their summer in Seaside. Most men would go back to Portland to work during the week, returning to the coast on Friday to visit the family. Every weekend the families would gather at the railroad station to greet him, then see him off again for his trip back to Portland. It wasn't long before the train became known as the "Daddy Train." As roads between Portland and the coast were constructed, the car took over, and the railroad carried its last dad in 1939.

In recent years, the town has become more than just a retreat for Portland families. Oregon's apostle of haute cuisine, the late James Beard, used to hold a celebrated cooking class here each summer. This opened the door for writers' retreats, art classes, and business conventions. If these occasions or a family outing should bring you to Seaside, you'll enjoy the spirit of fun if you don't mind plenty of company on summer weekends.

SIGHTS
The Promenade and Broadway

Sightseeing in Seaside means bustling up and down Broadway and strolling leisurely along the Prom. This three-mile-long concrete walkway, extending from Avenue U north to 12th Avenue, was initially constructed in 1908 to protect ocean properties from the waves. A pleasant walk alongside the beach, the boardwalk offers a fine vantage point from which to contemplate the sand, surf, frolicking beach-lovers, and the massive contours of 1,200-foot-high Tillamook Head to the south. The Prom is also popular for jogging, bicycle riding, and in-line skating.

Midway along the Prom is the **Turnaround,** a concrete-and-brick traffic circle that is the western terminus of Broadway. A bronze statue of Lewis and Clark gazing ever seaward proclaims this point the end of the trail for their expedition, though

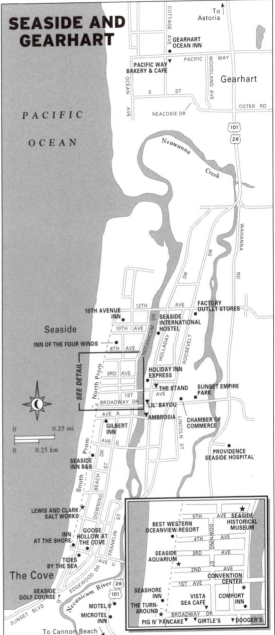

© AVALON TRAVEL PUBLISHING, INC.

THE GREAT NORTHWEST SHOE SWAP

Designer kites, Japanese glass fishing floats, berry jams, myrtlewood bowls, and objets d'art from galleries are among the gift-shopping treasures typically found on the Oregon coast. But in 1991, a unique event added a new wrinkle to the scene. It all started when a cargo of Nike athletic shoes washed up on north coast beaches, the result of the wreck of an Asian ship. The Japanese current swept the shoes down from the North Pacific to be deposited on Clatsop County beaches. Before long, beachcombers here were forming "shoe swap" clubs to match up sizes and styles in pairs. With extensive washing, these shoes were almost good as new, or at least good enough to sell for less than the $50-120 asking price at conventional outlets. From Cannon Beach north, the flotsam footwear was advertised on launderette bulletin boards, in community newspapers, and by hawkers on the street. Nike, Beaverton's multibillion-dollar shoemaker, did nothing to spoil this party, reveling instead in the publicity generated by the incident.

In March 1996, another beachcomber's bonanza hit the Oregon coast. This time, it was both athletic shoes and toys from a ship that burned in Asian waters 15 months before. These encounters with flotsam footwear have provided oceanographers with important data on ocean currents. Such incidents have also heartened proponents of "transoceanic diffusion," the theory that eons-old Asian boat migrations supplemented Eastern Hemisphere visitors crossing a land-ice bridge in the area of the present-day Bering Strait.

---

in fact they explored a bit farther south, beyond Tillamook Head. Eight blocks south of the Turnaround, between Beach Drive and the Prom, is a replica of the Lewis and Clark salt cairn.

Running east from the Turnaround, Broadway runs a half mile to Roosevelt Avenue (U.S. 101) through a dizzy gamut of tourist attractions, arcades, restaurants, and bars. Along Broadway, in a four-block area running west of U.S. 101 and bordered by the Necanicum River, First Avenue, and Avenue A, you'll find some fancy Victorian frame houses, some of the few old buildings that survived the 1912 fire that destroyed much of the town.

Today, the most notable sight in this busy section of Seaside is the enormous $73.3 million TrendWest time-share condo development containing nearly 300 living units. Condos in this outsized structure aren't available for rent directly from TrendWest, though vacation property rental companies can handle sublets.

Seaside Historical Museum

If you tire of having a good time on Broadway and the beach, make your way to the Seaside Historical Museum (570 Necanicum Dr., 503/738-7065, open 10 A.M.–4 P.M. Mon.–Sat. late Mar.–Oct., noon–3 P.M. the rest of the year; noon–3 P.M. Sunday year-round, $2 adults, $1 children), six blocks north of Broadway, where Clatsop artifacts and exhibits on early tourism in Seaside will impart more of a sense of history than anything else in town.

Seaside Aquarium

Right on the Prom north of the Turnaround is the Seaside Aquarium (200 N. Prom, 503/738-6211, open 9 A.M.–5 P.M. daily Mar.–Oct., 9 A.M.–5 P.M. Wed.–Sun. in winter, $3 ages 6–13, $6 ages 14 and up). It's not quite the Oregon Coast Aquarium in Newport, but if you're not going to make it that far south it's an OK introduction to sealife for young children. Back in the era of the Daddy Train, this place served as a natatorium but was converted to its current use in 1937. Today the pool is filled with raucously barking seals. In addition, a hundred species of marinelife here include 20-ray sea stars, crabs, ferocious-looking wolf eels and moray eels, and octopuses.

Lewis and Clark Salt Works

Near the south end of the Prom (at Lewis and Clark Way) are the reconstructed salt works of Lewis and Clark. While camped at Fort Clatsop during the winter of 1805–1806, the captains sent a detachment south to find a place suitable for rendering salt from seawater. Their supply was nearly exhausted, and the precious commodity was a necessity for preserving and seasoning their food on the expedition's return journey. At the south end of present-day Seaside, five men built a cairn-like stone oven near a settlement of the Clatsop and Killamox tribes and set about boiling seawater nonstop for seven weeks to produce three and a half bushels (about 112 quarts) of salt for the trip back east.

SPORTS AND RECREATION
Fishing and Boating

Just because you're smack-dab in the middle of a family resort town doesn't mean you can't enjoy some of nature's bounty; anglers can reel in trout, salmon, and steelhead from the Necanicum River right in the center of downtown. The **12th Avenue Bridge** is a popular spot for fishing and crabbing.

Cullaby Lake, on the east side of U.S. 101 about four miles north of Gearhart, offers fishing for crappies, bluegills, perch, catfish, and largemouth bass. At 88 acres, Cullaby is the largest of the many lakes on the Clatsop Plains. Two parks on the lake, **Carnahan Park** and **Cullaby Lake County Park,** have boat ramps, picnic areas, and other facilities. Cullaby is the only practical place to water-ski in the area.

A half mile west of the highway, **Sunset Beach Park** on Neacoxie Lake (also known as Sunset Lake) has a boat ramp, picnic tables, and a playground. Anglers come for warm-water fish species, plus rainbow trout stocked in the spring.

At Quatat Park, beside the Necanicum River in downtown Seaside, you can rent **kayaks, canoes,** and **pedal boats** for exploring the waterway.

Hiking

From the south end of Seaside you can walk in the footsteps of Lewis and Clark on an exhilarating hike over **Tillamook Head.** In January 1806, neighboring Native Americans told of a beached whale lying several miles south of their encampment. William Clark and a few companions, including Sacajawea, set off in an attempt to find it and trade for blubber and whale oil, which fueled the expedition's lanterns. Climbing Tillamook Head from the north, the party crested the promontory. Clark was moved enough by the view to later write about it in his journal:

> I beheld the grandest and most pleasing prospect which my eyes ever surveyed. Immediately in front of us is the ocean breaking in fury. To this boisterous scene the Columbia with its tributaries and studded on both sides with the Chinook and Clatsop villages forms a charming contrast, while beneath our feet are stretched the rich prairies.

They eventually found the whale, south of Tillamook Head. Ecola Point and State Park here are named for it, after the Chinook word for whale, *ecola* or *ekkoli*. By the time Clark arrived, however, the whale had been reduced to little more than a skeleton by the industrious Tillamooks, who used every part of the beast they could harvest. Clark measured the leviathan at 105 feet, which, if accurate, could only mean it was a blue whale, the largest animal on earth and an extraordinary windfall for the Native Americans. He found the Tillamooks busily engaged in boiling the blubber in a large wooden trough by means of hot stones. The oil, when extracted, was stored in bladders. He had to bargain hard for a share, and he wrote this of the negotiations:

> The Tillamooks, although they possessed large quantities of this blubber and oil, were so penurious that they disposed of it with great reluctance, and in small quantities only; insomuch that my utmost exertions, aided by the party, with the small stock of merchandise I had taken with me,

were not able to procure more blubber than about 300 pounds and a few gallons of oil. Small as this stock is, I prize it highly; and thank Providence for directing the whale to us; and think Him much more kind to us than He was to Jonah having sent this monster to be swallowed by us, instead of swallowing of us, as Jonah's did.

Today, you can experience the view that so impressed Clark on the **Tillamook Head National Recreation Trail,** which runs seven miles through Ecola State Park. Prior to setting out, you could arrange to have a friend drive south to **Indian Beach** to pick you up at the end of this three- to five-hour trek. Or you can be picked up another mile south at the Ecola Point parking lot. To get to the trailhead from Seaside, drive south, following Avenue U past the golf course to Edgewood Street and turn left; continue until you reach the parking lot at the end of the road.

As you head up the forested trail on the north side of Tillamook Head, you can look back over the Seaside townsite. In about 20 minutes, you'll be gazing down at the ocean from cliffs 1,000 feet above. A few hours later, you'll hike down onto Indian Beach.

Camping

One mile south of Seaside, in a lushly green meadow is **Circle Creek RV Park and Campground** (85658 Hwy. 101, 503/738-6070, tent spaces $20, RV sites $27–31). The campground is open mid-March through October and offers showers, a small store, picnic tables, and fire rings.

Other camping options convenient to Seaside include Fort Stevens State Park and Saddle Mountain State Park.

Surfing

The best surfing spot in the Seaside area is the beach just south of town simply referred to as **the Cove,** directly north of Tillamook Head and reached by parking areas along Sunset Boulevard. While prevailing winds favor winter surfing rather than summer, this

is in fact a popular boarding destination year round. Local surfers can be impatient with beginners, so this probably isn't a good spot for novices. For more information contact either **Seaside Surf Shop** (1116 S. Roosevelt, 503/717-1110) or **Cleanline Surf Co.** (719 1st Ave., 503/738-7888). Both shops rent and sell Boogie boards and surfboards, as well as wetsuits, boots, and flippers.

Wildlife Viewing

Bird-watchers gather at **Necanicum Estuary Park,** at the 1900 block of North Holladay Drive across the street from Seaside High School. Local students have built a viewing platform, stairs to the beach, a boardwalk, and interpretive signs. Great blue and green herons and numerous migratory bird species flock to the grassy marshes and slow tidal waters near the mouth of the Necanicum River. During the fall and winter, buffleheads and mergansers shelter in the estuary, while in summer the waters are often thronged with pelicans. Occasionally, Roosevelt elk, black-tailed deer, river otters, beavers, minks, and muskrats can also be sighted.

Swimming

Despite the lifeguard on duty in summer, swimming at Seaside's beach isn't the most comfortable unless you're used to the North Sea. Gearhart boasts a quieter beach than Seaside's, though the water's every bit as cool. Warm-blooded swimmers can head to the facilities at **Sunset Empire Park** (1140 E. Broadway, Seaside, 503/738-3311, open daily), which includes three pools, water slides, a 15-person hot tub, and fitness equipment.

Bike Rentals

Seaside has a bumper crop of places that rent bicycles, skates, and surreys, all for similar rates. The **Prom Bike Shop** (622 12th Ave., 503/738-8251) charges $3–6 per hour. Others are **Wheel Fun Rentals Spoke 1** (21 N. Columbia St., 503/717-4337), **Wheel Fun Rentals Spoke 2** (151 Ave. A, 503/738-7212), **Iron Coach Bike Rentals** (220 S. Columbia

St., 503/738-9458), and **Distinctive Outdoor Fun For All** (407 S. Holladay Dr., 503/738-8447).

Golf

Golfers can escape to public courses south of Seaside and north in the small town of Gearhart. At **Seaside Golf Course** (451 Ave. U, 503/738-5261), greens fees are $9–10 for nine holes. The **Highlands at Gearhart** (1 Highland Rd., Gearhart, 503/738-5248) is another public nine-hole course, with ocean views from most holes; $21 for 18 holes. The British links-style course at **Gearhart Golf Links** (1157 N. Marion Street, 503/738-3538) was established in 1882, making it one of the oldest on the West Coast and Oregon's oldest. Greens fees are $45 in summer for the 18-hole course.

ENTERTAINMENT AND EVENTS

Seaside predates any other town on the Oregon coast as a place built with good times in mind. A zoo and racetrack were among Seaside's first structures. Saturday afternoons, Quatat Park hosts **free concerts** downtown throughout summer. **Cannes Cinema** (U.S. 101 at 12th Ave.) is a five-screen multiplex showing first-run films.

The annual **Oregon Dixieland Jubilee** (800/394-3303, www.jazzseaside.com) takes place at the end of February. This event has been gaining momentum for more than 20 years and appeals to fans of Dixieland and traditional jazz. The town celebrates **July Fourth** with a parade, a picnic and social at the Seaside Museum, and a big fireworks show on the beach.

In early September, **Wheels and Waves** (503/717-1914) brings over 500 classic hot rods and custom cars (1962 and earlier, please) to downtown and the Civic and Convention Center (1st Ave. at Necanicum). The third week in September, the **Seaside Sandcastle and Beach Festival** is good fun.

SHOPPING

Seaside is a shopping hub not only for its own population but also for that of Cannon Beach, which oddly doesn't even have a grocery store, let alone a shopping mall. A number of shopping centers line U.S. 101 as it passes through Seaside, and the **Seaside Factory Outlet Center** (1111 N. Roosevelt Dr., 503/717-1603) has 25 discount stores, including outlets for Eddie Bauer and Nike.

ACCOMMODATIONS

Whatever your price range, you'll have to reserve ahead for a room in Seaside during the summer, weekends, and holidays (especially spring break). If you do, chances are you'll be able to find the specs you're looking for, given the area's array of lodgings and over 1,500 hotel rooms. The Seaside Visitors Bureau's helpful website provides comprehensive listings (www.seasideor.com).

Generally speaking, there are three lodging areas in Seaside. First, there are several modern motels along busy U.S. 101, about eight blocks from the beach. If you're just passing through or waited too long to call for reservations, these offer inexpensive rooms, but little in the way of beachside charm. A second grouping of hotels are in the center of Seaside, along the Necanicum River. These have a quieter riverside setting but still aren't beachfront (though you won't have to cross U.S. 101 to get to the beach). Finally, there are numerous hotels that face directly onto the beach or are just a short stumble to the strand. Even here, there's quite a difference in price between rooms that face the beach and those that face the parking lot.

$50-100

Out along U.S. 101 are two motels that provide good value and new rooms, but most people wouldn't consider them walking distance to the beach. **Motel 6** (2369 S. Roosevelt, 503/738-6269 or 800/466-8356, doubles from $75), on U.S. 101 about a half mile south of Broadway, isn't near the sand but does offer reasonably priced rooms. Just south is **Microtel Inns & Suites** (2455 S. Roosevelt, 503/482-7666 or 866/482-7666, doubles from $70), with free breakfast waffles, free high-speed Internet, and guest laundry. These two motels on the southern entry to Seaside are closest to Cannon Beach.

There's a clutch of motels south of the Broadway/Prom axis that offer easy beach access at fair prices—and a much quieter beachfront experience than town center. **The Tides by the Sea** (2316 Beach Dr., 503/738-6317 or 800/548-2846, www.thetidesbythesea.com, doubles from $82) is an older motel that's converted its large guest rooms and cottages into condos. About a quarter of the units face onto the Prom, but those that don't are just seconds away from the beach. If you can live without an ocean view, you'll save a bundle here. Each of the units is different, but most have kitchens and fireplaces.

Another good value are the rooms at **Seashore Inn** (60 N. Prom, 503/738-6368 or 888/738-6368, www.seashoreinnor.com, doubles from $65) right in the thick of it along the Promenade. Half the rooms face the beach, but half don't. These rooms are just steps from the beach but are a fraction of the cost of rooms on the other side of the building. All rooms have microwaves and mini-refrigerators, and some have full kitchens. There's also an indoor pool in case the weather turns foul.

$100-150

Also south of the bustling Broadway scene, the **Inn at the Shore** (2275 S. Prom, 503/738-3113 or 800/713-9914, www.innattheshore .com, doubles from $129) has nicely appointed rooms, each with gas fireplace, balcony, wet bar, microwave, coffeemaker, refrigerator, TV, and VCR, plus a balcony.

Best Western Oceanview Resort (414 N. Prom, 503/738-3264 or 800/234-8439, www .oceanviewresort.com, doubles from $129) is a large hotel right on the beach near the center of town. Amenities include an on-site restaurant and lounge, heated pool, and spa; the majority of rooms face the ocean. Non-oceanview rooms are about one-third less than view rooms.

In the center of Seaside, with balconies over the Necanicum River, the new **Holiday Inn Express Hotel Suites Seaside Convention Center** (34 Holladay Dr., 503/717-8000, dou-

bles from $105) has an indoor pool and spa, wireless high-speed Internet access, and rooms with fridge, microwave, coffeemaker, and CD and DVD player. Rates include a complimentary breakfast bar.

While motels dominate the lodging scene in Seaside, a few B&Bs offer an alternative. Our top award for creativity goes to the **Seaside Inn B&B** (581 S. Prom, 503/319-3300 or 800/772-7766, www.theseasideinn.com, doubles from $105). This four-story, shingle-sided structure stands right on the beach, with its north gable skewered by a clock tower. Each of the 15 guest rooms is decorated in a unique theme. The queen bed in the '50–'60s Rock and Roll room, for example, is incorporated into the tail end of a 1959 Oldsmobile ($115–195). Other themes include the Bubble Room ($120–199), and the Clock Tower Suite ($160–325). Most have a spectacular ocean view.

The **Gilbert Inn** (341 Beach Dr., 503/738-9770 or 800/410-9770, www.gilbertinn.com, doubles from $110) is a well-preserved 1892 Queen Anne, located just a block south of Broadway and a block from the beach. Period furnishings adorn the 10 guest rooms, which all have private bath, down comforters, and other nice touches. The third-floor "Garret" sleeps up to four in a queen and two twin beds, with ocean views from the dormer window.

North of Broadway, the **10th Avenue Inn** (125 10th Ave., 503/738-0643 or 800/745-2378, www.10aveinn.com, doubles from $100) is a comfortable 1908 home built just a few steps from the beach. In the parlor, a baby grand piano, guitar, and other instruments are available for musically inclined guests. The three guest rooms have king-size beds, attached baths, TVs, and small refrigerators. Next door and operated by the same folks is the **Doll House** (www.summerhouse-seaside. com), a sweet two-bedroom cottage (ideal for four adults plus two or three children) with full kitchen and a deck with barbecue grill. It goes for $850/week in summer (minimum week's rental), $160 per night off-season (two-night minimum).

Just north of the Necanicum River's mouth,

Gearhart offers a respite from the bustle of Seaside. The **Gearhart Ocean Inn** (67 N. Cottage St., 503/738-7373, www.gearhartoceaninn.com, doubles from $105) offers a choice of 12 New England–style wooden cottages with comforters, wicker chairs, and throw rugs, with beaches a short walk away. The two-story deluxe units have kitchens and hardwood floors. Pets are allowed in some units. This spruced-up old motor court is one of the best values on the North Coast.

$150-200

The **Comfort Inn** (545 Broadway, Seaside, 503/738-3011, doubles from $159), is right on the Necanicum River at the center of town. Rooms feature fireplaces, spa baths, microwaves, refrigerators, and balconies overlooking the river. The beach is a five-minute stroll from the hotel.

Seaside's most opulent rooms are at the **Inn of the Four Winds** (820 N. Prom, 503/738-9524 or 800/818-9524, doubles from $159). This 14-room boutique hotel has very comfortable rooms furnished with taste and style. All rooms have microwave, coffeemaker, refrigerator, DVD player, gas fireplace, and a deck or balcony with an ocean view. Best of all, the inn faces directly onto the beach eight blocks north of the frenetic Broadway strip.

Vacation Rentals

A good option for families and groups might be one of the several dozen vacation rentals. Check with the Seaside Visitors Bureau, or contact one of the rental agencies: **Beach Property Management** (503/738-9068); **Oceanside Vacation Rental** (503/738-7767 or 800/840-7764); **D. B. Rentals** (503/717-9516 or 800/203-1681); or **Northwind Property Management** (503/738-5532 or 800/488-3301).

Hostel

The cheapest place in town is the **Seaside International Hostel** (930 N. Holladay Dr., 503/738-7911 or 800/909-4776, www.2oregonhostels.com, dorm-style rooms $22, private rooms $41–57 per person, add $3 for non-members). Unlike many hostels, it doesn't close down during the day and there's no curfew at night. There's an espresso bar on-site, and the Necanicum River runs through the backyard. Close by is the Necanicum Estuary Park.

FOOD

While a stroll down Broadway might have you thinking that cotton candy, corn dogs, and saltwater taffy are the staples of Seaside cuisine, several eateries here can satisfy more refined palates as well.

Casual Dining

For breakfast, the Swedish pancakes and crab-and-cheese omelettes at **Pig 'N Pancake** (323 Broadway, 503/738-7243, open for three meals daily) are tops. If you're seriously hungry, try the Frisbee-sized cinnamon rolls. For soup, salads, sandwiches, desserts, and, of course, bagels, go to **Bagels by the Sea** (210 S. Holladay Dr., 503/717-9145, open for breakfast and lunch daily).

The **Vista Sea Cafe** (150 Broadway, 503/738-8108, open for lunch and dinner daily) is known for pizza with ingredients such as artichokes, feta, chorizo, and pesto, plus top-notch clam chowder with homemade beer bread. Its location one block from the Turnaround makes it especially convenient.

Dooger's (505 Broadway, 503/738-3773, open for lunch and dinner daily), which also has an outlet in Cannon Beach, has won acclaim for its clam chowder. Local clams and oysters, fresh Dungeness crab legs, sautéed shrimp, and marionberry cobbler are also the basis of Dooger's do-good reputation.

Just looking for a pub with local microbrews and good sandwiches? Your destination should be **Goose Hollow at the Cove** (220 Ave. U, 503/717-1940, open for lunch and dinner daily). There's nice deck seating plus 14 beers on tap; it's a smoke-free environment. The Reuben sandwiches here are locally famed.

Mexican

The Stand (109 N. Holladay, 503/738-6592)

features the satisfying and inexpensive Mexican fare that you'd find on the street-cart *loncherias* of Guadalajara. The carnitas taco is a mouthful of seasoned pork only exceeded perhaps by its beefy counterpart, the carne asada taco. The chili verde burrito, as well as enchiladas, tamales, and other specialties, can be enjoyed in the tiled confines of the restaurant.

Cajun
A rarity in these parts, **Lil' Bayou** (20 N. Holladay Dr., 503/717-0624, open for lunch and dinner daily, main courses $12–21) dishes up authentic muffulettas, jambalaya, blackened catfish, gumbo, and a host of other Cajun and Creole standards, right down to side dishes of collard greens, at reasonable prices. Finish off with a slice of sweet potato pecan pie or Aunt B's cheesecake.

Steak and Seafood
For over 30 years, **Girtle's Seafood & Steaks** (311 Broadway, 503/738-8417, open for three meals daily, main courses $12–24) has maintained a big local reputation for beef and fresh seafood, prepared with traditional Northwest aplomb. Expect large portions and a high-spirited barroom atmosphere.

Northwest Cuisine
Should the frenetic ambience of Seaside on a holiday weekend begin to wear thin, try the **Pacific Way Bakery and Cafe** in Gearhart (601 Pacific Way, 503/738-0245, open for dinner nightly, open for lunch Thurs.–Mon., main courses $14–24). Gearhart is the area where famed food writer James Beard was raised; his finesse lives on in such dishes as smoked salmon and cream cheese with thin-sliced red onion on a croissant. Pasta, crusty pizzas, and seafood dishes (including thick seafood cioppino) as well as crepes pop up at lunch and dinner. Rib eye steak and local razor clams are other frequent dinnertime highlights in the surprisingly urbane little café hidden behind a rustic old storefront.

PRACTICALITIES
The **Seaside Chamber of Commerce and Visitors Bureau** (7 N. Roosevelt St., Seaside 97138, 503/738-6391 or 800/444-6740, www.seasidechamber.com) is open 8 A.M.–5 P.M. daily.

Providence Seaside Hospital (725 S. Wahanna Rd., 503/717-7000) has 24-hour service and an emergency room.

Seaside is very walkable, but for $2 you can ride around town on the brightly painted **Seaside Street Car,** which runs hourly. Sunset Empire Transportation District also operates **The Bus,** which serves Cannon Beach, Seaside, Astoria-Warrenton, and points in between. For schedule and fare info, call 503/861-7433.

Cannon Beach and Vicinity

In 1846, the USS *Shark* met its end on the Columbia River Bar. The ship broke apart, and a section of deck bearing a small cannon and an iron capstan drifted south, finally washing ashore south of the current city limits at Arch Cape. And so this town got its name, which it adopted in 1922. Replicas of the hardware now stand near that spot, while the originals are preserved at the Cannon Beach Historical Society Museum.

In 1873, stagecoach and railroad tycoon Ben Holladay helped create Oregon's first coastal tourist mecca, Seaside, while ignoring its attractive neighbor in the shadow of Haystack Rock. In the 20th century, Cannon Beach evolved into a bohemian alternative to the hustle and bustle of the family-oriented resort scene to the north. Before the recent era of development, this place was a quaint backwater attracting laid-back artists, summer-home residents, and the overflow from pricier digs in Seaside.

Today, the low-key charm and atmosphere conducive to artistic expression are threatened by a massive visitor influx and price increases. While such vital signs as a first-rate theater, a good bookstore, cheek-by-jowl art galleries, and fine restaurants are still in ample evidence, your view of them from the other side of the street might be blocked by a convoy of Winnebagos.

Nonetheless, the broad, three-mile stretch of beach dominated by the impressive monolith of Haystack Rock still provides a contemplative experience. And if you're patient and resourceful enough to find a space for your wheels, the finest gallery-hopping, crafts, and shopping on the coast await. The city is small enough for strolling, only 1.3 miles long, and its location removed from U.S. 101 spares it the kind of blight seen on the main drags of other coastal tourist towns.

Wood shingles and understated earth tones dominate the architecture of tastefully rendered galleries, bookstores, and bistros. Throngs of walkers along Hemlock Street, the main drag, also distinguish this burg from the typical coastal strip town whose heart and soul have been pierced by U.S. 101. You have to go clear to the north end of Cannon Beach to find a gas station, and even then you're liable to bypass its stone-cottage facade.

SIGHTS
◖ Haystack Rock

As you get closer to town, Haystack Rock looms large above the extensive sands of Cannon Beach. This is the third-highest sea stack in the world, measuring 235 feet high. As part of the Oregon Islands National Wildlife Refuge, it has wilderness status and is off-limits to climbing. Puffins and other seabirds nest on its steep faces, and intertidal organisms thrive in the tidepools around the base. The surrounding tidepools, within a radius of 300 yards from the base of the monolith, are designated a "marine garden"; it's open to exploration, but with strict no-collecting (of anything) and no-harassment (of any living organisms) protections in effect. Flanking the mountain are two rock formations known as the Needles. These spires had two other counterparts at the turn of the 20th century that have gradually been

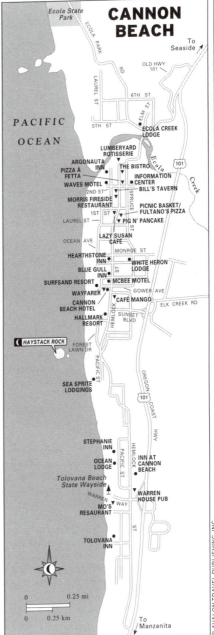

© AVALON TRAVEL PUBLISHING, INC.

© BILL MCRAE

Cannon Beach is one of Oregon's most upscale and beautiful beach towns.

leveled by weathering and erosion. Old-timers will tell you that the government dynamited a trail to the top of Haystack in 1968 to keep people off this bird rookery. It also reduced the number of intrepid hikers trapped on the rock at high tide.

The **Haystack Rock Awareness Program** (503/436-1581, www.haystackrock.org, June–Aug.), sponsors free interpretive programs. While these talks are interesting and informative, the beach also speaks to you with its own distinctive voices. You can't miss the cacophony of seabirds at sunset and, if you listen closely, the winter phenomenon of "singing sands" created by wind blowing over the beach.

Primary points for beach access are at the west end of Harrison Street downtown or at the end of Bower Street a mile north. A third beach access point is at Tolovana Beach Wayside, about three miles south of Cannon Beach along Hemlock Street.

Ecola State Park

Ecola State Park is just north of the Cannon Beach town site. Thick conifer forests line the access road to Ecola Point. This forested cliff has many trails leading down to the water. The view south takes in Haystack Rock and the overlapping peaks of the Coast Range extending to Neahkahnie Mountain. This is one of the most photographed views on the coast. Out to sea, the sight of sea lions basking on surf-drenched rocks (mid-April–July) or migrating gray whales (December and March) and orcas (May) are seasonal highlights.

From Ecola Point, trails lead north to horseshoe-shaped **Indian Beach,** a favorite with surfers. Some prefer to drive there as a prelude to hiking up Tillamook Head, considered by Lewis and Clark the region's most beautiful viewpoint (see *Hiking* in *Seaside and Gearhart*).

The name Ecola means whale in Chinook and was first used as a place-name by William Clark, referring to a creek in the area. Lewis and Clark journals note a 105-foot beached whale found somewhere within present-day Ecola Park's southern border, Crescent Beach.

Haystack Rock, Cannon Beach

© BILL MCRAE

This area represents the southernmost extent of Lewis and Clark's coastal Oregon travels.

There is a $3 day-use fee at the park. The Oregon Coast Annual Pass and Oregon Coast 5-Day Pass are honored.

South of Cannon Beach

Stunning beaches don't end with Cannon Beach. Sandy expanses stretch seven miles south to the Arch Cape tunnel on Hwy. 101, indicating the entrance to Oswald West State Park. Several of these beaches are reached via state park waysides. As you head south, views of **Hug Point State Park** and pristine beaches will have you ready to pull over. In summer, this can be a good escape from the crowds at Cannon Beach. Time your visit to coincide with low tide, when all manner of marinelife in tidal pools will be exposed. Also at low tide, you may see remains of an 800-foot-long, Model T–sized road blasted into the base of Hug Point, an early precursor to U.S. 101. The cliffs are gouged with caves and crevasses that also invite exploring, but be mindful of

the tides so you don't find yourself stranded. Hug Point got its name in the days when stage-coaches used the beach as highways; they had to dash between the waves, hugging the jutting headland to get around.

Cannon Beach History Center

Permanent exhibits at the small Cannon Beach History Center (1387 S. Spruce St., 503/436-9301, open 1–5 P.M. Wed.–Sat., free) chronicle the town's timeline, from prehistory to the modern expansion of tourism and recreation. The original, eponymous cannon from the ill-fated *Shark* is also on display here.

SPORTS AND RECREATION
Camping

Camping offers easier access to Cannon Beach's natural wonders at a bargain price. Although camping is not permitted on the beach or in Cannon Beach city parks, there are plenty of options for RV, tent, and outdoor enthusiasts.

The **Sea Ranch RV Park** (415 Old U.S. 101, 503/436-2815, www.cannon-beach.net/searanch) has grassy sites nestled among the trees, also home to horses, ducks, rabbits, and raccoons. It's open year-round with both full and partial hookups for RVs; campsites include a picnic table and fire ring (firewood sold on the premises) and access to restrooms with hot showers—all just three blocks from the beach and downtown. Sites run $23–27. Cabins are also available for $70. Pets are welcome but must be on a leash. Reservations recommended.

For a more pampered experience, check out the **RV Resort at Cannon Beach** (345 Elk Creek Rd., 503/436-2231 or 800/847-2231, www.cbrvresort.com). Open year-round, with 100 full hookups, indoor pool and spa, free cable TV, on-site convenience store, launderette, restrooms, and meeting room. This resort features a Saturday night weenie roast during the summer months. Call for rates.

The family-run **Wright's for Camping** (334 Reservoir Rd., 503/436-2347, www.wrightsforcamping.com) has quite a history. During the 1930s, the Wrights came from Portland to camp in this area. Then in 1946, Pop Wright bought 10 acres in Cannon Beach from a friend. After running a successful construction company in town, Wright and his wife turned their 10-acre site into a campground. Choose from 19 sites with picnic tables, restrooms, laundry, and fire rings. Wright's is wheelchair accessible; leashed pets are allowed. Rates run $20 and up.

Roughly 20 miles east of Cannon Beach, off U.S. 26, is Saddle Mountain State Park, which offers 10 tent camping sites at the base of 3,283-foot Saddle Mountain, one of the highest peaks in Oregon's Coast Range. This is a much more primitive campground than those listed above (though there are flush toilets and piped water, in addition to picnic tables and fire pits). However, this remote campground might just be the tonic if you're weary of the crowds along the beach. Sites are first-come, first-served and cost $9.

Horseback Riding

Sea Ranch Stables (415 Old U.S. 101, 503/436-2815), at the north entrance to Cannon Beach off U.S. 101, rents horses 9 A.M.–5 P.M. for beach rides mid-May–Labor Day. Horses are allowed on the beach anywhere along the coast using public access points. Sea Ranch offers a number of one- to two-hour guided rides, starting at $45 per hour, including night rides on the beach.

Mountain Biking

Mike's Bike Shop (248 N. Spruce St., Cannon Beach, 503/436-1266) has rentals for $3–6 per hour. Mike's specializes in mountain bikes, which can also be returned at a Warrenton outlet. You'll also find three-wheel beach-cycles for rent at the north end of town. These are fun for zipping up and down the hard-packed sand when the tide is out.

Surfing

The area around Cannon Beach has several good surfing beaches. The most popular, and the best bet for beginners, is **Short Sands Beach,** at the end of the trail to the beach at Oswald West State Park. It's a bit of a hike

down to the beach, but the sheltered cove is a great place to spend the day, even if you're just bobbing around in the waves.

Another good spot for somewhat more advanced surfers (and surf kayakers) is **Indian Beach,** at Ecola State Park. Up the road in Seaside, locals tend to control the surf breaks… if you're good enough to fit in, give it a go.

Two good surf schools operate in the Cannon Beach area. The instructors at **Oregon Surf Adventures** (1235 S. Hemlock, Cannon Beach, 503/436-1481, www.oregonsurf adventures.com) and **Northwest Women's Surf Camps** (1190 6th Ave., Seaside, 503/440-5782, www.nwwomenssurfcamps.com) will give you a bit of land training (the women's camp includes yoga to get you limbered up and in the right frame of mind) and then accompany you into the waves.

◖ Saddle Mountain State Park

A good reason to head east from Cannon Beach is the hike up 3,283-foot Saddle Mountain. To get to the trailhead, take U.S. 26 from its junction with U.S. 101 for 10 miles and turn left on the prominently signed Saddle Mountain Road. Although it's paved, this road is not suitable for RVs or wide-bodied vehicles. After seven twisting miles, you'll come to the trailhead of the highest peak in this part of the Coast Range. The trail itself is steep and gains more than 1,600 feet in 2.5 miles. Wet conditions can make the going difficult (allow four hours round-trip) and the scenery en route is not always exceptional, but the view from the top is worth it.

On a clear day, hikers can see some 50 miles of the Oregon and Washington coastlines, including the Columbia River. Also possible are spectacular views of Mounts Rainier, St. Helens, and Hood, and, unfortunately, miles of clear-cuts. If you go May–August you'll be treated to a wildflower display that'll surprise you. On the upper part of the trail, plant species that pushed south from Alaska and Canada during the last Ice Age still thrive. The cool, moist climate here keeps them from dying out as they did at lower elevations. Some early blooms include pink coast fawn lily, monkey-flower, wild rose, wood violet, bleeding heart, oxalis, Indian paintbrush, and trillium. Cable handrails provide safety on the narrow final quarter-mile trail to the summit.

The campground at Saddle Mountain is very pleasant and offers a secluded option for campers not attracted to the busy family scene at nearby Fort Stevens State Park.

ENTERTAINMENT AND EVENTS
Music and Theater

Going strong for more than 30 years, the **Coaster Theatre Playhouse** (108 N. Hemlock St., Cannon Beach 97110, 503/436-1242, http://coastertheatre.com) stages a varied bill of musicals, dramas, mysteries, comedies, concerts, and other entertainments. It's open year-round, in a building that started in the 1920s as a skating rink cum silent-movie house. Tickets run $14–16.

Beginning in July, the city park, at Spruce and 2nd streets, hosts **Concerts in the Park,** a series of jazz, rhythm and blues, and popular music, on Sunday afternoons at the bandstand 2–4 P.M. Well-chosen jazz and folk acts frequently grace the **Bald Eagle Coffee House** (1287 S. Hemlock St., 503/436-0522) on weekends.

Events

The **Puffin Kite Festival,** one of several kite events held on the coast, takes advantage of late April's blustery winds. Individuals and teams demonstrate flying techniques and compete for prizes; for kids, there's a treasure hunt, sandcastle building, and face painting. The festival is held just north of Haystack Rock, in front of the Surfsand Resort, which sponsors the event.

The half dozen or so other sand-sculpting contests that take place on the Oregon coast pale in comparison to Cannon Beach's annual **Sandcastle Day.** In 1964, a tsunami washed out a bridge, and the isolated residents of Cannon Beach organized the first contest as a way to amuse their children. Now in

its fifth decade, this is the state's oldest and most prestigious competition of its kind. Tens of thousands of spectators show up to watch 1,000-plus competitors fashion their sculptures with the aid of buckets, shovels, squirt guns, and any natural material found on the beach. The resulting sculptures are often amazingly complex and inventive. This event is free to spectators, but entrants pay a fee. Recent winners included Egyptian pyramids and a gigantic sea turtle. The event usually coincides with the lowest-tide Saturday in June. Call 503/436-2623 to find out the exact date of this collapsible art show, which takes place north of Haystack Rock. Building begins in the early morning; winners are announced at noon. The American Legion serves a big breakfast buffet at 1216 S. Hemlock Street, open to all.

The **Artist and Lecture Series** features notable regional writers, poets, artists, and others reading from their works or speaking on their craft in spring and fall. Dates and locations are posted around town, or contact the **Cannon Beach Arts Association** (1064 S. Hemlock St., Cannon Beach 97110, 503/436-0744) for a schedule.

In July and August, the well-regarded **Haystack Summer Program in the Arts** (503/464-4812, www.haystack.pdx.edu) offers classes and workshops in painting, music, gardening, and writing, including the annual Pacific Northwest Children's Book Conference. In addition, evening readings, art exhibits, and lectures are open to the public.

For a weekend in early November, writers, singers, composers, painters, and sculptors take over the town for the **Stormy Weather Arts Festival** (503/436-2623). Events include music on the streets, plays, a Saturday afternoon Art Walk, and the Quick Draw, in which artists have one hour to paint, complete, and frame a piece while the audience watches. The art is then sold by auction.

SHOPPING
Art Galleries

Cannon Beach has long attracted artists and artisans, and here art lovers and purchasers will find nearly two dozen outlets with high quality works. Most of the Cannon Beach galleries and boutiques are concentrated along Hemlock Street, where you can hardly swing a Winsor & Newton No. 12 hogbristle brush without hitting one. Not surprisingly, the seashore itself is the subject and inspiration of many works you'll see here, with Haystack Rock frequently depicted in various media. Cannon Beach Information Center has a guide to all the galleries in town, or you can just stroll and discover them for yourself.

At the north end of town, **Northwest by Northwest Gallery** (232 N. Spruce, 503/436-2428) has a new location to showcase its works of photography by Christopher Burkett and leading glass artists such as Duane Dahl. **White Bird Gallery** (251 N. Hemlock St., 503/436-2681), founded in 1971 and one of Cannon Beach's oldest galleries, casts a wide net with paintings, sculpture, prints, photography, glass, ceramics, and jewelry. Nearby, the **Artists Gallerie** (224 N. Hemlock St., 503/436-0336) is a working studio showing the works of 12 painters whose styles range from realist to pure abstraction. The **Uffelman Gallery** (271 N. Hemlock St., 503/436-2404) showcases the strikingly modern still lifes of Jeff Uffelman, which transform such mundane ingredients as a handful of peapods or peeled cucumbers into mesmerizing images. In midtown, **Icefire Glassworks** (at Gower and Hemlock St., 503/436-2359) is a working glass studio where you can watch glassblowers and artists shape their work and then shop for unique pieces in the gallery.

DragonFire Gallery (123 S. Hemlock St., 503/436-1533) is a teaching studio, offering weekend classes on various media. Throughout the summer, everyone is invited to come and express his or her creativity, tipple some wine, and listen to live music at the Saturday-night "Paint Party," hosted by local artists 6–10 P.M.

Specialty Shops

Much of the attraction in Cannon Beach is window shopping up and down Hemlock Street, which, in addition to galleries, is lined with clothing stores, gift shops, and other boutiques. Cannon Beach supports two fine kite stores one block apart, where you can gear up for the big Puffin Kite Festival: **Once Upon a Breeze** (240 N. Spruce St., 503/436-1112) and **Wind Dancer** (210 N. Hemlock St., 503/436-8612). The **Cannon Beach Book Company** (130 N. Hemlock St., 503/436-1301) is one of the better bookstores on the coast. This is the place to pick up regional titles or a good novel (lots of mysteries) for that rainy weekend.

In the **Cannon Beach Mall,** two shops specialize in European imports: **A Stór** (175 E. 2nd St., 503/436-0664) carries handcrafted items from Ireland, including hand-knit sweaters, pottery, and jewelry; **Aagesen's Imports** (183 N. Hemlock St., 503/436-1737) focuses on Scandinavian imports. **Ecola Square** (123 S. Hemlock St.) has a clutch of boutiques focused on nature and the outdoors: the **Wild Bird Shop** (bird feeders, birdhouses, etc.), **Shorelines, NW** (shells), and **Nature Arts & Sounds** (fountains and supplies).

ACCOMMODATIONS
$50-100

There aren't many inexpensive lodging options in Cannon Beach but the **McBee Motel** (888 S. Hemlock St., 503/436-0247, www.mcbeecottages.com, $45–130) is clean and perfectly comfortable. Nothing fancy and certainly not expansive, the McBee nonetheless is a favorite of those who like it simple and inexpensive. And it's just a minute from the beach and within walking distance of downtown. McBee accepts pets in its homey cottages.

$100-150

About a one-minute walk to the beach, with friendly management and a great vibe, the **Blue Gull Inn** (632 S. Hemlock St., 503/436-2714 or 800/507-2714, www.bluegullinn.net, doubles from $105) offers a choice between a beach house or less expensive motel units which come with housekeeping facilities. The modern cottages have in-room whirlpool tubs, fireplaces, and full kitchens. Cottages for larger groups are also available. On-site are a sauna and laundry room. Blue Gull Inn is one of four relatively inexpensive properties managed by Haystack Lodgings, which can be reached through the Blue Gull Inn website.

For a homey atmosphere, try the **Argonauta Inn** or the **The Waves Motel** (the office for both is located at 188 W. 2nd St., 503/436-2205 or 800/822-2468, www.thewavesmotel .com, doubles from $109). The Argonauta is made up of four houses in the middle of downtown and has five furnished units just 150 feet from the beach. A cluster of six buildings makes up The Waves, with units to fit the needs of families, couples, or larger groups. These are not cookie-cutter units but the kind of individual lodgings you'd expect in Oregon.

For a family-oriented beachfront lodgings try **Sea Sprite Guest Lodgings** (280 S. Nebesna St., 503/436-2266 or 866/828-1050, www .seasprite.com, doubles from $139), just south of Haystack Rock, with six cottages with kitchens, TV, and spectacular views, which hold up to two, six, or eight. These family-style beach cottages are a throwback to the Oregon coast of an earlier era. Inside you'll find such homey touches as fireplaces, games, books, periodicals, and rockers.

The **Cannon Beach Hotel** (1116 Hemlock St., 503/436-1392, doubles from $120) is a converted 1910 loggers' boardinghouse with 30 rooms and a small café and restaurant on the premises. The most expensive rooms have fireplaces, whirlpools, and partial ocean views. Meals are available in the restaurant adjacent to the lobby.

Just a few minutes' walk from downtown, **Ecola Creek Lodge** (208 E. 5th St., 503/436-2776 or 800/873-2749, www.cannonbeachlodge.com, doubles from $125) is a Cape Cod–style inn with 22 unique units set within four buildings. Accommodations range from simple queen-bed studios to two-bedroom suites. Special features include stained glass, lawns, fountains, flower gardens, and a lily pond. Les Shirley Park and Ecola Creek separate the lodge from the beach.

The enormous **Tolovana Inn** (3400 S. Hemlock St., 503/436-2211 or 800/333-8890, www.tolovanainn.com, doubles from $105) hotel complex sits at the southern end of the Cannon Beach sprawl. Tolovana Inn has a number of room types, ranging from studios to one- and two-bedroom condos, all with full kitchens, balconies, and fireplaces. To make up for the rather cookie-cutter design and furnishings, you'll get a swimming pool, spa and sauna, a number of restaurants sharing the same parking lots, and the beach right out the front door. The least expensive rooms have "mountain views," while oceanfront rooms are roughly $100 more per night.

The oceanfront **Hallmark Resort** (1400 S. Hemlock St., 503/436-1566 or 888/448-4449, www.hallmarkinns.com, doubles from $139) boasts romantic views of Haystock Rock. With convention and meeting facilities, a pool, and on-site massage available, this is a service-oriented resort geared to accommodate couples, families, and large groups. In-room fireplaces add a romantic touch.

$150-200

The handsome **Inn at Cannon Beach** (3215 S. Hemlock St., 503/436-9085 or 800/321-6304, www.atcannonbeach.com, doubles from $179) has large and stylish cottage-like rooms in a beautifully landscaped garden setting, with a courtyard pond, all just a block from the beach. All rooms include a gas fireplace, fridge, microwave, coffeemaker, and TV/VCR.

$200 and Up

The **Surfsand Resort** (148 W. Gower St., 503/436-2274 or 800/547-6100, www.surfsand.com, doubles from $239) offers a great combination of location and amenities in Cannon Beach. There are a number of room types, but most are spacious suites with kitchens, fireplaces, and spas. Guests may use the Cannon Beach Athletic Club and an indoor pool and spa. The rooms at the Surfsand have recently been stylishly upgraded, and another 50 units is scheduled to be added.

Two top-end hotels offer beachfront lodging and luxury. The ■ **Stephanie Inn** (2740 Pacific St., 503/436-3466 or 800/633-3466, www.stephanie-inn.com, doubles from $200) offers attentive, B&B-style service and attention to detail plus luxury-level rooms. All guest rooms have balconies, fireplaces, wet bars, Jacuzzi tubs, fine linens, and all the extras you'd expect in an upscale resort hotel—including a fine dining restaurant. Every room has outstanding views of the beach and Haystack Rock. The **Ocean Lodge** (2864 S. Pacific Dr., 503/436-2241 or 888/777-4047, doubles from $269) feels like a long-established beach getaway, though in fact it's recently built. The high-end furnishings also give a clue that despite its venerable design this rambling lodge isn't soaked in tradition. Rooms all have oceanfront views, balconies, DVD players, fireplaces, microwaves, and refrigerators.

For a more private experience just steps from the ocean, the **White Heron Lodge** (356 N. Spruce, 503/436-2205 or 800/822-2468, doubles from $279) comprises two fully furnished oceanfront Victorian-style homes, both of which sleep up to four. Each of the suites looks directly out to the Pacific. Wide sandy beaches and spacious front lawns make it a great location for families, especially those with small children. Located on a residential dead-end street, the lodge is only one block from the village.

Vacation Rentals

Several local property management companies offer a large selection of furnished rentals ranging from grand oceanfront homes to quaint secluded cottages. **Cannon Beach Property Management** (3188 S. Hemlock St., 503/436-2021 or 877/386-3402) allows visitors to virtually tour its list of homes (www.cbpm.com), as does **Cannon Beach Vacation Rentals** (P.O. Box 723, Cannon Beach 97110, 866/436-0940, www.visitcb.com). Rates for both range $65–400.

FOOD

If you're on a budget, keep dining prices down at the **Mariner Market** (139 N. Hemlock St., 503/436-2442), an antique-filled grocery that's fully stocked with fresh meat, fruit, and veg-

etables. It carries organic produce and natural food products as well as a deli with takeout items. Open 9 A.M.–9 P.M.

In the fishing business for more than 25 years, **Ecola Seafoods** (208 N. Spruce, 503/436-9130) features fresh-catch Dungeness crab and bay shrimp cocktails, as well as a decent clam chowder. Or sample the smoked salmon and fish and chips. You'll find it across from the public parking lots and information center.

Casual Dining

Try the wood-paneled, sky-lit **Lazy Susan Cafe** (126 N. Hemlock St., 503/436-2816, open for three meals daily) for anytime breakfast (eggs with a side of bread pudding), lunch (sandwiches and salads), and light dinner (hot seafood salad). There's also the fresh fish catch of the day and pizza. Head up the street to the **Lazy Susan Grill & Scoop** (156 N. Hemlock St.) to wash it all down with espresso or a soda fountain concoction at this spacious family-friendly establishment. Both restaurants are open until 5 P.M. (8 P.M. on weekends).

The local **Pig 'N Pancake** (223 S. Hemlock St., 503/436-2851, open for three meals daily) has large picture windows overlooking a leafy ravine. Breakfast, of which there are 35 varieties including homemade pancakes, is served anytime. For lunch, try the soups, chowder, or halibut fish and chips.

Brewpubs

Bill's Tavern (188 N. Hemlock St., 503/436-2202, open for lunch and dinner), once a legendary watering hole, is now a more traditional remodeled brewpub. Sweet thick onion rings, good fries, one-third-pound burgers, sautéed prawns, and grilled oysters are the bill of fare.

Farther south near Tolovana is the **Warren House Pub** (3301 S. Hemlock St., 503/436-1130, open for lunch and dinner daily) serves local beers from Bill's Tavern but in an English pub setting. The menu includes good smoked ribs, burgers, and seafood; in summer the beer garden is a lovely spot to relax.

American

Cafe Mango (1235 S. Hemlock St., 503/436-2393, open daily for breakfast and lunch) is another mainstay, locally famous for such dishes as Amish oatcake waffles, blueberry cornmeal pancakes, frittatas, bagels and lox, and creative omelettes. Such Mexican dishes as pozole soup, chilaquiles, and a breakfast burrito stuffed with homemade refried beans and eggs are also winners in this homey restaurant. Fresh fruit smoothies, homemade ketchup and jam, as well as extensive vegetarian options with organic ingredients also explain Mango's cult status.

The **Lumberyard Rotisserie and Grill** (264 3rd St., 503/436-0285, open for lunch and dinner daily, main courses $10–19) is a block away from busy downtown Cannon Beach, but this spacious newer restaurant offers high-quality food at good prices. The specialty is rotisserie meats, including turkey, chicken, and prime rib, but the pizza here is also good.

Pizza

Fultano's Pizza (200 N. Hemlock St., 503/436-9717) sits unobtrusively near the corner of 2nd and Hemlock on your way to the beach. If you're hungry, aromas of fresh cheese, garlic, and free-baked dough will draw you inside this brick enclave. Right downtown, **Pizza à Fetta** (231 N. Hemlock St., 503/436-0333) serves traditional hand-tossed gourmet pizzas, house salads, homemade pasta, minestrone soup, and Oregon and Italian micro-brewed beer and wines. All sauces and dressings are made in-house, meriting this little business a huge local following and inclusion in *Pizza Today Magazine's* Top 100 independent pizzerias in the United States.

Seafood

Hankering for some authentic West Coast chowder? Head to **Dooger's Seafood and Grill** (1371 S. Hemlock St., 503/436-2225, open for three meals daily, main courses $11–14) for award-winning seafood. **Mo's at Tolovana** (195 Warren Way, 503/436-1111), next to Tolovana Park, boasts a restaurant site

once selected by *Pacific Northwest* magazine as having the most romantic view on the Oregon coast. Add this to Mo's reliable formula of fresh fish and rich clam chowder at very reasonable prices in a family-friendly atmosphere, and you can't miss.

Fine Dining

Whether or not you're staying at the **Stephanie Inn** (2740 S. Pacific Dr., 503/436-2221 or 800/633-3466), you are welcome to join guests in the dining room for a four-course prix fixe dinner featuring innovative Northwest cuisine. The atmosphere boasts mountain views, open wood beams, and a river-rock fireplace. Since guests get first shot at tables, those staying elsewhere should reserve well ahead of time.

Cozy and refined, **The Bistro** (263 N. Hemlock St., 503/436-2661, open for dinner Wed.–Mon., main courses $14–25) is tucked back in a maze of shops and gardens in downtown Cannon Beach. The atmosphere is quintessentially French country inn, and the menu brings a taste of Provence to traditional fish and seafood dishes—the seafood stew is a wonderful blend of Northwest fish and shellfish prepared with Mediterranean zest. The dining room is truly tiny and the food superlative, so reservations are mandatory.

Half restaurant, half European-style charcuterie and deli, the **Gower Street Bistro** (1116 S. Hemlock St., 503/436-2729, open for brunch Mon., Wed., Fri., Sat. and Sun., dinner nightly, main courses $10–22) offers lots of goodies for impromptu picnics by day, then by night shifts gears and turns into a casual but well-honed dining room with a cocktail bar ambience. The salads are fantastic, and the garlicky, roast 40-Clove Chicken is delicious. It's located in the Cannon Beach Hotel.

Somewhat oddly, few of Cannon Beach's top restaurants have a view of the beach, so if fine dining and views of Haystack Rock and breaking waves are important to you, then call to reserve a table at **The Wayfarer** (1190 Pacific Dr., 503/436-1108, open for three meals daily), tucked above a beach entrance at Gower Street. Tables have great views, and the menu, which features classic steak and seafood main courses, is more than up to the task of competing for attention. The lounge here is a good spot for a drink.

INFORMATION AND SERVICES

The chamber of commerce operates the **Cannon Beach Information Center** (201 E. 2nd St., Cannon Beach 97110, 503/436-2623, www.cannonbeach.org, open 11 A.M.–5 P.M. Mon.–Sat., 10 A.M.–4 P.M. Sun.). This facility is close to the public restrooms (2nd and Spruce) and basketball and tennis courts. The **post office** (155 N. Hemlock St., 503/436-2822) is open 9 A.M.–5 P.M. Monday–Friday.

Sandpiper Medical Walk-in Clinic (171 N. Larch St., 503/436-1142) offers medical care for the whole family and minor emergency services. It's located in Sandpiper Square behind the stores on the main drag.

GETTING THERE AND AROUND

From U.S. 101, there's a choice of four entrances to the beach loop (also known as U.S. 101 Alternate, a section of the old Oregon Coast Highway) to take you into town. As you wade into the town's shops, galleries, and restaurants, the beach loop becomes Hemlock Street, the main drag of Cannon Beach. Sunset Empire Transportation District operates **The Bus** (503/861-7433), which serves Cannon Beach, Seaside, Astoria-Warrenton, and points in between. **Parking** can be hard to come by, especially on weekends, but you'll find public lots south of town at Tolovana Park and in town at Hemlock at 1st Street and on 2nd Street.

The free **Cannon Beach Shuttle** runs every half hour on a 6.5-mile loop, from Les Shirley Park on the north end of town to Tolovana Park; it operates 10 A.M.–6 P.M. daily, with extended summer hours.

Nehalem Bay Area

MANZANITA AND VICINITY

Just south of Arch Cape, **Neahkahnie Mountain** towers nearly 1,700 feet up from the edge of the sea. U.S. 101 climbs up and over its shoulders, to an elevation of 700 feet, and the vistas from a half dozen pullouts (highest along the Oregon coast) are spectacular—but do try to keep your eyes on the snaking road until you've parked your car.

This stretch of the highway, built by the WPA in the 1930s, was constructed by blasting a roadbed from the rock face and buttressing it with stonework walls on the precarious cliffs. The faint-hearted or acrophobic certainly couldn't have lasted long on this job. The handiwork of these road builders and masons can be admired at several pullouts, along with the breathtaking vista of Manzanita Beach, Nehalem Spit, and some 17 miles south to Cape Meares. Much of Neahkahnie Mountain and its rugged coastline are preserved in Oswald West State Park, one of the state's finest.

Immediately to the south, huddled along an expansive curve of beach at the foot of Neahkahnie Mountain, quiet Manzanita (pop. 785) makes a pleasant stop for lunch or for the weekend. As one of the few towns along the north Oregon coast that's not located directly on U.S. 101, Manzanita feels more peaceful and secluded than most others. When adjacent coastal areas are fogbound, the seven-mile-long Manzanita Beach usually enjoys sunshine because of the shelter of Neahkahnie Mountain. It also has good surfing and windsurfing.

Oswald West State Park

Most of Neahkahnie Mountain and the prominent headlands of Cape Falcon are encompassed within the 2,500-acre gem of Oswald West State Park. Whether or not you believe in the stories of lost pirate wealth buried somewhere on the mountain (see sidebar *The Lost Treasure of Neahkahnie Mountain*), there is real treasure today for all who venture here, in the

© JUDY JEWELL

Pitch your tent in a coastal old-growth forest at Oswald West State Park.

intangible currency of extraordinary natural beauty. The state park bears the name of Governor Oswald West, whose farsighted 1913 beach bill was instrumental in protecting Oregon's virgin shoreline. That same year, Neahkahnie Mountain was the site of another shipwreck, in somewhat mysterious circumstances (see sidebar *The Wreck of the Glenesslin*).

Several **hiking trails** weave through the park, including the 13 miles of the Oregon Coast Trail linking Arch Cape to the north with Manzanita. From the main parking lot on the east side of U.S. 101, a half-mile trail follows Short Sand Creek to **Short Sand Beach.** From Short Sand Beach, you can pick up the three-mile old growth–lined Cape Falcon Trail to the highway, or you might want just to linger at Smuggler's Cove, a popular spot for surfers year-round. Rainforests of hemlock, cedar, and gigantic Sitka spruce crowd the secluded, boulder-strewn shoreline. At daybreak or dusk, keep an eye out for Roosevelt elk.

A mile south of the main parking lot is the access road to the **Neahkahnie Mountain Summit Trail** on the east side of the highway. It's not well marked; look for a subdivision on the golf course to the west. Drive the gravel road up 0.25 mile to the trailhead parking lot and begin a moderately difficult 1.5-mile ascent. Allow about 45 minutes to get to the top. The summit view south to Cape Meares and east to the Nehalem Valley ranks as one of the finest on the coast.

To camp at Oswald West State Park (800/551-6949), walk 0.3 mile from the campers' parking lot to 30 primitive campsites in a grove of old-growth conifers surrounded by high cliffs. You can use the wheelbarrows at the parking lot and campground to cart your gear back and forth. Campsites are $14. There are flush toilets, but no electrical hookups.

Nehalem Bay State Park

Just south of Manzanita, and occupying the entire sandy appendage of Nehalem Spit, is scenic, sprawling Nehalem Bay State Park (503/368-5943 for information, 800/452-5687 or www.reserveamerica.com for reservations, open year-round), a favorite with beginning windsurfers, bikers, beachcombers, and anglers. Sandwiched between the bay and a four-mile beach stretching from Manzanita to the mouth of the Nehalem River is a vast campground (rates are $20) with hot showers. There are 18 yurts for $27. A $3 daily day-use fee applies to noncampers. Park amenities include evening programs, flush toilets, and piped water. As big as this park is, it does fill up in summer, so reservations are recommended (particularly during July and August). To get there, turn south at Bayshore Junction just before U.S. 101 heads east into the town of Nehalem.

Accommodations

Manzanita is a small town, without an abundance of lodgings. Advance reservations are a must, especially in summer, and many accommodations require two- to three-night stays during the high season and on some holidays. A good alternative to motels for families here are the rentals available from the several property

THE LOST TREASURE OF NEAHKAHNIE MOUNTAIN

Is there pirate gold on Neahkahnie Mountain? Local native legends tell of Spanish pirates burying a treasure at Neahkahnie Mountain. One story relates that the crew of a shipwrecked Manila galleon salvaged its cargo of gold and beeswax (a valuable commodity in trade with Asia) by burying it in the side of the mountain. To deter Indians from the site, the pirates killed a black man and buried him on top of the cargo. While this account taken from native histories has never been substantiated, a piece of crudely inscribed beeswax retrieved from the Neahkahnie region carbon-dated A.D. 1500-1700 (on display at Tillamook's Pioneer Museum) keeps speculation alive. Further intrigue was added by the 1993 discovery of an ancient wooden rigging block. Found in the mud at the mouth of the Nehalem River, it was determined by a Spanish maritime expert to have been from a Manila galleon during that same time period. Lewis and Clark's 1805 reports of a Chinook Indian with red hair, and similar accounts from the Vancouver Expedition's 1792 encounter with a redheaded native who claimed his late father had been a shipwrecked Spanish sailor, would tend to corroborate the shipwreck and treasure stories passed down in native oral histories.

management agencies in town. Among these is **Ribbon Investment Firm** (430 Laneda Ave., Manzanita 97130, 888/503-6009, www.ribbon vacationrentals.com), with more than 40 fully furnished homes to let, running $125–225 per night (most require weekly rentals in July and August).

If you're looking for an upscale retreat, the cedar-clad **Inn at Manzanita** (67 Laneda Ave., Manzanita 97130, 503/368-6754, www.innat manzanita.com, doubles from $120), set in a Japanese-accented garden just a short walk from the beach, promises guests (no children) the three Rs: recreation, relaxation, and romance. Each of its 13 wood-paneled rooms features a gas fireplace and two-person spa; most rooms have a balcony, offering glimpses through the evergreens of the nearby beach. Fresh flowers daily, robes, and other amenities help you feel pampered. Despite being in the middle of town near restaurants and the beach, a feeling of luxurious seclusion prevails. A two-night minimum stay is required on weekends and July 1–Labor Day, and discounts are available.

Six blocks from the beach, the five spacious, stylish, and airy cabins of **Coast Cabins** (635 Laneda Ave., 503/368-7113, www.coastcabins .com, doubles from $125) comfortably sleep one to two (two-story Cabin 5 is designed for up to four persons) and offer kitchenettes or full kitchens, satellite TV, and goose-down pillows and comforters. Two-night minimum for advance reservations in summer and weekends all year. Pets are allowed in some cabins for a $20 nightly fee.

The Arbors Bed-and-Breakfast (78 Idaho Ave., 503/368-7566 or 888/664-9587, doubles are $105–115), one block from the beach, offers two cozy rooms with private bath in a handsome, Craftsman-style cottage built in the early 1920s.

For a more standard motel experience, the **Sunset Surf** (248 Ocean Rd., 503/368-5224 or 800/243-8035, www.sunsetsurfocean.com, doubles from $95) offers guest rooms (many with kitchens) in three oceanfront units which share an outdoor pool.

Food

House renters, budget diners, and picnickers can take advantage of the excellent produce and impressive (for a coastal market) grocery section at **Manzanita Grocery & Deli** (2nd and Laneda Ave., open until 8 P.M.). One block away, **Mother Nature's Natural Foods Store** (10 A.M.–7 P.M. Mon.–Sat.) stocks natural groceries, coffees and teas, bulk foods, wine, and beer.

for a brew and a burger, the **San Dune Tavern** (127 Laneda Ave., 503/368-5080) is a friendly spot to hole up; it's smoke-free, too.

Up near U.S. 101, **Terra Cotta Cafe** (725 Manzanita Ave., 503/368-3700, open for dinner Wed.–Sun., main courses $9–28) offers French-influenced dining with charmingly low-key ambience. Parchment poached salmon is served with apples and blue cheese, while lamb chops are served with cranberry-jalapeño sauce. The **Manzanita Seafood and Chowder House** (591 Laneda Ave., 503/368-2722, open for lunch and dinner daily) serves pretty much what its name implies, plus sandwiches, burgers, and chicken.

NEHALEM

Tiny Nehalem (pop. 230), occupying just a few blocks along U.S. 101 on the north bank of the Nehalem River, has developed several gift and antique shops and restaurants and a few surprise attractions in keeping with its new identity as a tourist town. Sizable runs of spring and fall chinook salmon and winter steelhead make this a popular destination for anglers. In August, locals claim you could just about cross the river stepping from boat to boat when the fish are in. Just southwest of town, the county maintains a boat-launch facility and dock, providing access to the river and to the bay downstream. The bay and slow-moving river also invite exploration by kayak and canoe; bring your own, or rent them in Nehalem.

Accommodations

Nehalem offers a couple of interesting lodging choices. If you'd like to overnight close to the river—*on* the river—try the **Ripple Run Resort and Marina** (503/368-3865 or 877/655-0623, www.ripplerunresort.com, doubles from $100). Choose among four one-of-a-kind floating lodgings, including a 35-foot barge that sleeps 4–6 for $135 nightly) or a 47-foot converted tug that sleeps three. If a night on the water doesn't entice, opt for a room in a riverside cottage. All units include linens, towels, kitchenettes with dishes, gas barbecues,

© JUDY JEWELL

Public art or beach shelter? driftwood sculpture at Nehalem Bay State Park, Manzanita

Left Coast Siesta (288 Laneda Ave., 503/368-7997, closed Mon.–Tues.) specializes in design-your-own-burritos, the perfect takeout for a filling lunch or dinner. Options include spicy beef, spicy chicken, tequila-lime chicken, or black beans to put into a selection of flavored tortillas. It also serves tacos and enchiladas. Budget diners can eat well here for less than $6. And even though it advertises "fast, healthy, and fresh," Left Coast doesn't sacrifice flavor. And if you like it *caliente,* this is the place for you: Left Coast Siesta stocks a hot sauce bar with 200-plus different types of the hot stuff.

Even closer to the water, **Marzano's** (60 Laneda Ave., 503/368-5593) serves the coast's best slices of gourmet pizza, with prices to match—$15–24 for large-size whole pies. The roasted vegetable pizza is recommended, and the smoked prosciutto with aged Montegrappa cheese is another winner. The understated decor here is dominated by reproductions of French advertising posters. If you're looking

THE WRECK OF THE *GLENESSLIN*

The sea was calm and the winds mild along the north Oregon coast on the afternoon of October 1, 1913, when locals observed a square-rigged ship sailing perilously close to the Nehalem shore. The Liverpool-built three-master *Glenesslin*, bound for Portland, was one of a dying breed of large sailing ships on the high seas, which were quickly being replaced by steam-powered vessels. Built in 1885, it was a fine ship, and fast: Its 74-day passage from Portland, Oregon, to Port Elizabeth, South Africa, was never surpassed by another square-rigger. But on this day, in the twilight of sail, seasoned and reliable crews were scarce – the *Glenesslin*'s first and second officers were but 22 years old – and inexperience led to disaster.

According to maritime author James A. Gibbs, in his fascinating *Shipwrecks of the Pacific Coast*, the *Glenesslin*, under full sail, suddenly turned east toward the base of Neahkahnie Mountain. Losing the wind under the lee of Cape Falcon, Gibbs theorizes, the ship lost headway and the crew was unable to bring it about. As it neared the shore, an underwater reef ripped open the ship's bottom plates. The crew shot a line to shore, and, with the help of local rescuers, all 21 hands made it safely to land – many of them, it was said, under the influence of strong drink. As breakers pounded the stern, grinding the ship against the rocks, it soon began to break up. A Nehalem man bought the dying vessel for $100, but there was little hope of salvaging much.

In the lengthy official inquiry that followed, the captain and second mate were judged negligent in their duty, and the first mate reprimanded. The ship's underwriter initially balked at covering the loss, claiming that the ship had been intentionally wrecked in a scheme to collect the insurance, but the insurer eventually paid up. It was a heartbreaking end for a beautiful and storied ship.

cable TV, and videos, plus free use of kayaks, golf clubs, and boat moorage at Ripple Run's docks. Reservations are recommended.

An easily overlooked hideaway a short drive off U.S. 101 southeast of Nehalem is (**The Nehalem River Inn Lodge** (34910 Hwy. 53, 503/355-2301 or 800/368-6499, www .nehalemriverinn.com, doubles from $99). Perched right on the South Fork of the Nehalem, this one-time roadhouse dating back to the 1930s has been converted into a five-unit riverside retreat with a surprise trump card—an outstanding restaurant serving gourmet Northwest cuisine made from local ingredients. Each of the sunny, comfortable units has a private bath, cable TV, and a deck affording views of the river, the surrounding pasturelands, and mountains. The romantic white Riverside Cottage is a two-room suite with a kitchenette, fireplace, and a two-person spa. Eagle's Aerie also comprises two rooms, with a queen-size bed and twin hide-a-bed, plus kitchenette. The spacious Cormorant's

Watch features a fireplace, king-size bed, jetted tub, and sweeping views from large picture windows, while the smaller Heron's Lookout sleeps one to two in its queen-size bed. The inn also rents kayaks, which you can launch from the private dock to paddle up and down the river on a wildlife safari; you may spot otters, elk, bald eagles, and even seals that venture upriver from the bay.

Food

The (**Nehalem River Inn** (34910 Hwy. 53, 503/368-7708, www.nehalemriverinn.com, open for dinner Fri.–Mon., main courses $18–29) is one of the best places on the coast to experience fresh and inventive Northwest cuisine. The inn's sophisticated menu blends Northwest seafood, game, locally grown organic produce, wild mushrooms, and other ingredients to create dishes that will turn the heads of even the most discriminating diners—such as Muscovy duck breast served with black truffle potato gnocchi or Piedmontese Filet Mignon with potato and parsnip gratin. Complement your meal with a bottle from a well-selected wine list favoring Oregon wineries, including Nehalem River Inn's own private-label wines. Reservations are recommended.

On the riverside in Nehalem, **Currents** (35815 U.S. 101 N., 503/368-5557, open for lunch and dinner daily in summer, closed Mon. and Tues. the rest of the year, main courses $12–26) is an enjoyable spot for a casual lunch or dinner, with pastoral views from the dining room and adjoining deck. The menu features seasonal and local fish, seafood, and beef, but with hip and up-to-date preparations. Expect a strawberry, endive, and avocado salad and crispy crab cakes served with grapefruit beurre blanc.

Winery

The **Nehalem Bay Winery** (34965 Hwy. 53, 503/368-9463, www.nehalembaywinery.com) offers tastings and sales of its varietals, as well as fruit and berry wines (pinot noir, gewürztraminer, and blackberry). You can tour the grounds here and picnic 10 A.M.–6 P.M. daily or enjoy the tasting room's welcoming milieu. To get to the winery, look for the Highway 53 sign on U.S. 101 and head east 1.5 miles.

WHEELER

Wheeler (pop. 350) is a little town astride the Nehalem River where most accommodations are low-cost efficiencies for visiting fisherfolk, but the 10 rooms of the **Wheeler on the Bay Lodge and Marina** (580 Marine Dr., 503/368-5858 or 800/469-3204, $75–135), on U.S. 101 on the shore of Nehalem Bay, have more appeal. Seven rooms have bay views, five have jetted tubs, and all have different decor. There's also a video store, kayak rentals, dock tie-ups ($6 per night), and on-site massages, and they can help arrange fishing charters. Across the street, you can rent sea kayaks, recreational kayaks, surfboards, and other gear from **Nehalem Bay Kayak Co.** (503/368-6055). The company also organizes guided paddle tours of the bay on Saturday and Tuesday.

Nehalem Bay at Wheeler is popular with kayakers and fishers.

The Old Wheeler Hotel Bed & Breakfast (495 U.S. 101, Wheeler 97147, 503/368-6000 or 877/653-4683, $75–220 May–Sept.), a 1920s landmark across the road from the bay, has discounts available on weekdays and during the off-season. On weekends, a Swedish massage in the hotel's new massage room starts at $25 for a half hour—just the thing after a long day of kayaking or fishing.

In a tiny cottage with seven tables (and bayview outdoor seating on the deck when possible), the **Treasure Café** (92 Rorvik St., 503/368-7740, dinner Thurs.–Sun., main courses $19–28), just off U.S. 101, offers the unexpected: a French-trained chef who creates an inventive World Beat–type cuisine based on seasonal local ingredients. Don't let the humble appearance put you off—the food is very good here. Local shiitake mushrooms are stuffed with crab and crayfish, and Szechuan-style shrimp are bathed in mango and guava sauce. Note that the Treasure Café is no longer open for breakfast (this was once a highly esteemed stop for breakfast).

ROCKAWAY BEACH

This town of 1,200 was established as a summer resort in the 1920s by Portlanders who wanted a coastal getaway. And so it remains today—a quiet spot without much going on besides walks on the seven miles of sandy beach, a **Kite Festival** in mid-May, and an **Arts and Crafts Fair** in mid-August. Shallow **Lake Lytle,** on the east side of the highway, offers spring and early summer fishing for trout, bass, and crappie. While the town of Rockaway is unattractive from Highway 101—a lengthy stretch of tacky shops and modest motels—the beach is quite nice, anchored at the south by the impressive Twin Rocks formation. Several new and very large condo developments are going in along the highway, so if you liked Rockaway for its simple offerings and lack of pretense, now is the time to visit. The **Visitor Information Center** (503/355-8108), lodged in a bright red caboose in the center of town, can fill you in on other goings-on.

Accommodations

Rockaway's lodgings are basic and family oriented. Each of the following is on the ocean side of busy Highway 101, which dominates this long string bean of a town. **Surfside Resort Motel** (101 NW 11th, 503/355-2312 or 800/243-7786, www.surfsideocean.com, doubles from $109) is a large beachfront complex with an indoor pool. Some kitchen rooms are available. **Silver Sands Resort Hotel** (213 S. Pacific Ave., 503/355-2206 or 800/457-8972, www.oregonsilversands.com) is also right on the beach, with nicely furnished rooms, an indoor pool and hot tub, and sauna.

Food

Look to Rockaway's **Beach Pancake and Dinner House** (202 U.S. 101 N., 503/355-2411, open for three meals daily) for big portions at moderate prices. Locals tout the chicken and dumplings. Other features include Mexican dishes, fresh oysters, and breakfast all day. Photos and paintings by local artists cover the walls at **R and R Espresso & Morning Glory Café** (120 U.S. 101 N., 503/355-3315, open for breakfast and lunch daily), which offers coffee and baked goods in the morning and salads and panini sandwiches for lunch. **Cow Belle Cafe** (194 U.S. 101 S, 503/355-2441, open for lunch and dinner daily, breakfast Thurs.–Sun.) is a locals' favorite for good burgers and other American fare. The biscuits and gravy here is renowned, as is the bovine-rich decor.

Tillamook and the Tillamook Bay Area

GARIBALDI

Tillamook Bay's commercial fishing fleet is concentrated in this little port town (pop. 970) near the north end of the bay. Garibaldi, named in 1879 by the local postmaster for the Italian patriot, is a fish-processing center: Crabs, shrimp, fresh salmon, lingcod, and bottom fish (halibut, cabezon, rockfish, and sea perch) are the specialties here. At the marina, **Bayocean Seafood** (608 Commercial Dr., 503/322-3316) gets it right off the boats, so the selection is both low-priced and fresh. Likewise is the crab, fish, and other seafood available next door at **Oregon Gourmet** (606 Commercial Dr., 503/322-2544). If you want it fresher, you'll have to catch it yourself.

And the town's fishing and crabbing piers *do* attract hordes who want to catch their own. Rent crab traps, kayaks, and other gear at the **Garibaldi Marina** (302 Mooring Basin Rd., 503/322-3312). In addition to dock fishing, guide and charter services offer salmon and halibut fishing, bird-watching, and whale-watching excursions. North of Garibaldi on U.S. 101, the bay entrance is a good place to see brown pelicans, harlequin ducks, oystercatchers, and guillemots. The Miami River marsh, south of town, is a bird-watching paradise at low tide, when ducks and shorebirds hunt for food.

Garibaldi Maritime Museum

This small but interesting museum (112

NORTH COAST FONDUE

Here's a tasty way to enjoy the famous cheese, trees, and ocean breeze of Oregon's north coast: When visiting the Tillamook Cheese Factory, purchase a 10-ounce bar of Tillamook extra sharp cheddar. They are often on special for just a couple of bucks. These so-called seconds may look funky, but their cosmetic blemishes are actually an indication of additional aging that enrich the flavor, and they can be easily trimmed. You might consider getting an extra bar or two to keep in your cooler to take home with you. You'll also need a bottle of beer. Every beer imparts its own distinctive finish. The Oregon ales in particular work best for this recipe (some of our favorites are Newport Pale Ale, Bridgeport Blue Heron, or Bridgeport Coho). Finally, you'll need a good loaf of bread, preferably sourdough or a crusty baguette.

Rest assured that a fancy fondue pot with a denatured alcohol burner is not required to produce and enjoy this venerable dish. It can just as easily be prepared on a campfire in a well-blackened Boy Scout pot. A camp stove also works quite well if you don't have access to a kitchen.

Begin by slicing the French bread into pieces about an inch square, so that each piece has some crust to hold it together. Then cut up the entire cheese bar into small cubes and toss them into a saucepan. Add about a half cup of beer to start. You can add more later, depending on how thick or thin you like your fondue. Melt the cheese on low temperature, stirring to obtain a creamy texture. Season to taste with pepper. Grab a fork, stab a piece of bread, dip it in, and feast.

Garibaldi Ave., 503/322-8411, www.garibaldi museum.com, open noon–4 P.M. Thurs.–Mon., July–Sept.) retells the history of this longtime fishing village. It also focuses on the late 18th-century sailing world and the British sea captain Robert Gray and his historical vessels, the *Lady Washington* and the *Columbia Redivivia*, which explored the Pacific Northwest in 1787 and 1792. Among the museum displays are models of these ships, an eight-foot-tall reproduction of the Columbia figurehead, a half model of the Columbia showing how the ship was provisioned for long voyages, as well as reproductions of period musical instruments and typical sailors' clothing.

Fishing

The **Miami River** and **Kilchis River,** which empty into Tillamook Bay south of Garibaldi, get the state's only two significant runs of chum salmon, a species much more common from Washington northward. There's a catch-and-release season for them mid-September to mid-November. Both rivers also get runs of spring chinook and are open for steelhead most of the year.

Several charter companies have offices at the marina. **Garibaldi Charters** (607 Garibaldi Ave., 503/322-0007, www.garibaldicharters .com) offers fishing excursions (a full day of salmon fishing costs $100) and wildlife-viewing or whale-watching trips ($20 per person). **Troller Deep Sea Charters** (503/322-3666) also offers fishing charters.

Accommodations

If you want to wake up on the docks, spend the night at **Harbor View Inn** (302 S. 7th St., 503/322-3251, doubles from $65), a motel popular with fishers and sportsmen. The **Bayshore Inn** (227 Garibaldi Ave., 503/322-2552 or 877/537-2121, doubles from $75) offers pleasant rooms up along the highway, while **Comfort Suites** (502 Garibaldi Ave., 503/322-3338 or 800/547-0106, doubles from $90) has an indoor pool, sauna, hot tub, and free high-speed Internet access in all rooms.

Food

Just north of Garibaldi, **Pirate's Cove Restaurant** (14170 U.S. 101 N., 503/322-2092, open for lunch and dinner daily) is one of the best restaurants between Manzanita and Lincoln City, serving excellent seafood and steaks and offering a dramatic vista of the mouth of Tillamook Bay. Try the Hangtown Fry, local oysters and razor clams. The **Fisherman's Korner Restaurant** (306 Mooring Basin, 503/322-2033, open Thurs.–Mon. for breakfast and lunch) is right on the wharf and offers absolutely fresh fish and chips and excellent clam chowder. Breakfasts here are massive—meant for hungry sailors.

Four miles south, at the little enclave of Bay City is another temple to seafood. **Pacific Oyster** (5150 Oyster Bay Dr., 503/377-2323, open for lunch and dinner daily, main courses from $8) is mostly an oyster-processing center, but it's also an excellent spot for a quick meal of fish or seafood. The fish specials are posted on a chalkboard, or choose standbys like cod and chips or something more unusual, like salmon on a stick. Crab cakes, halibut burgers, and clam chowder are also highlights. Of course, the main draw is the oysters, which here are both for eating and entertainment. As you eat, you can watch the oyster-shuckers in action next door, as the dining area overlooks the oyster-processing area.

TILLAMOOK

Without much sun or surf, what could possibly draw enough visitors to the town of Tillamook (pop. 4,270) to make it one of Oregon's top three tourism attractions? Superficially speaking, tours of a cheese factory and a World War II blimp hangar, in a town flanked by mudflats and rain-soaked dairy country, shouldn't pull in more than a million tourists a year. But they do. As anyone who has driven to Tillamook via the scenic Three Capes Loop or past Neahkahnie Mountain on U.S. 101 can attest, those tasty morsels of jack and cheddar provide the perfect complement to the surrounding region's scenic beauty.

Tillamook County is home to more than 26,000 cows, which easily outnumber the county's human population. They're the foundation of the Tillamook County Creamery Association's famous cheddar cheese and other dairy products, which generate about $85 million in annual sales. Other important contributors to the local economy are fishing and oyster farming.

In 1933, a wildfire devastated forests in the Coast Range east of town in what was the worst natural disaster in the state's history. The Tillamook Burn raged for four weeks, reducing massive acreage of old growth to rows of charred stumps. The fire pushed a cloud of ash 40,000 feet into the air. Ashfall was recorded 500 miles out to sea and as far east as Yellowstone National Park in Wyoming, while Oregon's upper left edge lived in semidarkness for weeks. Fires in 1939 and 1945 further ravaged the area, leaving a total of 355,000 acres destroyed by the three blazes. More than 72 million seedlings planted by a community reforestation effort in the years that followed have produced an impressive stand of trees in these forests today.

In 1940–1942, partially in response to a Japanese submarine firing on Fort Stevens in Astoria, the U.S. Navy built two blimp hangars south of town, the two largest wooden structures ever built, according to *The Guinness Book of World Records.* One of five naval air stations on the Pacific coast, the Tillamook blimp guard patrolled the waters from Northern California to the San Juan Islands and escorted ships into Puget Sound. While all kinds of blimp stories abound in Tillamook bars, only one wartime encounter has been documented. Recently declassified records confirm that blimps were involved in the sinking of what was believed to be two Japanese submarines off Cape Meares. In late May 1943, two of the high-flying craft, assisted by U.S. Navy subchasers and destroyers, dropped several depth charges on the submarines, which are still lying on the ocean floor.

Until 1946, when the station was decommissioned, naval presence here created a boomtown. Bars and businesses flourished and civilian jobs were easy to come by. After the war years, Tillamook County returned to the economic trinity of "trees, cheese, and ocean breeze" that has sustained the region to the present day.

Tillamook Cheese Factory

With over a million visitors a year, the Tillamook Cheese Factory (4175 U.S. 101 N., Tillamook, 503/842-4481, open 8 A.M.–8 P.M. daily in summer and 8 A.M.–6 P.M. Labor Day–mid-June, free admission) is far and away the county's biggest drawing card. The plant welcomes visitors with a reproduction of the *Morningstar,* the schooner that transported locally made butter and cheese in the late 1800s and now adorns the label of every Tillamook product. The quaint vessel symbolizing Tillamook cheesemaking's humble beginnings stands in contrast to the technology and sophistication that go into making this world-famous gourmet product today.

Inside the plant, a self-guided tour follows the movement of curds and whey to the "cheddaring table." Whey is drained from the curds, which are then cut and folded. These processes are coordinated by white-uniformed workers in a stadium-sized factory. As you look down on the antiseptic scene from the glassed-in observation area, it's hard to imagine this as the birthplace of many a pizza and grilled-cheese sandwich. Tastes of a few samples, however, prove it's true. Tillamook ice cream has been touted by the *New York Times* as superior to Häagen-Dazs, and its extra premium aged sharp white cheddar was rated the country's best cheese by the National Milk Producers in 1997.

User-friendly informational placards and historical displays recount Tillamook Valley's dairy history from 1851, when settlers began importing cows. The problem then was how to ship the milk to San Francisco and Portland. Even though salting butter to preserve it allowed exportation, ships still faced the difficulty of negotiating the treacherous Tillamook bar. In 1894, Peter McIntosh introduced techniques here to make cheddar cheese, whose long shelf life enabled it to be transported overland.

In the early 1900s, the Tillamook County Creamery Association absorbed smaller operations and opened the modern plant in 1949. Today, Tillamook produces tens of millions of pounds of cheese annually, including Monterey jack, swiss, and multiple variations of the award-winning white cheddar. Pepperoni, butter, cheese soup, milk, and other products are also available. There's a gift shop (more Holstein-themed tchochkes than you've probably dreamed of) and a full-service restaurant, but the big attraction is the ice cream counter. Have a double-scoop chocolate peanut butter cone—worth every penny.

Blue Heron French Cheese Company

A quarter-million people a year visit Tillamook County's *second*-most-popular attraction, Blue Heron French Cheese Company (2001 Blue Heron Dr., 503/842-8282, open 8 A.M.–8 P.M. daily in summer and 8 A.M.–6 P.M. Labor Day–mid-June, free admission), located a mile south of the Tillamook Cheese Factory. Housed in a large white barn, Blue Heron is famous for its brie-style cheese, though it's no longer produced on-site. In addition to cheeses and other gourmet foods, the shop sells gift baskets; over 90 varieties of Oregon wines are available in the wine-tasting room. A deli serves lunches of homemade soups and salads. For kids, there's a petting farm with the usual barnyard suspects.

Tillamook Air Museum

South of town off U.S. 101 you can't possibly miss the enormous Quonset hut–like building east of the highway. The world-class aircraft collection of the Tillamook Air Museum (6030 Hangar Rd., Tillamook, 503/842-1130, www.tillamookair.com, open 10 A.M.–5 P.M. daily, $11 adults, $10 seniors, $6 ages 6–17) is housed in and around Hangar B of the decommissioned Tillamook Naval Air Station. At 1,072 feet long, 206 feet wide, and 192 feet high, it's the largest wooden structure in the world. During World War II, this and another gargantuan hangar on the site (which burned down in 1992) sheltered eight K-class blimps, each 242 feet long.

Inside the seven-acre structure, you can learn about the role the big blimps played during wartime as well as how they are used today. In addition, there's a large collection of World

War II fighter planes (many one-of-a-kind models) as well as photos and artifacts from the naval air station days. Be sure to check out the cyclo-crane, a combination blimp/plane/helicopter. This was devised in the 1980s to aid in remote logging operations; it ended up an $8 million bust.

If possible, bring binoculars here to see the interesting latticework of rafters and Navy-uniformed mannequins on the catwalks 20 stories up. To get there from downtown, take U.S. 101 south two miles, make a left at the flashing yellow light, and follow the signs.

Tillamook County Pioneer Museum

East of the highway in the heart of downtown, Tillamook County Pioneer Museum (2106 2nd St., Tillamook, 503/842-4553, open 9 A.M.–5 P.M. Mon.–Sat., 11 A.M.–5 P.M. Sunday, $3 general admission, $2.50 for seniors) is famous for its taxidermy exhibits as well as memorabilia from pioneer households. Particularly intriguing are hunks of ancient beeswax with odd inscriptions recovered from near Neahkahnie Mountain, which are thought to be remnants from 18th-century shipwrecks. The old courtroom on the second floor has one of the best displays of natural history in the state. There are many beautiful dioramas, plus shells, insects, and nests. The Beals Memorial Room houses a famous rock and mineral collection along with fossils.

The main floor and the basement highlight human history with antique kitchen tools, old-time logging equipment, Native American artifacts and basketry, historic modes of conveyance (from stagecoaches to cars), and simulated pioneer households.

Oregon Coast Explorer Trains

The Port of Tillamook Bay (503/842-8206, www.potb.org/oregoncoastexplorer.htm) operates a number of rail excursions between the fishing village of Garibaldi (eight miles north of Tillamook) to points north along the coast and west to Banks, on the other side of the Coast Range. The selection of trips and the schedule are both complex, so it's a good idea to check the website or call the office to find out what is on the calendar during your visit. The least expensive option is the 1.5-hour round-trip between Garibaldi and Rockaway Beach, which operates on Saturdays and Sundays from Memorial Day weekend to mid-September, and Fridays from July 4 through August, plus Memorial Day, July 4, and Labor Day. This train is pulled by a 1910 Heisler Locomotive Works engine. Tickets for this run are $13 adults, and $7 for children 3 to 10. Check the online schedule for dinner and brunch trips between other destinations.

Munson Creek Falls

Seven miles south of Tillamook, a 1.5-mile access road turns east from U.S. 101, leading to the highest waterfall in the Oregon Coast Range. Munson Creek Falls drops 266 feet over mossy cliffs surrounded by an old-growth forest. The very narrow, bumpy dirt road then takes you to the parking lot. A quarter-mile trail leads to the base of the falls, while another, slightly longer trail leads to a higher viewpoint; wooden walkways clinging to the cliff lead to a small viewing platform. This is a spectacle in all seasons, but come in winter when the falls pour down with greater fury. Note that motor homes and trailers cannot get into the park; the lot is too small.

Tillamook State Forest

A series of intense forest fires in the 1930s and 1940s burned vast amounts of land in the northern Coast Range. Most of this land was owned by private timber companies, who walked away from the seemingly worthless "Tillamook Burn," leaving property rights to revert to the counties, who then handed the land over to the state. A massive replanting effort ensued, and in 1973 the Tillamook Burn became the Tillamook State Forest. In 2006, the Tillamook Forest Visitor Center opened in a soaring timbered building in the middle of the once-burned, now-lush forest. Be sure to stop in to see the short movie about the area's history; the vivid fire scenes are a bit frightening, a sensation that's enhanced when the smell

A footbridge connects the Tillamook Forest Visitor Center with hiking trails.

of smoke is released into the auditorium. Don't leave without walking out through the center's back door, crossing the footbridge, and taking at least a short hike, where you'll see an assortment of native wildflowers, shrubs, and trees. If you head west from the bridge, Wilson Falls is about two miles away.

If a short hike outside the Forest Center leaves you hankering for more, head east along Highway 6 to the Kings Mountain trailhead. On a clear day (ha!) there are good views from the top. Several more trails start at the summit of the Coast Range. The campgrounds along Highway 6, including **Jones Creek,** which is right next to the Tillamook Forest Center, are popular with off-road vehicle drivers, who have their own trail network back in the hills.

Fishing

Among Oregon anglers, Tillamook County is known for its steelhead and salmon. Motorists along U.S. 101 can tell the fall chinook run has arrived when fishing boats cluster outside the Tillamook Bay entrance at Garibaldi. As the season wears on, the fish—affectionately called "hogs" because they sometimes weigh in at more than 50 pounds—make their way inland up the five coastal rivers—the Trask, Wilson, Tillamook, Kilchis, and Miami—that flow into Tillamook Bay. At their peak, the runs create such competition for favorite holes that the process of sparring for them is jocularly referred to as "combat fishing," as fishing boats anchor up gunwale to gunwale to form a fish-stopping palisade called a "hogline." Smokehouses and gas stations dot the outer reaches of the bay to cater to this fall influx.

The **Guide Shop Inc.** (12140 Wilson River Hwy., Tillamook, 503/842-3474) can arrange for a full day of fishing for chinook and silver salmon, steelhead, sturgeon, or trout; rates are about $150 per person, for one to four anglers. Nearby Garibaldi is home base for several charter operations.

Hiking

The Tillamook State Forest offers plenty of recreational opportunities. From a distance, the forest seems like a tree plantation, but hidden waterfalls, old railroad trestles from the days of logging trains, and moss-covered oaks in the Salmonberry River Canyon will convince you otherwise. Bird-watchers and mushroom-pickers can easily penetrate this thicket thanks to 1,000 miles of maintained roads and old railroad grades.

Two challenging trails off Highway 6, **King Mountain,** 25 miles east of Tillamook, and **Elk Mountain,** 28 miles east of Tillamook, climb through lands affected by the Tillamook Burn, but with scenic views throughout. Thanks to salvage logging in the wake of the disaster and subsequent replanting, myriad trails crisscross forests of Douglas and noble fir, hemlock, and red alder. Pick up the helpful pamphlet *Tillamook Forest Trails* put out by the **Oregon Department of Forestry,** Tillamook District (4907 E. 3rd St., Tillamook 97141, 503/842-2543).

Wildlife Viewing

Bird-watchers flock to Tillamook Bay June–November to view pelicans, sandpipers, tufted puffins, blue herons, and a variety of shorebirds. Prime time is before high tide, but step lively because this waterway was originally called "quicksand bay."

Golf

Golfers choose between two public courses in Tillamook. About two miles north of town, east of U.S. 101, **Bay Breeze Golf Course** (2325 Latimer Rd., Tillamook, 503/842-1166) charges $10 for nine holes on weekends. Another two miles north, **Alderbrook Golf Course** (7300 Alderbrook Rd., Tillamook, 503/842-6413) charges $52 on weekends for 18 holes.

Accommodations

Most travelers seem to pass through Tillamook on their way to someplace else, but a good local choice is **Best Western Inn & Suites** (1722 N. Makinster Rd., Tillamook, 503/842-7599 or 800/299-4817, doubles from $129), close to the cheese factories. Rooms have dataports, refrigerator, microwave, iron and ironing board,

coffeemaker, and cable TV. Amenities include indoor pool, sauna, and hot tub, plus complimentary continental breakfast. The **Western Royal Hotel** (1125 N. Main Ave., 503/842-8844 or 800/624-2912, doubles from $69) has clean comfortable rooms and an on-site restaurant and takes pets.

There's not a lot going on in downtown Tillamook, but if you'd like to stay in town, as opposed to the lengthy and busy commercial strip north of town, then book a room at the **Mar-Clair Inn** (11 Main Ave., 503/842-7571 or 800/331-6857, doubles from $65), a pleasant motor court with and outdoor pool and a restaurant.

Food

To sample the county's freshest produce, visit the **Tillamook Farmers Market** in downtown Tillamook. It runs every Saturday, late June–early October, on Laurel Avenue.

The **Farmhouse Cafe** at the Tillamook Cheese Factory serves breakfast and lunch (open at 8 A.M. daily). The **deli** at the Blue Heron French Cheese Company fixes sandwiches, soups, and salads daily; in polls conducted by the local paper, this is one of the locals' favorite lunch spots. The same survey rated **La Mexicana** (2203 3rd St., 503/842-2101, open for lunch and dinner daily) as the town's best Mexican restaurant. This restaurant, located in a vintage home on the edge of downtown, goes way beyond tacos and burritos, preparing local fish and seafood with south-of-the-border zest and finesse.

On the west side of U.S. 101, between the two cheese meccas, lunchtime do-it-yourselfers might check the locally raised and cured meat and smoked salmon at **Debbie D's Sausage Factory** (503/842-2622).

Information

The **Tillamook Chamber of Commerce** (3705 U.S. 101 N., Tillamook 97191, 503/842-7525, www.tillamookchamber.org) is located across the parking lot from the cheese factory. It's open 9 A.M.–5 P.M. Monday–Friday, 10 A.M.–3 P.M. Saturday, 10 A.M.–2 P.M. Sunday mid-June–September.

Three Capes Scenic Loop

The Three Capes Scenic Loop, a 35-mile byway off U.S. 101 between Tillamook and Pacific City, is considered one of the preeminent scenic areas on the north coast. While the beauty of Capes Kiwanda, Lookout, and Meares certainly justifies leaving the main highway, it would be an overstatement to portray this drive as a thrill-a-minute detour on the order of the south coast's Boardman Park or the central coast's Otter Crest Loop. Instead of fronting the ocean, the road connecting the capes winds mostly through dairy country, small beach towns, and second-growth forest. What's special here are the three capes themselves, and unless you get out of the car and walk on the trails, you'll miss the aesthetic appeal and distinctiveness of each headland's ecosystem. The wave-battered bluffs of Cape Kiwanda, the precipitous overlooks along the Cape Lookout Highway, and the curious Octopus Tree at Cape Meares are the perfect anti-dotes to the inland towns along U.S. 101. The majority of the Three Capes lodging and dining options are clustered in Pacific City and at the other end in Netarts and Oceanside. In between, it's mostly sand dunes, isolated beaches, rainforest, and pasture. To reach the Three Capes Scenic Loop from the north, turn west at Tillamook and follow signs to Cape Meares. From the south, follow signs north of Neskowin to Pacific City.

CAPE MEARES SCENIC VIEWPOINT

With stunning views, picnic tables, a newly restored lighthouse, and a uniquely contorted tree a short walk from the parking lot, Cape Meares Scenic Viewpoint is the user-friendliest site on the Three Capes Loop. The park was named for English navigator John Meares, who mapped many points along this coast in a 1788 voyage. The famed **Octopus Tree** is less than

© BILL MCRAE

Three Arch Rocks Wildlife Refuge from Cape Meares

a quarter mile up a forested hill. The tentacle-like extensions of this Sitka spruce have also been compared to candelabra arms. Another writer likened this tree to a gargantuan spider in a near-fetal position.

The 10-foot diameter of its base supports five-foot-thick trunks, each of which by itself is large enough to be a single tree. Scientists have propounded several theories for the cause of its unusual shape, including everything from wind and weather to insects damaging the spruce when it was young. A Native American legend about the spruce contends that it was shaped this way so that the branches could hold the canoes of a chief's dead family. Supposedly, the bodies were buried near the tree. This was a traditional practice among the tribes of the area, who referred to species formed thusly as "council trees."

Beyond the tree you can look south at Oceanside and Three Arch Rocks Refuge. The sweep of Pacific shore and offshore monoliths makes a fitting beginning (or finale, if you're driving from the south) to your sojourn along the Three Capes Loop, but be sure to also stroll the short paved trail down to the lighthouse, which begins at the parking lot and provides dramatic views of an offshore wildlife refuge, Cape Meares Rocks. Bring binoculars to see tufted puffins, pelagic cormorants, seals, and sea lions. The landward portion of the refuge protects rare old-growth evergreens.

The restored interior of **Cape Meares Lighthouse,** built in

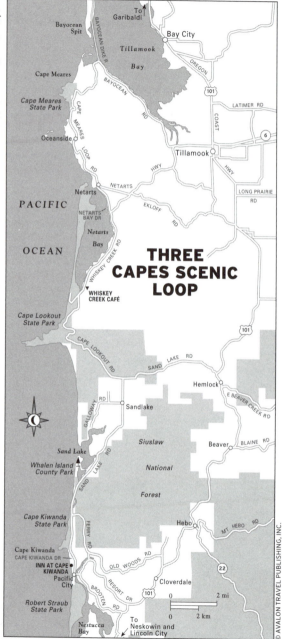

THREE CAPES SCENIC LOOP

© AVALON TRAVEL PUBLISHING, INC.

1890, is open 11 A.M.–4 P.M. daily May–September. This beacon was replaced as a functioning light in 1963 by the automated facility located behind it, and it now houses a gift shop. A free tour is occasionally offered by volunteers who might tell you about how the lighthouse was built here by mistake and perhaps offer a peek into the prismatic Fresnel lenses.

OCEANSIDE

The road between Cape Meares and Netarts heads into the beach-house community of Oceanside (pop. about 250). Many of the homes are built into the cliff overlooking the ocean, Sausalito style. This motif reaches its apex atop Maxwell Point. You can peer several hundred feet down at **Three Arch Rocks Wildlife Refuge,** part-time home to one of the continent's largest and most varied collections of shorebirds. A herd of sea lions also populates this trio of sea stacks from time to time.

While low prices and a window on the water can be found at **Ocean Front Cabins** (1610 Pacific Ave., Oceanside, 503/842-6081 or 888/845-8470, www.oceanfrontcabins .com), the older, smallish rooms here might give some travelers pause. Nonetheless, for as little as $60 (a sleeping unit without a kitchenette)—or two-bed rooms with full kitchens for $90—you'll find yourself literally a stone's throw from Oceanside's beachcombing and dining highlights.

The aptly named **House on the Hill** (P.O. Box 187, Oceanside 97134, 503/842-6030, www.houseonthehillmotel.com, doubles from $95), also called the Clifftop Inn, is perched on a bluff at Maxwell Point, with both seclusion and cliffside ocean grandeur. Most of the 16 units here are not especially elaborate, but the sweeping view is easily worth whatever you pay for the room. The office maintains a little museum with sea specimens and newspaper articles about the area, as well as a telescope focused on the offshore Three Arch Rocks Wildlife Refuge.

Another good lodging option is **Bender Vacation Rental Properties** (503/233-4363), boasting six units with cliffside ocean views, large private decks, and full kitchens (except for

© BILL MCRAE

Oceansides's quiet beach is protected by Three Arch Rocks.

one unit). Other amenities include fireplaces, TVs, VCRs, and microwaves. Pets are welcome at most locations. For $90–225 per night with a two-night minimum, this is a great deal.

A popular draw for hungry Three Capes travelers, **■ Roseanna's Oceanside Cafe** (1490 Pacific Ave. N.W., Oceanside, 503/842-7351, open 10 A.M.–9 P.M. daily, main courses $14–22) garners high marks from just about everyone. At first, the weather-beaten cedar-shake exterior might lead you to expect an old general store, as indeed it was decades ago. Once you're inside, however, the ornate decor leaves little doubt that this place takes its new identity seriously. From an elevated perch above the breakers, you'll be treated to expertly prepared local oysters, fresh salmon, a bevy of chicken dishes, and interesting pastas, such as gorgonzola and pear with penne noodles. Be sure to save room for blackberry cobbler; order it warm so the Tillamook Vanilla Bean ice cream on top melts down the sides, and watch the waves over a long cup of coffee.

The **Anchor Tavern** (1495 Pacific Ave., Oceanside, 503/842-2041) is a nearby alternative for food by the beach. Along with microbrews, specialties are smoked meats, barbecued ribs, clam chowder, pizza, and burgers. Hanging above the bar is a wide-angle photo of Hartford, Connecticut. The four-foot-long picture depicts the kind of urban sprawl that will make you glad you're here.

NETARTS

Tiny Netarts (pop. about 200) has an enviable location overlooking Netarts Bay and the Pacific beyond. Along with nearby Oceanside, it's the closest coastal settlement from Tillamook and makes for a fine quiet getaway. Netarts Bay and seven-mile-long Netarts Spit are popular with clamdiggers and fishermen crabbers, who can launch boats from Netarts Landing, at the northeast corner of the bay. **Netarts Bay RV Park and Marina** (2260 Bilyeu St., Netarts, 503/842-7774) and **Big Spruce RV Park** (4850 Netarts Hwy. W., 503/842-7443) rent motorboats and crabbing supplies.

Accommodations and Food

The **Terimore** (5105 Crab Ave., Netarts, 503/842-4623 or 800/635-1821, motel rooms from $55, cabins from $68) is situated a short walk from the water at the north end of Netarts Bay. Other than some units with fireplaces and kitchens, there are few frills here, but for fair rates you'll find yourself close by the water, within easy driving distance of the Cape Lookout trail, and a beach walk away from Roseanna's, the best restaurant on the Capes Loop.

For more up-to-date comforts, **Edgewater Motel and Vacation Rentals** (1st St. and Crab Ave., 503/842-1300 or 888/425-1050, doubles from $279) offers four luxury two-bedroom rentals directly above Netarts Bay. Each unit has two massive stone fireplaces (one in the master bedroom, one in the "great room"), a 650-gallon Jacuzzi tub, two balconies, and a well-equipped kitchen. Each unit sleeps up to eight people (with two queen-size fold-out couches). The views can't be beat. If you don't require this level of sophistication, there are also vintage cabins on the same property, each with kitchens and TVs with DVD, and some have fireplaces (doubles from $100).

You'll find several lunch and dinner spots to choose from. The view of Cape Lookout is tops at **The Schooner** (2065 Netarts Bay Rd., 503/842-4988), which serves breakfast (starting at 8 A.M.), lunch, and dinner (seafood and steak) daily. Five miles south of Netarts, along a woodsy stretch of the Three Capes route, **Whiskey Creek Cafe** (503/842-5117, open for lunch and dinner daily, main courses $8–19)is an unexpectedly sophisticated restaurant in a remote but lovely setting. The Whiskey Creek Cafe is a 21st-century example of the classic country diner, with excellent pies, sandwiches, and burgers but with the addition of noteworthy and up-to-date dishes that attract diners from far and wide. The café specializes in oysters—the bivalves are from the Pearl Point Oyster Farm, just next door—with such specialties as smoked oyster pâté and pan-fried oysters with chili-lime sauce. This is a friendly and unpretentious spot with excellent food; no alcohol is served.

CAPE LOOKOUT

One of the scenic highlights of the Three Capes route, Cape Lookout juts out nearly a mile from the mainland, like a finger pointing out to sea. The cliffs along the south side of the cap rise 800 feet from the Pacific's pounding waves. The best way to take in the vista and the thrill of the location is on foot.

Cape Lookout State Park

At the southern end of Netarts Spit is the campground and beach extension of expansive Cape Lookout State Park (13000 Whiskey Creek Rd. W., Tillamook, 503/842-4981 for information, 800/452-5687 or www.reserveamerica .com for reservations), which also encompasses the entire cape and the seven-mile-long Netarts Spit within its boundaries. The park has 176 tent sites ($16) and 38 full-hookup sites ($20), as well as 10 yurts ($27), three cabins (with bathrooms, kitchen, and TV/VCR, $66), and a hiker-biker camp ($4); discounts apply October–April. Amenities include showers, flush toilets, a laundry, and evening programs. Reservations and deposit are required at this popular campground. There is a $3 day-use fee, covered by the Coast Passport.

Cape Lookout Hikes

Hiking to the end of mile-wide Cape Lookout is one of the top coast hikes in Oregon. The trail begins either at the campground, where it climbs 2.5 miles up to a ridge-top trailhead with parking lot, or you can drive up the Three Capes route to the well-signed trailhead. An orientation map at the trailhead details the trail options. The main 2.5-mile trail out to the land's end, along the narrowing finger of land, can give hikers the impression that they're on the prow of a giant ship suspended 500 feet above the ocean on all sides. Here, more than anywhere else on the Oregon coast, you get the sense of being on the edge of the continent. Giant spruce, western red cedars, and hemlocks surround the gently hilly trail to the tip of the cape. In March, Cape Lookout is a popular vantage point for whale-watching. June through August, a bevy of wildflowers

and birds further enhance the rolling terrain en route to the tip of this headland, and in late summer red huckleberries line the path.

Halfway to the overlook, there are views north to Cape Meares over the Netarts sandspit. Even if you settle for a mere 15-minute stroll down the trail, you can look southward beyond Haystack Rock to Cascade Head. Right about where the trees open up, look for a bronze plaque commemorating the crash of a World War II plane (with nearly a dozen casualties) embedded in the rock wall bordering the right-hand (north) side of the trail at eye level. If you're unable to take this hike, two unmarked turnouts along the highway between the sand dunes and Cape Lookout parking lot let you survey the terrain south to Cape Kiwanda.

Another popular trail in the state park heads north from the campground through a variety of estuarine habitats along the sandspit separating Netarts Bay from the Pacific. The former is a popular site for agate hunters, clammers, and crabbers.

Sand Lake

South of Cape Lookout, the terrain suddenly changes. Extensive sand dunes surrounding the Sand Lake estuary suddenly appear, drowning the forest in sand. The dunes and beach attract squadrons of dune buggy enthusiasts. Camping is available year-round at **Sand Beach Campground** (five miles south of Cape Lookout on Galloway Rd., 877/444-6777), which has basic sites for tenters and RVs. This dramatic area is popular with hikers, too.

PACIFIC CITY AND CAPE KIWANDA

As you approach the shore in Pacific City, the sight of **Haystack Rock** will immediately grab your attention. At 327 feet, this sea stack is nearly 100 feet taller than the like-named rock in Cannon Beach. Standing a mile offshore, this monolith has a brooding, enigmatic quality that constantly draws the eye to it. Look closely, and you'll understand why some folks called it Teacup Rock.

The tawny sandstone escarpment of Cape Kiwanda juts one-half mile out to sea from Pacific City and frames the north end of the beach. In storm-tossed waters, this cape is the undisputed king of rock-and-roll, if you go by coffee-table books and calendar photos. While other sandstone promontories on the north coast have been ground into sandy beaches by the pounding surf, it's been theorized that Kiwanda has endured thanks to the buffer of Haystack Rock. In any case, hang-gliding aficionados are glad the cape is here. They scale its shoulders and set themselves aloft off the north face to glide above the beach and dunes.

The small town of Pacific City, with about 1,000 citizens, is at the base of Cape Kiwanda. It attracts growing numbers of vacationers and retirees but remains true to its 19th-century origins as a working fishing village. In addition to the knockout seascapes and recreation, if you come here at the right times of day you may be treated to a unique spectacle—the launch or return of the **dory fleet.**

It's a tradition dating back to the 1920s, when gillnetting was banned on the Nestucca River to protect the dwindling salmon runs. To retain their livelihood, commercial fishermen began to haul flat-bottomed, double-ended dories down to the beach on horse-drawn wagons, then row out through the surf to fish. These days, trucks and trailers get the boats to and from the beach, and outboard motors have replaced oar power, enabling the dories to get 50 miles out to sea. If you come around 6 A.M., you can watch them taking off. The fleet's late afternoon return attracts a crowd that comes to see the dory operators skidding their crafts as far as possible up the beach to the waiting boat trailers. Others meet the dories to buy salmon and tuna.

In late July, the **Dory Festival** celebrates the area's fleet. The three-day fete includes craft and food booths, a pancake breakfast, a fishing derby, and other activities. Visitors also have the opportunity to ride out through the surf in a dory, for about $10 per person. For more information, call the chamber of commerce (503/965-6161). If you want to join the an-

glers other times of year, contact the **Haystack Fishing Club** (888/965-7555), across from the beach near the Inn at Cape Kiwanda.

In addition, the Pacific City area is besieged by surfers, who enjoy some of the longest waves on the Oregon coast. **Robert Straub State Park,** just south of town, offers access to Nestucca Bay and to the dunes and a long uninterrupted stretch of beach.

Accommodations

The nicest motel on the Three Capes Loop is the ◖ **Inn at Cape Kiwanda** (33105 Cape Kiwanda Dr., Pacific City, 503/965-6366 or 888/965-7001, www.innatcapekiwanda.com, doubles from $179). All rooms face a beautiful beach and Cape Kiwanda's giant sand dune. If it's too rainy to go outside, fireplaces and spacious well-appointed rooms make for great storm-watching. Whirlpool tub rooms are available here, and pets are permitted in some rooms.

Food

Los Caporales (35025 Brooten Rd., Pacific City, 503/965-6999, open at 11 A.M. Wed.–Sun., main courses $7–10) serves up bountiful plates of Mexican food and seafood; the combination plates could feed several people. The restaurant's name refers to foremen at a cattle ranch, perhaps explaining portions fit for wrangler-sized appetites.

If hanging plants, a piano, and Nestucca River frontage don't make you feel at home, the apple pie and other wholesome fare at the **Riverhouse** (34450 Brooten Rd., 503/965-6722, www.riverhousefoods.com, main courses $8–27) probably will. The burgers and open-faced sandwich combinations are the perfect pick-me-ups after a morning of fishing or beachcombing along the Nestucca River estuary. Dinners focus on steak, pasta, burgers, fish, and shellfish. Steamer clams simmered in vermouth make a hearty starter, or try a salad with the sweet blue cheese dressing, which has such a following throughout western Oregon that it's sold in regional supermarkets. Come early, as seating is limited in this 11-table restaurant.

Close by, at the **Grateful Bread Bakery** (34085 Brooten Rd., 503/965-7337, open 8 A.M.–8:30 P.M. Thurs.–Mon.), the challah bread, carrot cake, marionberry strudel, and other homemade baked goods deserve special mention. The full breakfast menu offers a range of tasty omelettes, served with oven-roasted spuds at great prices. Lunch here might include thin-crust New York–style pizza, paying homage to the owners' East Coast roots, Tillamook cheese chowder, or a dilled shrimp salad sandwich. Dinners feature dory-caught cod, prepared breaded and grilled or blackened, plus salmon, chicken, and steak.

A popular and well-known Pacific City hangout is the **Pelican Pub and Brewery** (33180 Cape Kiwanda Dr., Pacific City, 503/965-7007, www.pelicanbrewery.com, open for three meals daily). Set in a most enviable spot right on the beach opposite Cape Kiwanda and Haystack Rock, this place boasts the best coastal view of any brewpub in Oregon. Halibut fish and chips, gourmet pizzas, steamed clams, barbecued pork ribs, and hazelnut-crusted salmon are some of the standouts. The pub's brews, including Tsunami Stout, Doryman's Dark Ale, India Pelican Ale, and MacPelican's Scottish Style Ale, have garnered stacks of awards.

Neskowin and Cascade Head

NESKOWIN

The tiny vacation village of Neskowin (rhymes with "let's go in") has a quiet appeal based on a beautiful beach and two golf courses in the shadow of 1,500-foot-high Cascade Head. It's the polar opposite of busy Lincoln City, 15 miles south. There's not much to do here but relax on the uncrowded beach and enjoy the views of Cascade Head and the dark beauty of **Proposal Rock,** a stony, forested hillock that stands right at the edge of the surf, with Neskowin Creek curving around it. The feature was named by Neskowin's first postmistress, whose daughter received a marriage proposal nearby.

Sleepy Neskowin has only one art gallery, and it's a good one. **Hawk Creek Gallery** (48460 U.S. 101 S., 503/392-3879, open 11 A.M.–5 P.M. daily in summer, and weekends only in spring and fall) is the studio and showroom for the works of painter Michael Schlicting, who exhibits his work internationally but has made the Hawk Creek Gallery his home base for the past 30 years.

Golf

Neskowin boasts twice as many golf courses as restaurants, which is to say, two. **Hawk Creek Golf Course** (48480 U.S. 101 S., 503/392-

4120, green fees $58) is a hilly, nine-hole course on the east side of the highway. West of the highway, **Neskowin Beach Golf Course** (48405 Hawk St., 503/392-3377, green fees $28) has streams and water hazards adding a challenge to most of the nine holes.

Accommodations

From the outside, **The Chelan** (48750 Breakers Blvd., 503/392-3270, www.rentoregoncoast .com, $119–185) resembles a lovingly landscaped Mediterranean villa perched on a dune above the Pacific. The nine two-bedroom condo units are well worth the price, with fireplaces, kitchens, and views. **Proposal Rock Inn** (48988 U.S. 101 S., Neskowin 97149, 503/392-3115, rooms $44–89, suites $89–135) backs up on Hawk Creek and commands a fine view of the beach and the eponymous rock. Two-room oceanview suites with a full kitchen fetch higher prices than the standard rooms.

To rent a home in the Neskowin or Pacific City area, contact the property management firm **Grey Fox Vacation Rentals** (888/720-2154, www.oregoncoast.com/greyfox).

Free, rustic **campsites** can be found just south of Neskowin. To get there, just look for the Scenic Drive sign east of U.S. 101 and follow County Road 12 for four miles. From there, travel about 100 yards west on Forest Service Road 12131, and you'll see the campground set along Neskowin Creek. To find out about the trails in the surrounding rainforest, call or write the **Siuslaw National Forest** (Hebo, OR 97121, 541/392-3161). The campground is open mid-April to mid-October—bring your own water or water-purification kit. The nearby scenic drive continues up into an area of huge trees captioned by Forest Service placards explaining the ecology.

Food

The **Neskowin Marketplace** is a grocery-deli-general store right off the highway. Neskowin's only restaurant, fortunately, serves great food at moderate prices. The **Hawk Creek Cafe** (503/392-3838, open 8 A.M.–9 P.M. daily, main courses $8–19) has a friendly atmosphere and an inviting deck perched right over the creek. Count on filling omelettes for breakfast; sandwiches, burgers, and wood-fired pizza for lunch; and grilled fish and steaks for dinner.

CASCADE HEAD
Cascade Head
Scenic Research Area

About 10 miles north of Lincoln City, the 11,890-acre Cascade Head Experimental Forest was set aside in 1934 for scientific study of typical coastal Sitka spruce and western hemlock forests found along the Oregon coast. In 1974, Congress established the 9,670-acre Cascade Head Scenic Research Area, which includes the western half of the forest, several prairie headlands, and the Salmon River estuary. In 1980, the entire area was designated a Biosphere Reserve as part of the United Nations Biosphere Reserve system.

The headlands, reaching as high as 1,800 feet, are unusual for their extensive prairies still dominated by native grasses: red fescue, wild rye, and Pacific reedgrass. The Nechesney Indians, who inhabited the area as long as 12,000 years ago, purposely burned forest tracts around Cascade Head to provide browse for deer and to reduce the possibility of larger,

uncontrollable blazes. These human-made alterations are complemented by the inherent dryness of south-facing slopes that receive increased exposure to sun. In contrast to these grasslands, the northern part of the headland is the domain of giant spruces and firs because it catches the brunt of the heavy rainfalls and lingering fogs. Endemic wildflowers include coastal paintbrush, goldenrod, streambank lupine, rare hairy checkermallow, and blue violet, a plant critical to the survival of the Oregon silverspot butterfly, a threatened species found in only six locations. Deer, elk, coyote, snowshoe hare, and the Pacific giant salamander find refuge here, while bald eagles, great horned owls, and peregrine falcons may be seen hunting above the grassy slopes. Today, in addition to its biological importance, the area is a mecca for some 6,000 hikers annually and for anglers who target the salmon and steelhead runs on the Salmon River.

On the north side of the Salmon River, turn west from U.S. 101 onto **Three Rocks Road** for a scenic driving detour on the south side of Cascade Head. The paved road curves about 2.5 miles above the wetlands and widening channel of the Salmon River estuary, passes Savage Road, and ends at a parking area and boat launch at Knight County Park. From the park, the road turns to gravel and narrows (not suitable for RVs or trailers) and continues about another 0.5 mile to its end, at a spectacular overlook across the estuary.

Cascade Head also offers some rewardingly scenic hikes, with rainforest pathways and wildflower meadows giving way to dramatic ocean views. The **Cascade Head Trail** runs six miles roughly parallel to the highway, with a south trailhead near the intersection of Three Rocks Road and U.S. 101 and a north trailhead at Falls Creek, on U.S. 101 about one mile south of Neskowin. It passes through old-growth forest and offers coastal views near its north end.

A short but brisk hike to the top of the headland on a **Nature Conservancy trail** begins near Knight County Park. Leave your car at the park and walk 0.5 mile up Savage Road to the trailhead. It's 1.7 miles one-way, with a 1,100-foot elevation gain. No dogs or bicycles are allowed on the trail.

About three miles north of Three Rocks Road, gravel Cascade Head Road (Forest Service Rd. 1861) leads four miles west of U.S. 101 to the **Hart's Cove trailhead.** The first part of the trail runs through arching red alder treetops and 250-year-old Sitka spruces with five-foot diameters. The understory of mosses and ferns is nourished by 100-inch rainfalls. Next, the trail emerges into open grasslands. The hilly, five-mile round-trip hike finally leads to an oceanfront meadow overlooking Hart's Cove, where the barking of sea lions might greet you. This trail can have plenty of mud, so boots are recommended as you tromp through the rainforest. Note that the trail is closed Janurary 15–July 15.

Sitka Center for Art and Ecology

The region in the shadow of Cascade Head can be explored in even greater depth thanks to the Sitka Center for Art and Ecology (P.O. Box 65, Otis 97368, 541/994-5485, www .sitkacenter.org), located off Savage Road on the south side of the headland. Classes are offered June–August in art and nature as an expression of the strong relationship between the two. Experts in everything from local plant communities to Siletz Indian baskets conduct outdoor workshops on the grounds of Cascade Head Ranch. Classes can last from a couple of days to a week, and fees vary as well.

CENTRAL COAST

Oregon's central coast, from Lincoln City to Reedsport and Winchester Bay, embraces such contrasts that it's difficult to generalize about the region.

In the north, Lincoln City's dense mix of lodgings and shopping opportunities, combined with its Indian-run casino, generates the coast's worst traffic jams, especially on holidays and weekends. The sprawling town isn't everyone's first choice for a quiet getaway, but it must be doing something right. Depoe Bay—built around the world's smallest navigable natural harbor—is headquarters for the coast's busiest whale-watching fleet—and one of the largest and most sprawling condo developments.

A necklace of small state parks adorns the shore every couple of miles all the way from southern Lincoln City on south; inland, the Siuslaw Na-

tional Forest safeguards several wilderness areas and groves of rare old-growth coastal forest, beckoning hikers to explore the primeval landscapes. Just north of Newport, Yaquina Head Outstanding Natural Area offers excellent vantage points for up-close whale-watching and bird-watching, plus tidepools accessible to wheelchair users.

The bustling harbor at Newport is home to the state's largest commercial fishing fleet and second-largest recreational fleet, which runs charters year-round for rockfish and seasonally for salmon, tuna, and halibut. Newport also boasts the state-of-the-art Oregon Coast Aquarium, former residence of Keiko the beloved orca, and the bohemian resort community of Nye Beach, which has been attracting tourists since the 19th century.

Just south of Yachats, the panoramic view

© BILL MCRAE

HIGHLIGHTS

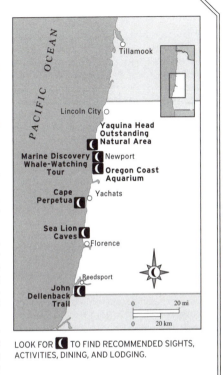

◖ **Oregon Coast Aquarium:** Explore the life of Oregon's shores and oceans at this excellent aquarium (page 105).

◖ **Yaquina Head Outstanding Natural Area:** A soaring lighthouse stands above a tidepool-studded inlet at this small park, the quintessence of the Oregon Coast (page 109).

◖ **Marine Discovery Whale-Watching Tour:** Thar she blows! Newport is a great departure point for gray whale-watching tours (page 112).

◖ **Cape Perpetua:** One of the most dramatic natural areas along the Oregon Coast, Cape Perpetua features mountains that edge out to directly front the Pacific. A top spot for hiking and exploring tidepools (page 122).

◖ **Sea Lion Caves:** Every so often, it pays to visit a roadside attraction. Here you'll take an elevator ride down to the caves at cliff's bottom to get a close look at the Steller sea lion rookery. During the spring and summer, the animals are outside, and you can get a good look from the roadside (page 128).

◖ **John Dellenback Trail:** Explore 400-foot dunes in the Oregon Dunes National Recreation Area on this hiking trail that's like trekking the Sahara to reach Pacific beaches (page 140).

LOOK FOR ◖ TO FIND RECOMMENDED SIGHTS, ACTIVITIES, DINING, AND LODGING.

from Cape Perpetua can, on a clear day, extend 75 miles in each direction. Down at sea level, the tidepools here are some of the most fascinating on the coast. At Sea Lion Caves, a touristy but unique experience between Yachats and Florence, the world's largest sea cave is the only mainland rookery of Steller sea lions in the lower 48 states. Close by, photographers spend more time trying to capture the perfect image of Heceta Head Lighthouse than any other sight along the entire coast.

PLANNING YOUR TIME

Plan to spend at least a few days exploring the central coast. In Florence's restored Old Town, visitors can easily explore the shops, restaurants, and riverside docks on foot. Florence also marks the start of dune country: Hikers, horseback riders, and off-road-vehicle enthusiasts flock to the 32,000-acre Oregon Dunes National Recreation Area, a fantastical landscape of dazzling white sand mountains and jewel lakes stretched along nearly 50 miles of shoreline. The sportfishing fleet at Winchester Bay draws thousands of anglers eager to tackle a brawny Umpqua River salmon or sturgeon, and a short drive away the Dean Creek Elk Viewing Area offers an excellent chance to view wild Roosevelt elk in a natural setting.

Lincoln City

Back in 1964, five burgs that straddled seven miles of beachfront between Siletz Bay and the Salmon River came together and incorporated as Lincoln City. In commemoration, a 14-foot bronze statue of Abraham Lincoln was donated to the city by an Illinois sculptor. *The Lank Lawyer Reading in His Saddle While His Horse Grazes* originally occupied a city park; Governor Mark Hatfield and actor Raymond Massey, who portrayed Honest Abe in a 1940 film, attended the dedication. Today the statue stands in a nondescript lot at N.E. 22nd Street and Quay Avenue. Look for the sign on U.S. 101 near the Dairy Queen.

In the following decades, what were discrete towns have grown and melded into an uninterrupted conurbation with a population of about 6,800 (which can balloon to 30,000 on a busy weekend). While the resulting sprawl and "zoned commercial" signs can be maddening at times, the most visited town on the coast must be doing something right. Perhaps it's the proximity to Portland and Salem, or the area's two tribal-run casinos. Perhaps it's the long, broad sandy beach, or the superlative wildlife-viewing around Siletz Bay. Or maybe it's the attraction of Devil's Lake State Park, a gem without equal among coastal freshwater playgrounds. Add prime kite-flying, some of the coast's better restaurants, and bibliophilic and antiquing haunts, and it's clear that there's more to the area than the pull of saltwater taffy and outlet malls.

SIGHTS AND RECREATION
Lincoln City Beach

Lincoln City boasts seven uninterrupted miles of sandy beach. From Siletz Bay north to Road's End State Recreation Area, there are more than a dozen access points. You can head west from U.S. 101 on just about any side street to get there. High coastal bluffs lining the north-central portion of town, though, may mean a climb down (and back up) long flights of stairs cut into the cliff. For something approaching

solitude on a crowded day, follow Logan Road west from the highway near the north end of town to **Road's End State Recreation Area;** tidepools and a secluded cove add to the allure. This stretch is also popular with sailboarders.

Tidepool explorers should also check out the rock formations at S.W. 11th Street (Canyon Drive Park), N.W. 15th Street, and S.W. 32nd Street.

The **D River Wayside,** a small park on the beach in more or less the middle of town, is a state park property where you can watch what locals claim is the "world's shortest river" empty into the ocean. Flowing just 120 feet from its source, Devil's Lake, to its mouth at the Pacific, it's short, all right; despite its unspectacular appearance, it was a cause célèbre when *The Guinness Book of World Records* withdrew the D's claim to fame in favor of a Montana waterway, the Roe. Local schoolkids rallied to the D's defense with an amended measurement, but the Roe, at a mere 53 feet long, carries the *Guinness* imprimatur as the most diminutive stream. In addition to seeing D River flow from "D" Lake into "D" ocean, you can fly a kite on the beach here. It's one of the easier beach-access points, between stretches of high, motel-topped bluffs, so it can get a little crowded here.

Another convenient beach-access point is off S.W. 51st Street at the south end of town, just before **Siletz Bay.** A large parking area here in what's known as the Taft District stands beside the driftwood-strewn shore of the bay, where you can often see a group of harbor seals chasing their dinner or coming in for a closer look at you. It's a short walk to the ocean.

Time was when it was common for storms and currents to wash up that ultimate beachcomber's prize—**glass fishing floats**—on the Oregon coast. Lincoln City improves the beachcomber's odds by distributing over 2,000 glass floats along its beaches October–Memorial Day. Handcrafted by Northwest glass artists, each of the colorful floats is signed and numbered and placed by volunteers on the beaches above the high-tide line. If you find one, you can call or stop in at the visitors center for a certificate and information about the artist who created it.

Devil's Lake

Devil's Lake, just east of town, is the recreation center of Lincoln City. In addition to windsurfing and hydroplaning, you can catch eight species of fish here, including catfish, yellow perch, crappie, largemouth bass, and trout. Chinese grass carp were introduced to the lake to help control the rampant aquatic weeds. There's also good bird-watching on and around this shallow, 678-acre lake, which attracts flocks of migratory geese, ducks, and other waterfowl. Species to look for include canvasbacks, Canada geese, widgeons, gadwalls, grebes, and mallards. Bald eagles and ospreys also nest in the trees bordering the lake.

The lake takes its name from a local Native American legend. The story tells that when Siletz warriors paddled a canoe across the lake one moonlit night, a tentacled beast erupted from the still water and pulled the men under. It's said that boaters today who cross the moon's reflection in the middle of the lake tempt the same fate, but the lake's devil has remained silent for years.

Of the five access points, East Devil's Lake Road off U.S. 101 northeast of town offers a scenic route around the lake's east side before rejoining U.S. 101 near the day-use portion of the state park at the south end of the lake. To reach the camping area of **Devil's Lake State Recreation Area,** take N.E. 6th Drive east from U.S. 101, about 0.25 mile north of the D River. The day-use area has a boat ramp, while there's a moorage dock across the lake adjacent to the campground.

Mountain bikes, canoes, and paddleboats can be rented at the **Blue Heron Landing** (4006 W. Devil's Lake Rd., Lincoln City, 541/994-4708).

Casinos

One of the biggest draws in town is the **Chinook Winds Casino** (1777 N.W. 44th St.,

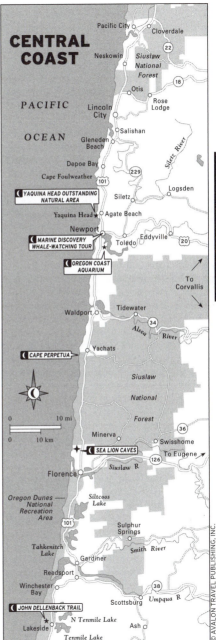

© AVALON TRAVEL PUBLISHING, INC.

CENTRAL COAST

CENTRAL COAST

Lincoln City, 541/996-5825 or 888/244-6665, www.chinookwindscasino.com), operated by the Confederated Tribes of Siletz Indians, near the north end of town. In addition to slots, blackjack, poker, keno, bingo, craps, and roulette, the casino has two on-site restaurants and a busy schedule of big-name (or formerly big-name) entertainment. Recent shows have included David Cassidy, Dionne Warwick, and Don McLean. Open 24 hours daily.

About 25 miles east of Lincoln City is the state's number one visitor attraction, **Spirit Mountain Casino** (P.O. Box 39, Grand Ronde 97347, 800/760-7977, http://spiritmountain. com), operated by the Confederated Tribes of Grand Ronde. Games of chance include slots, craps, blackjack, poker, keno, and bingo. It's open every day, 24 hours.

North Lincoln County Historical Museum

This modest museum (4907 S.W. U.S. 101, 541/996-6614, open noon–4 P.M. Tues.–Sat., free admission) tells the story of this area through exhibits of old-time logging machinery, homesteading tools, fishing, military life, and Native American history. Check out the early fashion mannequins and a World War II mine that washed ashore.

Camping

Several wilderness retreats are worth noting in the Lincoln City area. One remote escape is at **Van Duzer Wayside,** about 12 miles east of town on Highway 18, which offers a dozen primitive (and free) hike-in sites in a beautiful forest near the Salmon River.

More free rustic sites can be found about eight miles north of town and just south of Neskowin. To get there, look for the Scenic Drive sign east of U.S. 101 and follow County Road 12 for four miles. From there, travel about 100 yards west on Forest Service Road 12131 and you'll see the campground set along **Neskowin Creek.** The campground is open mid-April–mid-October. Bring your own water or water-purification kit. The nearby scenic drive continues up into an area of huge

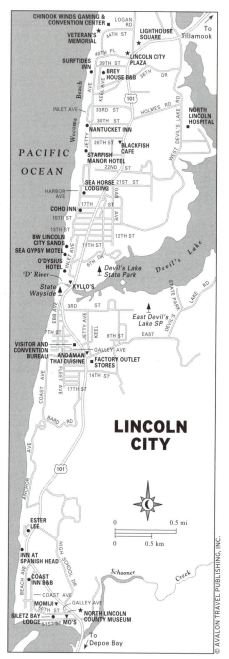

© AVALON TRAVEL PUBLISHING, INC.

KESEY'S LEGACY

Two miles south of Lincoln City, you'll come to the turnoff for Highway 229 along the Siletz River. If you drive down the north side of the river about 1.25 miles, on the opposite shore you'll note a Victorian-ish house that was built to last. It was constructed for the movie version of *Sometimes a Great Notion*. The 1971 film, a so-so adaptation of Ken Kesey's memorable novel, starred Paul Newman, Lee Remick, Henry Fonda, and Michael Sarrazin. The plot concerns the never-say-die spirit of an anti-union timber baron, his not-always-supportive family, and life in the mythical Coast Range logging community of Wakonda. A huge porch once fronted the riverbank, heavily reinforced against the elements. It was taken down in the decade after the movie was made, but it lives on in the pages of the book. Much of the movie was shot in this area, with café scenes taking place at Mo's on Newport's bayfront. Other scenes were shot near Florence.

trees captioned by forest service placards explaining the ecology.

More elaborate camping is available at **Devil's Lake State Park** (1452 N.E. 6th St., Lincoln City, 541/994-2002 information, 800/452-5687 reservations, www.reserveamerica.com) with 68 tent sites and 32 RV sites with full hookups. Amenities include showers, a café, and a laundry. The fee is $17–22 per night, $29 for yurts, $4 for hiker-biker spaces, mid-April–late October. This campground is just off U.S. 101 at the northeast end of town, between the ocean and Devil's Lake.

Golf

The big golfing news in Lincoln City is the beautifully laid out 18-hole **Chinook Winds Golf Resort** (3245 N.E. 50th St., 541/994-8442, http://chinookwindscasino.com/golf_resort). Set amidst towering coastal mountains on the edge of Lincoln City, this course is an-

other venture of the highly successful Chinook Winds Casino, operated by the Confederated Tribes of the Siletz Indians. The golf course spans just 5,000 yards with men's par 65 and women's 72, though plans include taking the current executive level course to a resort level, which means increasing the course size to 6,640 yards and the par to 71. The club offers all services with restaurant, lounge, pro shop, and lessons, plus the largest indoor driving range in the Northwest. Greens fees range $45–54 for 18 holes.

The area's other serious golf resort is seven miles south of Lincoln City at Gleneden Beach. **Salishan Spa and Golf Resort** (7760 U.S. 101, Gleneden Beach, 541/764-3632 or 800/890-8037) is an award-winning 18-hole course set in the foothills of the Coast Range and bordered by Siletz Bay and the sea. This challenging 6,470-yard, par-71, championship-layout course has recently reopened following a major redesign by Jacobsen Hardy Golf Course Design. The redesign includes 18 new green complexes, an additional 400 yards, and stunning new views. The greens fees for 18 holes are $99 in summer. Keep in mind that this is a Scottish-links course, where the roughs are really rough.

ENTERTAINMENT
Eden Hall

Housed within the renovated Gleneden Brick and Tile Factory, five miles south of Lincoln City in Gleneden Beach, Eden Hall (6645 Gleneden Beach Loop Rd., 541/764-3826 for performance info, 541/764-3825 for restaurant, www.edenhall.com) stages live theater and hosts an impressively eclectic roster of regional and touring musicians. This spacious, airy warehouse has an excellent sound system and is a wonderful place to take in a concert, with an emphasis on jazz, folk, and blues. Enjoy dinner at the adjacent Side Door Café.

Theater and Movies

Lincoln City's homegrown theater company, **Theatre West** (3536 S.E. U.S. 101, 541/994-5663, www.theatrewest.com), stages a half dozen productions each year, with an emphasis on comedies, plus musicals and drama.

Catch first-run flicks at the **Bijou Theatre** (1624 N.E. U.S. 101, 541/994-8255), an old-time movie house dating back to the 1930s, making it a rare old survivor around here. The six-screen **Regal Cinemas** (3755 S.E. High School Dr., 541/994-7649), just east of U.S. 101 in the south end of town, is its modern competitor.

EVENTS

Lincoln City calls itself the kite capital of the world, pointing to its position midway between the pole and the equator, which gives the area predictable wind patterns. The town holds not one but two kite fiestas at the D River Wayside each year. The spring **Kite Festival** takes place the first weekend in May; the fall festival is held the third weekend in September (541/994-3070 or 800/452-2151). The event is famous for giant spin socks, some as long as 150 feet.

The **Cascade Head Chamber Music Festival** (P.O. Box 605, Lincoln City 97367, 541/994-5333 or 877/994-5333, www.cascade headmusic.org) is another Oregon culture-fest that brings together world-class artists in an informal setting. Events are hosted at St. Peter the Fisherman Lutheran Church (1226 S.W. 13th St., 541/994-2007), under the direction of Sergiu Luca, a famed violinist who draws on decades of international experience and the friendship of virtuosi who fly in from all corners of the globe to make music on the Oregon coast. Old World artists such as Beethoven and Brahms as well as contemporary composers are featured in a series of June concerts (usually two a week over several weeks). Order tickets from the festival ticket office (541/994-5333) or get them at the gallery in Salishan or the Lincoln City Visitor and Convention Bureau. Tickets cost around $15 and may not always be available at the door.

Lincoln City's popular **Sandcastle Building Contest** happens the first Saturday in August, off S.W. 51st Street, in the historic Taft District alongside Siletz Bay. Call 541/996-3800 for details.

SHOPPING

A couple of miles south of town, **Alder House III** (611 Immonen Rd., 541/996-2483) is a glass-blowing operation and gallery open to the public. The variety of shapes and colors produced are fascinating aspects of this ancient craft that the artisans here will explain to you. Alder House is open 10 A.M.–5 P.M. daily, mid-March through November. The high-quality creations are on sale at bargain prices. The road to this establishment is indicated by signs on U.S. 101 three miles south of Lincoln City, 0.75 mile east on Immonen Road.

To sample the work of area artists, check out the **Ryan Gallery** (4270 N. U.S. 101, 541/994-5391) and **Earthworks Galleries** (620 N.E. U.S. 101, 541/557-4148).

With some 65 shops, the **Tanger Outlet Center** (1500 S.E. East Devil's Lake Rd., 541/996-5000), near the south end of town, is the largest outlet mall on the Oregon coast and has become something of a regional destination. Shops here include the ones you'd expect—London Fog, Samsonite, Eddie Bauer—plus such regional treats as the tasting room/espresso shop at **Chateau Benoit** (541/996-3981), where you can sample Oregon wines, and **Pendleton Woolen Mills** (541/994-2496).

Catch the Wind (266 S.E. U.S. 101, 541/994-9500) has a shop here, as well as in Newport and Florence, selling kites, windsocks, and all the materials you need to create your own colorful flying contraption. This one is conveniently close to the D River Wayside, site of Lincoln City's twice-annual kite festivals.

ACCOMMODATIONS

Lincoln City has, next to Portland, the most hotel rooms in the state. There are plenty to choose from, and many are very similar—basic hotel rooms within walking distance of the beach. However, there are some distinctions. No one would purposefully choose to stay on the east side of U.S. 101, necessitating an unpleasant fording of that great vehicular river just to walk to the beach, so all the following hotels are on the beach side of the highway.

Also, just because a hotel is new doesn't mean that it's preferred over older models. Some vintage hotels and motels have the best locations, and their slightly worn-in atmosphere is perfect for a summer holiday.

$50-100

The **Ester Lee** (3803 S.W. U.S. 101, 541/996-3606 or 888/996-3606, www.esterlee.com, doubles from $85) is a decades-old family motel complex, with some cottages on a bluff above miles of beachfront. All rooms have ocean views and fireplaces; some have kitchens and hot tubs. Pets are allowed. It's nothing fancy, but it's just fine and a good value.

Another pet-friendly place, the **Coho Inn** (1635 N.W. Harbor, 541/994-3684 or 800/848-7006, www.thecohoinn.com, doubles from $69) has 50 oceanfront units with fireplaces, kitchens, and continental breakfast.

$100-150

At the northern edge of Lincoln City, hugging the beach is the **Surftides Inn** (2945 N.W. Jetty Ave., 541/994-2191 or 800/452-2159, www.surftidesinn.com, doubles from $107), a large complex with 135 rooms, restaurant, lounge, and meeting rooms for business or family gatherings. All of the oceanfront rooms have balconies and most have fireplaces. The rather utilitarian rooms are pleasantly if simply furnished; all include a small refrigerator, microwave oven, and coffeemaker, as well as cable TV with DVD player. Prices vary considerably by view; ask about partial or no-view rooms for up to 30 percent in savings.

Overlooking the confluence of the Pacific and the tiny D River, the **Sea Gypsy Motel** (145 N.W. Inlet Ave., 541/994-2552 or 800/452-6929, www.theseagypsymotel.com, oceanview rooms from $104) is pretty much at the epicenter of beach life in Lincoln City. Recently remodeled units range from standard oceanfront rooms with queen-size beds and kitchenettes to a three-bed, two-bath suite with full kitchen. If price means more than view, the Sea Gypsy also has non-view units on a side street that are roughly half the price of view rooms (no kitchens, though). Each unit has cable TV, DVD player, and wireless Internet. The Sea Gypsy has an indoor pool and sauna.

On the bluff above the beach, with fine views and easy access to the sand, **Sea Horse Oceanfront Lodging** (2039 N.W. Harbor Dr., 541/994-2101 or 800/662-2101, www.seahorsemotel.com, oceanview doubles from $129) has a dizzying selection of lodging options, from simple motel rooms to cottages, houses, and two- and three-bedroom units, all in an extensive and quiet oceanfront compound. While it's a bit hard to generalize, most rooms have kitchens, some have fireplaces, and all guests are welcome at the breakfast bar, indoor pool, and outdoor hot tub. There are a handful of discounted non-view and partial-view rooms available. This friendly and venerable operation is one of the reasons Lincoln City is so popular with families.

Best Western Lincoln City Sands Suites (535 N.W. Inlet Ave., 541/994-4227 or 800/445-3234, www.visitlam.com, doubles from $139) is an imposing beachfront hotel near the mouth of the D River. The rooms are large and well furnished, more like condos than typical motel rooms, and have ocean views and patios or balconies directly above the beach; the kitchenettes have basic appliances and utensils. There's also an outdoor pool, hot tub, and sauna, plus patio area with fireplace and pond. This hotel is newer than many Lincoln City lodgings.

The **Siletz Bay Lodge** (1012 S.W. 51st St., 541/996-6111 or 888/430-2100, www.siletzbaylodge.com, doubles from $118), on the north end of Siletz Bay on a driftwood-strewn beach, is a family-friendly and wheelchair-accessible (with elevators) lodging in a location ideal for bird-watching and viewing seals. About half of the standard rooms have balconies, with delightful views of the bay and the sun going down over Salishan Spit. Spa rooms and spa suites are also available if you happen to be in town for a romantic getaway. Such in-room amenities as microwaves, refrigerators, and coffeemakers abound, and a continental breakfast is offered.

CENTRAL COAST

Close to the beach, **Brey House B&B** (3725 N.W. Keel Ave., 541/994-7123, www.brey house.com, doubles from $103) is one of the oldest bed-and-breakfast inns on the Oregon coast, a 1940-built three-story Cape Cod–style home with four bedrooms (all with private baths and entrances). You'll love the excellent breakfast, which is served in a light-filled room overlooking the ocean. This lodging is not appropriate for children.

The light and bright **Coast Inn B&B** (4507 S.W. Coast Ave., 541/994-7932 or 888/994-7932, www.oregoncoastinn.com, doubles from $100) offers nonsmoking guest rooms and a hot breakfast in a sprawling Craftsman-style home located in historic Taft Heights, south of Spanish Head. Siletz Bay is a short walk away, as is public beach access. Entirely remodeled in 2001, this home features comfortable new furnishings and homey decor.

$150-200

More a small boutique hotel than the typical sprawling motel complex that typifies Lincoln City, **Starfish Manor Hotel** (2735 N.W. Inlet Ave., 541/996-9300 or 800/972-6155, www.onthebeachfront.com, doubles from $169) has just 17 oceanfront rooms and suites perched above the beach. All units have large oceanview whirlpool tubs, fireplaces, oceanfront decks, kitchenettes, tasteful furnishings, and fine linens. Some units have two bedrooms. The Starfish is in a quiet part of town, perfect for a romantic getaway. The folks who own the Starfish have two other small boutique hotels with even more upscale suites; see the Starfish website for links.

If you've been fantasizing about rolling out of bed, slipping on your robe—coffee in hand—and walking out onto a semi-private stretch of beach, then the **Inn at Spanish Head** (4009 S.W. U.S. 101, 541/996-2161 or 800/452-8127, www.spanishhead.com, doubles from $185) may be your best bet. Oregon's only resort hotel right on the beach, the inn takes its place—large and looming—against the backdrop of rugged cliffs. Whether in a suite, studio, or bedroom unit, every room has an ocean

view. On-site amenities include Fathoms, the 10th-floor restaurant/bar, a fireplace lounge, meeting rooms, heated outdoor pool, saunas, spa, and exercise room.

For a small oceanfront luxury hotel, the **O'dysius Hotel** (120 N.W. Inlet Ct., 541/994-4121 or 800/869-8069, www.odysius.com, doubles from $155) offers 30 units furnished with period antiques. Guests meet in the lobby every afternoon to sample Oregon wine. The hotel accepts pets and provides concierge, massage, and a continental breakfast. Wheelchair accessible.

When asked to choose *the* place to stay on the Oregon coast, most Oregonians would recommend the **Salishan Lodge** (7760 N. U.S. 101, Gleneden Beach, 541/764-2371 or 888/SALISHAN, www.salishanlodge.com, doubles from $159). Named for a widespread native dialect in the Oregon Territory, this resort a couple of miles south of Lincoln City is one of a dozen properties in the nation that consistently receives a four-star as well as a five-diamond rating. Almost every year, *Condé Nast Traveler* rates Salishan one of the country's top resorts.

While there are distant Siletz Bay views, Salishan isn't a beachfront resort, and most folks quickly learn to appreciate the peace of the forest and golf course here. This paradigm shift is facilitated by art and landscape architecture that convey the vision of John Gray, who built Salishan and such other Northwest properties as Skamania Lodge (on the Washington side of the Columbia Gorge) and Sunriver (south of Bend) from native materials with respect for the surrounding environment.

Even if you don't stay here, the grounds and facilities are worth a look. The art gallery is free and features works by top Oregon artists (also check out master woodcarver Leroy Setziol's bas-relief panels in the dining room). In addition to the recreational and aesthetic appeal of the resort, the Dining Room contributes to Salishan's lofty reputation. The forested trails behind the golf course (rated among the top 75 in the United States) showcase the rainforested foothills of the Coast Range and the waterfowl

CENTRAL COAST

near Siletz Bay. Across the street, the Salishan Marketplace features first-rate galleries and a good bookstore, Allegory Books.

In high season, Salishan attracts well-heeled nature lovers, corporate expense-account clientele, folks enjoying a special occasion, and serious golfers. You'll also find everyday folks and seminar attendees on winter weekend specials at half the summertime rates. Ask about multiday packages for big savings on your room rate.

Vacation Rentals

To rent vacation homes throughout Lincoln County, contact the **Lincoln City Visitor and Convention Bureau** (800/452-2151). Or, try **Pacific Retreats** (3126-A N.E. U.S. 101, 800/473-4833, www.pacificretreats. com), which features a selection of vacation home rentals.

FOOD

Lincoln City offers many affordable and palate-pleasing dining options, most of them very busy and family-dining focused. There are a few fine dining options, but fish and chips and chowder are favorites here.

Brewpubs

The **Lighthouse Brew Pub** (4157 U.S. 101 N., 541/994-7238, open for lunch and dinner daily) is a welcome rehash of the McMenamin formula so successful in the Willamette Valley. Just look for a lighthouse replica in a parking lot on the northwest side of U.S. 101 across from McDonald's. Pizza bread, burgers, sandwiches, and chili can be washed down by McMenamins' own ales or some other quality brew, as well as hard cider and wine. Live music at night is an added plus.

Seafood

If coastal restaurants are eating a hole in your wallet, there's always tried-and-true **Mo's** (860 S.W. 51st St., 541/996-2535, open for lunch and dinner daily, main courses $8–18). As usual, count on good clam chowder and full fish dinners as well as superlative views of the water.

Dory Cove Restaurant (5819 Logan Rd.,

541/994-5180, open for lunch and dinner daily, main dishes $8–22), near Road's End State Park, has prices a little higher than Mo's, but the range of deep-fried and sautéed seafood main courses (halibut fish and chips are recommended) is impressive, as is the fact that in a place so clearly dominated by seafood, so many people come here for steaks and burgers. Save room for the homemade pies. This is an extraordinarily popular spot, so expect lines on weekends and in summer.

Kyllo's (1110 N.W. 1st Ct., 541/994-3179, open for lunch and dinner daily, main courses $16–20) specializes in broiled, sautéed, and baked seafood, plus excellent homemade desserts and Oregon microbrews and wines. The restaurant is visible from U.S. 101 as you drive by the D River Wayside. With views of the water on all sides, this restaurant is a good place to linger, though waits can be long in the evening as no reservations are taken.

Asian

Lincoln City is lucky to have several good Asian restaurants. Our favorite is **Andaman Thai Cuisine** (660 S.E. U.S. 101, 541/996-8424, open for lunch and dinner daily), in a strip mall midway through town. In addition to traditional and well-prepared Thai favorites, Andaman offers zippy updates that include local seafood and seasonal ingredients. One bite of the appetizer called Oh My God, golden fried tortilla rolls with crab meat, basil, and cream cheese, served with homemade siracha sauce, and you'll understand the dish's apt title. Grilled wild salmon is served with panang curry sauce, and the Garlic Lovers' Stirfry, loaded with wild mushrooms, might be just what you want after a diet of bland clam chowder and fish and chips.

At the south end of town, **Momiji** (5045 S.W. U.S. 101, 541/994-8886, open for lunch and dinner daily, sushi rolls $5–11) offers both Chinese and Japanese cooking, but the reason this restaurant is so popular is the excellent sushi rolls and sashimi served here. The sushi partakes of both Japanese tradition and Oregon invention: The Salem Roll, for example, is made with crab, cream cheese, and avocado, then deep fried and served with a sweet and spicy sauce. Also excellent is the Broiled Oyster Misoyaki, a half-shell oyster topped with homemade red miso paste, green onion, and smelt roe. You're welcome to watch at the bar as the sushi is made, or eat family-style in the restaurant.

Northwest Cuisine

The 🄲 **Blackfish Cafe** (2733 N.W. U.S. 101, 541/996-1007, www.blackfishcafe.com, open for lunch and dinner Wed.–Mon., main courses $13–18) is a great find. Presided over by former Salishan Resort executive chef Rob Pounding, who has longstanding relationships with local farmers, anglers, and mushroom foragers, the Blackfish Cafe is dedicated to fairly priced and delicious regional cooking. The emphasis is on what's fresh, homegrown, and creative—Willamette Valley pork medallions in huckleberry compote and troll-caught chinook salmon with Oregon blue cheese mashed potatoes. There is no shortage of humbler fare, either, such as the self-proclaimed best clam chowder on the coast and halibut fish and chips.

American

If you're en route to the wine country or the Willamette Valley or just want a respite from resort traffic, a place that appeals to everybody is 🄲 **Otis Cafe** (1259 Salmon River Hwy., 541/994-9560, open for three meals daily, main courses $7–14), at the Otis Junction on Highway 18 two miles east of U.S. 101. Here, innovative variations on American road food have been warmly embraced by everyone from local loggers to yuppies (and *New York Times* food critics) stopping off on the drive between Portland and the coast. In September, salmon-fishing devotees can be seen lining up here at 6:30 A.M. Breakfast in this unpretentious café, five miles northeast of Lincoln City, is such an institution that long waits on the porch are the rule on weekend mornings. The reasons for the wait include the thick-crusted molasses bread, buttermilk waffles, and legendary hash browns under a crust of melted Rogue Valley white

cheddar. Large portions, low prices, and a culinary touch that turns pork chops and rhubarb pie into epicurean delights are in full evidence at lunch and dinner.

A half mile south of Salishan (five miles equidistant from Depoe Bay and Lincoln City) is a Gleneden Beach eatery with considerable appeal. The **Side Door Café** (6675 Gleneden Beach Loop, 541/764-3825, www.edenhall .com) combines a gourmet restaurant with a musical venue. The airy yet cozy-feeling dining room features a menu where peach barbecue-glazed salmon and chanterelle mushroom hazelnut lasagna exemplify the menu offerings. The adjoining state-of-the-art Eden Hall theater might feature a Northwest artist with a national reputation, such as jazz singer Nancy King or Portland-based Delta blues artist Kelly Joe Phelps.

Two Indian gaming casinos are located within 25 miles of one another and offer dining alternatives to the coast-bound traveler. Both **Chinook Winds** (1777 N.W. 44th St., Lincoln City, 541/966-5825 or 888/CHI-NOOK, 888/244-6665), and **Spirit Mountain** (800/760-7977), about 25 miles east of Lincoln City on Highway 22 in Grand Ronde, have many dining options. Each offers generous full buffets for breakfast, lunch, and dinner, and both have fine-dining, full-service restaurants offering moderate to expensive prices. Both casinos have nightly buffets in the $15 range. Chinook Winds also offers a Friday night seafood buffet and a Sunday champagne brunch. Chinook Winds' ocean views are also worth noting. Both casinos have outlets for 24-hour dining.

Fine Dining

Some of coastal Oregon's top dining experiences are found just south of Lincoln City. The reasonable prices at the Salishan Lodge's **Sun Room Restaurant** (7760 N. U.S. 101, Gleneden Beach, www.salishanlodge.com) are a welcome surprise. This casual restaurant might be less elaborate and half the price of Salishan's five-star Dining Room, but its Northwest cuisine comes from the same kitchen.

At Salishan's **Dining Room** (800/452-2300, open for dinner, main courses $25–58) special emphasis is placed on seasonal seafood, game, and other regional delicacies. The elegance of the setting, expansive wine list, and creative dishes have long made this a coastal dining destination. Dishes may include salmon with wild mushrooms and blue cheese soufflé or duck breast with pecan and pear bread pudding. For decades the Dining Room has been the top rated restaurant in Oregon, famed for its creative interpretations of seasonal Northwest delicacies and a 12,000-bottle wine cellar (noted for the world's largest collection of Oregon pinot noir).

The **Bay House** (5911 S.W. U.S. 101, 541/996-3222, www.bayhouserestaurant.com, open for lunch Tues.–Sat., dinner nightly, main courses $26–49) combines oceanfront views with exquisite Northwest cuisine. Alaskan halibut is parmesan-crusted and served with sorrel velouté, and the signature crab cakes come with lemon aioli. Oenophiles will want to look at the wine list, praised by *Wine Spectator*. Dinner here with a bottle of Oregon pinot noir can easily set you back $75 a person, but for a special occasion the setting and the food can't be beat. The Bay House is now open for lunch, offering a less costly and formal opportunity to sample the restaurant's near legendary cuisine.

PRACTICALITIES

A little south of the D River is the helpful **Lincoln City Visitor and Convention Bureau** (801 S.W. U.S. 101, 541/994-8378 or 800/452-2151, open 9 A.M.–5 P.M. Mon.–Sat. and 10 A.M.–4 P.M. Sun.) **Driftwood Public Library** (541/996-2277) is in the same municipal complex.

The **Central Oregon Coast Association** (541/265-2064 or 800/767-2064, www.coast visitor.com) maintains a useful website with details on Lincoln City and the rest of coastal Lincoln County.

The **Traveler's Convenience Center** (660 S.E. U.S. 101), a mile south of the D River, has a coin-operated laundry. The **post office** (541/994-2128) is two blocks east of U.S. 101 on East Devil's Lake Road.

Lincoln City–bound travelers from Portland (via Hwy. 99 W) and Salem (via Hwy. 22) pass through the scenic wine and orchard country to connect with Highway 18. This is one of the most dangerous roads to drive in the state, so extra care is called for on this two-laner.

Peak traffic times in Lincoln City can result in 25,000 cars a day crawling through town. As an alternative to rush hour on U.S. 101, you could try detouring on N.E. West Devil's Lake Road or N.E. East Devil's Lake Road, which bypass the worst congestion.

Lincoln County Transit (541/265-4900, www.co.lincoln.or.us/transit/) buses stop in town for weekday service only. The line goes as far south as Yachats and does not run on major holidays.

CENTRAL COAST

Depoe Bay

In *Blue Highways,* William Least Heat-Moon characterized Depoe Bay thusly: "Depoe Bay used to be a picturesque fishing village; now it was just picturesque. The fish houses, but for one seasonal company, were gone, the fleet gone, and in their stead had come sport fishing boats and souvenir ashtray and T-shirt shops."

To be fair, tourists have come here since the establishment of the town. In fact, for all intents and purposes, the town didn't really exist until the completion of the Roosevelt Highway (U.S. 101) in 1927, which opened the area up to car travelers. Prior to that time, the area had been occupied mainly by a few members of the Siletz Reservation. One of the group, who worked at the U.S. Army depot, called himself Charlie Depot. The town was named after him, eventually taking on the current spelling.

Depoe Bay is in the heart of the so-called Twenty Miracle Miles, describing the attractive stretch of rockbound coast from the broad beaches of Lincoln City south past Depoe Bay

Depoe Bay's Harbor is linked to the Pacific by a narrow passage.

© BILL MCRAE

north. Regardless of what you think of the short commercial strip along the highway here, the scenic appeal of Depoe's location is impossible to ignore. The rocky outer bay, flanked by headlands to the north and south, is pierced by a narrow channel through the basalt cliffs leading to the inner harbor. It's home to an active sportfishing fleet as well as the whale-watching charters that have earned Depoe Bay its distinction as whale-watching capital of the state.

SIGHTS AND RECREATION
The Bayfront and Harbor

Depoe Bay is situated along a truly beautiful coastline that cannot be fully appreciated from the highway. A quarter-mile-long seawall and promenade invite a stroll. For a panorama of the harbor, continue along the sidewalks across the gracefully arching concrete bridge, designed by Conde McCullough and built in 1927. Other nice perspectives are offered from residential streets west of U.S. 101; try Ellingson Street, south of the bridge, and Sunset Street at the north end of the bay.

Two "spouting horns," natural blowholes in the rocks north of the harbor entrance, can send plumes of spray 60 feet into the air when the tide and waves are right.

East of the bridge is Depoe Bay's claim to international fame, the world's smallest navigable natural harbor. This boat basin is also exceptional because it's a harbor within a harbor. This topography is the result of wave action cutting into the basalt over eons until a 50-foot passageway leading to a six-acre inland lagoon was created. In addition to whale-watching, folks congregate on the bridge between the ocean and the harbor to watch boats maneuver into the enclosure. Depoe Bay's Harbor was scenic enough to be selected as the site from which Jack Nicholson commandeered a yacht for his mental patient crew in *One Flew Over the Cuckoo's Nest.*

Boiler Bay State Scenic Viewpoint

A half mile north of town is Boiler Bay, so named because of the boiler left from the 1910 wreck of the *J. Marhoffer.* The ship caught fire three miles offshore and drifted into the bay.

DRAKE'S LOST HARBOR?

In 1996, the media exploded with stories raising the possibility that the tiny hamlet of Whale Cove, two miles south of Depoe Bay, could supplant Plymouth Rock as the birthplace of a nation. Rotting timbers from what is theorized to have been a stockade built by Sir Francis Drake in 1579 were unearthed in an area where stories have long circulated that the English privateer made landfall.

Over the years, these notions have been fueled by several tantalizing pieces of evidence: an unsigned ship log from Drake's voyage in a museum in England that identified 44 degrees north latitude – the same as Whale Cove – as a landing site; an English shilling dating from 1560 found on the central Oregon coast in 1982; a photo from the 1930s showing a local resident with a distinctly English sword he unearthed; and a ship's cutlass found in Newport in the early 19th century bearing the markings of a 16th-century English arsenal. Moreover, excavations of a nearby Indian village thought to have been buried in the year 1600 turned up brass items, blades, and Venetian beads.

An amateur British historian, Bob Ward, makes a compelling case for Whale Cove as the place where Drake spent five weeks in summer 1579. In his flagship *Golden Hynde,* the only one of his five-ship fleet to survive the stormy straits around Cape Horn, Drake harassed Spanish settlements throughout Latin America and plundered Spanish ships wherever he met them. Sailing west from Mexico on its return to England via the Cape of Good Hope, the treasure-laden *Golden Hynde* was beset by storms, and Drake had to retreat to land to

make repairs. Conventional history has held that he made landfall around San Francisco, most likely on the Marin County coast.

Ward, however, believes that Drake continued his voyage farther north and sailed into the Strait of Juan de Fuca, thinking he had found the fabled Northwest Passage. Turning around before he realized his mistake, Drake then headed south down the Washington and Oregon coasts, where he found a sandy cove in which to drop anchor and make repairs before the long journey home.

On Drake's return to England after four years at sea, news of his exploits were suppressed. Queen Elizabeth confiscated the logs and charts, and it would be 10 years before an official account of the voyage would be published. Then, Drake's New Albion was described as being around 38 degrees north latitude (in northern California), in an attempt, Ward believes, to fool the Spanish into thinking the Northwest Passage was much farther south.

After Elizabeth's death in 1603, however, new charts began to appear that placed the landing site much farther north, and early 17th-century charts show a small, shallow bay labeled Novus Albionis (New Albion), which is an uncannily accurate depiction of Whale Cove.

Since the initial blizzard of publicity, there has been no final word from the archaeologists and historians involved in corroborating these claims. Because most history books have placed New Albion, Drake's fabled lost settlement, near San Francisco, researchers will not be too quick to claim otherwise without definitive research.

The remains of the boiler are visible at low tide. This rock-rimmed bay is a favorite spot for rock fishing, birding, and whale-watching. A trail leads down to some excellent tidepools.

Whale Cove

Half a mile south of Depoe Bay, a picturesque bay has been scooped out of the sandstone bluffs. The tranquility of this calendar-photo-come-to-life is deceptive. There's considerable evidence to suggest that this tiny embayment—and not California's Marin County—was the site of Francis Drake's 1579 landing (see sidebar *Drake's Lost Harbor?*), but the jury is still out. During Prohibition, bootleggers used the protected cove as a clandestine port.

Rocky Creek State Scenic Viewpoint overlooks Whale Cove. There are picnic tables, and it's a good spot for whale-watching, but there's no beach access.

Otter Crest Loop

The rocky bluffs of this coastal stretch take on an even more dramatic aspect as you leave the highway at the Otter Crest Loop, a winding three-mile section of the old Coast Highway, two miles south of Depoe Bay.

From atop **Cape Foulweather,** the visibility can extend 40 miles on a clear day. The view south to Yaquina Head and its lighthouse is a photographer's fantasy of headlands, coves, and offshore monoliths. Bronze plaques in the parking lot tell of Captain Cook naming the 500-foot-high headland during a bout with storm-tossed seas on March 7, 1778. Comic relief from the coast's parade of historical plaques comes with another tablet bearing the inscription, "On this site in 1897, nothing happened."

The Lookout gift shop on the north side of the promontory is a good place to buy Japanese fishing floats for a few bucks. The million-dollar view from inside the shop is easily one of the most spectacular windows on the ocean to be found anywhere.

Another mile south, in the hamlet of **Otter Rock,** you'll find another of the Oregon coast's several diabolically named natural features, the **Devil's Punchbowl.** The urnlike sandstone formation, filled with swirling water, has been sculpted by centuries of waves flooding into what had been a cave until its roof collapsed. The inexorable process continues today, thanks to the ebb and flow of the Pacific through two openings in the cauldron wall. A state park viewpoint gives you a ringside seat for this frothy confrontation between rock and tide. When the water recedes, you can see purple sea urchins and starfish in the tidepools of the **Marine Gardens** 100 feet to the north.

To the south of the Punchbowl vantage point are picnic tables and a wooden walkway down to the beach. Close by, in the tiny Otter Rock **Mo's** restaurant (221 1st St.), a seat occupied by "The Boss" himself, Bruce Springsteen, on June 11, 1987, is enshrined. Also in Otter Rock, the **Flying Dutchman Winery** (915 1st St., 541/765-2553) makes limited batches of

handcrafted wines. It is open 11 A.M.–6 P.M. daily for tastings and tours.

Back on U.S. 101, a mile's drive south brings you to Beverly Beach State Park.

Fishing and Whale-Watching Charters

With the ocean minutes from Depoe Bay's port, catching a salmon or seeing a whale is possible as soon as you leave the harbor. Most charter operators here offer both fishing and whale-watching excursions. Bottom-fishing trips average $55 for a five-hour run, salmon fishing about $100 for a seven- or eight-hour day; whale-watching excursions run $15–25 per person per hour.

Dockside Charters (541/765-2545 or 800/733-8915, www.docksidedepoebay.com) offers 1.5-hour whale-watching trips aboard its 50-foot excursion boat for $20/adult and on 25-foot rigid-hull inflatables for $25/adult. **Tradewinds Charters** (541/765-2345 or 800/445-8730, www.tradewindscharters.com) hosts one- and two-hour trips Decem-

Whale-watchers depart from Depoe Bay.

CENTRAL COAST

ber–May. Rates run $15–45/adult on its fleet of 30- to 52-foot boats and 18-foot Zodiac. A 12-hour tuna charter costs $160.

Surfing

If you're itching to actually get into the water and catch a few waves, the beach at Otter Rock, a few miles south of Depoe Bay, is a good place to surf. The beach here is protected, and there's a pretty large area where beginners tend to hang out. (There's also a section that gets bigger waves and better surfers.) Stop by the **Otter Rock Surf Shop** (488 N. U.S. 101, 541/765-2776, www.otterrocksurf.com) for rental equipment or lessons. (It's best to call ahead if you want a lesson.)

EVENTS

The **Depoe Bay Classic Wooden Boat Show, Crab Feed, and Ducky Derby** is held the last weekend in April. Several dozen wooden craft, both restored and newly constructed vessels, ranging from kayaks to skiffs and dinghies to larger fishing boats, are displayed in the harbor and the adjacent Depoe Bay City Park. Rowing races, boat-building workshops, crab races, and other activities are scheduled. The big Crab Feed, held 10 A.M.–5 P.M. both Saturday and Sunday, sees some 1,500 pounds of crab, plus side dishes, devoured at the Community Hall; it costs $14 for a full dinner. The Ducky Derby is a raffle in which you purchase "tickets" in the form of rubber duckies, which race down the harbor's feeder stream vying for prizes. For more information, contact the chamber of commerce.

The **Fleet of Flowers** happens each Memorial Day in the harbor to honor those lost at sea and in military service. More than 20,000 people come to witness a blanket of blossoms cast upon the waters.

The **Depoe Bay Salmon Bake** takes place on the third Saturday of September, 10 A.M.–5 P.M. at Depoe Bay City Park, flanking the rear of the boat basin. Some 3,000 pounds of fresh ocean fish are caught, cooked Native American–style on alder stakes over an open fire, and served with all the trimmings, to be savored to the accompaniment of live entertainment. Cost is $14 for adults, $8 children. It always seems to rain on the day of this event, but that's life on the Oregon coast.

ACCOMMODATIONS

Lodgings in popular Depoe Bay require advance reservations on most weekends and holidays.

The **Surfrider Resort** (3115 N.W. U.S. 101, 541/764-2311 or 800/662-2378, www.surfriderresort.com, doubles from $114) is a few miles north of town on picturesque Fogarty Creek's rockbound coast. While it's been around for a while and is not too elaborate, its setting and other appeals mandate a mention. Oceanfront suites and rooms have decks; some feature whirlpool tubs, kitchens, and fireplaces. A good restaurant, an indoor pool, and midweek specials are also noteworthy.

The **Inn at Arch Rock** (70 N.W. Sunset St., 800/767-1835, www.innatarchrock.com, doubles from $79) comprises a cluster of white clapboard buildings that overlook the bay from their clifftop perch at the north end of town. In addition to 13 oceanfront rooms, there are three two-bedroom condo units next door that sleep six, for $239.

Located about three miles south of Depoe Bay, at one of the most scenic spots on the central coast, is the **Inn at Otter Crest** (301 Otter Crest Loop, Otter Rock, 541/765-2111 or 800/452-2101, www.innatottercrest.com, hotel rooms from $129, studios from $139, suites from $199), a condo resort perched near the sandstone bluffs at the ocean's edge. Hotel rooms have two queen-size beds, refrigerator, coffeemaker, and private deck with picture windows, while studios have a queen-size Murphy bed, full kitchen, fireplace, and dining area. Suites have one to two bedrooms, plus full kitchens and balconies.

Harbor Lights Inn (235 S.E. Bay View Ave., 541/765-2322 or 800/228-0448, www.gracieslanding.com, doubles $89–135), a small inn overlooking the harbor, has the distinct advantage of being distant from U.S. 101. This homey inn affords views of sea otters, ducks, and geese while the whale-watching and fishing boats come and go. All rooms have a harbor view; rates include a hot breakfast. Pets are allowed.

The **Channel House** (35 Ellingson St., 541/765-2140 or 800/447-2140, www.channel house.com, rooms from $100, suites from $235) features three rooms and nine spacious suites boasting expansive dramatic views of the ocean, private decks with outdoor whirlpool tubs (in the majority of rooms), fireplaces, plush robes, and other amenities. This blufftop B&B (there isn't a beach below, just miles of ocean and surrounding cliffs) may not look prepossessing from the outside, but inside the place is all windows and angles. Imagine *Architectural Digest* in a nautical theme. This is the best place on the Oregon coast to commune with whales, passing boats, winter storms, and the setting sun. A continental breakfast with tasty baked goods in an oceanside dining area is included in the rates.

FOOD

Tidal Raves (279 N.W. U.S. 101, 541/765-2995, open for lunch and dinner daily, main courses $15–19) boasts the best views in town and a casual ambience. In addition to fresh fish and other seafood dishes such as Thai prawns and oyster spinach bisque, the restaurant's pasta specialties are uniformly excellent. The Pasta Rave features crab, shrimp, lingcod, snapper, and more on a bed of linguine with pesto. The Dungeness crab casserole is also noteworthy. For dessert don't miss the warm chocolate chunk cookie with Tillamook Vanilla Bean ice cream.

Oceanus (177 U.S. 101, 541/765-4553, open for lunch and dinner Thurs.–Tues., main courses $11–22) is a real gem of a seafood restaurant. The windows overlook the bay but the real action is on your plate. Eclectic preparations borrow from many cuisines, including fish tacos, Thai prawns, Cajun shrimp, and cioppino fish stew—though the traditional clam chowder is excellent. The key lime pie is locally renowned.

PRACTICALITIES

On the east side of the highway, opposite the seawall, the **Depoe Bay Chamber of Commerce** (70 N.E. U.S. 101, Depoe Bay 97341, 541/765-2889 or 877/485-8348, www.depoebay chamber.org) offers literature about the town and the central coast in general. Open 11 A.M.–3 P.M. weekdays, 9 A.M.–4 P.M. weekends.

On weekdays, **Lincoln County Transit** (541/265-4900, www.co.lincoln.or.us/transit/) runs buses four times daily, north to Lincoln City and south to Yachats.

Newport

In January 1852, a storm grounded the schooner *Juliet* near Yaquina (pronounced yah-KWIN-nah) Bay, where her captain and crew were stranded for two months. When they finally made their way inland to the Willamette Valley, they reported their discovery of an abundance of tiny, sweet-tasting oysters in the bay. Within a decade, commercial oyster farms were established here, the first major impetus to growth and settlement in Newport. The tasty morsels that delighted diners in San Francisco and at New York's Waldorf-Astoria Hotel are almost gone now, but the oyster industry continues by harvesting introduced species.

The port bustles with the activity of Oregon's largest commercial fishing fleet and second-largest recreational fleet. New factories to process *surimi* (a fish paste popular in Japan) and whiting have provided hundreds of jobs here, and a state-of-the-art aquarium that once housed Keiko the whale (from *Free Willy*) brings in the tourist dollar. In this vein, new wildlife observation facilities and improved access to tidal pools north of town at Yaquina Head make this park a highlight of the coast.

The shops, galleries, and restaurants along Newport's historic Bayfront, together with the Performing Arts Center and quieter charm of Nye Beach, keep up a tourism tradition that goes back to when this town was the "honeymoon capital of Oregon."

SIGHTS
◖ Oregon Coast Aquarium

There are 6,000 miles of water between the Oregon coast and Japan—the largest stretch of open ocean on earth. You can hear *our* side of the story at the Oregon Coast Aquarium (2820 S.E. Ferry Slip Rd., Newport, 541/867-3474, www.aquarium.org, open 9 A.M.–6 P.M. daily Memorial Day weekend–Labor Day weekend and 10 A.M.–5 P.M. daily the rest of the year (closed Christmas day), $12 adults, $10 seniors, $7 for ages 4–13), one of the state's most popular attractions.

The aquarium initially featured 40,000 square feet of galleries devoted to wetland communities, near-shore and marine ecosystems, and an environmental center. While it was respected as a top-notch educational facility, it lacked "star power" until the 1996 arrival of Keiko, a 7,720-pound, 32-foot-long orca who starred in *Free Willy.* Understandably, the whale's presence overshadowed four acres of sea lions, sea otters, tidepools, and undersea caves, as well as the largest walk-in seabird aviary in the Americas. Keiko was moved to Iceland for re-entry into the wild, where he died in 2003. Keiko or no,

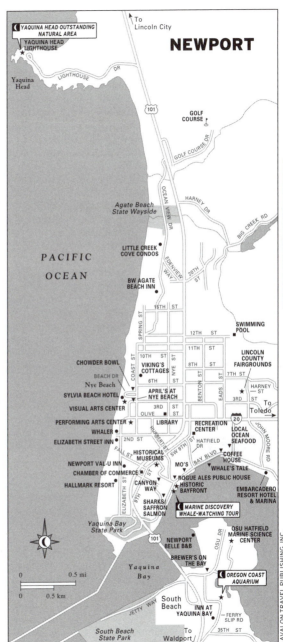

CENTRAL COAST

© AVALON TRAVEL PUBLISHING, INC.

there are still many attractions at the Oregon Aquarium to hold your interest.

One of the gems of the aquarium is Passages of the Deep, a 200-foot-long acrylic tunnel offering 360-degree underwater views in three diverse habitats, from Orford Reef to Halibut Flats to Open Sea, where you're surrounded by free-swimming sharks. The Jewels of the Sea exhibit showcases several dozen kinds of jellyfish in an almost psychedelic display.

At the Jetty is the aquarium's largest permanent indoor exhibit to date. Visitors look through a window into a 35,000-gallon tank to watch white sturgeon and coho and chinook salmon swimming among large basalt boulders that simulate a coastal jetty, such as these anadromous fish in the wild might pass through on their upriver journey to their spawning grounds.

Of the several hundred species of Pacific Northwest fish, birds, and mammals on display in the rest of the facility, don't miss the sea otters, wolf eel, leopard sharks, lion's mane jellyfish, and tufted puffins. The younger set

© BILL MCRAE

seals loafing in Newport harbor

will enjoy the sea cave with simulated wave action and resident octopus.

Indigenous simulated ecosystems help articulate the region's biology. The centerpiece of the Wetland's Gallery, for example, is a cross section of the salt marsh subject to the periodic ebb and flow of tides. Another ecological niche is illustrated by a 4,730-gallon tank in the Sandy Shores exhibit. Here, you can see smelt, perch, and leopard sharks navigate amid human-made rocks and piers. The Rock Shores Gallery adds another dimension to the experience with an open tidal pool that allows visitors to handle starfish, sea anemones, and the like. In the outside aviary and sea mammal pools, latex molds of rocky outcroppings provide perches for birds, otters, and sea lions (some of these animals were rescued from such debacles as the *Exxon-Valdez* oil spill).

In addition to gaining a heightened understanding of the coast biome, you might also come away with something from the museum shop's first-rate collection of regional books and oceanographic tomes or perhaps a crystal or gemstone. The on-site Mermaid Cafe emphasizes such Oregon fare as Tillamook dairy products, seasonal fruits, and seafood. Outside in the summer, enjoy barbecued burgers and hot dogs and teriyaki shish kebabs.

Advance tickets are recommended on weekends, major holidays, and during the summer. To get there from U.S. 101, turn east on OSU Drive or 32nd Street, south of the Yaquina Bay Bridge, and follow Ferry Slip Road to the parking lot.

Oregon State University Hatfield Marine Science Center

Just south of the Yaquina Bay Bridge, head east on the road that parallels the bay to the OSU Hatfield Marine Science Center (Marine Science Drive, Newport, 541/867-0100, http://hmsc.oregonstate.edu, open 10 A.M.–5 P.M. daily in summer and 10 A.M.–4 P.M. Thurs.–Mon. the rest of the year, donation $3 adult). This research and education facility is a low-key but interesting complement to the very popular Oregon Coast Aquarium, located half a mile south. At the door to greet you is an octopus in an open tank pointing the way to oceanography exhibits and a "hands-on" area where you can experience the feel of starfish, anemones, and other sea creatures. The back hallway has educational dioramas and a theater shows marine-science films throughout the day. If you proceed left from the octopus tank, you'll see tanks with different sea ecosystems. Beyond the walls of the museum, guided field trips (a fee is charged) explore estuary, beach, and coastal forest habitats at various times of the year (check with the front desk or the website for details). The bookstore has a good selection of nature books, posters, games, and gifts.

During Whale Watch weeks (Christmas break and spring break), the center temporarily returns to its summer hours. Admission is free, but a $3 donation is suggested to support the center and its programs.

Oregon Coast History Center

For a glimpse into the rich past of Lincoln County, stop at the Oregon Coast History Center (545 S.W. 9th St., Newport, 541/265-7509, www.oregoncoast.history.museum, open 10 A.M.–5 P.M. Tues.–Sun. June–Sept., 11 A.M.–4 P.M. Oct.–May, free admission), which incorporates the Log Cabin Museum and the adjacent Queen Anne–style Burrows House, a former boardinghouse built in 1895. It's located a half block east of the chamber of commerce on U.S. 101. The logging, farming, pioneer life, and maritime exhibits (particularly Newport shipwrecks) are interesting, but the Siletz baskets and other Native American artifacts steal the show.

Here you can learn the heartbreaking story of the hardships—forced displacement, inadequate housing, insufficient food, and poor medical facilities—that plagued the diverse tribes that made up the Confederated Siletz Indian Reservation.

The Bayfront

Newport's Old Town Bayfront District can be easy to miss if you're not alert. At the north end of the Yaquina Bay Bridge, look for the signs

Newport's Bay Boulevard is busy with both commercial fishers and tourists.

© BILL MCRAE

pointing off U.S. 101, which lead you down the hill to Bay Boulevard, the Bayfront's main drag. Alternatively, turn southeast off the highway a few blocks north onto Hurbert Street; this runs into Canyon Way, which ends at Bay Boulevard. On summer weekends, forget about parking anywhere near here unless you arrive early. Spots close by the boulevard can often be found, however, along Canyon Way, the hillside access route to downtown.

Until 1936, ferries shuttled people and vehicles to and from Newport's waterfront. With the completion of the Yaquina Bay Bridge that year, however, traffic bypassed the old town area. Commerce and development moved to the highway corridor, and the Bayfront faded in importance. Within the last couple of decades, the pendulum has swung back, and the Bayfront District is now one of Newport's prime attractions, with some of its best restaurants and watering holes, shopping, and tourist facilities.

One of the first things that'll strike you about the Bayfront today is that it's still a working neighborhood, not a sanitized recreation of a real seaport. Chowderhouses, galleries, and shops stand shoulder to shoulder with fish-processing plants and canneries, and the air is filled with the cries of fishmongers purveying wharfside walkaway cocktails and the harmonious discord of sea lions and harbor seals. On the waterfront, sport anglers step off charter boats with their catches, and vessels laden with everything from wood products to whale-watchers ply the bay. Unfortunately, the severe catch limits and cost of equipment make this less of a working port every year. In deference to the Oregon commercial fisherman and other endangered species, wall murals memorialize fishing boats and whales here on the Bayfront.

Yaquina Bay State Park

In 1871, a lighthouse was built here on a bluff overlooking the mouth of Yaquina Bay, and the lighthouse keeper, his wife, and seven children moved into the two-story wood-frame structure. It soon became apparent, however, that

The Yaquina Bay Bridge spans the entrance to the harbor in Newport.

© ELIZABETH OPENSHAW

the location was not ideal, as the light could not be seen by ships approaching the harbor from the north. The station was abandoned after just three years, once the nearby light at Yaquina Head was completed. The building was slated for demolition in 1934, when local residents formed the Lincoln County Historical Society to preserve it. In 1997, the government decided to turn Yaquina Bay's beacon back on.

Today, the handsome restored structure and surrounding grounds make up Yaquina Bay State Park (541/574-3129 or 800/551-6949), in a beautiful location at the north end of the Yaquina Bay Bridge. The oldest building in Newport, it's the last wooden lighthouse on the Oregon coast. The living quarters, replete with period furnishings, are open noon–4 P.M. daily. Admission is free. Be sure to ask the volunteers about the resident ghost.

From the parking area, you have an excellent photo-op of the bay and the bridge. The park is a good place to have a picnic, or you can descend the trails to the beach and dig for razor clams or hunt for agates and petrified wood.

Nye Beach

The 1890s-era tourism boom that came to Newport's Bayfront spilled over into Nye Beach. In 1891, the city built a wooden sidewalk connecting the two neighborhoods and soon "summer people" were filling the cedar cottages here. In the next century, thanks to an improved river-and-land route from Corvallis, health faddists (who came for hot seawater baths in the sanatorium) and honeymooners soon joined the mix.

Located a mile north from the Bayfront, to the west of U.S. 101 (look for signs on the highway), this one-time favorite retreat for wealthy Portlanders has undergone a revival in recent years. Rough times and rougher weather had reduced luxurious beach houses here to a cluster of weather-beaten shacks until a performing arts center went up two decades ago. On the heels of the development of this first-rate cultural facility, the conversion of a 1910 hotel into a kind of literary hostel has encouraged

other restorations and plenty of new construction. Culture vultures, beach lovers, and people-watchers now flock to Nye Beach.

Some larger resort and chain hotels have sprung up among the Cape Cod cottages, aging hippies, artists, and friendly fisherfolk, and not everyone is happy about the developments here, as such signs as The Real Nye Beach—R.I.P. attest. Still, there's plenty of character and charm in this neighborhood, which feels a world away from the Coast Highway commercial strip just a few blocks to the east.

◖ Yaquina Head Outstanding Natural Area

Five miles north of Newport, rocky Yaquina Head juts out to sea. Tools dating back 5,000 years have been unearthed at Yaquina Head. Many were made from elk and deer antlers and bone, as well as stone. Clam and mussel shells from middens in the area evidence a diet rich in shellfish for the area's ancient inhabitants.

Today, much of the headland is encompassed

The recently renovated Yaquina Head Lighthouse is in a beautiful natural setting.

© PAUL LEVY

in the Yaquina Head Outstanding Natural Area (P.O. Box 936, Newport 97365, 541/574-3100, admission $5 per vehicle, managed by the BLM. "Outstanding" is indeed the word for this place; a visitor could easily spend several hours exploring all the site has to offer.

At its outer tip stands **Yaquina Head Lighthouse,** the coast's tallest beacon. In the early 1870s, materials intended for construction of a lighthouse several miles north at Otter Crest were mistakenly delivered here. The 93-foot tower began operation in 1873, replacing the poorly located lighthouse south of here at the mouth of Newport's harbor. Walk up the 114 cast-iron steps for a spectacular panorama of the headland and surrounding coast. The lighthouse is open daily, weather permitting.

Below, an observation deck provides views of seals, sea lions, gray whales, and seabirds. Of the half dozen varieties of pelagic birds that cluster on Colony Rock—a large monolith in the shallows 200 yards offshore—the tufted puffin is the most colorful. It's sometimes called a sea parrot because of its large yellow-orange bill. Puffins arrive here in April and are most visible early in the day on the rock's grassy patches. The most ubiquitous species here are common murres, pigeon guillemots, and cormorants. The murre's white breasts and bellies contrast with their darker bills and elongated backs. The guillemots resemble pigeons with white wing patches and bright red webbed feet. The cormorants look like prehistoric pelicans.

East of the lighthouse, the large **Interpretive Center** (541/574-3116, open 10 A.M.–5 P.M. daily in summer, until 4 P.M. the rest of the year) features exhibits on local ecosystems, Native American culture, and historical artifacts such as a 19th-century lighthouse keeper's journal. Other highlights include a life-size replica of the Fresnel lens that shines from the top of the nearby lighthouse, a sea cave simulation with a life-size mural of a California gray whale (accompanied by an exhibit detailing its migratory pattern), statues of birds and harbor seals, and information on tidepool inhabitants.

Close by, wheelchair-friendly paths give access to tidal pools, augmented by the hand of man, in an abandoned basalt quarry on the south side of the headland. Enjoy sea stars, purple urchins, anemones, and hermit crabs at low tide.

Beaches

North of town, **Agate Beach** is a broad swath of coastline famed for its agate-hunting opportunities and its views of nearby Yaquina Head. In addition to the semiprecious stones, the contemplative appeal of Agate Beach inspired no less a figure than Ernest Bloch, the noted Swiss composer, who lived here from 1940 until his death in 1959. Famed violinist Yehudi Menuhin spoke of Bloch and the locale thusly: "Agate Beach is a wild forlorn stretch of coastline looking down upon waves coming in all the way from Asia to break on the shore, a place which suited the grandeur and intensity of Bloch's character." Each summer, the Ernest Bloch Music Festival pays tribute to the spirit and music of this man.

Moolack Beach, two miles north of Yaquina Head, is a favorite with kite flyers and agate hunters. Another 1.5 miles north, at **Beverly**

AGATE-HUNTING

Hunting for agate after winter storms is a passion at several Oregon beaches, particularly around Newport. Deep in the earth, metals, oxides, and silicates fused together to create this type of quartz. Red, amber, blue, and other tones sometimes form stripes or spots in the translucent rocks. One of the best places to find these treasures is on the beach north of Hotel Newport, appropriately called Agate Beach. Nearby Moolack Beach and the beach at Seal Rock, north of Waldport, as well as area estuaries and streambeds, are more spots worth a look October–May. Procure the free pamphlet *Agates: Their Formation and How to Hunt for Them* from the Greater Newport Chamber of Commerce before setting out.

Beach, 20-million-year-old fossils have been found in the sandstone cliffs above the shore. Beverly Beach also attracts waders, unique for Oregon's chilly waters. Offshore sandbars temper the waves and the weather, so it's not as rough or as cold as many coastal locales. This long stretch of sand (panoramic photos are best taken from Yaquina Head Lighthouse looking north) is rated among America's 50 best beaches in a list that considers both scenic and recreational appeal.

The beach at **Yaquina Bay State Park,** accessible via a trail from the bluff-top parking area, is a popular spot for clamdigging and agate hunting. Two miles south of the Yaquina Bay Bridge, **South Beach State Park** draws beachcombers, anglers, and picnickers to its miles of broad, sandy beach. The large campground here is the closest available to Newport.

Toledo

Aficionados of antiquities can head east of Newport six miles up the Yaquina River on U.S. 20 to Toledo, where "junque" shops abound. This small town's fortunes have risen and fallen with the timber cut. At one time, the world's largest spruce mill was here, but in the era of big timber's swan song, dealers of collectibles have sprouted up to take advantage of coast-bound traffic from the Willamette Valley. Most of the antique shops are located on Main Street. Timber has enjoyed a resurgence here with the mill getting old-growth logs submerged in Yaquina Bay during World War II.

SPORTS AND RECREATION
Fishing

Newport is one of the top spots on the coast for charter fishing, and opportunities abound here at the home port of Oregon's second-largest recreational fleet. Bottom fishing (year-round), tuna fishing (Aug.–Oct.), crabbing (year-round), and salmon and halibut fishing (seasonal) are all possible. Typical rates here are $65 for a half day of bottom fishing, $100 for a full day; $110 for an eight-hour salmon outing; $190 for 12

CENTRAL COAST

Newport is one of Oregon's busiest fishing ports.

hours of tuna fishing; and $165 for a 12-hour halibut charter.

In addition to a full menu of fishing excursions, most Newport operators also offer whale-watching charters. **Newport Marina Store and Charters** (2212 OSU Dr., South Beach, 541/867-4470 or 877/867-4470, www .newportmarinacharters.com) offers a combination crabbing/fishing trip ($90 for six hours). Two-hour whale watching trips are $25. Two other local operators are **Newport Tradewinds** (653 S.W. Bay Blvd., 541/265-2101 or 800/676-7819, www.newporttradewinds.com) and **Sea Gull Charters, Inc.** (343 S.W. Bay Blvd., 541/265-7441 or 800/865-7441, www.seagull-charters.com).

For those who prefer to take matters into their own hands, the clamming and Dungeness crabbing are superlative in Yaquina Bay. If you haven't done this before, local tackle shops, such as the Newport Marina Store in South Beach, rent crab pots or rings and offer instruction. The best time to dig clams is at an extremely low tide. At that time, look for clammers grabbing up cockles in the shallows of the bay. Tide tables are available from the chamber of commerce and many local businesses.

Camping

The campgrounds at Beverly Beach State Park and South Beach State Park could well be the most popular places of their kind on the Oregon coast. Their proximity to Newport, the absence of other camping in the area, and the special features of each explain their appeal.

Beverly Beach State Park (541/265-9278 or 800/452-5687 for information, 800/452-5687 or www.reserveamerica.com for reservations) rents 152 tent sites and 127 RV spaces (both $17–21), as well as yurts, set seven miles north of Newport on the east side of the highway in a mossy glade. Across the road is a tunnel leading to a beach. **Devil's Punchbowl** and **Otter Crest** are one and two miles up the highway, respectively. Fees include all amenities; there is an on-site café. Campground is open year-round.

South Beach State Park (541/867-4715 or 800/551-6949 for information, 800/452-5687 or www.reserveamerica.com for reservations), located just south of the Yaquina Bay Bridge, occupies a long beach with opportunities for fishing, agate hunting, windsurfing (for experts), horseback riding, and hiking. It has the full range of creature comforts, including a laundry. It's open mid-April–late October at $17–21 per night (hiker and biker spaces $5).

Marine Discovery Whale-Watching Tour

In addition to the fishing charter companies noted above, which all offer whale-watching tours, the best company on the coast in terms of state-of-the-art equipment and natural history interpretation is **Marine Discovery Tours** (345 S.W. Bay Blvd., 800/903-BOAT, www .marinediscovery.com). Whale-, seal-, and bird-watching, an oyster bed tour, estuary and ocean exploration, and a harbor tour, narrated by naturalist guides, exemplify the offerings. The 65-foot *Discovery* features videocameras that magnify the fascinating interplay between smaller life forms, but the real attractions can be appreciated by the naked eye. Landlubbers will especially relish the full crab pots pulled up from the deep and the resident pod of whales often visible north of Yaquina Bay off Yaquina Head. The two-hour SeaLife tour costs $30 for adults, $28 seniors, $15 for ages 4–13.

During the prime whale-watching weeks of late December and late March, volunteers from Whale Watching Spoken Here staff the **Don A. Davis City Kiosk** in Nye Beach, to answer questions and help you spot whales.

Golf

The public course closest to Newport is nine-hole **Agate Beach Golf Course** (4100 North Coast Hwy., 541/265-7331), just north of town. Just the views of Yaquina Head are worth a visit. Open year-round. Greens fees are $16 for nine holes, $32 for 18.

ENTERTAINMENT

Overlooking the sea in Nye Beach, the **Newport Performing Arts Center** (777 W.

Olive St., 541/265-2787, www.coastarts.org/ pac), the coast's largest performance venue, hosts local and national entertainment in the 400-seat Alice Silverman Theatre and the smaller Studio Theatre. At the same address is the **Oregon Coast Council for the Arts** (541/265-9231 or 888/701-7123, www.coast arts.org), which puts out a free monthly newsletter and has ticket information on the PAC venues. It also has updates on the **Newport Visual Arts Center** (777 N.W. Beach Dr., 541/265-6540), located right above the beach two blocks north at the Nye Beach turnaround. The two floors and two galleries here offer art-education programs and exhibition space for paintings, sculpture, and other works, often with a maritime theme. Runyan Gallery is open 11 A.M.–6 P.M. Tuesday–Sunday; Upstairs Gallery is open noon–4 P.M. Tuesday–Saturday. All exhibits are free.

In addition to its impressive schedule of music, dance, drama, and other arts, the Performing Arts Center screens a series of imported and art films—the ones you probably won't find at the multiplex **Newport Cinema** (5836 North Coast Hwy., 541/265-2111).

In the Bayfront District, Mariner Square (250 S.W. Bay Blvd., 541/265-2206) is a complex of three attractions that mostly appeal to kids: **Ripley's Believe It or Not!, The Waxworks,** and the **Undersea Gardens.** Admission per attraction is $9.95 for adults, $5.95 for children; discounts are offered to hardy souls who want to take in all three.

EVENTS

The biggest bash here (and one of the largest events of its kind in the country) is late February's **Newport Seafood and Wine Festival** (541/265-8801 or 800/262-7844, www.sea foodandwine.com), which features dozens of food booths and scores of Oregon wineries serving up these palate pleasers, along with music and crafts, at the South Beach Marina (across Yaquina Bay from the Bayfront). A huge tent joins the exhibition hall wherein festival-goers wash down delights from the deep with Oregon vintages. Admission runs

$6–12, and the event is open only to the 21-and-over crowd.

The second event of note is **Loyalty Days and Sea Fair** (541/265-8801 or 800/262-7844) in early May, featuring sailboat races, a chicken feed, and a parade. What began during the Depression as the Crab Festival, intended to stimulate the market for Dungeness crab, was recast during the depths of the Red Scare of the 1950s as a public expression of patriotism. Although that aspect still undergirds the events, as evidenced by visiting naval vessels, it's really just a big community party stretching over four days, with carnival rides, boat tours, yacht races, bed races, a car show, a parade, and the coronation of the Crab Queen. Admission fee charged.

Each summer, the lectures, recitals, and concerts of the **Ernest Bloch Music Festival** (541/574-0614 information, 541/265-ARTS tickets, www.baymusic.org) are eagerly anticipated by classical music lovers. The festival usually takes place late June–mid-July, at the **Newport Performing Arts Center** (777 W. Olive St.), with related performances at other central-coast locales. Along with Bloch's compositions, works by Schubert, Ravel, Saint-Saëns, and other icons of classical music are performed by top musicians in this acoustically superior hall. Ticket prices range from free to $25.

The **Fourth of July fireworks** display, shot off from the South Beach Marina, is a crowd-pleasing spectacle. Vantage points include Yaquina Bay State Park, the bridge, and the beach. July is also the month for the **Lincoln County Fair and Rodeo** (541/265-6237), held over four days on the third weekend of the month, at the Lincoln County Fairgrounds, on the east side of town a block north of U.S. 20.

Suds and Surf is the theme of the annual mid-October **Newport Microbrew Festival** (541/265-8801 or 800/262-7844), held at the Rogue Ales Brewery (2320 OSU Dr., Newport, 541/867-3660), at South Beach Marina, just south of the bridge. This event, Oregon's second-largest microbrew festival, brings together 30 of the Northwest's finest craft breweries, complemented by musical entertainment and a variety of food and arts and crafts booths. The festival also features commercial and home-brew competitions. Admission is $6, ages 21 and over only.

ACCOMMODATIONS
$50-100

Viking's Cottages (729 N.W. Coast St., 541/265-2477 or 800/480-2477, www.vikings oregoncoast.com, rooms $85–165, condos $115–195) has until recently offered simple beachfront Cape Cod–style cottages originally built in the 1920s. However, time and the weather have been harsh to these venerable structures, and in 2007 they were replaced with a series of modern shake-sided four-plex units with kitchens. These spacious rooms still offer great beach access, and most have ocean views. In addition, Viking's offers oceanfront condos with full kitchens and access to an indoor pool.

Within easy walking distance of Nye Beach, the **Newport Val-U Inn** (531 SW Fall St., 541/265-6203 or 800/443-7777, www.newport valuinn.com, doubles from $85) is a new hotel in a good location. While these aren't ocean-front rooms, the Val-U Inn is just minutes from the beach and the rooms are comfortable and inexpensive.

If you're staying in Newport mostly to see the aquarium, consider staying at the new **Inn At Yaquina Bay** (2633 South Pacific Way, 541/867-7055 or 888/867-3100, www.innaty-aquinabay.com, doubles from $69), south of town and within easy walking distance of the aquarium. Located at the south end of the Yaquina Bay Bridge, the Inn at Yaquina Bay has 51 rooms and suites, some with balconies with bay views and fireplaces. All rooms are equipped with VCR, microwave, mini-fridge, and hair dryer. A guest laundry is also available.

$100-150

For location, you can't beat the **The Whaler** (155 S.W. Elizabeth St., 541/265-9261 or 800/433-9444, www.whalernewport.com, doubles from $105). Each of the 73 rooms has

a view, and some have fireplaces, wet bars, and private balconies. Guests are treated to fresh-popped popcorn, pool facilities, and continental breakfast.

The **Hallmark Resort** (744 S.W. Elizabeth St., 541/265-2600 or 888/448-4449, www.hallmark inns.com, doubles from $139) is a large hotel complex sitting atop the Newport bluffs, looking westward over the Pacific and miles of sandy beach. Of the many modern hotels that share this vista, the Hallmark has the largest rooms and is the best maintained. Facilities include an indoor pool, spa, and restaurant.

If you want to get away from it all, **Little Creek Cove Condominiums** (3641 N.W. Oceanview Dr., 541/265-8587 or 800/294-8025, www.littlecreekcove.com, studios from $129, one-bedroom units from $169) is a small condo resort that might be what you're looking for. Little Creek Cove resort is two miles north of Newport, perched above an isolated stretch of beach. You have a choice of studio, one-, and two-bedroom units, each with private deck, full kitchen, and fireplace.

The **Best Western Agate Beach Inn** (3019 N. Coast Hwy., 541/265-9411 or 800/547-3310, www.newportbestwestern.com, doubles from $132) is yet another oceanfront hotel, with a fine view overlooking Yaquina Head Lighthouse and Agate Beach. Replete with a grill and sports bar, this inn features guest rooms with all of the imaginable amenities, including a data port.

You may not find any riverboat gamblers aboard the **Newport Belle Bed & Breakfast** (H Dock, Newport Marina, 541/867-6290 or 800/348-1922, www.newportbelle.com, doubles $125–145), a recently constructed stern-wheeler designed as a floating inn, but this 97-foot-long B&B evokes the ambience of the sternwheeler heyday. Choose from five generous staterooms, each with its own personality and private bath. Three of the rooms have queen-size beds, one has a king, and the family room has a full and a twin. Most have fabulous vistas of the bustling marina and bridge area. In the evening, guests either retire to their staterooms, enjoy the open afterdeck, or socialize in the main salon, where a gourmet breakfast is served every morning. No pets, children, or smoking allowed. Soft-soled shoes required.

The ☪ **Sylvia Beach Hotel** (267 N.W. Cliff St., 541/265-5428, www.sylviabeachhotel.com, doubles $94–183) combines the camaraderie of a hostel with the intimate charm of a bed-and-breakfast. Built in the era when the Corvallis-to-Yaquina Bay train and seven-seater Studebaker touring cars from Portland ferried the summer folks to Nye Beach, the hotel and its National Historic Landmark designation and literary theme have attracted an enthusiastic following. The 20 guest rooms, named after different authors, are furnished with decor evocative of each respective literary legacy. The Edgar Allen Poe Room, for instance, has a pendulum guillotine blade and stuffed ravens, while the Agatha Christie Room drops such clues as shoes underneath the curtains and capsules marked Poison in the medicine cabinet.

Most of the rooms ("bestsellers") run $131, with several oceanfront suites ("classics") featuring a fireplace and deck going for $183. "Novels" go for $94. All rates include a full breakfast and reflect double occupancy. At breakfast, you have a choice of entrées and share a table with eight other guests, so misanthropes beware! No smoking, pets, or radios are allowed on the premises, and small children are discouraged. If you're looking for a budget room, Sylvia Beach features dormitory bunk beds for $25 per night.

To get there, turn off U.S. 101 onto N.W. 3rd Street and follow it down to the beach, where N.W. 3rd and Cliff Streets meet. Look for a large four-story dark green vintage wooden structure with a red roof on a bluff above the surf.

$150-200

Elizabeth Street Inn (232 S.W. Elizabeth St., 541/265-9400 or 877/265-9400, www.elizabeth streetinn.com, doubles from $169) sits on a bluff overlooking the ocean. All of the rooms in this newer property face the ocean and have private balconies. They come fully equipped with fireplaces, refrigerators, microwaves, and coffeemakers. Guests also get a complimentary continental breakfast and have use of the indoor pool, spa, and fitness room.

The ever-popular **Embarcadero Resort Hotel & Marina** (1000 S.E. Bay Blvd., 541/265-8521 or 800/547-4779, www.embarcadero-resort.com, studio suites from $155, one-bedroom suites from $179) is bayfront but not beachfront, as it overlooks Yaquina Bay and the soaring bay bridge, arguably one of the best views in Oregon. The Embarcadero has an assortment of suites and townhouses with full kitchens and fireplaces. Facilities include an indoor pool, sauna, two outdoor hot tubs, restaurant and bar, private dock, and boat rentals.

FOOD

This is a town for serious diners—folks who know good food and don't mind paying a tad more for it. It's also the kind of place where wharfside vendors do it on the cheap. June through October, you can pick up the freshest garden produce the area has to offer, plus baked goods, honey, and other delectables at the Lincoln County Small Farmers' Association's **Saturday Farmers Market,** held in the parking area of the Newport Armory (41 S.W. U.S. 101, 541/574-4040), on the east side of the highway just behind City Hall. It kicks off at 9 A.M.

About seven miles east of the Bayfront, the **Oregon Oyster Farms** (6878 Yaquina Bay Rd., Newport, 541/265-5078) is the only remaining commercial outlet for Yaquina Bay oysters, on sale daily 9 A.M.–5 P.M. Visitors are welcome to observe the farming and processing of these succulent shellfish. Try oysters on the half-shell, or sample smoked oysters on a stick. To get there, follow Bay Boulevard east six miles from the Embarcadero Resort.

Because you'll probably be spending most of your time at either Nye Beach or the Bayfront, eateries in those neighborhoods highlight this section.

Casual Dining

Down along the Bayfront is a wonderful breakfast haunt, the **Coffee House** (156 S.W.

Bay Blvd., 541/265-6263, open for breakfast and lunch daily). Gourmet pastry and such creative brunch fare as a wild mushroom omelette, crab cakes Florentine, various crepes, and oysters lightly breaded with Japanese panko breadcrumbs are complemented by the best espresso drinks in Newport. In fair weather, the outside deck is a relaxing spot for soaking in some rays while you gaze out on the harbor.

Near Nye Beach, the spot for lattes, breakfast pastries, and lunch sandwiches is **Café Stephanie** (411 Coast St., 541/265-8082, open for breakfast and lunch daily), a bustling cubbyhole with friendly service.

Seafood

The Newport Bayfront is where Mohava Niemi first opened the original **Mo's** (622 S.W. Bay Blvd., 541/265-2979, www.moschowder.com) several decades ago. When word got out about the good food and low prices, Mo's small homey place soon had more business than it could handle. In response to the overflow, **Mo's Annex** (541/265-7512) was created across the street. While both establishments feature such favorites as oyster stew and peanut butter cream pie, the Annex bay windows have the best view. Both are open for lunch and dinner daily.

Lighthouse Deli (640 U.S. 101, South Beach, 541/867-6800, open 8 A.M.–8 P.M. daily, main courses $8–12) has fish and chips in a batter that's light enough not to obscure the flavor of fresh salmon, halibut, or cod. If you're looking for a family stop after visiting the Oregon Coast Aquarium (just south of the Aquarium turnoff), this is it.

Another solid choice for those who crave fresh seafood is the **Whale's Tale** (452 S.W. Bay Blvd., 541/265-8660, open for lunch and dinner daily, main courses $9–22). A Newport institution, the Whale's Tale is a venerable and friendly seafood restaurant that perfectly captures a moment of early 1970s charm, when even loggers and fishermen wanted to be hippies. The woodsy maritime decor creates a gastronomic time capsule that's

well suited to a plate of grilled local oysters or a piece of grilled halibut. This is excellent food in a fun atmosphere.

Chowder Bowl at Nye Beach (728 N.W. Beach Dr., 541/265-7477, open for lunch and dinner daily, main courses $5–18) is perfect after a long beach walk. A first-rate salad bar, garlic bread, and award-winning chowder make an excellent lunch.

Right on the bayfront, with windows overlooking the active fishing port, **C Saffron Salmon** (859 S.W. Bay Blvd., 541/265-8921, open for lunch and dinner Wed.–Mon., main courses $16–26) is one of Newport's finest choices for expertly prepared, sophisticated seafood. The restaurant's namesake dish is pan-seared chinook salmon with saffron cream sauce, while calamari are sautéed with olive oil and red cabbage. There's also a selection of organic steaks and rack of lamb.

Also in the old town harbor area, **Sharks Seafood Bar & Steamer Co.** (852 S.W. Bay Blvd., 541/574-0590, www.sharksseafoodbar.com, open for dinner Fri.–Wed., main courses $12–26) provides a tasty antidote to the heavy breaded and fried seafood omnipresent in most Oregon coast restaurants. All Shark's main courses are sautéed, steamed, or braised, resulting in dishes that are not only more delicate tasting but better for you. But don't worry—this isn't tasteless health food. The Catalina bouillabaisse packs a wallop—1.5 pounds of seafood in every spice-filled bowl. You'll also find a savory seafood gumbo, oyster stew, and a mix of stewed and sautéed fish called a pan roast. Fresh fish gets the steam treatment—in season, try halibut, salmon, and rockfish steamed and served with the chef's special sauces.

If you're hankering for a broad selection of fresh seafood but don't need a fancy dining room to enjoy it in, the **Local Ocean Seafood** (213 S.E. Bay Blvd., 541/574-7959, open for lunch and dinner daily, main courses $7–19) is the place for you. Part fish market, part seafood grill, this new operation is bright and bustling, offering impeccably fresh fish and a lively atmosphere. Each item in the fish case is identified by name, where it was caught, how it was harvested, and who caught it. The menu items change depending on what's fresh, but count on great fish and chips, chowder, and seafood salads plus the house-specialty fish tacos and albacore tuna kabobs.

Georgie's Beachside Grill (744 S.W. Elizabeth St., 541/265-9800, open for three meals daily, main courses $12–22) in Nye Beach's Hallmark Resort has the best ocean view in town, as well as good food. The salmon hash and smoked seafood pasta are highlights. The restaurant also features Cajun (try the catfish or shrimp Creole) and Jamaican seafood specials.

Italian
(April's at Nye Beach (749 N.W. 3rd St., 541/265-6855, open for dinner Wed.–Sun., main courses $12–25) is a small, stylish café with big Mediterranean flavors close to the Sylvia Beach Hotel. Fish soup and portobello mushrooms in cheese-laden cannelloni are standouts in a creative menu. House-made bruschetta and steamed Manila clams are excellent appetizers. For dessert, have an éclair dipped in chocolate ganache and topped with slivered almonds. Affordable wines by the glass (around $5) add to one of Newport's best dining experiences.

Northwest Cuisine
(Canyon Way Bookstore and Restaurant (1216 S.W. Canyon Way, 541/265-8319, open for lunch Mon.–Sat., for dinner Tues. –Sat., main courses $12–25) has been a mainstay of Newport's culinary and cultural scene since 1971. A combination restaurant, art gallery, clothing boutique, and 20,000-title bookstore, it offers something for everybody. Stay for haute cuisine or carry out homemade quiche, croissants, and espresso. Early-dinner prices halve the later ones, which average $20, for the same order. Menu highlights include prawns Provençal, Yaquina Bay oysters, crab cakes, local lamb and beef, and a good Oregon-centered wine list. You'll also appreciate

extras such as outdoor patio dining and works by local artists adorning the walls.

You don't have to be a guest to have a meal at the **Tables of Content** (267 N.W. Cliff St., 541/265-5428, www.sylviabeachhotel.com, four-course prix fixe meals for $19) the excellent restaurant at the Sylvia Beach Hotel. There's a nice view of the breakers, good company, and it's a good value for creatively prepared Northwest cuisine. Each night features several entrée selections with an appetizer, salad, bread, beverages (alcohol not included), and dessert. Diners share tables and are encouraged to break the ice with a game called Two Truths and a Lie, in which they regale each other with several stories, the object being to distinguish which one is untrue. Reservations are mandatory.

Brewpubs
Rogue Ales Public House (748 S.W. Bay Blvd., 541/265-3188, open for lunch and dinner daily, main courses $7–16) is along the Bay in Old Town, serving seafood salads, shrimp melt sandwiches, pizza, fish and chips, and seasonal fish dishes. A new dinner menu and expanded dining area offer a more upscale though still casual dining experience. In addition to the renowned Rogue ales, there's Keiko draft root beer, a creamy concoction laced with honey and vanilla. Another Rogue Ales brewery, called **Brewers on the Bay** (320 OSU Dr., 541/867-3660), is across Yaquina Bay near the Oregon Coast Aquarium and offers a brewpub experience and light dining.

INFORMATION AND SERVICES
Information
The **Greater Newport Chamber of Commerce** (555 S.W. U.S. 101, Newport, 541/265-8801 or 800/541/262-7844, www.newportchamber. org) has lots of literature and helpful staff. The office is open 8:30 A.M.–5 P.M. Monday–Friday year-round; it's also open weekends 10 A.M.– 4 P.M. June–September.

The **Central Oregon Coast Association**

(541/265-2064 or 800/767-2064, www.coast visitor.com) maintains a useful website with details on Newport and the rest of Lincoln County. The City of Newport operates another informative website, **Get to Know Newport** (www.discovernewport.com).

A public radio station, **KLCO,** a local translator station for Eugene's KLCC, is heard on your dial at 90.5 FM.

Services

Given the size of this city, there's more likelihood of needing to call the **police** (541/265-5352) than in many other coastal locales. Other useful numbers include **Pacific Communities Hospital** (930 S.W. Abbey, 541/265-2244) and the **Lincoln County Ambulance** (541/265-3175). The Coast Guard **marine conditions** line is 541/265-5511.

Eileen's Coin Laundry (1078 N. Coast Hwy., 541/265-5474) is open 6 A.M.–11 P.M. daily. The **Newport Public Library** (35 N.W. Nye St., 541/265-2153) is open 10 A.M.–9 P.M. Monday–Thursday, 10 A.M.–6 P.M. Friday–Saturday, and 1–4 P.M. Sunday. The **post office** (310 S.W. 2nd St., Newport 97365, 541/265-5542) is one block west of the highway. For ATM services, head to **Bank of America**'s walk-up teller on 10 S. Coast Highway at Olive Street.

GETTING THERE AND AROUND

Newport is one of the few places on the Oregon coast that's reached by public transportation. **Valley Retriever** (541/265-2253) buses connect Newport with Corvallis Monday–Saturday. On weekdays, **Lincoln County Transit** (541/265-4900, www.co.lincoln.or.us/transit/) runs buses four times daily, north to Lincoln City and south to Yachats, with numerous stops en route through Newport. A brochure with schedules and fare info is available in commercial establishments all over town.

Newport's car rental agency of choice is **Enterprise Rent A Car** (533 E. Olive St., 541/574-1999).

Waldport and Vicinity

Originally a stronghold of the Alsea Indians, Waldport also has had incarnations as a gold rush town, salmon-canning center, and lumber port. This town of about 2,000, whose name means forest port in German, is pretty quiet today. The chamber of commerce touts Waldport's livability, suggesting that the town's "relative obscurity" has spared it the fate of more crowded tourist hot spots. This may also be explained by a nondescript main drag that gives no hint of surrounding beaches and prime fishing and crabbing spots. A recent influx of retirees has spurred new home-building, particularly on the Alsea spit across from the town, but this place is still decidedly low-key. For those passing through, Waldport provides a low-cost alternative to the big-name destinations; in Waldport, you won't have to fight for a parking spot or make reservations months in advance.

SIGHTS AND RECREATION
Alsea Bay Bridge Historical Interpretive Center

This small museum-cum-visitors center (541/563-2002, open 9 A.M.– 5 P.M. daily in summer, 9 A.M.–4 P.M. Tues.–Sat. the rest of the year, free), operated by the Oregon Parks and Recreation Department and Waldport Chamber of Commerce, stands along the highway on the south side of the river. Exhibits here tell the story of how the sleek 1991 bridge replaced the aging Conde McCullough span across the bay, which has since been demolished. Displays about transportation methods along the central coast since the 1800s, information on the Alsea tribe, and a telescope trained on the seals and waterfowl on the bay are worth a quick stop. In addition, Oregon Parks and Recreation guides lead bridge tours and give clamming and crabbing demonstrations during the summer.

Seal Rock State Recreation Site

Four miles north of town, Seal Rock attracts beachcombers and agate-hunters, as well as folks who come to explore the tidepools and observe the seals on offshore rocks. The park's name derives from a seal-shaped rock in the cluster of interesting formations in the tidewater. The picnic area is set in a shady area behind the sandy beach. During Christmas and spring breaks, the volunteers of Whale Watching Spoken Here are on hand to help visitors spot passing grays 10 A.M.–1 P.M. The park is open for day use only; call 800/551-6949 for information.

Ona Beach State Park

A couple of miles north of Seal Rock, this beguiling park on the west side of the highway includes a forested picnic area with a quarter-mile trail and a footbridge over Beaver Creek leading to a fine stretch of beach. The park is open for day use only; call 800/551-6949 for information.

Drift Creek Wilderness

Seven miles east of Waldport are the nearly 5,800 acres of the Drift Creek Wilderness, which protects the Coast Range's largest remaining stands of old-growth rainforest. Here you can see giant Sitka spruce and western hemlock hundreds of years old, nourished by up to 120 inches of rain per year. These trees are the "climax forest" in the Douglas fir ecosystem. They seldom reach old-growth status because the timber industry tends to replant only fir seedlings after logging operations. There is also perhaps the largest population of spotted owls in the state here, along with bald eagles, Roosevelt elk, and black bears. Drift Creek sustains wild runs of chinook, steelhead, and coho, which come up the Alsea River.

Steep ridges and their drainages, as well as small meadows, make up the topography, which is accessed via a couple of hiking trails. The trailhead closest to Waldport is the **Harris Ranch Trail,** which descends 1,200 feet in two miles to a meadow near Drift Creek. The local

© PAUL LEVY

The wind can be strong on the Oregon coast, and dedicated beachgoers sometimes build elaborate shelters.

CENTRAL COAST

access to Harris Ranch and Horse Creek trails leaves Highway 34 at the Alsea River crossing seven miles east of Waldport. Here, pick up Risely Creek Road (Forest Service Road 3446) and Forest Service Road 346. The wilderness is administered by the Siuslaw National Forest–Waldport Ranger Station (541/563-3211), which can supply directions to the different trailheads into this increasingly rare ecosystem.

Fishing

Waldport's recreational raison d'être is fishing. World-class clamming and Dungeness crabbing in Alsea Bay and the Alsea River's famous salmon, steelhead, and cutthroat trout runs account for a high percentage of visits to the area. Before commercial fishing on the river was shut down in 1957, as much as 137,000 pounds of chinook was netted in a season. The wild fall chinook run remains healthy and starts up in late August. Catch-and-release for sea-run cutthroats starts in mid-August, while steelhead are in the river December–March. Crabbers without boats can take advantage of the Port of Waldport docks.

Gene-O's Guide Service (P.O. Box 43, Waldport 97374, 541/563-3171) calls on four decades of experience to help you reel in salmon and steelhead. **Dock of the Bay Marina** (1245 N.E. Mill, 541/563-2003) and **Kozy Kove Marina** (9646 Alsea Hwy.) rent and sell crabbing and fishing supplies and can guide you to the best spots.

Camping

Two excellent campgrounds sit about four miles south of Waldport on U.S. 101 along the beach. **Beachside State Park** (541/563-3220 or 800/551-6949 for information, 800/452-5687 or www.reserveamerica.com for reservations) is located near a half mile of beach not far from Alsea Bay and Alsea River. This is a paradise for rock fishers, surfcasters, clammers, and crabbers. For $17–21 a night mid-April–mid-October, there are 50 tent sites, 32 sites for RVs up to 30 feet long, and some hiker-biker sites. Beachside fills up fast, with such amenities as a laundry and hot showers, so reserve early for space Memorial Day–Labor Day.

A half mile down U.S. 101, the forest service operates **Tillicum Beach** (877/444-6777 or www.reserveusa.com for reservations). Set right along the ocean, the campground is open all year but requires reservations. For $20 a night you have flush toilets plus ranger campfire programs in summer. Forest service roads from here access Coast Range fishing streams, which are detailed in a forest service map. You'll also appreciate the strip of vegetation blocking the cool evening winds that whip up off the ocean here.

Should Beachside and Tillicum be filled to overflowing, you might want to set up a base camp in the Coast Range along Highway 34—especially if you have fishing or hiking in the Drift Creek Wilderness in mind. Just go east of Waldport 17 miles on Highway 34 to the Siuslaw National Forest's **Blackberry Campground** (877/444-6777 or www.reserve-usa.com for reservations). The 33 sites ($15 a night) are open year-round for tents and RVs, most of them on the river. A boat ramp, flush toilets, and piped water are on-site.

Golf

Crestview Hills Golf Course (1680 Crestline Dr., Waldport, 541/563-3020 or 888/538-4463, open year-round, greens fees $14 for 9 holes, $20 for 18 holes) is a public nine-hole course one mile south of Waldport.

ACCOMMODATIONS

Cottage is a word often used to describe accommodations between Yachats and Waldport. It may be a duplex or self-contained cabin, generally by a beach.

$50-100

The **Terry-a-While Motel** (7160 S.W. U.S. 101, 541/563-3377, www.terry-a-while.com, doubles $50–110) has well-appointed rooms that range in style from modern to vintage and in size (the newer four-plex is ideal for families).

The vintage **Cape Cod Cottages** (4150 S.W. U.S. 101, 541/563-2106, www.dreamwater.com, doubles $70–100) offer one- and two-bedroom oceanfront units with complete kitchens, cozy fireplaces, cable television, spectacular views, and private decks. A three-night minimum stay is required in summer.

At the **Howard Johnson Inn Waldport** (902 N.W. Bayshore Dr., 541/563-7700 or 877/327-6500, doubles from $81) half of the 84 rooms enjoy sweeping views of the bay, bridge, and town, and all are equipped with either one or two queen-size beds and the usual amenities. There's also a dining room and cocktail lounge, with occasional entertainment, and a fitness room.

$100-150

The historic **Cliff House** (1450 Adahi Rd., 541/563-2506, www.cliffhouseoregon.com, doubles $110-225) may appear rustic, but in fact this is a beautifully restored historic home, and the location can't be beat to set a romantic mood. Four rooms, some with whirlpools, are decorated with antiques; even the woodstoves are period. (No pets are allowed, and children are best left home with grandma or the sitter.)

FOOD

Forget fine dining in Waldport—this is an eat 'n' run town. Unless you want to drive to the Yachats branch, **Leroy's Blue Whale** (541/563-3445) located right on U.S. 101 is one of few choices.

Grand Central Pizza (245 U.S. 101, 541/563-3232, open for lunch and dinner daily) is a favorite with the locals, across the street from the 76 gas station—you can't miss it. *Oregon Coast* magazine voted this the best pie on the coast. In addition to spaghetti dinners, lasagna, and pizza, the homemade garlic rolls, selection of microbrews, fish and chips, and grinder sandwiches are also noteworthy. Best of all, the largest appetites can be sated here for less than $10.

For a hearty breakfast and other meal specials served in a sport-lovers' atmosphere, replete with big-screen TV, the **Flounder Inn Tavern** (180 S.W. Arrow St., 541/563-2266) offers customers lots of pub grub choices, including fish and chips and a popular roasted chicken dinner.

Eight miles south of Newport and five miles north of Waldport in the village of Seal Rock, **Yuzen** (10111 U.S. 101, 541/563-4766, lunch 11:30 A.M.–2 P.M. and dinner 4–9 P.M. Tues.–Sun.), is a well-regarded Japanese restaurant with an oddly Bavarian facade.

PRACTICALITIES
Information and Services

The Walport Chamber of Commerce operates a **visitors center** (P.O. Box 669, Waldport 97394, 541/563-2133, www.pioneer .net/~waldport) in the Alsea Bay Bridge Historical Interpretive Center, just south of the river. The chamber is open 9 A.M.–5 P.M. daily in summer, 9 A.M.–4 P.M. Tuesday–Saturday the rest of the year.

The **Siuslaw National Forest-Waldport Ranger Station** (1094 S.W. U.S. 101, Waldport 97394, 541/563-3211) can provide information on area camping and hiking, including the trails in the Drift Creek Wilderness.

For banking and walk-up ATM, the Waldport branch of **Bank of Newport** (433 Hwy. 34) can provide these services.

Getting There and Around

Highway 34 runs east from Waldport, following the Alsea River for several miles before veering northeast to Corvallis, about 65 miles away.

The Lincoln County buses run four times a day Monday–Saturday between Yachats and Newport.

Yachats and Cape Perpetua

Yachats (pronounced "YAH-hots") is derived from an Alsea word meaning "dark waters at the foot of the mountain." The phrase aptly describes the location of this picturesque resort village of 635 people, clustered on the hillsides and coastal shelf beside the Yachats River mouth in the shadow of Cape Perpetua. Word of mouth has helped to spread the popularity of Yachats as a place for a quiet getaway and a base for enjoying the 2,700-acre Cape Perpetua Scenic Area and nearby beaches.

SIGHTS AND RECREATION
🅲 Cape Perpetua

The most notable sight near Yachats, indeed on the whole central coast, is the view from 803-foot-high Cape Perpetua. The name derives from Captain Cook's sighting of the promontory on March 7, 1778, St. Perpetua's Day. It's too bad the British explorer didn't make landfall here to enjoy one of the world's preeminent coastal panoramas. Oregon's highest paved public road this close to the shoreline affords 150 miles of north-to-south visibility from the top of the headland. On a clear day, you can also see 39 miles out to sea.

Prior to hiking the 23 miles of foot trails or driving to the top of the cape, stop off at the **Cape Perpetua Visitor Center** (541/547-3289), three miles south of Yachats on the east side of the highway. A picture window framing a bird's-eye view of rockbound coast, along with exhibits on forestry and marinelife, begin your introduction to the region. Cataclysms such as the forest fire of 1846, the monsoons and 138 mph winds unleashed by the 1962 Columbus Day Storm, and 1964 Hurricane Frieda are artfully explained by exhibits. An excellent 15-minute film about Oregon's intertidal biome will also hold your interest.

Personnel at the desk have maps and pamphlets about such trails as Cook's Ridge, Rig-

Yachats offers quiet beaches and rocky tidepools.

© BILL MCRAE

gin' Slinger, and Giant Spruce, as well as directions for the auto tour to the summit. In addition, they can point the way to tidepools and berry patches. Two naturalist-guided hikes a day are offered to coastal rainforest and tidepools. The center is open 9 A.M.–5 P.M. early May–October, and it opens during peak whale-watching weeks from Christmas to New Year's and in late March. Admission is $5 per car. The Pacific Coast Passport, Northwest Forest Pass, and Golden Passports are honored here.

The awe-inspiring 1.5-mile **Saint Perpetua Trail** from the visitors center to the cape's summit is of moderate difficulty, gaining 600 feet in elevation. En route, placards explain the role of wind, erosion, and fire in forest succession in this mixed-conifer ecosystem.

At the crest of Cape Perpetua the **Trail of the Whispering Spruce** begins, a quarter-mile loop through the grounds of a former World War II Coast Guard lookout built by the Civilian Conservation Corps (CCC) in 1933. The southern views from the crest take in the highway and headlands as far as Coos Bay. Halfway along the path, you'll come to a WPA-built rock hut called the West Shelter that makes a lofty perch for whale-watching, one of the best spots on the entire coast. Beyond this ridgetop aerie the curtain of trees parts to reveal fantastic views of the shoreline between Yachats and Cape Foulweather.

The two-mile drive up the cape (where the Whispering Spruce Trailhead can be accessed) is complicated by a not-so-prominent sign on U.S. 101 (mile marker 188.5) indicating the turnoff onto Forest Service Road 55. To begin your auto ascent, drive a hundred yards north on U.S. 101 from the visitors center and look for the steep winding spur road on the right. As you climb, you'll notice large Sitka spruce trees abutting the road. Halfway up, you'll come to a Y in the road. Take a hard left and follow the road another mile to the top of Cape Perpetua. If you miss the left turn and go straight ahead, you'll soon find yourself on a 22-mile loop through the Coast Range to Yachats. Along the way, 18 placards annotate forest ecology.

State Parks and Coastal Waysides

In this part of the coast, state parks and viewpoints abound with attractions. There's so much to see here that keeping your eyes on the road in this heavily traveled section is a challenge.

A mile south of Cape Perpetua, **Neptune State Park** has a beautiful beach and is near the 9,300-acre **Cummins Creek Wilderness** east of U.S. 101. Just north of Neptune Park, Forest Service Road 1050 leads east to the Cummins Creek Trailhead. A half-mile south, gravelly Forest Service Road 1051 can take you to a point where a moderately difficult 2.5-mile hike leads to Cummins Ridge Trailhead. This pathway has some of the last remaining coastal old-growth Sitka spruce stands. Get maps and detailed directions for these and other area trails at the Cape Perpetua visitors center.

Close by, there's a chance to explore tidepools and sometimes observe harbor seals at **Strawberry Hill.** Scenic shorelines can also

Sealife is especially abundant along Oregon's central coast.

CENTRAL COAST

© BILL MCRAE

be found in the next few miles farther south at **Stonesfield Beach State Recreation Site** and **Muriel O. Ponsler State Scenic Viewpoint.**

A mile north of town, **Smelt Sands State Recreation Site** gives access to tidepools and the 0.75-mile 804 Trail, which follows the rocky shore to a broad, sandy beach to the north. In Yachats, turn west onto 2nd Street to loop around wave-battered **Yachats State Recreation Area,** overlooking Yachats Bay. The route heads north along the ocean, where it becomes Marine Drive. After going through a residential community, it eventually takes an easterly turn to reconnect with U.S. 101.

On the south bank of the Yachats River is a short but beautiful beach loop off U.S. 101 (going south, look for the Beach Access sign). The road runs between the landscaped grounds of beach houses and resorts on one side and the foamy sea on the other. A wide beach, tidepools, and blowholes on the bank by the river's mouth are a special treat.

Hiking

Another hike from the Cape Perpetua visitors center goes down to a geological blowhole (called a spouting horn), where sea water is funneled between rocks and explodes into spray. This is the **Captain Cook Trail,** which goes six miles through a dense wind-carved forest and the remains of an old CCC camp under U.S. 101 to an ancient lava deposit on the shore. Given enough wave action, water bubbles up through fissures in the basalt. There are also Native American shell middens built up 300–2,000 years ago in the area.

Just north of the turnoff for the top of Cape Perpetua (Forest Service Road 55) and U.S. 101 is the turnout for **Devil's Churn,** on the west side of the highway. Here, the tides have cut a deep fissure in a basalt embankment on the shore. You can observe the action from a vertigo-inducing overlook high above, or take the easy, switchbacking trail down to the water's edge. While watching the white-water torrents in this foaming cistern, beware of "sneaker waves," particularly if you

venture beyond the boundaries of the **Trail of the Restless Waters.** The highlights here are the spouting horns and acres of tidepools. All along this stretch of the coast, many trees appear to be leaning away from the ocean as if bent by storms. This illusion is caused by salt-laden westerlies drying out and killing the buds on the exposed side of the tree, leaving growth only on the leeward branches.

Camping

Set along Cape Creek in the Cape Perpetua Scenic Area, the Forest Service's **Cape Perpetua Campground** (877/444-6777 or www.reserveusa.com for reservations) has 38 sites for tents, trailers, or motor homes up to 22 feet long. Picnic tables and fire grills are provided. Flush toilets, piped water, and sanitary services are available. The campground is open May–October; sites cost $20. Reservations are necessary for groups. The forest service rangers put on slide-illustrated campfire talks here during summer months.

ENTERTAINMENT AND EVENTS

This little village seems to be busy with some festival or other event just about every weekend. For a full schedule, see the local chamber of commerce website (www.yachats.org/events .html). Below are some highlights.

Spring brings two arts and crafts festivals to the Yachats Commons (U.S. 101 and W. 4th St.): In late March, the chamber-sponsored **Original Yachats Arts and Crafts Fair** (541/547-3530 or 800/929-0477) exhibits the work of some 75 Pacific Northwest artists and artisans. Admission is free. If you miss that one, come back in late May for **Crafts on the Coast** (541/547-4738 or 541/547-4664).

Yachats pulls out all the stops for the **Fourth of July.** Events include the short and silly La De Da Parade at noon, the Yachats Yamboree (food booths, beer gardens, live music), a farmers market, a musical variety show, and a fireworks show on the bay when darkness falls.

During the Yachats **Smelt Fry,** held the second Saturday of July, up to 750 pounds of this sardinelike fish are served on the grounds of Yachats Commons on 4th Street (just follow the signs to this refurbished schoolhouse). Yachats used to be one of the few places in the world blessed with a run of oceangoing smelt, but they have declined drastically due to changing ocean conditions. Nonetheless, the town's traditional "welcome to summer" event has continued thanks to imported Northern California smelt, which augment the local catch. For $8 you get all the deep-fried, delicately flavored smelt you can eat ($3 for children 12 and younger) with side dishes and a beverage. Or choose a sausage plate for $5. What you're really paying for is a classic small-town festival where you get to rub elbows with a spirited community. More info is available from the chamber of commerce.

The same weekend, the **Yachats Music Festival** takes place several blocks north at the Presbyterian Church (360 W. 7th St., 541/547-3141 or 510/601-6184). Admission is $15 for each performance. The lineup features classical virtuosi and vocalists from the San Francisco Bay Area for evening concerts and a Sunday matinee performance.

A relatively new but popular event here is the **Yachats Village Mushroom Fest** (541/547-3530 or 800/929-0477), held the third weekend in October. Native mushrooms abound in the temperate rainforests of the Cape Perpetua region, and fall is the season to harvest them. Chef John Ullman started the Yachats event, inspired by similar festivals in Italy. Activities over the weekend include the Friday-night Yachats Rainforest Fungi Feast, mushroom-cooking demonstrations, guided mushroom walks at Cape Perpetua visitors center, and the last farmers market of the season.

SHOPPING

Yachats has long been a center for artists and Bohemians, and for proof of this you need go no further than **Earthworks Gallery** (2222 U.S. 101 N., 541/547-4300). This excellent gallery displays the work of local painters, glass artists, and jewelers, as well as high-quality crafts. **Touchstone Gallery** (2118 U.S. 101 N.,

541/547-4121) is another gallery with unique Northwest arts and crafts.

ACCOMMODATIONS
$50-100

At the beginning of the beach loop (on the south bank of the Yachats River and west of U.S. 101) are the **Shamrock Lodgettes** (105 U.S. 101 S., 541/547-3312 or 800/845-5028, www.shamrocklodgettes.com, cabins $79–179, motel and one-bedroom units $79–149). Shamrock's beautiful parklike landscape frames a selection of individual log cabins plus redwood motel rooms and one- and two-bedroom units. Stone fireplaces, in-room movies, and ocean or bay views all contribute to a relaxed get-away-from-it-all feeling. The sauna and whirlpool tub on the premises also enhance the mellowing-out process. Ask about midwinter specials. Pets are allowed in some units.

A short drive farther south, the **Yachats Inn** (331 U.S. 101, 541/547-3456 or 888/270-3456, www.yachatsinn.com, doubles from $80) offers basic summer shelter with unfussy rooms that have a TV but no phone, though some have kitchens and fireplaces. There's great access to the beach. The best bets here are the newly constructed suites, which have full kitchens and fireplaces. The indoor pool overlooks the beach.

For those looking for a budget place close to the center of town, try **Rock Park Cottages** (431 W. 2nd St., 541/547-3214 or 541/343-4382, www.trillian.com/rockpark, doubles from $65), adjacent to Yachats State Recreation Area. Consisting of five rustic cottages arranged around a courtyard, Rock Park has to be one of the better bargains on the coast. The kitchens are well equipped, and the vintage cottages couldn't be better located.

The **Dublin House Motel** (U.S. 101 and 7th Street, 866/922-4287, www.dublinhousemotel.com, doubles from $69) offers large guest rooms and ocean views, each with microwave, refrigerator, coffeemaker, and cable TV; some kitchen units are also available. The indoor heated pool is especially nice in the winter months.

The aptly named **SeeVue** (95590 U.S. 101, 541/547-3227, www.seevue.com, doubles from $75) has long been a favorite window on the Pacific for storm- and whale-watchers. This 10-room complex thrives today thanks to an eminently affordable combination of comfort and location, just six miles south of Yachats and three miles south of Cape Perpetua. Assuming you can pull yourself away from watching the waves, there's also prime beachcombing and wildlife-viewing close by. All units here boast Pacific perspectives and the decor is funky and charming in equal measures. There are nonsmoking rooms as well as some housekeeping units. Pets are allowed.

For the ultimate in seclusion, the **Oregon House** (94288 U.S. 101, 541/547-3329, www .oregonhouse.com, doubles from $95), eight miles south of Yachats, overlooks the Pacific from a bluff and offers guests a reflective phone- and TV-free atmosphere. Twelve apartments (housed in five different buildings, including a carriage house and gate house) with baths and kitchens, some with fireplaces and whirlpool tubs, are perfect for groups. In fact, Oregon House specializes in groups but also rents the apartments to individuals. No pets are allowed; quiet children are permitted. Stroll the three acres of gardens or head down the private path to the beach.

$100-150

A little north of the town center, the imposing **Adobe Resort** (155 U.S. 101 N., 541/547-3141 or 800/522-3623, doubles from $104) overlooks Smelt Sands Beach. If you appreciate all services in one compound, from dining room to gift shop, the Adobe gets the nod. All units have refrigerators, microwaves, satellite TV, DVD players, and phone with voice mail. Pets are accepted in some rooms. Brand new, two-bedroom, hot tub suites are 1,400 square feet and have all the comforts of a small home.

$150-200

A mile north of Yachats, above a thrust of wave-pounded tidepools, the ◖ **Overleaf Lodge** (280 Overleaf Lodge Ln., 541/547-4880 or 800/338-0507, www.overleaflodge.com, doubles from $159) offers the newest and nicest rooms in the Yachats area. Most rooms have balconies, hot tubs, and fireplaces, and all have fantastic views. Rates include a breakfast buffet, plus access to an indoor pool and fitness area. New in 2007 is a 3,000 square foot spa with treatment rooms, steam rooms, and saunas, plus oceanview hot tubs. Adjacent to the lodge are six newly built cottages tucked into the forest. Ranging from two- to four-bedroom, these charming units with Craftsman-style decor have full kitchens and everything a family or small group will need for a great beach vacation.

The **Sea Quest Inn** (95354 U.S. 101, 541/547-3782 or 800/341-4878, www.seaq.com, doubles from $170) is an antique-filled but contemporary inn of cedar and glass, with private entrances and a location adjacent to Ten Mile Creek, about seven miles south of Yachats. The "Tis Sweete" is a 1,000-square-foot suite with a king-size canopy bed, a wood-burning fireplace, 25-foot-high windows, and wraparound deck all located on a private wing ($375 a night for two people). With the fine cognac and wines in the evening; the fruit, scones, and popcorn in the commons; and the chocolates and bottled water in your room, the inn is well stocked with quality goodies catering to your whim and pleasure. Breakfasts are delicacy-laden presentations superior to that of many hotel fine dining rooms. The wraparound deck affords superlative views of the beach, and telescopes and binoculars are always on hand for spotting whales and other marinelife. Many guests return each year, so be sure to book well in advance. Not appropriate for pets or children under 12 years of age.

Vacation Rentals

If you're planning a long stay, check out **Yachats Village Rentals** (541/547-3501, www.97498.com), which offers a varied stable of vacation homes ($110–215) for rent.

FOOD

For a town its size, Yachats has particularly good restaurant choices.

Casual Dining

Start the day at **Green Salmon Bakery and**

Cafe (220 U.S. 101, 541/547-3077, open for breakfast and lunch Tues.–Sun.) for fresh breads and pastries plus soup and sandwiches for lunch. This lively café doubles as a hangout for the local alternative community. **Toad Hall Coffee Gallery** (237 W. 3rd St., 541/547-4044) offers coffee, tea, and scones in an art-filled café or in a lovely garden setting.

At the other end of the day, enjoy evening light snacks and flights of wine at **Yachats Wine Trader** (125 Ocean View Dr., 541/547-5100, open Tues.–Sun., with food 5–8 P.M.) which is a wine shop by day, wine bar by night. The views are stunning.

Grand Occasions Deli (84 Beach St., 541/547-4409, open for lunch and dinner daily) is a quintessential Yachats business. This tiny shop serves soup, sandwiches, and wonderful pies in a modest little store that fronts the bay. Grab a cup of coffee and a patio chair and watch the waves roll in. Everything is homemade and served with charm and care; check for extended evening hours in summer. Ask about picnic baskets—Grand Occasions will fix up an excellent feast for the beach. Oh, and if this place weren't already delightful enough, it also serves as the local florist shop.

The carefully restored but fun-loving **Drift Inn Pub** (124 U.S. 101 N., 541/457-4477, open daily for lunch and dinner) offers seafood dishes, crunchy salads, fish and chips, and other well-prepared pub grub in a casual atmosphere. There's often really good live music here, making this a lively spot whether you're here to eat or to quaff a pint or two. Families are welcome.

Northwest Cuisine
Right off U.S. 101 is **La Serre** (2nd and Beach Sts., 541/547-3420, open for dinner Wed.–Mon., main courses $12–22), a bright sky-lit restaurant with lots of plants (*La Serre* means The Greenhouse) that creates a relaxing setting for well-prepared Northwest cuisine. The salmon or crab cakes, oven-roasted free-range chicken, poached wild salmon, steaks, bouillabaisse, and clam puffs appetizer are all welcome choices after a day of hiking or exploring

tidepools. For dessert, try the flourless chocolate cake.

On a bluff overlooking Smelt Sands Beach is the glass-enclosed **Adobe Resort** (1555 U.S. 101, 541/547-3141, open for three meals daily, main courses $12–28). Two side-by-side semicircular dining rooms, with windows on the crashing surf, are a great place to start the day for breakfast or end it with a romantic evening repast, with such favorites as pan-fried oysters, salmon, and steaks. Ask about the loft, where elevated coastal views provide photo-ops; this is the perfect place to nurse a drink. A Sunday champagne brunch is served 9 A.M.–1 P.M.

The newest Yachats dining room is **Yachats River House** (131 U.S. 101 N., 541/547-4100, www.yachatsriverhouse.com), a wonderful addition to an already beguiling dining scene. In this bay-view restaurant, expect seasonal, organic cuisine like halibut coated in bread crumbs and Dijon mustard, served with tomato-tarragon beurre blanc, and cumin-crusted lamb with saffron aioli. For diners along the central coast, this restaurant, with excellent service and an amazing view, is good news indeed.

INFORMATION AND SERVICES
The **Yachats Area Chamber of Commerce** (241 U.S. 101, P.O. Box 728, Yachats 97498, 541/547-3530 or 800/929-0477, www.yachats.org) has a central location on the highway (next to Clark's Market) and a loquacious staff. Ask them about fishing, rockhounding, bird-watching, and beachcombing in the area. Open 10 A.M.–4 P.M. daily March–September, Thursday–Sunday the rest of the year.

The **Central Oregon Coast Association** (541/265-2064 or 800/767-2064, www.coastvisitor.com) maintains a useful website with details on Yachats and the rest of coastal Lincoln County.

The bus stop is also in the parking lot of the Clark's Market complex (U.S. 101 and W. 2nd St.). Here you can catch **Lincoln County Transit** buses (541/265-4900), which run four times a day, Monday–Saturday, between Yachats and Newport, with a link to Lincoln City.

Florence and Vicinity

If you study the map of the central Oregon coast, you'll see that Florence is oriented along the Siuslaw River; a spit of dunes reaches up from the south, barring quick access from downtown to the ocean. But don't dismiss this riverfront town for its lack of oceanfront real estate; the views onto the river are plenty scenic, and Old Town is charming and easy to navigate on foot.

Florence began shortly after the California gold rush of 1849 put a premium on the lumber and produce shipped out via the Siuslaw River estuary here. Several decades later, the town's name was inspired by a remnant from a French shipwreck that floated ashore, bearing the ship's name, *Florence*. The townspeople either recognized an omen when they saw it or just couldn't come up with anything better.

SIGHTS

If first and last impressions are enduring, Florence is truly blessed. A short ways to the north of town, U.S. 101 passes over Heceta Head, with great views back onto the lighthouse there. As you leave the city to the south, a graceful bridge over the Siuslaw ushers you away.

The Siuslaw River Bridge is perhaps the most impressive of Conde McCullough's WPA-built spans. The Egyptian obelisks and art deco styling characteristic of other McCullough designs are complemented by the views to the west of the coruscating sand dunes. To the east, the riverside panorama of Florence's Old Town beckons further investigation.

Old Town itself is a tasteful restoration, with all manner of shops and restaurants and an inviting boardwalk along the river. The quickest access to the beach and dunes is south of the bridge via South Jetty Road.

◖ Sea Lion Caves

Ten miles north of Florence, you can descend into the world's largest sea cave to observe the only U.S. mainland rookery of Steller sea lions (*Eumetopias jubatus*). Sea Lion Caves (91560 U.S. 101, 541/547-3111, open 9 A.M.–7 P.M. daily in summer, 9 A.M.–4 P.M. daily in winter, closed Christmas, $8 adults, $4.50 ages 6–15, free for children five and under) is home to a herd that averages 200 individuals of this species, although the numbers change from season to season. These animals occupy the cave during the fall and winter, which are thus the prime visitation times. The Steller sea lions you'll see at those times are cows, yearlings, and immature bulls. In spring and summer, they breed and raise their young on the rock ledges just outside the cave. In addition, California sea lions (*Zalophus californianus*), common all along the Pacific Coast, are found at Sea Lion Caves from late fall to early spring.

Enter Sea Lion Caves through the gift shop on U.S. 101. A steep downhill walk reveals stunning perspectives of the coastal cliffs, as well as several kinds of gulls and cormorants that nest here. The final leg of the descent is facilitated by an elevator that drops an additional 208 feet. After disembarking the lift into the cave, your eyes adjust to the gloomy subterranean light and you'll see the sea lions on the rock shelves amid the surging water inside the enormous cave. Flash photography is forbidden, so study your camera's settings if you wish to take pictures inside. You have a better chance of seeing these animals inside during fall and winter. A set of stairs here leads up to a view of Heceta Head Lighthouse through an opening in the cave.

Steller sea lions were referred to as *lobos marinos* (sea wolves) in early Spanish mariners' accounts of their 16th-century West Coast voyages, and their doglike yelps might explain why. You'll notice several shades of color in the herd, which has to do with the progressive lightening of their coats with age. Males sometimes weigh more than a ton and dominate the scene here with macho posturings to scare off rivals for harems of as many as two dozen cows. Their protection as an endangered species enrages many commercial anglers, who

© BILL MCRAE

For a close-up view of sea lions, ride the elevator down to Sea Lion Caves.

claim that the sea lions take a significant bite out of fishing revenues by preying on salmon. In any case, the close-up view of these huge sea mammals in the cavernous enclaves of their natural habitat should not be missed—despite an odor not unlike sweat-soaked sneakers.

If you can't observe the animals to your satisfaction in the cave, go 0.25 mile north of the concession entrance to the "rockwork" turnout, where the herd sometimes populate the rocky ledges several hundred feet below. It's also a good place to snap a shot of the picturesque Heceta Head Lighthouse across the cove to the north from the turnout.

Heceta Head State Scenic Viewpoint and Devil's Elbow

About 11 miles north of Florence, Heceta Head State Scenic Viewpoint is located in a lovely cove at the mouth of Cape Creek, at the base of thousand-foot-high Heceta Head. From here you can get a good look at the graceful arc of Conde McCullough's Cape Creek Bridge, spanning the chasm more than 200 feet above you. Across the cove, photogenic **Heceta Head Lighthouse** (541/547-3416, tours 11 A.M.–5 P.M. daily May–Sept., 11 A.M.–3 P.M. daily March, April, and Oct., $3 day-use fee), completed in 1894, beams the strongest light on the Oregon coast, from a shelf 205 feet up the rocky headland. An easy half-mile trail leads up from the park's picnic and parking area to the tower. Admission is free, but donations aid restoration work here. A little below the lighthouse is Heceta House, where the lighthouse keepers used to live. Today, it's a B&B.

Heceta Head is said to be the most photographed lighthouse in the country; that may be difficult to verify, but it's impossible to quibble with the magnificent sight of the gleaming white tower and outbuildings on the headland, particularly when viewed from a set of highway pullouts just south of the bridge. The vistas from the lighthouse and network of trails on the headland are no less dramatic: See murres, tufted puffins, and other seabirds, as well as sea lions, on the rock islands below, bald eagles

CENTRAL COAST

soaring overhead, and, in spring, northbound female gray whales and their calves as they pass close to shore. A trail leading to the north side of Heceta Head offers views to Cape Perpetua, 10 miles to the north.

Just south of Heceta Head is a trail down to the beach at adjoining Devil's Elbow State Park. Be conscious of tides here if you climb along the rocks adjoining the beach.

Darlingtonia Botanical Gardens

Three miles north up the Coast Highway from Florence, in an area noted for dune access and freshwater lakes, are the Darlingtonia Botanical Gardens (east side of U.S. 101, five miles north of Florence, 800/551-6949, www.oregon stateparks.org, free). In a sylvan grove of spruce and alder are a series of wooden platforms that guide you through a bog where carnivorous *Darlingtonia californica* plants thrive. Shaped like a serpent head, the darlingtonia is variously referred to as the cobra orchid, cobra lily, or pitcher plant. The sweet smell the plant pro-

duces invites insects to crawl through an opening into a chamber.

Inside, thin transparent "windows" allow light to shine inside the chamber, confusing the bug as to where the exit is. As the insect crawls around in search of an escape, downward-pointing hairs within the enclosure inhibit its movement to freedom. Eventually, the tired-out bug falls to the bottom of the stem, where it is digested. The plant needs the nutrients from the trapped insects to compensate for the lack of sustenance supplied by its small root system. If you still have an appetite after witnessing this carnage, you might want to enjoy lunch at one of the shaded picnic tables here.

Siuslaw Pioneer Museum

To fill yourself in on the early history of Florence and the Siuslaw River valley, and get some notion of Native American and pioneer life, spend an hour or so at the Siuslaw Pioneer Museum (85294 U.S. 101, Florence, 541/997-7884, open noon–4 P.M. Tues.–Sun. year-round, $3 adults). You'll find it south of the Siuslaw River on the west side of the highway in a converted church. Along with exhibits on early logging and farming, read an account of how the U.S. government doublecrossed the Siuslaw tribespeople, who sold their land to the feds and never received the promised recompense.

Jessie M. Honeyman Memorial State Park

Honeyman State Park ($3 day-use fee or Oregon Coast Passport), three miles south of Florence, has a spectacular dunescape and then some. Come here in May when the rhododendrons bloom along the short, sinuous road heading to the parking lot. A short walk west of the lot brings you to a 150-foot-high dune overlooking Cleawox Lake. From the top of this dune, look westward across the expanse of sand, marsh, and remnants of forest at the blue Pacific, some two miles away. See *Camping* under *Sports and Recreation* for details on an overnight at this huge state park.

Darlingtonia, a carnivorous plant, thrives at the Darlingtonia Botanical Gardens.

© BILL MCRAE

South Jetty

The northern boundary of the Oregon Dunes National Recreation Area is at the South Jetty ($5 per car or Northwest Forest Pass), where the Siuslaw River flows into the Pacific Ocean. From May through September (and on all weekends and holidays), the beach at the South Jetty is closed to motor vehicles, and even though there are no marked trails, it's a great place to explore the dunes in near solitude. The road into the jetty has several staging areas for off-highway vehicles; during the summer months, the area south of the road is open to motor vehicles. South Jetty Road is less than a mile south of the Siuslaw River bridge.

SPORTS AND RECREATION
Hiking

Find some incredibly scenic hiking in the area around Heceta Head and Carl Washburne State Park. You'll probably feel like a hobbit, the furry-footed characters in J. R. R. Tolkien's works, when peering up at the high walls woven of roots, peat, and sand that loom above the **Hobbit Trail,** cut deep into the forest floor at the southern end of Carl Washburne State Park. The path winds 0.4 miles through dense forest thickets of pine, fir, and rhododendrons from the highway down to the beach. From the same trailhead, a trail takes off uphill to the **Heceta Head** lighthouse. In its 1.75-mile run, the trail gains quite a bit of elevation and passes some outstanding viewpoints. Also starting at the same U.S. 101 parking area, the China Creek Trail (a.k.a. the Valley Trail) runs 1.7 miles on the east side of the highway to the Washburne campground. The parking area for all these hikes is on the east side of U.S. 101 about 13 miles north of Florence (or 14 miles south of Yachats). It's also possible to park in the day-use lot across the highway from the campground, catch the Valley Trail near the campground entrance, and hike to the Hobbit and Heceta Head trails.

Up the North Fork of the Siuslaw River is the **Pawn Old-Growth Trail,** a half-mile pathway through several-hundred-year-old, 100-inch-diameter, 275-foot-tall Douglas fir and hemlock. The trailhead, located at the confluence of the North Fork of the Siuslaw and Taylor's Creek, is a good place to see salmon spawning in the fall and observe water ouzels (also called dippers). It follows the creek and offers interpretive placards along the way. At one point in the trail, visitors walk through fallen Douglas fir logs 260 inches in diameter. Placards explain the science of tree rings. From Florence, take Highway 126 east for one mile, then turn north onto Forest Road 5070 and take it 12 miles to Forest Road 5084; stay right and go another five miles to the trailhead.

An excellent and not terribly difficult introduction to dune hiking can be found about 10 miles south of Florence at the **Oregon Dunes Day-Use Area.** The Overlook Beach Trail runs for about a mile from a viewing platform to the beach. Follow the blue-topped wooden posts that mark the trail through the sand. To turn this into a more strenuous 3.5-mile loop, continue one mile south along the beach and head back inland (again following the posts) along the more rugged Tahkenitch Creek Loop. Find the turnoff from U.S. 101 near milepost 201.

Another good place to explore the dunes is along **Carter** and **Taylor Dunes Trails.** Carter Dunes Trail starts near Carter Lake and heads west 1.5 miles to the beach. The first half of the mile-long Taylor Dunes Trail is wheelchair accessible; the trail passes some of the oldest (and gnarliest) conifers in the area. Both of these trails are good places to view wildlife, especially in the winter and spring, when the dunes take on wetland characteristics. The two trails link up, forming a Y rather than a loop. The turnoff for both trails is 7.5 miles south of Florence. Carter Lake also has a campground.

Hike the **Waxmyrtle Trail** along the Siltcoos River; the 1.5-mile trail travels along the estuary and ends up at the beach. The trail is closed March 15–September 15 to protect nesting snowy plover. This is a good spot for bird-watching. Find the trailhead near the Waxmyrtle campground about eight miles south of Florence at the Siltcoos Recreation Area.

CENTRAL COAST

Camping

There are some excellent campgrounds around Florence. Camping here offers recreational opportunities comparable to those at the Oregon Dunes National Recreation Area (NRA), with more varied scenery.

Carl G. Washburne State Park (93111 U.S. 101 N., 541/547-3416 information, 800/452-5687 reservations, open year-round, $17–22, $4 hiker-biker spaces) is popular with Oregonians because of its proximity to beaches, tidepools, Sea Lion Caves, and elk. The eight tent sites and 58 RV sites have such modern conveniences as showers, laundry, electricity, and piped water. There are also two yurts, which can be reserved. It's 14 miles north of Florence on U.S. 101 (several miles past Sea Lion Caves), then one mile west on a park road. This state park offers fine camping and nearby forest pathways such as the Hobbit Trail.

Three miles south of Florence's McCullough Bridge and on both sides of U.S. 101 is **Honeyman State Park** (84505 U.S. 101 S., 541/997-3641 information, 800/452-5687 reservations). This exceedingly popular campground gets very crowded in the summer—reservations are a must—but it empties out enough during spring and autumn to make a stay here worthwhile. There are 240 tent sites with the basics, a large number of RV spaces with all the amenities, and many hiker-biker spots as well (more than 400 in total). Ask about canoe rentals to savor the serenity of Cleawox Lake. Fishing, swimming, hiking, and dune buggies are available nearby, so there's always something to do. In spring, pink rhododendrons line the highway and park roads. Advance reservations are accepted Memorial Day through Labor Day, and the sites cost $13–22, depending on the season and the type of site.

An ideal place to escape from the summertime coastal crowds is the **North Fork of the Siuslaw** campground. Chances are you'll see mostly locals here—if anybody. From Florence follow Highway 126 about 15 miles to Mapleton and the junction with Highway 36. The latter road takes you 13 miles to County Route 5070. Then it's a short drive to the riverside campsite (or you can drive the North Fork Siuslaw River Road from Florence for 14.5 miles). The fee is $4 between July and early September. Picnic tables, fire pits, and crawdads are other reasons to come. Contact the **Siuslaw National Forest Ranger Station** (4480 U.S. 101 N., Florence, 541/902-8526) for more information. This campground is near the Pawn Old-Growth Trail. By the way, nearby Highway 36 makes an interesting access road back to the Willamette Valley if you're not in a hurry. Its circuitous route passes through Deadwood and ends up in the Junction City area.

Dune Rides

Ride into the dunes with the folks from **Sand Dunes Frontier** (83960 U.S. 101, Florence, 541/997-3544). This company rents vehicles for travel in specially designated areas within the Dunes NRA. Odysseys, small one-person dune buggies, go for $45 per hour and a $100 deposit. You must be strapped in, with a helmet, stay within the marked territory, and be especially careful going uphill. If you lose power on an incline, it's possible to roll over when turning around to go back down. The 20-person dune buggy rides cost $12 for adults, $10 for children 4–11 years old. Protective goggles are provided, along with a driver. Go in the morning when the sand tends to blow around less.

Sandboarding

Dude, it's a natural! Wax up a board, strap it onto your bare feet, and carve your way down the dunes. Rent a board and try out the rails and jumps at **Sand Master Park** (87541 U.S. 101, 541/997-6006, www.sandmasterpark .com, 9 A.M.–7 P.M. daily June–Aug., 10 A.M.– 5 P.M. Thurs.–Tues., Sept.–May, board rentals from $16 including admission) on the northern outskirts of Florence. If you're more of a do-it-yourselfer, a number of roadside shops are beginning to rent sandboards, and the dunes are certainly plentiful.

Water Sports

Although only the hardiest swimmers go into

the ocean without wetsuits, Cleawox and Woahink Lakes warm up sufficiently to make summertime swimming enjoyable. Cleawox, the smaller of the two, is especially well suited for swimming. Woahink, which has a boat ramp and canoe rentals, is good for paddling. Both lakes are located within Honeyman State Park, three miles south of Florence.

If you want to learn to scuba dive, Florence's **Central Coast Watersports** (1901 U.S. 101, 541/997-1812 or 800/789-3483) offers scuba instruction at Woahink Lake. But the most popular local dive spot is at the North Jetty, off Rhododendron Drive, which has been designated an underwater park. Divers typically go after crabs and clams and must pay careful attention to the tides.

Surfers head to the beaches at South Jetty; the waves here are best when small—they can often become overwhelming and unsuitable for novices. Look for more protection from the wind at the mouth of the river. Check with Central Coast Watersports for conditions and rentals.

Horseback Riding

Riding across the dunes into the sunset on a trusty steed sounds like a fantasy, but you can do it, too, thanks to **C&M Stables** (90241 U.S. 101, Florence, 541/997-7540). Rates range $35–55 per person for trips of 1–2 hours (with discounts for larger parties). The stables are open daily and are located near 14 miles of horse trails that wind through the forest on a bluff above the beach. With beach rides, dune trail excursions, and sunset trips, there's something for everybody. Call for times and reservations.

Golf

Ocean Dunes Golf Links (3345 Munsel Lake Rd., 541/997-3232, $25 for 9 holes, $40 for 18 holes) lets you tee off with sand dunes (some more than 60 feet tall) as a backdrop. The manicured 18-hole course has a driving range, a full pro shop, and equipment rentals on-site. For the ultimate in golfing by the dunes, however, try **Sandpines Golf Course** (1050 35th St., 541/997-1940). This was voted

Florence is on the banks of the Siuslaw River. A riverside boardwalk is a good place for a morning stroll.

© JUDY JEWELL

Golf Digest's number one new public course in 1993. To get there, go west off U.S. 101 on 35th Street. In May and June rhododendrons line this drive, which heads into dune country as you move toward the sea. Follow the signs until you see a water tower not far from the pro shop. Sandpines's layout features fairways lined with Douglas fir and beach grass on gently undulating terrain. Coastal winds that kick up in the morning can figure prominently in your shot selection. Summertime greens fees are $80 weekdays, $95 weekends, carts $30.

Siltcoos Lake

Oregon's largest coastal lake, six miles south of Florence, 3,100-acre Siltcoos Lake offers excellent fishing and other recreation. Rainbows are stocked in the spring, and steelhead, salmon (closed to coho fishing), and sea-run cutthroat trout move from the ocean into the lake via the short Siltcoos River in late summer and fall, but the real excitement here is the fishing for warm-water species, which is some of the best in the Northwest. Bluegill, crappie, yellow perch, and brown bullhead action is good through the summer, while fishing for largemouth bass can be good year-round. Access points include several public and private boat ramps on the lake, as well as a wheelchair-accessible fishing pier at Westlake Resort.

In addition, the Siltcoos River invites kayakers and canoeists to explore the two-mile stretch between the lake and the sea. Meandering two miles through dunes, forest, and estuary, the Siltcoos is a gentle, Class-I paddle with no white water or rapids, although a small dam midway must be portaged. Wildlife that you may encounter along the way include mink, raccoons, otters, beavers, and even bears. In the estuary, sea lions and harbor seals are common.

For more information on the Siltcoos area, contact the **Oregon Dunes National Recreation Area Visitor Center** (541/271-3611) in Reedsport.

Other Activities

Huckleberry picking is another attraction just outside town. Some prime pickings are found about five miles north of Florence at the Sutton Creek Trail, which begins in the campground with the same name just off U.S. 101. During late summer or fall, these berries flourish below the dense canopy of shorepines here. Rhododendrons bloom in profusion mid-May to early June. In addition to these delights, you can hike through the dunes, which are broken up by several freshwater lakes.

ENTERTAINMENT AND EVENTS

Art shows, classical concerts by acclaimed virtuosi (including performances as part of the Ernest Bloch Music Festival—see *Events* in the *Newport* section for more details), ballet, theater, and community events can be enjoyed within the warm, welcoming, and spacious **Florence Events Center** (715 Quince St., 541/997-1994 or 888/968-4086, www.eventcenter.org). An on-site gallery displays the works of local artists.

The **Dune Mushers Mail Run,** held the first weekend of March, is the world's longest organized dry-land run for dogsled teams, which mush up the dunes from North Bend. On Sunday, the teams pass through Florence's South Jetty area, to finish up with a parade through Old Town Florence.

During the third weekend of May, Florence celebrates the **Rhododendron Festival,** coinciding with the bloom of these flowers that proliferate in the area. It's a tradition that goes back to 1908, when the festival was started as a way to draw attention and commerce to the area. A parade, carnival, flower show, 5K and 10K "Rhody Run," and the crowning of Queen Rhododendra are highlights of the festivities. Today, the event attracts more than 15,000 visitors each year. Contact the chamber of commerce (541/997-3128) for more information.

Fourth of July celebrations include live outdoor music and a barbecue in Old Town, and a fireworks display over the river.

Chowder, Brews, and Blues (541/997-1994, admission $6–10) in late September is a three-day event honoring several things the community relishes. A coastwide clam chowder contest here is a highlight, along with live music and microbrew-tasting at the Florence Events Center.

SHOPPING

A nice selection of Oregon food products and crafts is available in Old Town Florence at **Incredible Edible Oregon** (1350 Bay St., 541/997-7018). One place to stop if you're looking for regional titles is next door, at **Old Town Books and Country Gifts** (1340 Bay St., 541/997-6205). The friendly staff here will also gladly direct you to local attractions and answer any questions you might have about the region.

ACCOMMODATIONS

As just about everywhere else, there are budget motels on the main drag, but to experience the coast fully, try one of the romantic getaways between Florence and Yachats. There are many romantic B&Bs north of town, covered in detail in the *Yachats and Cape Perpetua* section.

$50-100

One of the best bargains in town is the **Lighthouse Inn** (155 U.S. 101, 541/997-3221 or 866/997-3221, doubles from $55), a Cape Cod–style two-story motel on the highway close to the bridge and convenient to Old Town. With neatly kept rooms in an untouched 1938 lodging, decorated with bric-a-brac and other homey touches, it may give you the feeling that you're spending the night at your grandmother's house. There are no in-room kitchens, but a common refrigerator and microwave are available for guest use. Most rooms have a queen- or king-size bed and sleep two; some are considered suites, with two rooms and a connecting bath, and they sleep up to five guests. Ask about the plushest of all, the honeymoon/anniversary suite.

Just around the corner from Old Town, and across the highway from the Lighthouse Inn, the pet-friendly **Old Town Inn** (170 U.S. 101 N., 541/997-7131 or 800/570-8738, www.old-town-inn.com, doubles from $71) provides guests with spacious rooms a short walk away from the river and Old Town. Although this motel is on U.S. 101, the rooms are fairly quiet.

For a river experience, try the 【 **River House Motel** (1202 Bay St., 541/997-3933 or 888/824-2750, www.riverhousemotel.com, doubles from $89, from $109 for riverfront). It's worth paying extra for a riverfront balcony. The motel, which also has good views of the pretty Siuslaw River bridge, is just a block away from the heart of Old Town.

If it's not important for you to be an easy walk from Old Town, consider staying three miles south of town at the charming and pet-friendly 【 **Park Motel** (85034 U.S. 101, 541/997-2634 or 800/392-0441, www.parkmotelflorence.com, doubles $60–128), a classic mom-and-pop place set well back from the highway in a stand of Douglas firs. The rooms are paneled in knotty pine and come in a variety of sizes and configurations, including a few cabins, making it a good place for families or groups of friends.

$100 and Up

【 **The Edwin K B&B** (1155 Bay St., 541/997-8360 or 800/8-EDWINK, www.edwink.com, doubles $130–150) has six units with private bath two blocks from Old Town just across the street from the Siuslaw River. River views, period antiques, and multicourse breakfasts with locally famous soufflés and home-baked breads on fine china have established this gracious 1914 home as Florence's preeminent B&B. Add private baths and whirlpool tubs in some units, a private courtyard and waterfall in back, and the reasonable rates, and you'll understand the need to reserve well in advance.

On the south bank of the river, just across the bridge from Old Town, the **Best Western Pier Point Inn** (85625 U.S. 101, 541/997-7191, doubles from $135) offers spacious rooms, bay views, sand-dune hiking across the street, and a good restaurant on-site (Lovejoy's offers fish and chips and selection of English ales and microbrews). There is also a beach house for rent along the Siuslaw River that sleeps six. Rates at this large luxury motel drop by about half in the off-season.

CENTRAL COAST

Nine miles north of Florence and just a short walk from Heceta Head Lighthouse is **Heceta Head Lighthouse B&B** (92072 U.S. 101, 541/547-3696 or 866/547-3696, www.heceta lighthouse.com, doubles $157–251), built in 1893. It used to be the lighthouse keeper's home; today, it's a B&B with antique furnishings and vintage photos, which help re-create the lives of the keepers of the flame. Among the bedrooms, the two Mariners' rooms command the finest view and have private baths (two of the other rooms share a bathroom down the hall). The current caretakers maintain a garden on the grounds, as did the actual lighthouse keepers of yesteryear, and use some of the produce to turn out amazing seven-course breakfasts, glorious several-hour affairs replete with such dishes as d'Anjou pear with chevre and Oregon honey and vol-au-vent stuffed with eggs, chives, and asparagus. The innkeepers are more likely to tell you about resident ghosts during breakfast than right before bedtime.

At Heceta Beach, on the northern edge of Florence, **Driftwood Shores Resort** (88416 1st Ave., 541/997-8263 or 800/422-5091, www.driftwoodshores.com, doubles $98–299) is unique among Florentine lodgings in that it is oceanside. It is also a huge complex, and in a pretty isolated area, far from Old Town and restaurants (except the resort restaurant). All rooms face the ocean and have decks or patios, as well as microwaves and refrigerators (some suites have full kitchens).

Vacation Rentals

The properties listed highlight Siuslaw Bay and/or Old Town and will enhance your appreciation of this estuarine environment. Another alternative is renting a house out in the dunes through **Dolphin Property Management** (508 Kingwood St., 541/997-7368, www.oregon vacationproperties.com). For other rental locations, try **Elson Shields Property Management** (1287 Bay St., 541/997-6235, www.florencerentals.com).

FOOD

A Zen master once said, "If you can make a cup of tea right, you can do anything." The same aphorism seems to apply to clam chowder in coastal restaurants, if Florence eateries are any indication.

Steak and Seafood

Most of the places to eat in Old Town are fairly predictable high-volume tourist places. Not to say they're not good, but they may not ooze with personality. Lack of personality is not a problem at the **❰ Waterfront Depot** (1252 Bay St., 541/902-9100, open for dinner nightly, main courses $10), a friendly, bustling place with good views onto the river and lovely filtered evening light. Wait for a table or sit at the bar, where you're likely to be next to a local regular, in for the saucy crab-encrusted halibut fillet. If you want to shy away from extra-rich food, try ordering from the tapas menu, which, like all the offerings, is written on a chalkboard up on the wall.

In Old Town, the local **Mo's** (1436 Bay St., 541/997-2185, $4.25 bowl of chowder, $15 bouillabaisse) is the largest outlet of this famed Oregon chowderhouse, and its fresh fish, fast service, fair prices, and Siuslaw River frontage make it this neighborhood's most popular restaurant. Even if you don't eat here, you might want to stock up on Mo's clam chowder base packaged to go.

For yet another chowder champ, **Ruby Begonia** (1565 9th St., 541/997-1821, open 8 A.M.– 9 P.M. daily) has one of the best seafood chowders on the coast, according to *Sunset* magazine. This golden-hued soup has salmon, halibut, prawns, and clams. The tasty homemade pie and the Mexican entrées add another dimension to the Florence dining scene.

The **Bridgewater Seafood Restaurant and Oyster Bar** (129 Bay St., Old Town, 541/997-9405, main courses $10–20) is what passes for "fine dining" in Old Town. But with its rattan furniture and tropical motif, it's much less stuffy than most white-tablecloth joints. Fresh fish, often with a Cajun flair, dominates the menu, which is so wide-ranging that almost everyone can find something to his or her liking. Be aware that this is a place where simpler is often better—the fancier dishes sometimes sound better than they taste.

The **International C-Food Market** (1498 Bay St., 541/997-9646, open for lunch and dinner daily, dinner $17–30), perched out over the river, gets good word-of-mouth from locals. This combination restaurant and retail market offers seafood right off the boat. Try the smoked salmon pizza—it's excellent.

Thai
Sick of clam chowder? **Thai Talay** (2515 U.S. 101, 541/997-7227, open for lunch and dinner daily, main courses $8–19) might come as a welcome change, especially if you go for the spicy mango-and-broccoli stir fry. If you can't be away from seafood for too long, try one of the seafood specialties here.

Italian
Another good place to take a break from chowder (though not necessarily seafood) is **Pomodori's** (1415 7th St., 541/902-2525, open for lunch Tues.–Fri., dinner Tues.–Sat., dinner about $20), an intimate Northern Italian restaurant. Specialties include fresh shrimp and halibut and pasta, as well as a pork chop stuffed with shrimp, pancetta, scallions, and tomatoes.

Casual Fare
Traveler's Cove (1362 Bay St., 541/997-6845, open 9 A.M.–9 P.M. daily) is a good lunch or casual dinner stop in Old Town, with homemade clam chowder and interesting salads and sandwiches. Fresh Dungeness crab makes an appearance here with crab quiche, crab enchiladas, and "crabby" Caesar salad. Best of all, the patio out back provides riverfront views to enjoy along with your meal. A full bar with flavored margaritas might also enhance your appreciation of the river frontage. Weekend nights often bring live music.

Stock up on organic produce and bulk grains at **Salmonberry** (812 Quince St., 541/997-3345, open daily).

Coffee, Tea, and Ice Cream
After dinner, have dessert at either of **BJ's Ice Cream Parlor**'s two locations (2930 U.S. 101 or 1441 Bay St., 541/997-7286, 10 A.M.–11 P.M. daily during summer, 11 A.M.–10 P.M. daily during winter). BJ's churns out hundreds of flavors, with 48 on display at any given time, famous all over Oregon. Full fountain service, ice cream cakes, cheesecakes, gourmet frozen yogurt, and pies complement the cones and cups.

Close to the bridge, **Siuslaw River Coffee Roasters** (1240 Bay St., 541/997-3443, 7 A.M.–8 P.M. or 9 P.M. daily during summer; 7 A.M.–5 P.M. Sun.–Wed., 7 A.M.–6 P.M. Thurs.–Sat. during winter) serves good coffee and pastries. There's a little deck out back overlooking the river, and lots of books and hobnobbing inside.

If you're visiting on a rainy afternoon, a good place to while away the time is **Lovejoy's Tea Room** (129 Nopal St., 541/997-9118, open 11 A.M.–6 P.M. daily), a branch of a San Francisco tearoom. Dine on a Cornish pasty or sausage roll ($7) or go for tea service, available at several levels of decadence.

In Mapleton
Driving east on Highway 126 en route to Eugene from the coast lets you follow the Siuslaw past isolated farms and lush forests topped by clear-cut ridges. Fourteen miles east of Florence, you come to Mapleton. Set at the base of the Coast Range, it's one of the rainiest burgs in the whole state. It also has a restaurant that evokes remembrances of things past. **The Alpha Bit Crafts Café** (10780 Hwy. 126, Mapleton, 541/268-4311, main dishes $3–7) is only a 20-minute drive from Florence, but it exists in a different time and space. Started by a group of 20 or so people who share land in the nearby town of Deadwood, the restaurant serves good veggie sandwiches and home-baked treats (try the date bar) at reasonable prices. The preparations frequently include produce grown on Alpha Farm. Also don't miss the December 1991 *Life* magazine article about the creators, available upon request. The unusual local crafts and fine selection of books make Alpha Bit the cultural center of Mapleton.

INFORMATION AND SERVICES

The **Florence Area Chamber of Commerce** (270 U.S. 101, Florence, 541/997-3128, www.florencechamber.com, open 9 A.M.– 5 P.M.), is three blocks north of the Siuslaw River Bridge.

The **Siuslaw National Forest Ranger Station** (4480 U.S. 101 N., Florence, 541/902-8526) is located near the BiMart on Florence's main drag. Tune into radio station **KCST,** at 106.9 FM or 1250 AM, for coastal news, weather, and a whole lotta Paul Harvey.

Peace Harbor Hospital (400 9th St., Florence, 541/997-3128) is open 24 hours, with a dozen specialists and an emergency room. The **post office** (770 Maple Street, Florence 97439, 541/997-2533), near the junction of Highway 126 and U.S. 101, is close to the library.

GETTING THERE AND AROUND

Greyhound (www.greyhound.com) still runs to Florence, but its service is limited (don't count on checking luggage). The bus stop, at the 37th Street Laundry (1857-1 37th St., 541/997-5111), sees twice-daily service. **Porter Stage Lines** (541/269-7183) runs along the southern Oregon coast, then turns inland at Florence and goes to Eugene, Bend, and Ontario.

Reedsport and Winchester Bay

If you're going fishing or are coming back from a dunes hike, you'll appreciate a hot meal and a clean, low-priced motel room in Reedsport. Otherwise, this town of 5,000 people might seem like a strange mirage of cut-rate motels, taverns, and burger joints in the midst of the Oregon Dunes National Recreation Area. To find the more interesting side of Reedsport, turn off U.S. 101 up the Umpqua River.

Jedediah Smith explored this country in 1828, after the Hudson's Bay Company's Peter Skene Ogden theorized that the Umpqua River—the largest river between San Francisco Bay and the Columbia—might be the fabled Northwest Passage. It wasn't, of course, but this river is still one of the great fishing streams of the state. Zane Grey avoided writing about it, lavishing the publicity instead on the Rogue to divert people from his favorite steelhead spots here.

Cargo ships from Scottsburg, a hamlet some 17 miles upriver from Reedsport, supplied San Francisco markets with meat, milk, and produce between 1856 and the early 20th century. In its 1850s heyday, Scottsburg was larger than Portland, with some 5,000 residents, before an 1861 flood destroyed much of the town.

Two miles north of Reedsport, the little burg of Gardiner was created in the wake of a shipwreck. The *Bostonian* (owned by a Mr. Gardiner) was dashed against the rocks at the mouth of the Umpqua in 1856, and from its remnants the first wood-frame structure in this area was built. It was soon joined by other white-painted homes and facilities for a port on the Umpqua. Although this "white city by the sea" declined in importance when the highway elevated Reedsport to regional hub status, the homes still bear the same color scheme from the earlier era.

Three miles southwest of Reedsport, Salmon Harbor Marina in Winchester Bay (pop. 1,000), a busy port for commercial sport fishing at the mouth of the Umpqua, has given the whole area new life in recent years, following hard times precipitated by the decline in timber revenues.

SIGHTS
Umpqua Discovery Center

In Reedsport's Old Town on the south bank of the river, the Umpqua Discovery Center (409 Riverfront Way, 541/271-4816, open 9 A.M.– 5 P.M. daily June–Sept., 10 A.M.–4 P.M. daily Oct.–May, $8 adults, $4 children) interprets the regional human and natural history of this area through multimedia programs, dioramas, scale models, and helpful staff. The boardwalk and observation tower give a good view of the broad lower reaches of the Umpqua. In summer, free Friday evening concerts are staged here, and the center is the site of the September Tsalila festival.

Dean Creek Elk Viewing Area

Three miles east of Reedsport, and stretching three miles along the south side of Highway 38, the Dean Creek Elk Viewing Area provides parking areas and viewing platforms for observing the herd of some 120 wild Roosevelt elk that roam this 1,100-acre preserve. The elk move out of the forest to graze the preserve's marshy pastures, sometimes coming quite close to the highway. Elk can reach 1,100 pounds at maturity, and the majestic rack on a fully grown bull can spread three feet across. Early mornings and just before dusk are the most promising times to look for them; during hot

© PAUL LEVY

the Umpqua Lighthouse, just south of Winchester Bay

weather and storms the elk tend to stay within the cover of the woods.

Umpqua Lighthouse State Park

Less than one mile south of Winchester Bay is Umpqua Lighthouse State Park (460 Lighthouse Rd., Winchester Bay, 541/271-4118). Tour the red-capped 1894 lighthouse (541/271-4631, open 10 A.M.–4 P.M. daily May–Sept., $2) or admire it from the roadside. Adjacent, in a former Coast Guard building, the **visitors center and museum** (541/271-4631, open 10 A.M.–5 P.M. Wed.–Sat., 1–5 P.M. Sun. May–Sept.) has marine and timber exhibits. Directly opposite the lighthouse, overlooking the mouth of the Umpqua and oceanfront dunes, is a whale-watching platform with a plaque explaining where, when, and what in the world to look for.

Lake Marie, just south near the camping area, has a swimming beach and is stocked with rainbow trout. A one-mile forest trail around the lake makes for an easy hike. A trail from the campground leads to the highest dunes in the United States (elev. 545 feet), west of Clear Lake.

SPORTS AND RECREATION
Fishing

Winchester Bay and the tidewater reaches of the lower Umpqua River comprise Oregon's top coastal sturgeon fishery and one of the best areas for striped bass, particularly near the mouth of the Smith River, which enters the Umpqua just east of Reedsport. The best action for the Umpqua's spring chinook tends to be inland, below Scottsburg. Fall chinook enter the bay July–September. Other notable fisheries here are the huge runs of shad, which peak May–June, and smallmouth bass offer action upstream from Reedsport. Crabbing and clamming are also popular and productive pastimes in Winchester Bay and the lower reaches of the river. Every year from August 1 to mid-September, tagged crabs are released into the water in and around Winchester Bay, one of them worth a cash prize of $5,000 to whomever catches it.

CENTRAL COAST

DUNE COUNTRY: COOS BAY TO FLORENCE

Even though the 47-mile stretch of U.S. 101 between Coos Bay and Florence does not overlook the ocean, your eyes will be drawn constantly westward to the largest and most extensive oceanfront dunes in the world.

How did they come to exist in a coastal topography otherwise dominated by rocky bluffs? A combination of factors created this landscape over the past 12,000 years, but the principal agents are the Coos, Siuslaw, and Umpqua rivers. The sand and sediment transported to the sea by these waterways are deposited by waves on the flat, shallow beaches. Prevailing westerlies move the particulate matter exposed by the tide eastward up to several yards per year. Over the millennia, the dunes have grown huge, with some topping 500 feet.

Constantly on the move, the shifting sands have engulfed ancient forests, a fact occasionally corroborated by hikers as they stumble upon the top of an exposed snag. The cross section of sandswept woodlands seen from U.S. 101 demonstrates that this inundation is still occurring. Nonetheless, the motorist gets the impression that the trees are winning the battle because the dunes are only intermittently visible from the road.

The Oregon Dunes National Recreation Area (NRA) is home to more than 400 species of flora and fauna, but the only dangerous animal within this ecosystem is possibly the American teenager. This species migrates here during summer vacation to assault the dunes with a variety of all-terrain vehicles. Of the 31,500 acres within the NRA, nearly half are designated open sand and riding trails for off-highway vehicles such as dune buggies.

GETTING ORIENTED

Reedsport and the nearby fishing village of Winchester Bay have carved out identities as refueling and supply depots for excursions into Oregon's Sahara-by-the-Sea. A great place to start your explorations is the **Oregon Dunes NRA Visitor Information Center** (885 U.S. 101, Reedsport 97467, 541/271-3611, www.fs.fed.us/r6/siuslaw), at the junction of the Coast Highway and Highway 38. In addition to the printed information on hiking, camping, and recreation, the Siuslaw Forest Service personnel are very helpful.

Note that a $5 day-use fee is charged per vehicle at most facilities and access points within the NRA. You can purchase an annual pass at the Dunes Visitor Center for $30.

Because the dunes are difficult to see from the highway in many places, the most commonly asked question in the visitors center is "Where are the dunes?" To answer it for everybody, the National Forest Service opened **Oregon Dunes Overlook** just south of Carter Lake, midway between Florence and Reedsport, at the point where the dunes come

Charter services operating in the area include: **Salmon Harbor** (541/271-2010, www.salmonharborcharterfishing.com); **Reel Fishing Trips** (541/271-3850); **Strike Zone Charters** (541/271-9706 or 800/230-5350, www.strikezonecharters.com); **River's End Guide Service** (541/271-3125, www.umpquafishing.com); and **Jerry Jarmain** (541/271-5583 or 800/653-5583, www.umpqua-river-guide.com).

💽 John Dellenback Trail

A spectacular dunes landscape can be found 10.5 miles south of Reedsport along the John Dellenback Trail, 0.25 mile south of the Eel Creek Campground near Lakeside. After you emerge from a half-mile hike through coastal evergreen forest, you'll be greeted by dunes 300–400 feet high. It's said that dunes near here can approach 500 feet high and one mile long after a windblown buildup. The trail, marked by blue-banded wooden posts, continues another 2.5 miles to the beach. Dune hiking can be a bit disorienting. If you lose the trail, climb to the top of the tallest dune and scan for the trail markers.

closest to U.S. 101. In addition to four levels of railing-enclosed platforms connected by wooden walkways, there are trails down to the sand. It's only about a quarter mile to the dunes and, thereafter, a mile through sand and wetlands to the beach.

You can hike a loop beginning where the sand gives way to willows. Bear right en route to the beach. Once there, walk south 1.5 miles. A wooden post marks where the trail resumes. It then traverses a footbridge going through trees onto sand, completing the loop. If you go in February, this loop has great bird-watching potential. A day-use fee is charged for cars.

Other sites for easy introductions to the dune topography are (from south to north): Spinreel Campground, Umpqua Dunes Trail, Honeyman State Park, and Florence's South Jetty.

RECREATION IN THE DUNES
There are three excellent state parks and a dozen Siuslaw National Forest Campgrounds within the NRA. Although joyriding in noisy dune buggies and other off-road vehicles doesn't lack for devotees, the best way to appreciate the interface of ecosystems is on foot. Dunes exceeding 500 feet in height, wetland breeding grounds for animals and waterfowl, evergreen forests, and deserted beaches can be encountered in a march to the sea. Numerous designated hiking trails, ranging from easy half-mile loops to six-mile round-trips, give visitors a chance to star in their own version of *Lawrence of Arabia* as they moonwalk through this earthbound Sea of Tranquility. The soundtrack can be provided by the 247 species of birds here – along with your heartbeat – as you scale these elephantine anthills. Deserted beaches and secret swimming holes are among the many rewards of the journey.

Before setting out, pick up the *Hiking Trails Recreation Opportunity Guide* from the Oregon Dunes NRA Visitor Center. This and other publications will correct the superficial impression that the dunes are just a domain for all-terrain vehicles and day hikers.

To ensure a *bon voyage*, it's important to understand this terrain. Carry plenty of water and dress in layers – there are hot spots in dune valleys and ocean breezes at higher elevations. Expect cool summers and wet, mild winters. Although rainfall here can average more than 70 inches per year (with 75 percent of it falling Mar.–Nov.), a string of dry, 50–60°F days in February is not uncommon. Another surprise is summertime morning fog, brought in by hot weather inland. These fogs, together with the inevitable confusion caused by dunes that don't look much different from each other, make a compass necessary. The lack of defined trails also compels such measures as marking your return route in the sand with a stick. Binoculars can help with visual orientation, not to mention bird-watching opportunities galore.

A shorter and easier one-mile loop trail leads through woodlands to the dunes for a quick introduction to this landscape.

Camping
Choices abound in this recreation-rich area. Just south of Winchester Bay is **Umpqua Lighthouse State Park** (460 Lighthouse Rd., Winchester Bay, 541/271-4118 information, 800/452-5687 reservations). The campground alongside Lake Marie has firewood, flush toilets, showers, picnic tables, electricity, and piped water. The 20 RV sites go for $20, 24 tent sites for $16, two basic yurts for $27, six deluxe yurts (with shower, small kitchen, refrigerator, microwave, and TV/VCR) for $66, and two rustic cabins for $35. The lake offers fishing, boating, and swimming. Trails from here lead to the highest dunes in the United States (elev. 545 feet), west of Clear Lake.

William A. Tugman State Park (541/759-3604 information, 800/452-5687 reservations) is eight miles south of Reedsport, in the heart of dune country. This larger campground, with 115 sites, has a similar range of creature comforts, price, and recreation. It sits on the west shore of Eel Lake, east of U.S. 101 across from the widest point of the dunes, two miles to the sea.

Windy Cove Campground (541/271-4138) is a county park with 24 full hookup sites and four other sites with electric service only. Located on the south side of Salmon Harbor Drive, across from the Winchester Bay marina, it has restrooms, picnic tables, grass, and paved site pads. No reservations are accepted. It is legal to drive your off-highway vehicle (OHV) from this campground directly to the dunes, but it requires a couple of miles on the pavement.

About nine miles south of Reedsport, set along Eel Creek near Eel Lake and Tenmile Lakes, is **Eel Creek Campground,** a Siuslaw National Forest facility with 51 basic tent and RV sites. It's open mid-May through September, and reservations (877/444-6777, www.reserveusa.com, $17) are advised. The Umpqua Dunes Trail offers access to the dunes and beach.

Eight miles north of Reedsport, the **Tahkenitch Campground** (877/444-6777 reservations, www.reserveusa.com, open mid-May–Sept., $17) is another Forest Service facility, set among ancient Douglas firs and conveniently located near Tahkenitch and other lakes, dunes, and ocean beaches. A network of trails branch out from here through the dunes, along Tahkenitch, and to the beach.

Winchester Bay's **Discovery Point Resort** (242 Discovery Point Lane, 541/271-3443, www.discoverypointresort.com) offers dunes enthusiasts dune access and all-terrain vehicle (ATV) rentals, and provides one- to three-bedroom cabins (sleep up to six) and 60 RV spaces. To get there from Reedsport, head two miles south on U.S. 101 to Winchester Bay, then turn right at Pelican Market onto Salmon Harbor Drive. Go one mile, and you'll see Discovery Point Resort on the left. Reservations are highly recommended.

Skate Park
Near the south end of Reedsport on the east side of U.S. 101 is a world-class skate park (www.reedsportskatepark.com). Here you'll find a funnel-shaped full pipe and a 360-degree full loop as well as many more approachable features.

Lakeside-Area Recreation
Ten miles south of Reedsport, the sleepy resort town of Lakeside hosted visits from Bob Hope, Bing Crosby, and the Ink Spots, among other luminaries, back in its 1930s and 1940s heyday. Today, it's still a popular destination, primarily for its proximity to the sprawling, many-armed Tenmile and North Tenmile Lakes. These large, shallow lakes offer waterskiing and excellent fishing for stocked rainbow trout and warm-water species, including crappie, yellow perch, bluegill, and lunker largemouth bass up to 10 pounds. A quarter-mile channel connects the two lakes, and a county park on Tenmile Lake has a paved boat ramp, fishing docks, sandy swimming beach, and picnic area.

EVENTS
Every June, over Father's Day weekend, chainsaw sculptors compete for $10,000 in prizes as they transform pieces of raw western red cedar into grizzly bears, giant salmon, and other rustic works of art during the **Chainsaw Sculpture Championships** (800/247-2155) at the Rainbow Plaza Old Town Reedsport.

An interesting annual event is **Tsalila** (800/247-2155). Named for the Coos Indian word for river (pronounced sa-LEE-la), this festival features interpretive tours of the Umpqua, alder-baked salmon with squash and corn-on-the-cob dinners, and a traditional Indian village on the waterfront at the Umpqua Discovery Center. Music and food service appear here on the second weekend in September. There's no charge except dinner prices of $10 for adults and $5 for kids.

ACCOMMODATIONS
$50-100
Of the half-dozen motels that sit along U.S. 101 in Reedsport, the **Fir Grove Motel** (2178 Winchester Ave., 541/271-4848, doubles $44

and up) is slightly less expensive but comparable in comfort (i.e., clean with no frills) to its counterparts.

A cluster of budget motels along the highway includes the following: **Anchor Bay Inn** (1821 Winchester Ave., 541/271-2149 or 800/767-1821, doubles $57 and up) with suites and kitchenettes available; **Best Budget Inn** (1894 Winchester Ave., 541/271-3686, doubles $50 and up); and the **Economy Inn** (1593 Highway Ave., 541/271-3671 or 800/799-9970, doubles $65 and up).

Anglers, or anyone who'd rather be in a location off the main drag, should consider the **Winchester Bay Motel** (4th and Broadway, Winchester Bay, 541/271-4871 or 800/246-1462, www.winbayinn.com, doubles $72 and up), located just across from the docks. Be sure to reserve ahead of time in fishing season. Pets are permitted in some rooms.

A few miles north of Reedsport in Gardiner is another lodging with more character than those along motel row for not significantly more money. The **Gardiner Guest House** (401 Front St., 541/271-4005, www.gardiner bedandbreakfast.com, $65–75) is located in a sleepy former paper-mill town that sits close by the confluence of the Smith and Umpqua rivers. The 1883 home was built by local bigwig and state senator Albert Reed, for whom Reedsport was named. The recently remodeled home still has the Victorian feel, without lacking in modern conveniences. If you like to peruse old books by a fire or watch bald eagles from a bay window above the Umpqua River, you'll love this place. Choose between a cheaper room with the facilities down the hall and a higher-priced view room with private bath. A large home-cooked breakfast is included in the rate.

Over $100

If you're interested in this area's ultimate get-away-from-it-all alternative, try the ℂ **Salbasgeon Inn of the Umpqua** (45209 Hwy. 38, Reedsport, 541/271-2025, doubles $80–145) with nicely appointed rooms on the Umpqua and a romantic location about seven

© JUDY JEWELL

Stop by the docks at Winchester Bay to catch a charter or just buy a can of delicious tuna.

miles upstream from town. The name was inspired by the trio of most popular sportfishing species (i.e., salmon, bass, sturgeon) in the region. Pets are permitted for an extra fee.

In town, the **Best Western Salbasgeon Inn** (541/271-4831 or 800/528-1234, $100 and up) is a separate place, located on U.S. 101 just south of the Umpqua River bridge.

FOOD
Reedsport

There is no shortage of basic but decent places to eat here. A popular place on U.S. 101 is **Don's Main Street Restaurant** (2115 Winchester Ave., 541/271-2032, breakfast, lunch, and dinner daily), whose burgers and soup are good enough to get you to Florence. After a bite of Umpqua ice cream (touted by many to be the best in the state), however, you might stick around until you're hungry again.

The **Schooner Café** (423 Riverfront Way, 541/271-3945, open 10 A.M.–3 P.M. daily, lunch about $10), on the boardwalk next door to the Discovery Center, has a pleasant riverside patio and a good selection of salads and sandwiches. The food here is a little fancier than you'll find at other places in town, with excellent homemade coleslaw and good salad dressings.

Winchester Bay

For the best fresh seafood in the dune country, head down to the Salmon Harbor marina at Winchester Bay, where there are a number of casual seafood restaurants.

The friendly staff at the **Sportsmen's Cannery and Smokehouse** (Bay Front Loop, 541/271-3293, shop open daily, seafood barbeque Sat. and Sun. afternoon and evening, $12–17) hosts a weekend seafood barbecue that features salmon, halibut, and crab (and whatever else is fresh) and all the trimmings. Don't expect indoor seating for this meal—you'll eat at picnic tables set up in the parking lot. Peek inside and you may see cannery employees cutting up the day's catch. Visit the adjoining shop to purchase fresh, smoked, or canned fish; they'll even smoke your catch for you.

Just across the parking lot from Sportsmen's is **Griff's Seafood** (Bay Front Loop, 541/271-2512, open for lunch and dinner daily), where you can sit inside for your extra-tasty fish and chips or bucket of steamer clams.

Once you've filled up on fish, wander over to the **Village Roastery** (140 Coho Point, 541/271-3424) for good coffee and a wide selection of teas. Head out the back door to the adjoining business, which serves ice cream and homemade desserts.

INFORMATION AND SERVICES

The **Oregon Dunes NRA Visitor Information Center** (885 U.S. 101, Reedsport 97467, 541/271-3611, www.fs.fed.us/r6/siuslaw) and **Reedsport Chamber of Commerce** (541/271-3495 or 800/247-2155, www.reedsportcc.org) share a building at the junction of U.S. 101 and Highway 38. Mid-May through mid-September, it's open 8 A.M.–4:30 P.M. weekdays and 10 A.M.–4 P.M. weekends; open weekdays only the rest of the year.

SOUTH COAST

Stretching from the Coos Bay area to the California border, the southern Oregon coast is far from the population centers of Oregon's interior valleys, but the south coast amply rewards visitors who make the effort to get here. The foothills of the Klamath Mountains tumble down the narrow coastal plain and fall off in precipitous headlands at the ocean's edge. Close to shore, the waters are a rocky garden of sea stacks and islets that are home to uncounted flocks of pelagic birds. With half a dozen wild rivers slicing through the mountains to the sea, the south coast is famed for its outstanding salmon fishing, especially on charters from the harbors of Charleston, Gold Beach, Bandon, and Brookings.

In addition, the southern region is blessed with the fairest weather on the Oregon coast and generally gets the most sunshine, least rain, and warmest temperatures—attributes as appealing to visitors as to the area's many retirees and other transplants.

Scenic highlights of the south coast include the weather-beaten bluffs and formal gardens at Cape Arago and Shore Acres State Parks, the gorgeous scenery of Boardman and Harris Beach State Parks, and just about every inch of the drive between Brookings and Port Orford.

In addition to fishing, recreational opportunities are seemingly endless: Outstanding courses draws golfers to Bandon (*Golf* magazine hailed Bandon Dunes as one of the country's top three courses) and Brookings (where the Salmon Run Golf Course is alongside the Chetco River), some of the coast's top windsurfing is near Cape Sebastian, and popular

© STEFANO BONI

HIGHLIGHTS

◖ South Slough Estuarine Research Reserve: Here, where freshwater meets saltwater, is a nutrient-rich environment that supports many wildlife species. Hike or paddle, but either way, pay attention to the tides (page 152).

◖ Bandon Dunes Golf Resort: This links-style course on the coastal headlands is evocative of Scotland. There are three golf courses here now, each expertly designed in a strikingly gorgeous setting, even for the Oregon coast (page 165).

◖ Humbug Mountain: The three-mile trail to the top of Humbug Mountain passes a spectacular array of native plants. Even if the promised mountaintop view is shrouded in fog, it's a great hike (page 172).

◖ Cape Sebastian: Hike up Cape Sebastian for some of the most expansive views on the southern coast and a front-row seat for springtime whale-watching (page 178).

◖ Rogue River Jetboat Ride: Even diehard paddlers won't regret succumbing to a jetboat tour up the Rogue River. Boaters often get to see ospreys and eagles fishing along this stretch of river; even if wildlife doesn't show up, your tour operator will point out all sorts of interesting sights (page 179).

◖ Samuel H. Boardman State Scenic Corridor: North of Brookings, the roadbed winds hundreds of feet above the surf, allow-

ing you to peer down at one of the most dramatic meetings of rock and tide in the world. Trails lead down to secluded, often nearly deserted, beaches (page 188).

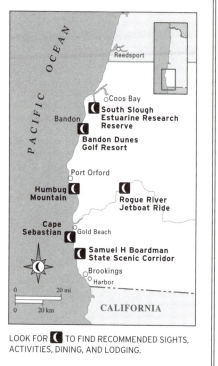

LOOK FOR ◖ TO FIND RECOMMENDED SIGHTS, ACTIVITIES, DINING, AND LODGING.

jetboat tours run up the Rogue River from Gold Beach.

PLANNING YOUR TIME

Coos Bay is the only real city along the southern coast and, like Tillamook to the north, it's a gateway to some spectacular areas, but pretty workaday itself. Be sure to head west and south from town to explore the coastal estuary at South Slough National Estuarine Research Reserve, south of Coos Bay. Bandon Marsh National Wildlife Refuge protects the largest remaining tract of salt marsh within the Coquille River estuary. Major habitats include undisturbed saltmarsh, mudflat, and Sitka spruce and alder riparian communities, which provide resting and feeding areas for migratory waterfowl, shore and wading birds, and raptors.

Of course, Bandon is now best known for its world-class Bandon Dunes Golf Resort, but there's also a real community here. Bandon's beachfront, along with the Coos Bay sandspit, the beaches on the western side of Humbug Mountain, and the isolated shorelines of Boardman State Park are choice beachcombing spots.

Port Orford is often overlooked, but it's one of our favorite spots, with great ocean vistas from town, and lots of hiking at nearby Humbug Mountain. It also doesn't hurt that there's good eating here.

Jetboat tours start in Gold Beach and head up the Rogue River, offering those with just a morning to spare the chance to explore this lush river. Between Gold Beach and Brookings, save some serious time to explore beaches sequestered between steep cliffs and pounding surf at the 11-mile-long Boardman State Scenic Corridor.

Charleston, Coos Bay, and North Bend

The towns around the harbor of Coos Bay—Charleston, Coos Bay, and North Bend—refer to themselves collectively as the Bay Area. In contrast to its namesake in California, the Oregon version is not exactly the Athens of the coast. Nonetheless, visitors will be impressed by the area's beautiful beaches, the largest oceanfront dunes in North America, and three wonderfully scenic and historic state parks. Because much of this natural beauty is on the periphery of the industrialized core of the Bay Area, away from U.S. 101, it's easy to miss. All that many motorists see upon entering Coos Bay/North Bend on the Coast Highway are the dockside lumber mills and foreign vessels anchored at the onetime site of the world's largest lumber port.

The little town of Charleston (pop. 700) to the southwest makes few pretenses of being anything other than what it really is—a bustling commercial fishing port. Processing plants here can or cold-pack tuna, salmon, crab, oysters, shrimp, and other kinds of seafood. The town might occasionally smell of fish, but the few restaurants and lodgings here are good values, and the town is the gateway to a trio of extraordinary state parks: Sunset Bay, Shore Acres, and Cape Arago.

To reach Charleston from points south, or to head south from town, take the interesting **Seven Devils Road,** which has its southern terminus about three miles north of Bandon. This route runs 13 miles alongside beaches, state parks, and an estuarine preserve.

SIGHTS
Coos Bay Harbor
A good place to take in the bustling bayfront is the **waterfront boardwalk and overlook pier** (U.S. 101 and Anderson Avenue) where you can check out the oceangoing freighters, visit a restored tugboat, and learn of the harbor's history courtesy of interpretive placards. A 400-gallon saltwater aquarium holds fish and other marinelife of Coos Bay. This is the largest coastal harbor between San Francisco and Puget Sound (more than 100 deepwater vessels call here each year), and it's fun to watch the ships docking and the portside wood-chip piles growing by dozens of feet overnight. Wood chips are Oregon's primary forest-product export. What had been considered surfeit slivers can now be made into a low-grade paper with the addition of chemicals during processing aboard the Japanese factory ships in the harbor.

Coos Art Museum
The Coos Art Museum (235 Anderson Ave., Coos Bay, 541/267-3901, www.coosart.org, open 10 A.M.– 4 P.M. Tues.–Fri., 1–4 P.M. Sat., $5 adults, $2 students and seniors), in downtown Coos Bay, is the Oregon coast's only art museum and features primarily 20th-century and contemporary works by American artists, including pieces by Robert Rauschenberg and Larry Rivers. Etchings, woodcuts, serigraphs, and other prints make up a large part of the permanent collection, which includes several of Janet Turner's richly detailed depictions of birds in natural settings. Other highlights include

SOUTH COAST

SOUTH COAST

To Florence
Gardiner
Reedsport
Umpqua R
38
Winchester
Bay
Eel Lake
Lakeside
N Tenmile
Lake
Oregon Dunes
National Recreation
Area
Tenmile Lake
101
PACIFIC
Allegany
North Bend
OCEAN
Coos Bay
Charleston
Coos
Bay
S Fork Coos R
Cape Arago
SOUTH SLOUGH ESTUARINE
RESEARCH RESERVE
Sumner
Coquille
Point
Coquille
Dora
425
Bandon
Norway
Myrtle Point
BANDON DUNES
GOLF RESORT
42
Bridge
To Roseburg
Langlois
South Fork Coquille R
Denmark
Powers
Cape
Blanco
Sixes
Port Orford
Siskiyou
National
River
HUMBUG MOUNTAIN
Forest
Ophir
Agness
Rogue
Illinois River
Wedderburn
ROGUE RIVER
JETBOAT RIDE
Gold Beach
101
Kalmiopsis
Wilderness
CAPE SEBASTIAN
River
Carpenterville
Klamath
SAMUEL H BOARDMAN
STATE SCENIC CORRIDOR
Mountains
Brookings
Harbor
0   10 mi
OR
CA
0   10 km
To Crescent City
© AVALON TRAVEL PUBLISHING, INC.

Kirk Lybecker's photo-realistic watercolors. Don't miss the Prefontaine Room on the second floor of the museum. Photos, trophies, medals, and other memorabilia of this native-son world-class runner illustrate his credo: "I want to make something beautiful when I run."

In addition to the permanent collection, recurring events worth detouring for are the May–June juried show of artists from the western states, and the Maritime Art Exhibit, August–mid-September.

Coos County Historical Museum

The Coos County Historical Museum (1220 Sherman Ave., North Bend 97459, 541/756-6320, www.cooshistory.org, open 10 A.M.–4 P.M. Tues.–Sat., $2) is located near the south end of the Conde McCullough Bridge, one of several distinctive Depression-era high-wire acts by Oregon's master bridge-builder. The museum houses more than the usual bric-a-brac from earlier eras, thanks largely to the region's heritage as a shipping center. An early-1900s Regina music box, a piano shipped around Cape Horn, miniature boat models, and a jade Chinese plaque, as well as Coos Indian beadwork and other artifacts, make this collection especially memorable. Outside, old-time logging equipment and a 1920s steam train are also worth a look.

Sunset Bay State Park

The Cape Arago Highway west of Charleston leads to some of the most dramatic beaches and interesting state parks on the coast. Among the several beaches on the road to Cape Arago, the strand at Sunset Bay State Park (13030 Cape Arago Hwy., 541/888-4902 information, 800/452-5687 reservations) is the big attraction because its sheltered shallow cove, encircled by sandstone bluffs, is warm and calm enough for swimming, a rarity in the Pacific Ocean north of Santa Barbara, California. In addition to swimmers, divers, surfers, kayakers, and boaters, many people come here to watch the sunset. Local legend tells that pirates hid out in this well-protected cove.

A four-mile cliffside segment of the Oregon

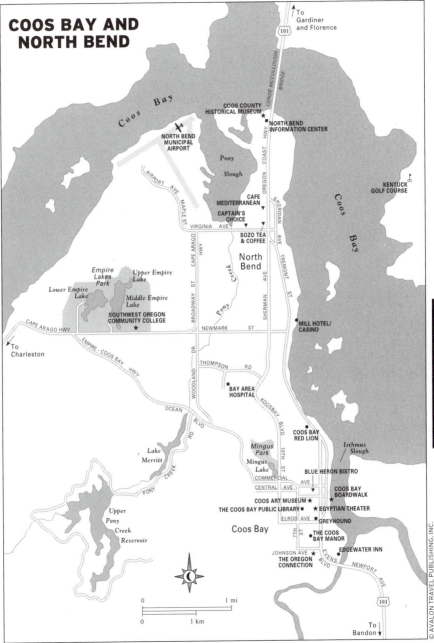

COOS BAY AND NORTH BEND

Coos Bay

To Gardiner
and Florence
101

COOS COUNTY
HISTORICAL MUSEUM

NORTH BEND
INFORMATION CENTER

NORTH BEND
MUNICIPAL
AIRPORT

Pony
Slough

KENTUCK
GOLF COURSE

Coos Bay

CAFE
MEDITERRANEAN

CAPTAIN'S
CHOICE

VIRGINIA AVE

SOZO TEA
& COFFEE

North Bend

AIRPORT AVE

MAPLE ST

CAPE ARAGO HWY

SHERIDAN AVE

TREMONT ST

Empire
Lakes
Park

Upper Empire
Lake

Lower Empire
Lake

Middle Empire
Lake

SOUTHWEST OREGON
COMMUNITY COLLEGE

Pony Creek

BROADWAY ST

SHERMAN AVE

NEWMARK ST

MILL HOTEL/
CASINO

To
Charleston

EMPIRE - COOS BAY HWY

WOODLAND DR

THOMPSON RD

BAY AREA
HOSPITAL

OCEAN BLVD

KOOSBAY BLVD

COOS BAY
RED LION

Isthmus
Slough

Lake
Merritt

PONY CREEK RD

Mingus
Park

Mingus
Lake

10TH ST

BLUE HERON BISTRO

COMMERCIAL

CENTRAL AVE

COOS BAY
BOARDWALK

COOS ART MUSEUM

THE COOS BAY PUBLIC LIBRARY

EGYPTIAN THEATER

ELROD AVE

GREYHOUND

Upper
Pony
Creek
Reservoir

Coos Bay

7TH ST

THE COOS
BAY MANOR

EDGEWATER INN

JOHNSON AVE
THE OREGON
CONNECTION

EVANS BLVD

NEWPORT AVE

0   1 mi

0   1 km

To
Bandon
101

SOUTH COAST

© AVALON TRAVEL PUBLISHING, INC.

© PAUL LEVY

Sunset Beach, west of Coos Bay, is known for its relatively warm water and calm conditions.

Coast Trail from Sunset Beach south is the best way to appreciate the sea stacks and islands between here and Cape Arago. Good views of Cape Arago Lighthouse across the water can be had along this route. Listen for its unique foghorn. For a shorter hike, follow the signs from the mouth of Big Creek to the viewpoint overlooking Sunset Bay.

Shore Acres State Park

Less than one mile south of Sunset Bay at Shore Acres State Park (541/888-3732, open 8 A.M.–sunset year-round, $3 per vehicle or Oregon Coast Passport), the grandeur of nature is complemented by the hand of man. The park is set on the grounds of lumber magnate and entrepreneur Louis J. Simpson's early-1900s mansion, which began as a summer home in 1906 and grew into a three-story mansion complete with an indoor heated swimming pool and large ballroom. Originally a Christmas present to his wife, Shore Acres became the showplace of the Oregon coast, with formal and Japanese gardens even-

tually added to the 743-acre estate. After a 1921 fire, a second, larger (two stories high and 224 feet long) incarnation of Simpson's "shack by the beach" was built. Over the following years the building fell into disrepair; the house and grounds were ceded to the state in 1942. Because of the high cost of upkeep, the mansion had to be razed, but the gardens have been lovingly maintained.

The gardens here are compelling attractions, but the headland's rim is more dramatic. Perched near the edge of the bluff, on the site formerly occupied by the mansion, a glass-enclosed observation shelter makes a perfect vantage point from which to watch for whales or marvel at the crashing waves. When there's a storm, the waves really slam into the sandstone reefs and cliffs, hurling up tremendous fountains of spray. It's not uncommon to feel the spray atop the 75-foot promontory. The history of the Simpson family is really the history of the Bay Area, and their story is captioned beneath period photos in the observation gazebo and in the garden

COOS BAY SHIPWRECKS

The *Captain Lincoln*, whose grounding on the treacherous North Spit of Coos Bay led to settlement of the area, would not be the last ship to meet its end on these dangerous shores. In 1910, the *Czarina* foundered in heavy seas on the bar; 24 people were killed in one of the worst shipwrecks on Oregon's south coast. The *Claremont* and the *Santa Clara* both wrecked on the bar in 1915, and the *Sujameco* grounded on Horsfall Beach in 1929. Although most of the ship was removed during salvage operations, iron projections can still sometimes be seen in the sand at the low tide.

The most recent and infamous shipwreck here, though, was the February 4, 1999 grounding of the 640-foot wood-chip carrier *New Carissa*, on the North Spit. After the Coast Guard firebombed the freighter in an attempt to burn off the 150,000 gallons of fuel oil on board, the vessel broke into two parts. After weeks of failed attempts, the bow section was finally towed out to sea and sunk in 10,000 feet of water by a Navy torpedo. Most of the stern was finally removed, but a section of it remains mired in the sand on the North Spit, just beyond the surf. During the shipwreck and months of salvage efforts, the hulk leaked some 70,000 gallons of oil, which killed an estimated 2,400 seabirds and destroyed oyster beds. The media circus that sprang up around the site generated a temporary economic boomlet for the region, but the long-term ecological damage is still to be determined.

in a small enclosure at the west end of the floral displays.

In the seven acres of neatly tended gardens, set back from the sea, the international botanical bounty culled by Simpson clipper ships and schooners is still in its glory, complemented by award-winning roses, rhododendrons, tulips, and azaleas. A restored gardener's cottage with antique furnishings stands at the back of the formal gardens. It's open for special occasions and during the winter holidays. Also in the garden, note the copper egret sculptures at the pond and the greenhouse for rare plants from warmer climes.

From Thanksgiving through New Year's, during the annual **Holiday Lights and Open House,** the gardens are decorated with 250,000 colored lights and other holiday touches, open 4–10 P.M. daily. The gardener's cottage opens and serves free refreshments during this time.

If you bear right and follow the pond's contours toward the ocean, you'll come to a trail. Follow it north for cliffside views of the rock-studded shallows below. Southward, the trail goes downhill to a scene of exceptional beauty. From the vantage point of a small beach, you can watch waves crash into rocks with such force that the white spray appears to hang suspended in the air. Exploring tidepools and caves, as well as springtime swimming in a cove formed by winter storms on the south side of the beach, are pursuits for the active traveler here. In summer, thimbleberries and salal growing along the trail down to the beach can provide sustenance for these activities.

Cape Arago State Park

A little more than one mile south of Shore Acres is Cape Arago State Park (800/551-6949, day-use only, free), at the end of the Cape Arago Highway. Locals have made much of the fact that this was a possible landing site of the English explorer Sir Francis Drake in 1579, and they put a plaque here commemorating him.

Beachcombers can make their own discoveries in the numerous tidepools, some of the best on the coast. The south cove trail (find it past the picnic shelter) runs down to a sandy beach and the better tidepools. The north cove trail leads to more tidepools, good spots for fishing, and views of the colonies of seals and sea lions at Shell Island, including the most northerly breeding colony of enormous elephant seals.

SOUTH COAST

SOUTH COAST

© PAUL LEVY

Sir Francis Drake may have landed at rocky Cape Arago. Hike down and discover the beach for yourself.

Their huge pups, when just a month old, may already weigh 300–400 pounds. Note that the north trail closes March 1–June 30 to protect seal pups. The picnic tables on the headlands command beautiful ocean panoramas and are superbly placed for whale-watching.

South Slough Estuarine Research Reserve

Estuaries, where freshwater and saltwater interface, form some of the richest ecosystems on earth, capable of producing five times more plant material than a cornfield of comparable size, while supporting great numbers of fish, birds, and other wildlife. The South Slough of Coos Bay is the largest such web of life on the Oregon coast. The South Slough Estuarine Reserve Interpretive Center (Seven Devils Rd., 541/888-5558, www.southsloughestuary.org, open 8:30 A.M.–4:30 P.M. daily June–Aug., 8:30 A.M.–4:30 P.M. Mon.–Sat. Sept.–May, free), four miles south of Charleston, will help you coordinate a canoe trip through the estuary and offers guided hikes as well.

The center looks out over several estuarine arms of Coos Bay, the largest harbor between San Francisco Bay and the Columbia River. These vital wetlands nurture a variety of life forms, detailed by the placards captioning the center's exhibits. The coastal ecosystem is presented by the "10-minute trail" behind the interpretive center. The various conifers and the understory are clearly labeled along the gently sloping half-mile loop. Branch trails lead down toward the water for an up-close view of the estuary. Down by the slough, you may see elk grazing in marshy meadows and bald eagles circling above, while *Homo sapiens* harvest oysters and shrimp in these waters.

Beginning near the visitors center is the easy, three-mile **estuary study trail,** which follows Hidden Creek from the wooded uplands down the valley to a boardwalk that winds through fresh- and saltwater marshes and leads to several wildlife-observations points.

Whiskey Run Beach

Midway between Charleston and Bandon is

the quiet beach at Whiskey Run, whose ore-bearing sands spread gold fever down the south coast in the early 1850s. As many as 2,000 miners worked here until a storm washed away the deposit. Other forms of beachcombing at Whiskey Run and on the beaches to the north are still thriving, however. Agate-hunting after a season of winter storms and clamming at low tide make these solitary shorelines ideal places to forget worldly concerns. To get there, turn west from the lightly traveled Seven Devils Road onto Whiskey Run Road, and drive 1.5 miles to this county park.

New Carissa Shipwreck

In the winter of 1999, the freighter *New Carissa* ran aground off the north spit, north of the mouth of Coos Bay (see sidebar *Coos Bay Shipwrecks*). Although most of the wreckage has been removed, a large portion of the stern section was, in the summer of 2006, still mired in the sand. (Although plans are under way to remove the debris, many doubt it'll happen.) The site is accessible year-round via 4WD vehicle or by hiking 2.1 miles over sand from the paved road. To reach the shipwreck, turn west off U.S. 101 at the Oregon Dunes National Recreation area/ Horsfall Beach sign (north of the McCullough Bridge). Follow the road across the north bay and over the railroad tracks. At a fork in the road, take a left onto the Trans Pacific Parkway and follow the road south for a few miles to the Bureau of Land Management boat ramp. Go about 100 yards farther and the entrance to the North Spit road to the New Carissa is on the right. There are several openings along the road where you can get a glimpse of the New Carissa, but the best site is an overlook two miles down the road from the start of the North Spit access. During summer months, the dry sand areas of the North Spit beach are off limits, as this is one of the preferred nesting areas of the threatened snowy plovers. The Bureau of Land Management requires visitors to keep pets on leashes and stay in the wet sand portion of the beach to avoid disturbing the nesting shorebirds. Before making this drive, you might want to check with the **Coos Bay Visitor Center** (541/269-

0215 or 800/824-8486) to make sure the wreck is still visible.

Myrtlewood

To see Oregon coast folk art in the making, visit the **Oregon Connection** (1125 S. 1st St., Coos Bay, 541/267-7804), just off U.S. 101 at the south end of Coos Bay. The myrtlewood factory tour shows you how a myrtlewood log gets fashioned into bowls, clocks, tables, and other utensils. No admission is charged for this 25-minute guided run through a working factory. After you're done, the store is a delight, with Oregon gourmet foods and crafts supplementing the quality woodwork.

In 1869, the golden spike marking the completion of the nation's first transcontinental railroad was driven into a highly polished myrtlewood tie. Novelist Jack London was so taken by the beauty of the wood's swirling grain that he ordered an entire suite of furniture. Hudson's Bay trappers used myrtlewood leaves to brew tea as a remedy for chills.

During the Depression, the city of North Bend issued myrtlewood coins after the only bank in town failed. The coins ranged from $0.50 to $10 and are still redeemable, although they are worth far more as collector's items.

Five miles north of North Bend, **The Real Oregon Gift** (3955 U.S. 101, 541/756-2220) is another large myrtlewood factory and showroom.

SPORTS AND RECREATION
Fishing

Spring chinook salmon, which sometimes exceed 30 pounds and are renowned as an unrivaled dining treat, offer prime fishing in Coos Bay. However, their population levels and fishing rules vary from year to year. Fall chinook and hatchery-reared coho salmon runs have had generally healthy runs in recent years. Mid-August through November, Isthmus Slough sees a good return of fin-clipped cohos. In saltwater, chinook and coho are found in good numbers within a one- to two-mile radius of the mouth of Coos Bay May–September, although the legal season varies; carefully check the regulations. Remnant striped bass are still occasionally caught in Coos Bay's sloughs and upper tidewater, but their numbers are diminishing.

Coos Bay is also one of the premier areas for crabbing and clamming. The Charleston Fishing Pier is a productive spot for crabs, while the best clamming spots are found along the bay side of the North Spit.

Fishing charters, bay cruises, whale-watching, and the like can be arranged through a number of charter outfits based at the Charleston Boat Basin. **Betty Kay Charters** (541/888-9021 or 800/752-6303, www.bettykaycharters.com) charges typical per-person prices: five hours of rock fishing, $62; five hours of salmon fishing, $82; 12 hours of tuna or halibut fishing, $170; and bay cruise, whale-watching, or eco-tour, $30. **Bob's Sportfishing** (541/888-4241 or 800/628-9633, www.bobssportfishing.com) is another charter operator.

Hiking

Twenty-five miles northeast of Coos Bay in the Coast Range is **Golden and Silver Falls State Park** (800/551-6949, www.oregonstateparks.org). Two spectacular waterfalls are showcased in this little-known gem of a park. Getting there involves driving east of Coos Bay along the Coos River, crossing to its north bank, and continuing along the Millicoma River through the community of Allegany. To find your way from Coos Bay, look for the Allegany/Eastside exit off U.S. 101. Beyond Allegany, continue up the East Fork of the Millicoma River to its junction with Glenn Creek, which ultimately leads to the park. The narrow, winding gravel roads make this half-hour trip unsuitable for a wide-body vehicle.

You can reach each waterfall by way of two half-mile trails. The 100-foot cataracts lie about one mile apart, and although both are about the same height, each has a distinct character. For most of the year, Silver Falls is more visually arresting because it flows in a near semicircle around a knob near its top. During or just after the winter rains, however, the thunderous sound of Golden Falls makes it more awe-inspiring of the two. Along the

trails, look for the beautifully delicate maidenhair fern.

Camping

Bastendorff Beach County Park (63379 Bastendorff Beach Rd., Charleston, 541/888-5353) is a conveniently and beautifully located park two miles west of Charleston just off the Cape Arago Highway. It's open for camping year-round, with RV and tent sites ($16–20, less off-season), as well as cabins ($30) and some hiker-biker sites. Campsites have drinking water, wood stoves, flush toilets, and hot showers (for an extra $2). Fishing, hiking, and a nice stretch of beach are the recreational attractions, plus there's a good playground for toddlers.

Even though the crowds at **Sunset Bay State Park** (13030 Cape Arago Hwy., Coos Bay, 541/888-4902, 800/452-5687 reservations) can make it seem like a trailer park in midsummer, the proximity of Oregon's only major swimming beach on the ocean keeps occupants of the 66 tent sites ($16) and 65 trailer sites ($20) here happy. The eight yurts go for $27, and primitive hiker-biker sites are $4. Facilities include laundry and showers, and a boat launch at the north end of the beach. This site, located three miles southwest of Charleston, is popular with anglers, who can cast into the rocky intertidal area for cabezon and sea bass.

Northwest of the Bay Area—2.5 miles north of the McCullough Bridge—is the Trans-Pacific Parkway, a causeway west across the water leading to Coos Bay's North Spit and the south end of the Oregon Dunes National Recreation Area, with four Siuslaw National Forest campgrounds and expansive dunes that draw off-road vehicle enthusiasts. The main **Horsfall Campground** is popular with crowds of noisy all-terrain vehicles and RVs. For more quiet and privacy, continue another mile on Horsfall Beach Road to **Bluebill Lake.** The 18 tent/RV sites are equipped with picnic tables and bathrooms, and the campground is open all year. Ask the campground hosts about area trails and the nearby oyster farm for the ultimate in campfire fare. Close by, **Horsfall Beach Campground** is located in the dunes next to

© JUDY JEWELL

Most Oregon state park campgrounds have yurts for rent.

the beach. Off-highway vehicle (OHV) access and beachcombing are popular activities. Showers are available two miles east at Horsfall Campground. One-half mile away, **Wild Mare Horse Camp** has beach and dune access and a dozen primitive campsites, each with a single or double horse corral. Each of these Siuslaw National Forest campgrounds charges $20 nightly year-round. Only Horsfall Campground takes reservations (877/444-6777, www.reserveusa .com) May–September.

Paddling

From a canoe or sea kayak, as you pass tide flats, salt marshes, forested areas, and open water, you can really begin to grasp the richness of the estuarine habitat at the **South Slough Estuarine Reserve** (541/888-5558, www.southsloughestuary.org). The estuary here has two main branches, offering plenty of territory for a day of exploration.

Although the waters here are placid, they are strongly influenced by the tides—be sure to consult tide tables as you plan an outing here.

Wind can also affect your trip: Know that in the spring and summer, the prevailing winds are from the northwest; in the winter they're from the southwest. At all times of year, the wind blows hardest in the afternoon.

Surfing and Swimming

The best spot on the Oregon coast for swimming is at **Sunset Bay State Park.** The water is warm enough for most adults and gentle enough for most kids.

Surfing is best just northeast of Sunset Bay, at **Bastendorff Beach County Park** (63379 Bastendorff Beach Rd., Charleston, 541/888-5353). The beach at Cape Arago can also be a good bet, though it requires a fairly steep downhill hike to get there.

Golf

There are two inexpensive public golf courses in the Bay Area: **Sunset Bay Golf Course** (11001 Cape Arago Hwy., Charleston, 541/888-9301, $23 weekends for nine holes; $21 weekdays), a nine-holer close to Sunset Bay State Park, and the 18-hole **Kentuck Golf Course** (675 Golf Course Ln., North Bend, 541/756-4464, $25 weekends for 18 holes, $13 for nine holes; $23 weekdays for 18 holes, $12 for nine holes), across the bay from North Bend along the Kentuck Inlet. Neither can hold a candle to the lush (and quite expensive) courses just to the south at Bandon Dunes.

Mill Casino

Occupying the former bayside site of the Weyerhaeuser mill alongside U.S. 101 in North Bend, the Mill Casino (3201 Tremont Ave., North Bend, 541/756-8800 or 800/953-4800, www.themillcasino.com) is operated by the Coquille tribe. Open 24 hours a day, the casino offers blackjack, lots o' slots, poker, and bingo. A large hotel, lounge, and several restaurants are on-site. Nightly entertainment includes jazz and R&B, while headliners lean toward country performers such as Wynonna and Kenny Rogers.

Yoga

In Charleston, try to catch a yoga class with Donna, a friendly and experienced teacher who has set up a very nice studio in the back of her clothing resale store, **Thrifty Fashions** (Oyster Cove Square, 63330 Boat Basin Rd., 541/888-4007). Call to check on class times.

Other Outings

Wavecrest Discoveries (P.O. Box 1795, Coos Bay 97420, 541/267-4027, http://wavecrestdiscoveries.com) offers a cornucopia of guided outdoor activities around the Bay Area and beyond, including clamming and tidepooling excursions, sea kayaking, dune and estuary tours, and more.

ENTERTAINMENT AND EVENTS

The **Dune Mushers Mail Run** (541/269-0215) is a noncompetitive endurance dogsled run held annually the first weekend in March. This is the world's longest organized dry-land run for dogsled teams. Small teams of 3–5 dogs and larger teams of 5–10 dogs haul mushers on wheeled buggies over 70 miles of dunes from North Bend to Florence. The smaller teams start off from Horsfall Beach on Friday, while the larger teams leave the next morning. En route, spectators have opportunities to watch the teams as they pass through Spinreel Park, Winchester Bay, Gardiner, and Florence's South Jetty area, to finish up with a parade through Old Town Florence on Sunday. The "mail" carried by the dog teams are commemorative envelopes, which are sold as souvenirs to support the event.

The first event of note in summer is the **Oregon Coast Music Festival** (P.O. Box 663, Coos Bay 97420, 541/267-0938 or 877/897-9350, www.oregoncoastmusic.com, tickets $5–18), which runs for two weeks in mid-July and has been going on for more than 25 years. Coos Bay is the central venue for these south coast classical, jazz, pop, and world music concerts, but Bandon, North Bend, Charleston, and other neighboring burgs host some performances as well.

In late August, the ubiquitous Oregon blackberry is celebrated with the **Blackberry Arts Festival** (541/888-1095 or 541/888-6572). Food and wine-tasting booths, a juried arts-and-crafts show, and entertainers fill the Coos Bay Mall (Central Avenue in downtown Coos Bay).

In mid-September, perhaps the best-known Bay Area figure, Steve Prefontaine, is honored with a 10K race and two-mile walk in the annual **Prefontaine Memorial Run** (541/269-1103, www.prefontainerun.com). Prefontaine was a world-class runner whose gutsy style of running and record performances made him a major sports personality until his premature death at 24 years old in 1974. Many top-flight runners pay homage by taking part in the race. Events begin and end at the runner's alma mater, Marshfield High School (4th St. and Anderson Ave., Coos Bay).

Perhaps the best place to see migratory shorebirds in the Northwest each fall is the **Oregon Shorebird Festival** on Cape Arago, taking place the second weekend in September. Boat trips out to see albatrosses and other seldom-seen species that frequent the open ocean and excursions to the Bandon Marsh National Refuge and to Coos Bay to see plovers, loons, and a variety of other shorebirds are arranged through the **Cape Arago Audubon Society** (541/267-7208 or 541/756-5688).

The **Egyptian Theater** (229 S. Broadway, Coos Bay, 541/267-3456) is a movie house with a pharaonic motif that goes back to the 1920s, when many small towns took to emulating the opulence and foreign intrigue of such big-city movie houses as Graumann's Chinese Theater in Hollywood. Four first-run films are usually playing here.

Across the street, the players of the **On Broadway Theater** (226 S. Broadway, 541/269-2501) stage a changing program of live theater throughout the year, ranging from current Broadway hits to relatively unknown scripts to children's entertainment.

ACCOMMODATIONS

Some people take umbrage at the fact that many Bay Area accommodations face industrial sites. Nevertheless, there is no shortage of quiet places to stay, some of them quite nice. Unless you're just dropping off U.S. 101 for the night, consider staying in Charleston, for its fishing-village atmosphere and easy access to ocean beaches, South Slough, and fishing.

Charleston

C Captain John's Motel (63360 Kingfisher Dr., 541/888-4041, www.captainjohnsmotel.com, doubles from $50) is clean and quiet and has some units with kitchenettes. It's within walking distance of fishing, charter boats, clamming, and dock crabbing. Close by is a special fish- and shellfish-cleaning station and, with any luck, your dinner. Staying in Charleston also puts you close to state parks and within easy reach of laundry and postal services, as well as offering temperatures warmer than Coos Bay in winter and cooler in summer. The studio rates are a bit higher. Reserve well in advance for July and August; pets are allowed.

If you'd like to catch your own dinner, the

Plainview Motel (91904 Cape Arago Hwy., 541/888-5166 or 800/962-2815, http//plainviewmotel.com, doubles from $59) provides guests with crab rings and fishing poles. This small, older motel has 12 pet-friendly units, some with kitchens. Pets cost an extra $5.

Coos Bay

A costlier, more plush alternative is the **Coos Bay Red Lion** (1313 N. Bayshore Dr., 541/267-4141 or 800/RED-LION, doubles from $100). Large rooms with immense beds, thick pile carpets, and everything else in the way of little luxuries are characteristic of these units. This hotel is also distinguished by its restaurant, one of the best in town, as well as by a lounge with quality entertainment and a happy hour with complimentary hors d'oeuvres. A complimentary shuttle runs guests to and from the airport.

The Coos Bay Manor (955 5th St., 800/269-1224, doubles $135, full breakfast included) is the kind of place where a fluffy terrycloth robe and bubble bath sustain the first impressions made by the grand, high-ceilinged colonial-style home and eye-popping river views from the open-air second-floor breakfast balcony. The B&B's five spacious rooms have distinct decor; two of the rooms can become a suite for families.

The bayfront **Edgewater Inn** (275 E. Johnson Ave., 541/267-0423 or 800/233-0423, doubles $120–130) has loads of perks in addition to its location off the highway, facing the water. With 82 units, many with views and kitchens, the hotel also offers fitness and tanning rooms, indoor pool, spa and sauna, and meeting room.

North Bend

The Mill Hotel (3201 Tremont Ave., 541/756-8800 or 800/953-4800, www.themillcasino.com, doubles from $109) is located just south of the Mill Casino along the waterfront in a building that once housed a plywood mill. But rather than a mill-town ambience, this economic development project of the Coquille (pronounced ko-KWELL in native dialect) tribe expresses its owners' patrimony. The exterior of this three-story hotel is the same cedar that tribe members used to build their plank houses, and the fireplace in the lobby is made of Coquille River rocks. The canoe displayed behind the front desk was carved by tribal members and is part of an interpretive display that tells the story of the Coquilles. Rooms feature views of oceangoing ships and well-appointed furnishings, including Internet access. Look for discount deals throughout the year.

Also popular with the casino crowd is the **Ramada Inn** (1503 Virginia Ave., 541/756-3191 or 800/272-6232, doubles from $86), just five blocks from U.S. 101. With 96 units and the standard chain hotel amenities, this hotel provides a quiet escape.

A less expensive alternative just north of the McCullough Bridge is the **Bay Bridge Motel** (33 Coast Hwy., 541/765-3151 or 800/557-3156, doubles $60–80), a small motel with good views of the bay from the higher-priced rooms.

FOOD

Oregon's Bay Area has many eateries where your nutritional needs can be met, if not in fine style then at least at the right price. Oddly enough, prime rib is a recurring special in this coastal town. There is no shortage of seafood places along this part of the coast, but you'll find the freshest, cheapest maritime morsels close to where they're caught.

Charleston

You can't go too far wrong looking for a fresh seafood meal down at the docks—a number of casual restaurants (some more like shacks) cluster here, including one spot where the crab cooker is always on.

The hot restaurant of the moment in the Bay Area is casual but upscale **Oyster Cove Grill** (63346 Boat Basin Rd., 541/888-0703, open for dinner Tues.–Sun., main courses $18–35), with seafood every bit as fresh as it should be and tastier than you'll generally find it. The simple preparations of wild salmon or Alaskan halibut are delicious, and the chef also has a way with Cajun spices—a crab-stuffed

halibut loaded with cheese and topped with spicy sauce ($27) is a worthy splurge. Steaks are also taken seriously here.

The Sea Basket (63502 Kingfisher Rd., 541/888-5711, open for breakfast, lunch, and dinner daily) typifies the good seafood, fast service, and relatively low prices in these parts. Oysters are especially tasty in this restaurant, with noted breeding farms close by. It is also famous for its BIGMAN burgers. The fluorescent glare above the cafeteria-style tables frequented by anglers in work-blackened denims may not count much for atmosphere, but you'll leave satisfied.

Close by, the somewhat classier **Portside** (63383 Kingfisher Rd., Charleston Boat Basin, 541/888-5544, open for lunch and dinner daily, dinner $13–34) has won several Silver Spoon Awards from the Diners Club in recent years. Fine dining in Charleston might seem a contradiction in terms, but the chance to select your own lobsters and crabs out of a tank, along with the sight of the fleet unloading other dinners just outside the door, would whet the appetite of any gourmet. Reserve ahead for the Friday night all-you-can-eat seafood buffet at a reasonable price. You may want to pass on the karaoke, depending upon your singing prowess.

Just before the Charleston Bridge, the **Fisherman's Grotto** (91149 Cape Arago Hwy., 541/888-3251, open for lunch and dinner daily, main courses $8–20) is a good place for fish and chips or standard seafood dinners. If you're an oyster lover, you'll certainly want to visit **Qualman's** (4898 Crown Point Rd., 541/888-3145). Just look for the signs on the north side of the Charleston Bridge on the east side of the highway. Open 10 A.M.–5:30 P.M., it sells fresh, high-quality oysters. Several other oyster purveyors make this delicacy available at other Bay Area outlets.

Coos Bay

Even though the **Blue Heron Bistro** (110 W. Commercial Ave., 541/267-3933, open for lunch and dinner Mon.–Sat., dinner Sun.) is located in the heart of downtown Coos Bay, it evokes dining experiences in San Francisco, Portland, or some other place far from this logging port. This impression can come from opening the door to the restaurant or opening the menu. The restaurant's tile floors, newspapers on library-style posts, and international posters adorning the walls are in keeping with a European-influenced bill of fare. The extensive menu's eclectic array ranges from Greek salad to Cajun-style blackened fish and emphasizes the freshest ingredients (nitrite-free German sausage) and a creative interpretation whenever possible. An impressive list of microbrews and imports, as well as Oregon, California, and European wines, will complement whatever dish you order. Best of all, for not much more than you'd pay at Denny's, you can enjoy an oasis of refinement in Timbertown, U.S.A.

For old-school Italian food, try **Benetti's** (290 S. Broadway, 541/267-6066, dinner nightly, $9–19). Here the spaghetti can be tailored to satisfy the pickiest seafood-hater, and the less fussy can enjoy both the warm atmosphere (hang around long enough and you'll learn that Joe Benetti is the mayor of Coos Bay) and the lasagna.

The dining room at **Brickstones** at the Coos Bay Red Lion (1313 N. Bayshore Dr., 541/267-4141, ext. 305, breakfast, lunch, and dinner daily) offers extra-thick cuts of prime rib and flambéed items prepared tableside that are as much a treat to look at as to taste. This restaurant is an "in" place to eat out, so make reservations. The smoked prime rib is recommended. For a "logging camp breakfast," locals recommend the **Timber Inn Restaurant** (1001 N. Bayshore Dr., 541/267-4622), where it's served all day long.

North Bend

A prime rib special is usually on the menu at the **Mill Casino** (800/953-4800) on the east side of U.S. 101 in North Bend. The restaurant's windows on Coos Bay make the bargain meal of prime rib, salad, vegetables, dessert, and beverage taste even better. Even if you miss the special, you'll appreciate that the restaurant

is open 24 hours. A seafood buffet on Friday and other buffets are featured throughout the week for less than $12.

For sit-down or takeout seafood, the **Captain's Choice** (1210 Virginia Ave., 541/756-0125) serves enormous pots of clam chowder and oyster stew but also has plenty of "steak and [insert your favorite seafood here]" selections for about $10.

If you've had enough of the standard coastal fare, try ◖ **Cafe Mediterranean** (1860 Union St., 541/756-2299, 11 A.M.–9 P.M. Mon.–Fri., 3–9 P.M. Sat., $4–12) for Middle Eastern–style Mediterranean food, including a locally loved lentil soup, in a friendly, relaxed setting.

Stop in at **Sozo Tea and Coffee** (1955 Union St., 541/746-4634, 9 A.M.–9 P.M. Mon.–Thurs., 9 A.M.–11 P.M. Fri.–Sun.) and you may find yourself lingering with a pastry or dessert, just to absorb the warm atmosphere.

Natural-food fans converge at **Coos Head Natural Foods** (1960 Sherman Ave., 541/756-7264), which has the largest selection of certified organic produce and food on the south coast.

INFORMATION AND SERVICES

The **Bay Area Chamber of Commerce** (50 E. Central Ave., Coos Bay, 541/269-0215 or 800/824-8486, www.oregonsbayareachamber. com, open 9 A.M.–5 P.M. Mon.–Fri., 10 A.M.–4 P.M. Sat., noon–4 P.M. Sun.) is five blocks west of U.S. 101 off Commercial Avenue.

The Coos Bay World is the largest daily paper on the south coast. In May and August, catch its "Let's Go" section on area getaways.

For health care and emergencies, the **Bay Area Hospital** (1775 Thompson Rd., Coos Bay, 541/269-8111), one-half mile west of U.S. 101 via Newmark Street, is the south coast's largest medical facility.

The Coos Bay **post office** (4th St. and Golden, Coos Bay 97420, 541/267-4514) is two blocks west of the highway, just south of city center.

Wash-a-Lot (1921 Virginia Ave., North Bend, 541/756-5439) is the local version of a fast-disappearing American institution—the all-night launderette.

The **Coos Bay Public Library** (525 W. Anderson Ave., 541/267-1101) is open 10 A.M.–7 P.M. Monday–Thursday and noon–6 P.M. Friday and Saturday. For ATM or banking needs, the Coos Bay **Bank of America** (245 S. 4th St.) has it all.

GETTING THERE AND AROUND

Recent improvements to Highway 42 make it possible to get to and from Roseburg, 87 miles from Coos Bay, in less than two hours. Motorists should still be aware that this thoroughfare carries more truck traffic than any other interior-to-coast road in Oregon. But weekenders will usually encounter few trucks and light traffic.

Coastal Express buses (800/921-2871) run up and down the south coast weekdays only between North Bend and the California border. **Porter Stage Lines** (541/269-7183) also runs along the southern Oregon coast, then turns inland at Florence and goes to Eugene, Bend, and Ontario. If the bus doesn't fit into your plans (or your style), consider the **North Bend Airport** at the north end of town. **Horizon Air** (800/547-9308) flies between the Bay Area and Portland daily. To get to the airport, follow the signs on the road between Charleston and North Bend.

Public transportation in the Bay Area is limited. The one bus line makes a loop in Coos Bay and North Bend, and **Dial-A-Ride** (541/267-7111) operates on-call 8:30 A.M.–4:30 P.M. daily.

Bandon and Vicinity

In contrast to the glitzy tourist trappings of some of the larger coastal towns, Bandon-by-the-Sea (pop. 2,900) is characterized by the style and grace of an earlier era. The glory that was Bandon is alive and well in Old Town, a picturesque collection of shops, galleries, restaurants, and historical memorabilia. The coast highway finally re-encounters the coast at Bandon, after long inland stretches of pastureland and forests to the south and north.

Although logging, fishing, dairy products, and the harvest of cranberries have been the traditional mainstays of the local economy, in the early part of the 20th century Bandon also enjoyed its first tourism boom. In addition to being a summer retreat from the heat of the Willamette Valley, it was a port of call for thousands of San Francisco–Seattle steamship passengers. This era inspired such tourist venues as the Silver Spray dance hall and a natatorium with a saltwater swimming pool. The golden age that began with the advent of large-scale steamship traffic in 1900, however, came to an abrupt end following a devastating

fire in 1936 that destroyed most of the town. The blaze was started by the easily ignitable gorse weed, imported from Ireland (as was the town's name) in the mid-1800s. Dramatic descriptions of the townspeople fighting the flames with their backs to the sea earned the incident a citation as one of the Top 10 news stories of the year.

The facelift given Old Town decades later, and the subsequent tourist influx, conjured for many the image of the mythical phoenix rising from its ashes to fly again. On the wings of the recovery, Bandon has established itself as a town rooted in the past with its eyes on the future. Today, Bandon is a curious mixture of provincial backwater, destination resort, and new-age artist colony. Backpack-toting travelers from all over the world flock to this town because of its beaches, its cultural and recreational pursuits, and its European-style hostelry. They coexist happily with the large population of retirees, award-winning artisans, and locals who seem to have cornered the market on late-model pickups with gun racks.

SIGHTS

One of the appealing things about Bandon is that most of its attractions are within walking distance of each other. In addition, on the periphery of town is a varied array of things to see and do.

Old Town

Bandon's Old Town, much of which dates from after the 1936 fire, is a half dozen blocks of shops, cafés, and galleries squeezed in between the harbor and the highway. The renovated waterfront invites relaxed strolling, and crabbers and anglers pull in catches right off the city docks. The small commercial fleet based here pursues salmon and tuna offshore.

Preservation buffs should check out **Masonic Hall** (2nd St. and Alabama St.), one of the few buildings to have survived Bandon's 1914 and 1936 blazes. A photo in the historical museum shows the same building and surrounding structures on Alabama Street (then called

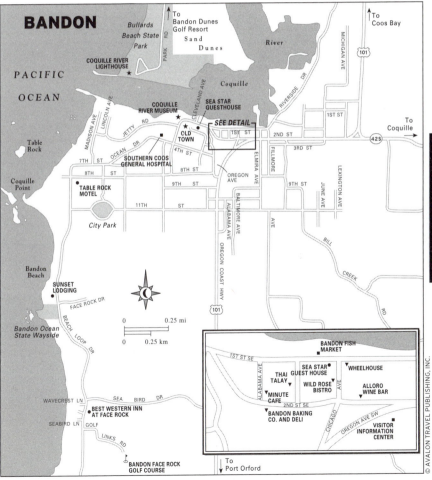

© AVALON TRAVEL PUBLISHING, INC.

SOUTH COAST

CRANBERRIES

From the vantage point of U.S. 101 between Port Orford and 10 miles north of Bandon, you'll notice what appears to be reddish-tinged ground in flood-irrigated fields. If you get close, you'll see cranberries, small evergreens that creep along the ground and send out runners that take root. Along the runners, upright branches 6-8 inches long hold pink flowers and fruits.

These berries are cultivated in bogs to satisfy their tremendous need for water and to protect them against insects and winter cold. Bandon leads Oregon in this crop, with an output ranking third in the nation. Oregon berries are often used in cranberry juice production by Ocean Spray because of their deep red pigment and high vitamin C content.

It is possible to arrange a visit to see some of these bogs – the most interesting time is during the late autumn harvest. **Faber Farms** (519 Morrison Rd., 541/347-1166) offers free tours through bogs 10 A.M.-4 P.M. Monday-Saturday from June through mid-November. A sweeter encounter can be found at **Cranberry Sweets** (1st St. and Chicago St., Bandon, 800/527-5748, open 9 A.M.-5:30 P.M. daily). Herein are confections ranging from cranberry fudge to cranberry truffles. Sugar fans will be glad it's open seven days a week.

Oregon bogs were producing wild cranberries when Lewis and Clark first traded with the Indians for them in 1805. Shortly thereafter, cultivated bogs were developed in Massachusetts, which, like Oregon, has acidic soils with lots of organic materials conducive to berry production. By the California gold rush of 1849, East Coast growing and harvesting techniques had transformed Bandon's marshes into commercial cranberry bogs. In the years to come, much of the modern equipment for harvesting these bogs was developed in Bandon. Wet-picking, for instance, is facilitated by the water reel, which is rotated to create eddies on the bog to shake berries off the vines. After they float to the surface, the cranberries are pushed by long booms toward a submerged hopper. They are then transferred by conveyor belt onto trucks. Walking through the bogs without trampling the berries is possible by fastening wooden platforms with short pegs to the soles of boots.

Without such innovations, Thanksgiving dinner wouldn't be the same. In order to bring the enormous annual volume of cranberries to the dinner table for the holidays, all of these harvesting techniques – as well as processing and packaging technology – are called into play.

Atwater) circa 1914. The photo depicts boardwalks leading to a woolen mill, old storefronts, a theater, and the Bandon Popular Hotel and Restaurant, outside which a horse and buggy await. The scene today has changed dramatically, but nonetheless an early-1900s charm still pervades the neighborhood.

Throughout Old Town are artists and artisans pursuing their crafts and selling their wares. **2nd Street Gallery** (210 2nd St., 541/347-4133, open 10 A.M.-5:30 P.M. daily) has a little of everything, from functional and art pottery to blown glass to paintings and sculptures. **Winter River Books and Gallery** (170 2nd St., 541/347-4111) has crystals, objets d'art, and a wide-ranging assortment of travel titles, photo essays, and fiction that makes this the best bookstore on the south coast.

Close by, the **Bandon Driftwood Museum and Art Gallery** (130 Baltimore Ave., 541/347-3719, open 9 A.M.-7 P.M. Mon.-Sat., 10 A.M.-6 P.M. Sun. in summer, call for winter hours) shows off an interesting collection of natural sculptures, from gnarly root balls to whole tree trunks. It's housed at the **Big Wheel General Store,** where you'll also find the Fudge Factory (24 flavors of homemade ice cream and butter fudge).

Bandon Historical Society Museum

This museum, at the corner of U.S. 101 and

© MICHAEL MCCLURE

Old Town Bandon

Fillmore Street (270 Fillmore St., 541/347-2164, open 10 A.M.–4 P.M. Mon.–Sat., 10 A.M.–3 P.M. Sun., closed Sun. in winter, $2 for adults, free for kids), in Bandon's former city hall, traces the history of the Coquille tribe and its forebears. The chronology continues with the steamers and the railroads that brought in white settlers. One room is devoted to Bandon's unofficial standing as the cranberry capital of Oregon. Black-and-white photos showing women stooping over in the bogs to harvest the ripe berries are captioned with such quips as this politically incorrect classic from an overseer: "I had 25 women picking for me, and I knew every one by her fanny." Color photos spanning five decades of Cranberry Festival princesses also adorn the walls.

Another room depicts Bandon's Resort Years, 1900–1931, when the town was called the Playground of the Pacific. The most compelling exhibits in the museum deal with shipwrecks and the fires of 1914 and 1936.

The Beach Loop

U.S. 101 follows an inland path for more than 50 miles between Coos Bay and Port Orford, but you can leave the highway in Bandon and take the four-mile Beach Loop for a lovely seaside detour south of town. Several access roads lead west from the highway to Beach Loop Drive (County Road 29), each about 0.25 mile from the others. Most people begin the drive by heading west from Old Town on 1st Street along the Coquille. Another popular approach is from 11th Street, which leads to Coquille Point. The south end of the drive runs through the northern portion of **Bandon State Natural Area,** providing parking, beach access, and picnic tables.

Along the fine stretch of beach are rock formations with such evocative names as Table Rock, Elephant Rock, Garden of the Gods, and Cat and Kittens Rocks. The whole grouping of sea stacks, included within the Oregon Islands National Wildlife Refuge, looks like a surrealist chess set cast upon the waters. The most eye-catching of all is **Face Rock,** Bandon's answer to New Hampshire's lately lamented Old Man of the Mountain. This basalt monolith resembles the face of a woman gazing skyward. An Indian legend says that she was a princess frozen by an evil sea spirit. Look for the Face Rock turnout 0.25 mile south of Coquille Point on the Beach Loop.

Despite its scenic and recreational attractions, the beaches south of town can be surprisingly deserted, perhaps because of the long, steep trails up from the water along some parts of the beach. In any case, this dearth of people can make for great beachcombing. Agates, driftwood, and tidepools full of starfish and anemones are commonly encountered here, along with bird-watching opportunities galore. Elephant Rock has a reputation as the Parthenon of puffins, while murres, oystercatchers, and other species proliferate on the other offshore formations.

Bullards Beach State Park

Two miles north of Bandon, bordering the Coquille River estuary and more than four miles of beachfront, Bullards Beach State Park (P.O. Box 25, Bandon 97411, 541/347-2209

or 800/551-6949 information, 800/452-5687 reservations) is a great place to fish, crab, bike, fly a kite, windsurf, picnic, or overnight in the large, sheltered campground. The beach and lighthouse are reached via a scenic three-mile drive paralleling the Coquille River. Look for jasper and agates amid the heaps of driftwood on the shore. Equestrian trails and horse camping facilities make this a popular destination for riders. The boat ramp gives anglers, kayakers, and canoeists access to the lower Coquille River and Bandon Marsh National Wildlife Refuge.

The riverside road going out to the Coquille's north jetty takes you through the dunes to the picturesque **Coquille River Lighthouse,** a squat tower with adjacent octagonal quarters. The last lighthouse built on the Oregon coast, it was completed in 1896 then abandoned in 1939 when the Coast Guard installed an automated light across the river. After years of neglect, the structure was restored in the late 1970s and is now open throughout the year. Etchings of ships that made it across Bandon's treacherous bar—and

waves at Bullards Beach State Park

© STEFANO BONI

some that didn't—greet you as you enter. Volunteers are on duty April–October to staff the gift shop and show you around.

West Coast Game Park

Seven miles south of Bandon is the West Coast Game Park (46914 U.S. 101 S., 541/347-3106, open 9 A.M.–7 P.M. daily June 15–August, 9 A.M.–5 P.M. spring and early fall, call for late fall and winter hours, $13 ages 13 and up, $8.50 ages 7–12, $5.50 ages 2–6, $12 seniors), the self-proclaimed largest wild-animal petting park in the country. There are 450 animals, represented by 75 different species, including tiger cubs, chimps, camels, zebras, bison, and snow leopards. Along with these exotics you'll also encounter such indigenous species as elk, bears, raccoons, and cougars. Visitors may be surprised to see a lion and tiger caged together, or a fox and a raccoon sharing the same nursery. The park tries raising different species together and often finds that animals can live harmoniously with their natural enemies. Free-roaming animals include deer, peacocks, pygmy goats, and llamas. An elk refuge is another popular area of the park. Even if you're not with a child, the opportunity to pet a pup, a cub, or a kit can bring out the kid in you. The park is open year-round, but call during winter because of restricted hours of operation.

SPORTS AND RECREATION

Bandon Marsh
National Wildlife Refuge

Bird-watchers flock to the Bandon Marsh National Wildlife Refuge (541/347-3683), especially in the fall, to take in what may be the prime birding site on the coast. The extensive mudflats attract flocks of shorebirds, including red phalaropes, black-bellied plovers, long-billed curlews, and dunlins, as well as such strays from Asia as Mongolian plovers.

Bandon Marsh lies a short paddle across the river from the state park, or via Riverside Drive, which runs from Bandon to U.S. 101 on the south side of the Coquille River bridge. The refuge protects more than 700 precious acres of the Coquille estuary's remaining saltmarsh habitat along the southeastern side of the river. Migrating waterfowl, bald eagles, California brown pelicans, and other birds feast on the rich food sources here. The refuge and its elevated observation deck are open daily from sunrise to sunset.

◖ Bandon Dunes Golf Resort

Bandon Dunes Golf Resort (57744 Round Lake Dr., Bandon, 541/347-4380 or 888/345-6008, www.bandondunesgolf.com) has drawn accolades from the golf press and is far and away the most spectacular place to golf in Oregon. The original course, Bandon Dunes has seven holes by the Pacific and unobstructed ocean views from all 18. Two other 18-hole courses, Pacific Dunes and Bandon Trails, give golfers a chance stay for a few days and keep encountering new territory.

To preserve the natural surroundings along the ocean bluffs, this Scottish links course doesn't allow carts (the only missing amenity here), so you'll have to hire a caddie or schlep your own bag. A luxurious resort with Pacific views from a sand dune and a restaurant are also here for those who come to worship in the south coast's Sistine Chapel of golf.

Golfers who have never played on the Oregon coast should come prepared for wind, especially in the afternoon. Oregon golfers, you may know about the wind, but we have a special piece of advice for you—dress up! This is one fancy place, and you'll feel out of place in your old baggy shorts and faded polo shirt.

It's one mile north of the Coquille River. Greens fees, June–September, are $185 for hotel guests, $240 for nonguests; during the rest of the year, rates run $75–130. Caddie fee is $50 per bag.

Other Golf

Duffers and other mortals may choose instead to tread the equally scenic seaside links two miles south of town at **Bandon Face Rock Golf Course** (3235 Beach Loop Rd., Bandon, 541/347-3818), where greens fees are a mere $10 for nine holes, $16 for 18 holes.

Fishing

The Coquille River runs 30 miles from its Siskiyou headwaters before meandering leisurely through Bandon. The north and south jetties are popular spots for perch and rockfish, while the city docks right in Old Town yield catches of perch and crab April–October and smelt July–September. The spring chinook run pales in comparison to those in the Rogue and Chetco to the south, but the fall runs of chinook (beginning Sept.–Oct.) and coho (Oct.–Nov.) are strong and productive. Steelhead usually arrive in November, and the run gathers steam January–February. A boat is necessary for the best steelhead and salmon water, but bank anglers can fish the mouth of Ferry Creek, just off Riverside Drive in Bandon. Fishing guides and gear can be arranged through the **Bandon Bait Shop** (1st St. and Alabama St., 541/347-3905), across from the boat basin. The shop also rents crab rings and other gear and can point you to productive spots for catching Dungeness crab.

Just off the south end of Beach Loop Drive, 30-acre **Bradley Lake,** protected from ocean winds by high dunes, offers good trout fishing and a boat ramp. Trophy rainbows averaging five pounds, reared at the Bandon Fish Hatchery east of town, are stocked here each spring.

Camping

Bullards Beach State Park (P.O. Box 25, Bandon 97411, 541/347-2209 or 800/551-6949 information, 800/452-5687 reservations) is a wonderful state park in a great location, between the Coquille River and four miles of beach. The park has 190 campsites ($16–20), 13 yurts ($27), eight horse-camping sites, and hiker-biker spaces. To get there, drive north of town on U.S. 101 for about one mile; just past the bridge on the west side of the highway is the park entrance. The beach is reached via a scenic two-mile drive paralleling the Coquille River. Electricity, picnic tables, and fire grills are provided. You'll also find a store, a café, a laundry room, horse-riding/camping facilities, an inviting sandy beach, summer evening campfire talks Tuesday–Saturday, and hiking trails.

Other Activities

On the waterfront in Old Town, **Adventure Kayak** (315 1st St., 541/347-3480, www .adventurekayak.com, open 10 A.M.–5 P.M. daily in summer) rents kayaks (from $30 for two hours), teaches classes on a variety of kayak techniques, and offers guided sea-kayak tours of the lower Coquille ecosystem (and farther afield) with a naturalist from $35 for a two- to three-hour paddle.

Bandon Beach Riding Stables (2640 Beach Loop Rd., 541/347-3423) is four miles south of Face Rock on the Beach Loop. Several beach rides are offered daily, plus sunset rides in the summer. Riders of all abilities are welcomed, including those with handicaps. Prices range $30–40 for a 1.5- to 2-hour ride. Reservations are advised. Open year-round.

ENTERTAINMENT AND EVENTS

The annual **Wine and Seafood Festival** happens every Memorial Day weekend at the Community Center in City Park off 11th Street West in Bandon. The event is free and includes live music, horse-drawn buggy rides, arts-and-crafts booths, and wine-tasting. Contact the chamber of commerce (541/347-9619) for details. The same weekend, competitors in the **Sandcastle Contest** create amazing sculptures out of sand, water, and imagination. This takes place on the beach off Beach Loop Drive at Seabird Lane. Construction starts at 9 A.M.; judging is at 1 P.M.

A fish fry, kayak and driftboat races, parade, and classic car and motorcycle show are highlights of Bandon's **Fourth of July** celebration; at dusk, fireworks are launched across the Coquille to burst above the river.

The biggest weekend of the year for Bandonians comes the second weekend in September, when the **Cranberry Festival** (541/347-9616) brings everyone together in Old Town for a parade, crafts fair, tours of a cranberry farm, and the Bandon High Cranberry Bowl—in which the local footballers take on traditional rival Coquille High.

During the late November to early January

holiday season, the merchants of Old Town and anglers deck their stores and boats with twinkling lights in the traditional **Festival of Lights.** Particularly striking is the Coquille River Lighthouse, lit up across the water like a Christmas tree.

ACCOMMODATIONS

For the best ocean views, often with nearby trails to the beach, look to the lodgings along the Beach Loop. If you want to be able to walk to dinner in Old Town, stay at one of the in-town locations. For the best of both worlds, bring a bike, and cycle into town from a Beach Loop room. Bandon bills itself as America's storm-watching capital, and special packages are often available October–March.

$50-100

Right in the heart of Old Town, the ◖ **Sea Star Guesthouse** (370 1st St., 541/347-9632 or 888/732-7871, www.seastarbandon.com, doubles $75–150) has a room and four suites with skylights, wood-beam ceilings, and views onto the harbor. Suites sleep two to six people and have cooking facilities. Sea Star also has hostel rooms facing a courtyard, including two rooms with bunk beds and a shared bath ($19 per person), a room with a private bath ($39), and a family room with kitchenette ($75). All units are nonsmoking, and no pets are permitted.

Head south of town along the Beach Loop to the pet-friendly **Table Rock Motel** (840 Beach Loop Rd., 541/347-2700 or 800/457-9141, www.tablerockmotel.com), which has nicely decorated and well-maintained older motel rooms for $55–90 and newer condo-type units from $109. Unfortunately, Bandon's construction boom is playing havoc with the views; ask when you make a reservation about the view from your room. Even if the view is of the new neighbor's trophy home, rest assured that there is a trail from the motel to an excellent stretch of beach.

Also on the Beach Loop is **Sunset Lodging** (1865 Beach Loop Rd., 541/347-2453 or 800/842-2407, www.sunsetmotel.com, dou-bles $60–150). With some units built right into the cliff above a scenic beach, the view here is hard to beat. Whether you're looking for rooms with a kitchen, rooms that accommodate pets, or rooms with a fireplace, there's something here for you. A hot tub, indoor pool, on-site laundry, and Lord Bennett's restaurant across the street also recommend this place. Nonetheless, the steep steps down the 80-foot-high bluff to the beach, the busy atmosphere of the place, and the rusticity of the least expensive rooms might not be to everyone's liking.

$100 and Up

Set on a bluff overlooking Old Town, the **Bandon Inn** (355 U.S. 101, 541/347-4417 or 800/526-0209, doubles from $109) has spectacular views and a path down to town. Pets are permitted in some rooms.

A favorite place to stay on the Beach Loop is the older-but-refurbished **Windermere Motel** (3250 Beach Loop Rd., 541/347-3710, www .windermerebythesea.com, doubles $105–170), where baby-boomers can relive their childhood beach getaways in cedar efficiencies or two-story condo-like units, situated on a bluff above a windswept beach. Housekeeping facilities and proximity to restaurants (Lord Bennett's) and West Coast Game Park also make this an ideal family vacation spot.

Another popular place is the **Best Western Inn at Face Rock** (3225 Beach Loop Rd., 541/347-9441 or 800/638-3092, doubles from $120). Part of its popularity has to do with the motel's location—set back from the road near the end of the beach loop, across the street from Bandon's coastline, and near the nine-hole golf course. Many of the modern, well-appointed rooms have magnificent ocean views. An indoor pool, fitness room, whirlpool, and restaurant also make this an especially good choice for active travelers. Some suites have fireplaces, kitchenettes, and private patios. There's an on-site restaurant and a short path to the beach.

For avid golfers, the **Lodge at Bandon Dunes** (57744 Round Lake Dr., 888/345-6008, www.bandondunesgolf.com, doubles

SOUTH COAST

from $180) is a deluxe resort at what is considered one of the country's finest courses. This is one of the most luxurious places on the Oregon coast. Lodging is in several different locations around the resort and includes single lodge rooms in various sizes, two- or four-bedroom suites, and cottages. View options vary from golf course and ocean views to dune and surrounding woods. Bandon Dunes is five minutes from Bandon, a mile north of the Coquille, and 30 minutes from the North Bend Airport, which is served by daily flights from Portland.

Vacation Rentals

Bandon is an easy place to spend a week, and there are several property-management companies that can help you find a house to rent.

Coastal Vacation Rentals (541/347-3009 or 800/336-5693, www.coastalvacationrentals.com) offers a broad range of properties, including a studio suitable for a single person or couple and several places that accept pets. Many of the places offered by **Exclusive Property Management** (541/347-3790 or 800/527-5445, www.visitbandon.com) are large and quite upscale, with great locations and lovely interior design. It also rents a few more modest homes, so don't be afraid to call or check the website.

Bandon Beach Vacation Rentals (54515 Beach Loop Rd., 541/347-4801 or 888/441-8030, www.bandonbeachrentals.com) has several units available, including one place that'll sleep 10 people.

The **Table Rock Motel** (840 Beach Loop Rd., 541/347-2700 or 800/457-9141, www.tablerockmotel.com) rents a couple of condos near the motel.

FOOD

Five miles south of Bandon, on the east side of U.S. 101, hit the brakes at **Misty Meadows Jams** roadside stand (48053 U.S. 101 S., 541/347-2575, open 8 A.M.–6 P.M.) for first-rate jams and jellies, including a variety of products incorporating Bandon cranberries. This family-owned and -operated business

has been making delicious concoctions from Oregon-grown fruits since 1970. In addition to preserves, the shop sells olives and fruit-based barbecue sauce, syrup, honey, and salsa.

Breakfast

If you're after a full breakfast, head to the **Minute Café** (145 2nd St., 541/347-2707, open 5:30 A.M.–8 P.M.), where locals and tourists settle in with the morning paper, omelettes, and pancakes. For coffee, granola, and excellent pastries, head across the street to the **Bandon Baking Co. and Deli** (160 2nd St., 541/347-9440).

Seafood

The unpretentious and extremely popular **Wheelhouse Seafood Grill** (1st St. and Chicago Ave., 541/347-9331, lunch and dinner daily, dinners about $20) uses fresh fish (which is, unfortunately, not always the case for the coast's high-volume restaurants) and does its deep frying with a beer batter that doesn't mask the taste of the food. The homemade soup is a specialty (as is the sirloin steak with prawns), especially the Cioppino Rick, using diverse shellfish and bottom fish in a marinara base. Meals here come with salad and side dishes, making it a relative bargain. This is a good bet for a family, or for a night when you're not up for a fancy restaurant.

For a more refined atmosphere, reserve a table at the **Wild Rose Bistro** (130 Chicago Ave., 541/347-4428, dinner nightly summer, Thurs.–Sun. winter, entrées $17–30), where abundant use is made of local produce. This place is small and intimate—it's probably the best choice in town for a romantic dinner. A tasty paella goes for $22; cioppino is $24.

Budget diners and smoked fish connoisseurs will appreciate the **Bandon Fish Market** (at the boat basin near the intersection of 1st St. and Chicago Ave., 541/347-4282). Heartier appetites call for the market's excellent fish and chips (takeout only). A picnic table outside by the harbor is the place to enjoy it all with a trip across the street to **Cranberry Sweets** for dessert.

If you don't want to leave the Beach Loop for dinner, **Lord Bennett's** (1695 Beach Loop Dr., 541/347-3663, open for lunch and dinner daily, dinner $15–20) cliffside aerie looks out over the breakers toward Bandon's most dramatic restaurant view. Lunch and dinner do justice to these surroundings with elegantly rendered seafood dishes. Recommended are the bouillabaisse, crab cakes, and blackened ahi. Jazz on selected evenings in the lounge is another nice touch.

The most elegant restaurant in Bandon is two miles north of town in the main lodge of the Bandon Dunes Golf Resort. Here, the **Gallery** (57744 Round Lake Rd., 541/347-4380, open for three meals daily, dinner $17–36) is a good place to eat an excellent steak, and the meatloaf is also a favorite. If you're not staying at the resort, lunch is an interesting time to get a feel for the place and to enjoy the views out onto the Bandon Dunes course, all for the price of a hefty $8 burger.

Italian
Although it's called a wine bar, ◖ **Alloro Wine Bar** (375 2nd St., 541/347-1850, open 3–10 P.M. Tues.–Sun., dinner $17–25) is the top choice in town for an Italian dinner and Oregon wine (you can also get a fine Barolo here). But don't come looking for spaghetti—the food is way more upscale than that. Look instead for duck breast served with cranberry salsa and polenta. The food here is excellent, and the pace relaxed. If you don't want a full dinner, there's a small bar where you can taste a flight of wines and nibble on olives or Italian cheeses.

Thai
Thai Talay (160 Baltimore St., 541/347-8074, open for lunch and dinner daily, closed Sunday in winter, lunch $6–9, dinner $8–13) serves surprisingly good Thai food, including excellent curries. This is probably the best deal in town for a delicious dinner in a simple, comfortable restaurant.

PRACTICALITIES
Information and Services
The **Bandon Chamber of Commerce** (300 W. 2nd St., Bandon, 541/347-9616, www.bandon .com), in Old Town, distributes a comprehensive guide and a large annotated pictographic map of the town. Ask about what they call "the best river fishing and crabbing docks on the coast."

Southern Coos General Hospital (900 11th St. S.E., 541/347-2426) features an ocean view that in itself is therapeutic, as well as an emergency room and facilities for coronary and respiratory care.

For banking services, the **Bank of America** (at U.S. 101 and 11th St.) should be able to accommodate you.

Getting There and Around
North- and southbound **Coastal Express** buses (800/921-2871) run three times daily, weekdays only, between North Bend and Brookings, stopping near the north end of Bandon at Ray's Food Place supermarket.

Between Bandon and Coos Bay, you can escape the tedium of U.S. 101's inland route by taking the **Seven Devils Road** about three miles north of Bandon. This route runs 13 miles to **Charleston,** a fishing village that sits closer to the ocean than its larger neighbors to the northeast, Coos Bay and North Bend. En route, beaches, state parks, and an estuarine preserve make the drive interesting, although the miles of heavily logged mountainsides may take you aback.

Port Orford and Vicinity

Port Orford marks the northernmost end of one of the most spectacular stretches of coastline in the nation. From Bandon, the highway runs inland; when it hits Port Orford, the road nearly runs into the Pacific. And what a splendid place to encounter the ocean! The beach here is perfect for long treasure-hunting walks, and the bluffs just to the north are also fun to explore. A few miles north, blustery Cape Blanco is the westernmost point of the continental United States; a short distance south, Humbug Mountain rises almost directly from the ocean. All of these places are great for a quick ogle and a snapshot, but even better for hiking and exploring. Port Orford is a good base for all of that, with a wide range of accommodations and a few good places to eat.

In spite of its knockout views and great recreation, the area is not especially prosperous. Commercial fishing and cedar logging were once the leading revenue producers. In recent years, tourism and many eclectic cottage industries have sprung up to supplement the boom/bust, resource-based economy. The outskirts of Port Orford host such diverse undertakings as an escargot-breeding farm, llama and sheep ranches, a goat-milk dairy, and commercial berry growers, as well as plots of land devoted to Christmas trees and exotic herbs. Offshore, divers harvest kelp for use as a food supplement and sea urchins to supply the Japanese with a popular aphrodisiac and seafood delicacy. In town, the stunning scenery and relatively low rents probably have played a role in the development of a passel of galleries here, evidencing a nascent artist colony.

SIGHTS AND RECREATION

Port Orford has an ocean view from downtown that is arguably the most scenic of any town on the coast. A waterfront stroll lets you appreciate the cliffs and offshore sea stacks, as well as the unique sight of commercial fishing boats being hoisted by large cranes into and out of the harbor. With only a short jetty on its north side, Port Orford's harbor, the only open-water port in Oregon, is unprotected from southerly swells, so boats can't be safely moored on the water. When not in use, the fleet rests on wheeled, trailer-like dollies near the foot of the pier.

A stroll or bike ride through town is a perfect way to visit Port Orford's **galleries.** These are, by and large, much different and far more interesting than the typical seaside-town collections of landscape paintings and sunset photos. Expect to find high-quality crafts, glass art, sculpture, and Internet-based art. Stop by the visitors center to pick up a gallery-walk brochure.

Battle Rock Park

As you come into town on U.S. 101, it's hard to ignore enormous Battle Rock on the shoreline, the site of the 1851 conflict between local Native Americans and the first landing party of white settlers. If you can make your way through the driftwood and blackberry bushes surrounding its base, you can climb the short trail to the top for a heightened perspective on the rockbound coast that parallels the town. You'll also notice the east-west orientation of the harbor. Once you get to the top of the rock, don't think that the battle is necessarily over. Bracing winds often chill you, and high tides can sometimes render this huge coastal extension an island. The rock is also the focus of a **Fourth of July Jubilee Celebration,** which reenacts the historic battle.

Even if you're not up for a scramble on Battle Rock, do walk the short path down to the beach, which is relatively sheltered from the wind and a good place for a walk. It's also a good spot for beachcombing, with agates and fishing floats being the prize finds.

If you'd rather do your scavenging inland, try searching the nearby foothills for the lost Port Orford meteorite. The meteorite was found in the 1860s by a government geologist, who estimated its weight at 22,000 tons.

PORT ORFORD INDIAN WARS

© PAUL LEVY

Boats are taken out of the water every night at Port Orford.

In 1850, the U.S. Congress passed the Oregon Donation Land Act, allowing white settlers to file claims on Indian land in western Oregon. This was news, of course, to the Indian nations of the region, who had not been consulted on the decision. William Tichenor, captain of the steamship *Gull*, hoping to exploit the new act, had ambitions to establish an outpost on the coast at what's now Port Orford. When Tichenor observed the hostility of the Quatomah band of Tututni Indians in the tidewater, he put nine men ashore on an immense rock promontory fronting the beach because of its suitability as a defensive position. The Indians besieged the rock for two weeks be-

fore the white men escaped under cover of night. Tichenor returned with a well-armed party of 70 men and succeeded in founding his settlement.

From this inauspicious beginning, "Awferd," as the locals call it, established itself as the first town site on the south coast. Shortly thereafter, the town became the site of the first fort established on the coast during the Rogue Indian Wars. This conflict started when gold miners and settlers came into Indian lands. As a result of the clashes, hundreds of local natives were rounded up and sent to the Siletz Reservation near Lincoln City in 1856.

Unfortunately, he was unable to locate the meteorite when he returned for another look.

Port Orford Heads State Park

Another shoreline scene worth taking in, featuring a striking panorama from north to south, is located up West 9th Street at what the locals call The Heads, Port Orford Heads State Park. If you go down the cement trail to the tip of the blustery headland, you look south to the mouth of Port Orford's harbor. To the north, many small rocks fill the water, along with boats trolling for salmon or checking crab pots. On clear days visibility extends from Cape Blanco to Humbug Mountain.

Also located here is the historic **Port Orford Lifeboat Station** (541/332-0521, open 10 A.M.–3:30 P.M. Thurs.–Mon. Apr.–Oct., free), built by the Coast Guard in 1934 to provide rescue service to the southern Oregon coast. After it was decommissioned in 1970, the officers' quarters, the pleasingly proportioned crew barracks, and other outbuildings were converted to a museum depicting the work of the station. A trail leads down to Nellie's Cove, site of the former boathouse and launch ramp.

◖ Humbug Mountain

Some people will tell you that 1,756-foot-high Humbug Mountain, six miles south of Port Orford on U.S. 101, is the highest mountain rising directly off the Oregon shoreline. Because the criteria for such a distinction varies as much as the tides, let's just say it's a special place. There's more than one version of how the peak, formerly called Sugarloaf Mountain, got its name. According to one version, gold miners who were drawn here in the 1850s by tales of gold in the black sands nearby soon discovered that the rumored riches proved to be "humbug."

Once the site of Native American vision quests, Humbug Mountain now casts its shadow upon an Eden-like state park campground surrounded by myrtles, alders, and maples. Just north is a breezy black-sand beach. A three-mile trail to the top of Humbug rewards

hardy hikers with impressive vistas to the south of Nesika Beach and a chance to see wild rhododendrons 20–25 feet high. Rising above the rhodies and giant ferns are bigleaf maple, Port Orford cedar, and Douglas and grand firs. Access the trail from the campground or from a trailhead parking area off the highway near the south end of the park. In addition, the **Oregon Coast Trail,** which follows the beach south from Battle Rock, traverses the mountain and leads down its south side to the beach at Rocky Point.

Prehistoric Gardens

What can we say about this unique roadside attraction, featuring a 25-foot-tall, Formica-green *Tyrannosaurus rex* standing beside the parking lot? Is it kitsch, or is it educational? You decide. In any case, if you've got children in the car, unless they're sleeping or blindfolded, you're probably going to have to pull over. Prehistoric Gardens (36848 U.S. 101, 541/332-4463, open 9 A.M.–dusk daily spring–fall, call for winter

The kids will make sure you don't miss the Prehistoric Gardens, south of Port Orford.

© MARK MORRIS

hours, $7 adults, $6 ages 11–17 and 65-plus, $5 children 3–10), about 10 miles south of Port Orford, is the creation of E. V. Nelson, a sculptor and self-taught paleontologist who began fabricating life-size dinosaurs here back in 1953 and placing them amid the lush rainforest on the backside of Humbug Mountain. Paths lead through the ferns, trees, and undergrowth to a towering brontosaurus, triceratops, and 20 other ferro-concrete replicas, painted in a dazzling palette of Fiestaware colors.

Cape Blanco State Park and Hughes House

Four miles north of Port Orford, west of U.S. 101, is Cape Blanco, whose remote appendages give you the feeling of being at the edge of the continent—as indeed you are, here at the westernmost point in Oregon. From the vantage of Cape Blanco, dark mountains rise behind you and the eaves of the forest overhang tidewater. Below, driftwood and 100-foot-long bull kelp on slivers of black-sand beach fan out from both sides of this earthy red bluff. Somehow, the Spaniards who sailed past it in 1603 viewed the cape as having a *blanco* (white) color. It's been theorized that perhaps they were referring to the fossilized shells on the front of the cliff.

With its exposed location, Cape Blanco really takes it on the chin from Pacific storms. The vegetation along the five-mile state park road down to the beach attests to the severity of winter storms in the area. Gales of 100-mph winds (the record winds were clocked at 184 mph) and horizontal sheets of rain have given some of the usually massive Sitka spruces the appearance of bonsai trees. An understory of salmonberry and bracken fern help evoke the look of a southeast Alaska forest.

Atop the weathered headland is Oregon's oldest, most westerly, and highest lighthouse in continuous use. Built in 1870, the beacon stands 256 feet above sea level and can be seen some 23 nautical miles out at sea. **Cape Blanco Lighthouse** (541/332-6774, open 10 A.M.–3:30 P.M. Tues.–Sun. Apr.–Oct., $2 adults, $1 children under 12) also holds the distinction of having had Oregon's first female lighthouse

© PAUL LEVY

Cape Blanco Lighthouse sits on a bluff at the westermost point of the continental United States.

keeper, Mabel E. Bretherton, who assumed her duties in 1903. Tours of the facility include the chance to climb the 64 spiraling steps to the top; this is the only operational lighthouse in the state that allows visitors into the lantern room, to view the working Fresnel lens.

Over the years, several shipwrecks have occurred on the reefs near Cape Blanco, including the *J. A. Chanslor,* an oil tanker that collided with the offshore rocks in 1919, with a loss of 36 lives.

Near Cape Blanco on a side road along the Sixes River is the **Hughes House** (541/332-0248, open 10 A.M.–3:30 P.M. Tues.–Sun. Apr.–Oct.), a restored Victorian home built in 1898 for rancher and county commissioner Patrick Hughes. Owned and operated today by the state of Oregon, the house serves as a museum and repository of antique furnishings. In addition to the regular season, it's also open during the winter holiday season, when punch and cookies are often served on the weekend before Christmas.

SOUTH COAST

Grassy Knob Wilderness

The Grassy Knob Wilderness encompasses 17,200 acres of steep, rugged terrain and protects rare stands of Port Orford cedar. The wood of this majestic, fragrant tree is light, strong, and durable. Its use in planes during World War II and in Japanese construction has made it highly valued, but a fatal root fungus spread by logging trucks accounts for its rarity and astronomically high price. (As you travel around the area, you may notice the dead or dying cedars.) During World War II, Japanese submarines used Cape Blanco Lighthouse as an orientation mark to aim planes loaded with incendiary bombs at the Coast Range. The Japanese hoped to ignite forest fires that would destroy the region's Port Orford cedar trees, which were used to construct airplanes then. Because of the perennial dampness, the results were negligible. A short (0.8 mile) but moderately difficult trail leads to the summit of Grassy Knob. To get there, follow U.S. 101 north of Port Orford about four miles, go east on County Road 196 to Forest Service Road 5105, which ends at the trailhead. For more information, contact the **Siskiyou National Forest, Powers Ranger District** (Powers, OR 97466, 541/439-3011).

Fishing

The **Elk River,** which empties on the south side of Cape Blanco, and the **Sixes River,** which meets the sea north of the cape, are two popular streams for salmon and steelhead fishing. Chinook and steelhead begin to enter both rivers after the first good rains of fall arrive, usually in November. Private lands limit bank access, with the exception of a good stretch of the Sixes that runs through Cape Blanco State Park. The salmon season runs to the end of the year, steelhead through the following March. **Lamm's Guide Service** (541/440-0558, www.umpquafishingguide.com) leads trips on both rivers.

Camping

Humbug Mountain State Park (541/332-6774), six miles south of Port Orford, features 80 tent sites and 30 sites for trailers and motor homes ($14–16), and wind-protected sites reserved for hikers and bikers ($4). Flush toilets, showers, picnic tables, water, and firewood are available.

Arizona Beach Campground (P.O. Box 621, Gold Beach 97444, 541/332-6491, www.arizonabeachrv.com, $14–20) is a 70-acre campground close to a beach with lots of driftwood. It has 31 tent sites and almost 100 RV spaces. You can camp on the beach, in an adjoining meadow, or back in the woods by a tiny stream. All the amenities are here, 15 miles north of Gold Beach on U.S. 101, but the closely spaced sites lack privacy. Nonetheless, there are few better places for kids because of the creek running though the site and the proximity of the Prehistoric Gardens. It's open all year. Reservations are needed during holidays only.

Cape Blanco State Park (39745 U.S. 101 S., 541/332-6774 information, 800/452-5687 for cabin reservations) can be reached by driving four miles north of Port Orford on U.S. 101, then heading northwest on the park road that continues five miles beyond to the campground. It features 54 tent sites ($16), four cabins ($35), trailer and motor home sites ($16), a horse camp ($14), and hiker-biker sites ($4); picnic tables, water, and showers are available. For horseback riders, there's a seven-mile trail and a huge open riding area; horses are also allowed on the beach. Regular sites are first-come, first-served.

Boating and Waterskiing

In the northwest of town, drive west of the highway on 14th or 18th streets to 90-acre **Garrison Lake** for boating, water-skiing, and fishing for stocked rainbow and cutthroat trout. **Buffington Memorial City Park,** at the end of 14th Street, has a dock for fishing or swimming, plus playing fields, tennis courts, picnic areas, hiking trails, and a horse arena. One-half mile north of the lake, look for agates on **Paradise Point Beach.**

Floras Lake Windsurfing and Kiteboarding

Between Port Orford and Bandon (just south

of Langlois) is **Floras Lake,** one of the southern Oregon coast's two great windsurfing and kiteboarding spots (the other is south of Gold Beach at Pistol River). The lake, just barely inland from the beach, catches incredible breezes. **Floras Lake Windsurfing School** (541/348-9912, www.floraslake.com) offers windsurfing and kiteboarding lessons and rentals; the proprietors also have a very nice B&B just above the lake. It's 11 miles north of Port Orford, about four miles west of the highway on Floras Lake Loop Road. On the lake is **Boice Cope County Park,** which has basic tent and RV sites and a boat ramp. When the wind's not blowing (fat chance of that!), explore the hiking trails from the campground to the beach. From Floras Lake north to Bandon, the most desolate beachfront on the coast can be found—ideal for beachcombing. Grasses, dunes, and shore pine usher you the 25 miles back to Bandon, and chances are good you won't see a soul.

Surfing

The south-facing beach at **Battle Rock Beach,** in downtown Port Orford, can be okay for surfing during the winter, when northwesterly winds blow in. Otherwise, surfers tend to go about a mile south of town to the beach at Hubbard Creek (best in the spring). What these spots may lack in intensity, they make up for in scenery.

ACCOMMODATIONS

With one notable exception, Port Orford is the kind of place where a room with a view will not break your budget.

$50-100

Battle Rock Motel (136 6th St., 541/332-7331, doubles $65), directly across the highway from Battle Rock, is a typical small-town budget place, but with outstanding views. The **Shoreline Motel** (206 6th St., 541/332-2903, doubles $40–60), also across the highway from Battle Rock but with somewhat less dramatic views, offers clean rooms and accommodates pets. Both of these places are convenient and adequate for a night's stay.

Just south of town, the **Seacrest Motel** (44 U.S. 101 S., 541/332-3040, doubles $57–79) features views of coastal cliffs and a garden from a quiet hillside on the east side of the highway. Pets are welcome at this older motel.

◖ **Castaway-by-the-Sea** (545 W. 5th St., 541/332-4502, www.castawaybythesea.com, doubles $65–135) features ocean/harbor views from high on a bluff, fireplaces, and housekeeping units, and it allows pets. In addition to the motel rooms, the Castaway has a two-bedroom lodge that'll sleep up to 10 (from $200). The rates on the upper-end lodgings go down significantly in the off-season. It's said that Jack London once stayed in an earlier incarnation of this place.

$100 and Up

Port Orford's serene luxury resort is ◖ **Wildspring Guest Habitat** (www.wildspring.com, doubles $199–249, including continental breakfast). The small (five-cabin) resort is in a forested setting on a bluff above the highway (but totally secluded from it), with views of the ocean. The cabins are meticulously designed and furnished (including a refrigerator, massage table, and Wi-Fi access in each cabin, but no telephones or TVs) and are as comfortable as they are perfect-looking. The main guest hall has a kitchen that's available to guests as long as it's not being used to prepare breakfast or the Saturday-night ice cream sundaes. The well-tended grounds include a labyrinth and several meditation nooks, but perhaps the best place to hang out is the slate-lined hot tub, which looks out over treetops to the ocean. It's not a bad idea to take binoculars, as Wildspring is a stop along the Oregon Coast Birding Trail. Bikes, backpacks, and hiking trail maps are available to all guests. Guided meditation, drumming, and tai chi are all offered one or two times a month (check website or call to inquire). This is a good place for a romantic retreat or a solo contemplative getaway.

Home-by-the-Sea (444 Jackson St., 541/332-2855 or 800/480-2144, www.home bythesea.com) includes a full breakfast at rates of $105–115 a night for two. The dramatic hillside view of Battle Rock seascape makes for excellent storm-watching. Wireless Internet access is available.

North of Port Orford, the **Floras Lake House B&B** (92870 Boice Cope Rd., Langlois, 541/348-2573, www.floraslake.com, doubles $135–155 including breakfast) is perfectly suited for windsurfers or others who want to explore the beaches in this unpopulated area. The spacious, light-filled house looks out onto Floras Lake and the ocean, and the proprietors also offer windsurfing and kiteboarding lessons.

Vacation Rentals

Neath the Wind (736 U.S. 101, 541/332-9463, www.neaththewind.com) can help you settle into a vacation house for a few nights.

FOOD

Port Orford doesn't have a lot of restaurants, but there are a few good places to eat.

Start the day at **Wild Wind Café and Bakery** (831 Oregon St., 541/332-0534, open for breakfast, lunch, and dinner daily), a cheery and popular spot with good pastries and full breakfasts.

You'll feel a little bit daring when you order fish and chips at **Dock Tackle** (490 Dock Rd., 541/332-8985, open 10 A.M.–6 P.M. daily in summer, 10 A.M.–3 P.M. daily in winter), a funky-looking shack down at the Port Orford dock. But the fish here is as fresh as it gets, and the atmosphere, with crusty old fishermen eating hot dogs and talking crabbing, is not a cookie-cutter idea of a fish and chips place.

More elaborate fare can be had across the street from Battle Rock at **Paula's Bistro** (236 6th St., 541/332-9378, open for dinner Tues.–Sat., main courses $17–20), with a fish-centric menu and a casual country atmosphere.

Aside from the tackle shop, the other really memorable place to eat in town is ◖ **Port Orford Breadworks** (190 6th St., 541/332-4022, open for lunch and dinner Wed.–Sat., dinner Sun., main courses $8–23, dinner reservations recommended) with great trattoria-style Italian food, good bread, and gourmet sandwiches. Dinner guests select from the evening's three entrées, which might include standard East Coast–style Italian dishes such as lasagna, as well as pork medallions or risotto with prawns. The view from the dining room is superb, and the wines are very reasonably priced. During the daytime, stop in for a sandwich or deli meats and cheeses to go.

Chow down on vegetarian soup and sandwiches at **Seaweed Natural Food and Grocery** (832 Oregon St., 541/332-3640).

PRACTICALITIES
Information and Services

Begin your travels here at **Battle Rock Information Center** (541/332-4106, www.discoverportorford.com), open daily on the west side of U.S. 101. The people here are especially friendly and helpful. Information is also available at www.portorfordoregon.com. The **library** (555 W. 20th St.) is open weekdays 10 A.M.–5 P.M.

The **Sterling Savings Bank** (716 U.S. 101 N., 541/332-0187) in Port Orford offers ATM and banking services.

Getting There and Around

Curry County's **Coastal Express** buses (in Port Orford, call 800/921-2871) run up and down the south coast weekdays only between North Bend and the California border, including local service in Port Orford.

Gold Beach and Vicinity

Despite the name Gold Beach, the real riches here are silver, and they swim up the Rogue River in great numbers every year. This town is one part of the coast where the action is definitely away from the ocean. To lure people from Oregon's superlative ocean shores, the Rogue estuary has been bestowed with many blessings. First, the gold-laden black sands were mined in the 1850s and 1860s. While this short-lived boom era gave Gold Beach its name, the arrival of Robert Hume, later known as the Salmon King of the Rogue, had greater historical significance. By the turn of the 20th century, Hume's canneries were shipping out some 16,000 cases of salmon per year and established the river's image as a leading salmon and steelhead stream. This reputation was later enhanced by outdoorsman Zane Grey in his *Rogue River Feud* and other writings. Over the years, Herbert Hoover, Winston Churchill, Ginger Rogers (who had a home on the Rogue), Clark Gable, Jack London, George H. W. Bush, and Jimmy Carter, among other notables, have come here to try their luck. During the last several decades, white-water rafting and jetboat tours focusing on the abundant wildlife, scenic beauty, and fascinating lore of the region have hooked other sectors of the traveling public.

Today, Gold Beach is a town of about 2,100 and the Curry County seat. Gold Beach serves as the south coast tourism hub, but a pulp mill and commercial ocean fishing industry round out the local economy. The seasonal nature of many local businesses creates serious wintertime unemployment. This fact, combined with torrential rains, drastically reduces the population of Gold Beach from Thanksgiving until spring. Thereafter, the wildflowers and warm weather transform this town into a vacation mecca.

At the north end of town, just before the road gives way to Conde McCullough's elegant

SOUTH COAST

© MICHAEL MCCLURE

This elegant bridge welcomes your entrance to Gold Beach.

© PAUL LEVY

Myers Creek Beach, south of Cape Sebastian

Patterson Bridge, the harbor comes into view on the left, full of salmon trawlers, jetboats, pelicans, and seals bobbing up and down. Across the bridge is **Wedderburn,** a baby sister to Gold Beach. Named for the Scottish birthplace of Robert Hume, its major claim to fame is as the home port of the Mailboat, which has been the mail carrier to upriver residents on the Rogue since 1895.

SIGHTS
Beaches

The driftwood-strewn strand of **South Beach,** just south of Gold Beach's harbor, is convenient but only so-so. You'll find more exciting stretches both north and south of town. Tidepoolers might want to stop at the visitors center before heading out and ask for the *Tidepools Are Alive* brochure, with tips and species descriptions. Two miles south, there's easy access to a nice beach and some tidepooling at tiny **Buena Vista State Park,** at the mouth of Hunter Creek. Seven miles south of Gold Beach, there's more tidepooling amid

the camera-friendly basalt sea stacks at beautiful **Myers Creek Beach,** part of Pistol River State Park south of Cape Sebastian. The south side of Cape Sebastian and **Pistol River State Park,** a couple of miles farther south, are the best places on the Oregon coast for windsurfers to enjoy wave sailing. The beaches around Pistol River are also productive areas for finding razor clams.

Bailey Beach, north of town between the Rogue River jetty and Otter Point, is another popular spot for razor clamming, and **Nesika Beach,** seven miles from Gold Beach, is another good tidepooling destination.

◖ Cape Sebastian

Seven miles south of Gold Beach is Cape Sebastian. This spectacular windswept headland was named by Sebastián Vizcaíno, who plied offshore waters here for Spain in 1602 along with Manuel d'Alguilar. At least 700 feet above the sea, Cape Sebastian is the highest south coast overlook reachable by paved public road. On a clear day, visibility extends

43 miles north to Humbug Mountain and 50 miles south to California. This is one of the best perches along the south coast for whale-watching. A trail zigzags through beautiful springtime wildflowers down the south side of the cape for about two miles until it reaches the sea. In April and May, Pacific paintbrush, Douglas iris, orchids, and snow queen usher you along. In addition, Cape Sebastian supports a population of large-headed goldfields, a summer-blooming daisylike yellow flower found only in coastal Curry County.

In 1942, a caretaker here heard Japanese voices drifting across the water through the fog. When the mist lifted he looked down from Cape Sebastian trail to see a surfaced submarine. This sighting, together with the Japanese bombing at Brookings and the incendiary balloon spotted over Cape Blanco, sent shock waves up the south coast. But the potential threat remained just that, and local anxiety eventually subsided.

Museums

At the **Curry County Historical Museum** (920 S. Ellensburg Ave., 541/247-6113, open 10 A.M.–4 P.M. Tues.–Sat., closed January, $2), the local historical society has assembled a small collection of exhibits on Indian and pioneer life, mining in the region's golden age, logging, fishing, and agriculture. It's located at the county fairgrounds at the south edge of town. Particularly interesting are a realistic reconstruction of a miner's cabin, vintage photos, and Indian petroglyphs.

In the harbor area on the west side of U.S. 101, Jerry's Jetboats has assembled the best regional museum on the south coast, the **Rogue River Museum** (541/247-4571, open 8 A.M.–9 P.M. summer, 8 A.M.–6 P.M. in other seasons, free). Centuries of natural and human history are depicted here. In addition to geologic history, the museum contains photos of pioneer families, arrowheads and other native artifacts, and a taxidermic collage of local critters to round out your introduction to the Rogue Valley. Jerry's river tour clientele will find that perspectives from the museum on the

local salmon industry in the 1920s and on early river travel are expanded upon in their jetboat guide's commentary. Museum photos of early river runs—hauling freight, passengers, and mail—can impart a sense of history to your trip upriver or up the road.

Scenic Drives

From U.S. 101, two miles south of town, you can pick up Hunter's Creek Road, which loops north through the forest, finally following the course of the Rogue back into Gold Beach along Jerry's Flat Road. The three-hour drive follows Hunter's Creek inland for several miles. The route goes past interpretive markers explaining "our national forest, land of many uses" and is mapped out in a free pamphlet available at the Gold Beach Ranger Station. This map shows several picnic areas and campgrounds.

Other roads less traveled include the old Coast Highway, which you can pick up near Pistol River and Brookings; the Shasta Costa Road paralleling the Rogue from Gold Beach to Galice; and an unpaved summer-only road into the Rogue Wilderness from Agness (a town upriver on the Rogue) to Powers. Despite most of these routes being paved (except the last one), they are all narrow, winding, and not suitable for trailers or motor homes. Maps and directions to these back roads can be obtained from the Gold Beach Ranger Station.

SPORTS AND RECREATION
Rogue River Jetboat Ride

The most popular way to take in the mighty Rogue is on a jetboat ride from Gold Beach harbor. Several different companies run this trip, and they all provide comparable service and prices. It's an exciting and interesting look at the varied flora and fauna along the estuary as well as the changing moods of the river. Most of the estimated 50,000 people per year who "do" the Rogue in this way take the 64-mile round-trip cruise. The more adventurous 104-mile cruise includes a stop for a sumptuous lunch at one of several secluded fishing lodges upriver. The pilots/commentators usually have grown up on the river, and their evocations of the diverse ecosystems and Native American and gold-mining history add greatly to your enjoyment. Bears, otters, seals, and beavers may be sighted en route, and anglers may hold up a big keeper to show off. Ospreys, snowy egrets, eagles, mergansers, and kingfishers are also seen with regularity in this stopover for migratory waterfowl.

In the first part of the journey, idyllic riverside retreats dot the hillsides, breaking up stands of fir and hemlock. Myrtle, madrone, and impressive springtime wildflower groupings also vary the landscape. Both the 64- and 104-mile trips focus on the section of the Rogue protected by the government as a Wild and Scenic River. Only the longer trips take you into the pristine Rogue Wilderness, an area that motor launches from Grants Pass do not reach. The 13 miles of this wilderness you see from the boat have canyon walls rising 1,500 feet above you. Geologists say this part of the Klamaths is composed of ancient islands and sea floor that collided with North America. To deal with the rapids upstream, smaller, faster boats are used that skim over the boulders with just six inches of water between hull and rock surface.

The season runs May–October 15. Remember that chill and fog near the mouth of the estuary usually give way to much warmer conditions upstream. These tour outfits have wool blankets available on cold days as well as complimentary hot beverages. Also keep in mind that the upriver lodges can be booked for overnight stays, and your trip may be resumed the following day. The following suppliers offer 64- and 104-mile trips; meals are included in the cost of the 104-mile trip (rates range $42–84 for adults, $16–37 for children).

Just south of the Rogue River Bridge, west of U.S. 101 on Harbor Way, is **Jerry's Rogue River Jetboats** (P.O. Box 1011, Gold Beach 97444, 541/247-4571 or 800/451-3645, www.roguejets.com). This heavily patronized company runs trips May–October. Jerry's is noted for personable, well-informed guides. If you forgot a hat to buffer the winds at the mouth of the Rogue, stop in at Jerry's gift shop.

While you're there, check out the local jams and critically acclaimed fish prints of local artist Don Jensen.

Rogue River Mailboats (P.O. Box 1165, Gold Beach 97444, 541/247-7033 or 800/458-3511, www.mailboat.com) is located 0.25 mile upstream from the north end of the Rogue River bridge. Besides human cargo, this boat also carries sacks of U.S. mail, ensuring a warm welcome in upriver locations.

Fishing

Fishing is a mighty big deal in Gold Beach, which has one of the highest concentrations of professional guides in the state. There's something to fish for just about year-round, but salmon and steelhead are the top quarry. When the spring chinook pour in, April–June, anglers will need to book guided trips well in advance to get a shot at them. Catches peak in May. Summer steelhead and fall-run chinook usually arrive July–September, then it's hatchery coho September–November (sometimes as early as August). In December, the first of the winter steelhead make their appearance and continue into March.

The **Rogue Outdoor Store** (560 N. Ellensburg Ave., Gold Beach, 541/247-7142) is well stocked with fishing, camping, and other gear, and its staff can advise on where, when, and what to fish. Typical rates for guided salmon trips here are $150–200 per person. Contact the **Gold Beach Visitor Center** or the **Curry Guide Association** (800/775-0886) for a list of over two dozen licensed guides.

Some well-established **guides** include: Darrell Allen (541/247-2082); Denny Hughson (541/247-2684, www.hughsons-rogueriver.com); Steve Beyerlin (541/247-4138 or 800/348-4138, www.fishoregon.com), for both conventional and fly-fishing; Shaun Carpenter (541/247-2049, www.endoftherogue.com), conventional and fly-fishing; Helen Burns (541/247-2441 or 541/290-8402, www.helensguideservice.com), one of the few women in a male-dominated club; Ron Smith (541/247-6046 or 800/501-6391, www.sportfishingoregon.com); and John Ward (541/247-2866).

Hiking

The 40-mile **Rogue River Trail** offers lodge-to-lodge hiking, which means you need little more in your pack than the essentials. The lodges here are comfortably rustic, serve home-style food in copious portions, and run $150–200 for a double room. They are also comfortably spaced, so extended hiking is seldom a necessity. Call **Rogue Quest** (888/517-1614) if you would like a guide (about $80 per day).

Before you go, check with the Gold Beach Ranger Station on trail conditions and specific directions to the trailhead. Pick up the western end of the trail 35 miles east of Gold Beach, about 0.5 mile from Foster Bar, a popular boat landing. Park there and walk east and north on the paved road until you see signs on the left marking the Rogue River Trail. Go in spring before the hot weather and enjoy yellow Siskiyou iris and fragrant wild azaleas. The trail ends at Graves Creek, 27 miles northwest of Grants Pass. Be careful of rattlesnakes on the trail.

Camping

There are no public campgrounds along the coast between Humbug Mountain, just south of Port Orford, and Harris Beach, at the northern entrance to Brookings. But campsites east of town up the Rogue River provide wonderful spots to bed down for the night. Those taking the road along the Rogue should be alert for oncoming log trucks, raft transport vehicles, and other wide-body vehicles. In addition to the public campgrounds listed here, there are *many* private RV resorts up the north bank of the Rogue.

Foster Bar Campground (Siskiyou National Forest, Gold Beach Ranger Station, 1225 S. Ellensburg Ave., 541/247-6651, www.fs.fed.us/r6/rogue-siskiyou, open year-round, flush toilets available May–Nov., $5) is located 30 miles east of Gold Beach on the south bank of the Rogue. Take Jerry's Flat Road east for 30 miles to the turnoff for Agness. Turn right on Illahe Agness Road and drive three miles to camp. Recently transformed from primitive to developed, campsites here now come equipped

with drinking water, toilets, handicapped-accessible facilities, picnic tables, fire rings, and a boat ramp. Sites are available on a first-come, first-served basis only. The campground is generally open March–October but may vary depending on the weather. This is a popular spot from which to embark on an eight-mile inner tube ride to Agness. It's also where rafters pull out, so the parking lot may be jam-packed. The rapids are dangerous—wear a life jacket. You are also within walking distance of the trailhead of the Rogue River Trail.

Lobster Creek Campground (541/247-3600, www.fs.fed.us/r6/rogue-siskiyou, $5) is nine miles east of Gold Beach via Forest Service Road 33. This campground is open year-round and has three tent sites, three trailer sites, one group site, picnic tables, fishing, and flush toilets—but no drinking water. Ask the Forest Service for directions to the Schrader old-growth trail nearby. It is a gentle one-mile walk through a rare and majestic ecosystem that is under siege in other forests throughout the state. Also nearby is the world's largest myrtle tree.

Honeybear Campground and RV Resort (P.O. Box 97, 34161 Ophir Rd., Ophir 97464, 541/247-2765 or 800/822-4444, www.honeybearrv.com, open year-round, $16–27) is not up the Rogue; it's nine miles north of Gold Beach on U.S. 101, then two miles north on Ophir Road—it but could just as well be in the Black Forest. The owners have built a large rathskeller with a dance floor. Six nights a week during the summer, there are dances here with traditional German music. Check out their version of Octoberfest. Locals praise the Honeybear's on-site delicatessen for its homemade German sausage. There are 20 tent and RV sites, picnic tables, flush toilets, hot showers, firewood, a launderette, and ocean views.

Windsurfing

Although beginners may want to hone their skills at Floras Lake, experienced windsurfers head out into the ocean near the debouchment of the Pistol River. Stop in the hamlet of Langlois, between Port Orford and Bandon, at **Big**

Air Windsurfing (541/347-2692, www.big-air .com) for equipment and tips.

Horseback Riding

Hawk's Rest Ranch at Siskiyou West Day Lodge (94667 N. Bank Pistol River Rd., Pistol River, 541/247-6423, www.siskiyouwest .com, rides $25–95), a working horse ranch, offers horseback riding through the forest and on the beach near the scenic Pistol River. The most popular ride is a 1.5-hour ride across the dunes and along the beach ($30). Rides leave several times daily, but it's best to call in advance for reservations.

Golf

Cedar Bend Golf Course (P.O. Box 1234, Gold Beach 97444, 541/247-6911, greens fees $15 for nine holes, $20 for 18 holes) is located in nearby Ophir. Eleven miles north of Gold Beach, pick up Ophir Road off U.S. 101. Follow it to Squaw Valley Road, turn right at the Old Ophir Store, and continue until you see the links. Woods line the fairways, and a winding creek offers a challenge on each of the nine holes.

ENTERTAINMENT AND EVENTS

The **Wild Rivers Coast Seafood, Art, and Wine Festival** is a two-day event that celebrates wine, fine dining, and arts and crafts of the southern Oregon coast, in mid-May at the Event Center on the Beach (29392 Ellensburg Ave., 541/247-4541).

People line the river for the annual **jetboat races,** which take place in mid-June. Contact Jot's Resort (800/367-5687) or the chamber of commerce for information.

The **Pistol River Wave Bash National Windsurfing Competition** brings four days of competitive riding to Pistol River State Park each June. For details, contact the Gold Beach Visitor Center (541/247-7526 or 800/525-2334).

In late July or early August, the **Curry County Fair and Rodeo** takes place at the Event Center on the Beach. Highlights in-clude Oregon's largest flower show and a lamb barbecue.

Since 1982, the Pistol River Concert Association (541/247-2848, www.pistolriver.com) has produced a top-notch **concert series,** encompassing bluegrass, folk, jazz, classical, and blues at the Pistol River Friendship Hall. Concerts are held roughly once a month throughout the year, and it's well worth fussing with your schedule in order to catch one. Past and present performers are a who's who of acoustic music, including Greg Brown, Mike Seeger, Peggy Seeger, Kevin Burke, Norman and Nancy Blake, Peter Rowan, and Tony Rice, to name a few. To get there from Gold Beach, take U.S. 101 10 miles south, to the second Pistol River exit (Pistol River/Carpenterville) and take the first right. The Pistol River Friendship Hall is .5 mile ahead on the right.

ACCOMMODATIONS

As in most coastal towns, there is no shortage of places to stay along the main drag, Ellensburg Avenue (a.k.a. U.S. 101). In fact, Gold Beach offers the largest number and widest range of accommodations on the south coast, with intimate lodges overlooking the Rogue as popular as the oceanfront motels. A discount of 20 percent or more on rooms is usually available during winter here, when 80–90 inches of rain can fall.

$50-100

The cheapest place in town is probably the **Oregon Trail Lodge** (550 N. Ellensburg Ave., 541/247-6030, doubles from $45), where you get no-frills accommodation close to the harbor. Be aware that the paper-thin walls may put you on more intimate terms with your next-door neighbor than you want to be.

Don't turn up your nose at the **Motel 6** (1010 Jerry's Flat Rd., 541/247-4533 or 800/759-4533, doubles from $70); the location here—perched above the Rogue River—is great, and the rooms are modern and comfy. Kitchenettes are available, as are spa suites. Pets are permitted.

If you're looking for a simple place to spend

a night or two and don't care about frills, the **Azalea Lodge** (29481 Ellensburg Ave., 541/247-6635 or 866/381-6635, www.azalea lodge.biz, doubles from $86) is a good bet, with friendly owners and clean rooms. No pets are allowed; all rooms are nonsmoking and have refrigerators.

$100 and Up

◖ **Ireland's Rustic Lodges** (29330 El-lensburg Ave., 541/247-7718, www.irelands rusticlodges.com, doubles $95–150) was started by two women who used to bring meals to the cabins. Although this is no longer the case, the touch of home has not been lost. Many of the rooms have fireplaces, knotty-pine interiors, and distinctive decor. Best of all, the grounds are lovingly landscaped with pine trees, flowers, and ocean views. A sandy beach is a short stroll to the west. There are 33 motel lodge units (some with kitchens), seven old but well-kept log cabins (recommended) that sleep up to five, and houses that sleep as many as 11. Ireland's also has an RV park close to the lodge.

Located on the Rogue River's north bank, the immense **Jot's Resort** (94360 Wedder-burn Loop, Wedderburn, 541/247-6676 or 800/FOR-JOTS, www.jotsresort.com, doubles from $100) can host a full vacation in one com-pound featuring pool and spa, sports shop, pri-vate dock, rental boats, and a restaurant across the street. The rooms here are at a premium in summer, when the motorcoach tours come through, leaving other travelers with the less desirable rooms. There are numerous room styles—from standard-view rooms to river-front condos big enough for six people—and a wide range of prices, so it's best to call for cur-rent rates and specials. The Rod 'n' Reel across the street features evening entertainment with low-stakes blackjack, a country music duo, and a big-band dance on weekends.

◖ **Tu Tu Tun Resort** (96530 N. Bank Rogue River Rd., 541/247-6664 or 800/864-6357, www.tututun.com, doubles from $195) emphasizes tranquility, reinforced by the ab-sence of TV in the rooms (except in the suites and houses). Although there is a TV in the cedar-planked lodge, most guests prefer to take in the river view through the floor-to-ceiling windows or enjoy a good book from the lodge's library in front of the massive river rock fire-place. As you sit on your patio overlooking the water along with two nearby resident bald ea-gles, only the sounds of an occasional passing boat may intrude upon your Rogue River rev-erie. The lodge is located seven miles up the Rogue River from Gold Beach.

A heated pool and other recreational facili-ties, the lodge's beautifully appointed interi-ors, and delicious meals served family style are other appeals of this acclaimed retreat. Meals are available on an inclusive Modified Amer-ican Plan, which includes hors d'oeuvres, a gourmet four-course dinner, and a bountiful breakfast buffet (for $53 per person).

The cuisine here is worth special mention. Whether it's blackberry muffins and house-cured pepper bacon at breakfast or a mesquite-grilled pork loin doused in Hood River apple juice for dinner, gustatory highlights abound. The dining room is open May–October only. In the off-season, guests are served a continen-tal breakfast only.

Spring is the best time to be here because much of the traveling public is still at home and the wildflowers are in their glory. Pink rhododendrons, native to Oregon, blossom at the edge of the forest in May. From early sum-mer to late fall, a huge dahlia garden at the lodge is in bloom. Although autumn is also beautiful, business meetings in September and October necessitate that bookings be made well in advance for stays after Labor Day.

A slightly less elaborate alternative to the Tu Tu Tun is the ◖ **Rogue River Lodge** (94966 North Bank Rogue River Rd., 541/247-9070, www.rogueriverlodge.com, doubles $160–295), an old riverside motel that has been completely refurbished into a rustic but upscale lodge. The extremely comfortable rooms are all suites, and the largest ones can house a group of six. All rooms have riverside decks and kitchen facili-ties ranging from rudimentary to full; most have hot tubs.

SOUTH COAST

Vacation Rentals

For vacation house rentals around Gold Beach, check out the offerings at **Rogue Reef Vacation Rentals** (www.roguereefvacation-rentals.com). A variety of condos and houses are available, starting at about $150 per day.

Upriver Lodges

Several lodges on the Rogue, some accessible only by boat or via hiking trails, lure visitors deep into the interior. Jetboat trips can drop you off for an overnight or longer stay. Advance reservations are essential.

Accessible by road or jetboat 32 miles inland from the coast, the **Cougar Lane Lodge** (4219 Agness Rd., 541/247-7233, doubles $45–65) was established in 1949 on the east shore of the Rogue. Spend the night in one of the simple lodge rooms or come for the day to fish (licenses and tackle available at the Cougar Lane store). Dine at the lodge restaurant, overlooking the Rogue, which serves standard American breakfast, lunch, and dinner every day. From here, hike the Rogue or Illinois trails. The Agness RV Park is nearby for overnight camping.

Also accessible by road and boat, the **Lucas Pioneer Ranch & Fishing Lodge** (3904 Cougar Lane, 541/247-7443, doubles $45–80) is also 32 miles east of Gold Beach. Cabins here come equipped with cooking and noncooking options. Lunch and dinner are served daily in the lodge—chicken, biscuits, and garden vegetables are standard fare. Reservations are required.

The more remote **Half Moon Bar Lodge** (3140 Juanipero Way, Medford, 541/842-2821 or 888/291-8268, www.halfmoonbarlodge.com, $150 adults, $65 children, includes three meals) is located in the wild and secluded piece of wilderness, once the site of Native American encampments. Choose from three private cabins or stay in the rustic lodge, which houses a sauna, dining room, and bar. Meals are served family-style and include fresh seasonal garden veggies and fruits. Tour boats take visitors 52 miles upriver; raft down with a white-water guide or fish for steelhead. To get there, hike in 11 miles from Foster Bar along the Rogue River Trail or five miles from Bear Camp near Agness. The lodge can also accommodate small planes on its private airstrip. Call to make arrangements.

Only accessible by helicopter, jetboat, or foot, the **Paradise Lodge** (541/247-6504 or 800/525-2161, www.go-oregon.com, $150 adults, $65 children, includes three meals) attracts nature enthusiasts interested in the "wildest" experience. Only the meals are scheduled here, where you can take an eco-tour, enjoy a sauna, raft or jetboat the rapids, or check out some of the old mining sites in the vicinity. A huge on-site garden provides ingredients for home-cooked meals. Jetboat round-trip rates are $95.

FOOD

You can't eat scenery, but Gold Beach restaurants charge you for it anyway. Still, this is one place where the oceanfront and riverside views are often worth it. Then, too, there's always the option of cheaper restaurants away from port. Spring chinook salmon, blackberry pie, and other indigenous specialties taste good anywhere.

Breakfast

Grant's Pancake House (29790 U.S. 101, 541/247-7208, open for breakfast and lunch daily) is the breakfast place of choice from the Rogue estuary to California. Omelettes, pancakes, waffles, and corned beef hash often make lunch (in the same price range) an afterthought. Nonetheless, locals consider the Thursday clam steaks lunch special (breaded East Coast sea clams in a spicy homemade sauce) one of the town's culinary highlights.

Stop by **Biscuits Café** (29707 Ellensburg Ave., 541/247-2495) in Gold Beach Books for coffee and pastries. Be sure to take a look in the rare book room after you finish eating.

Bistro

Just upriver on the north bank of the Rogue River, find **Rollin 'n Dough** (94257 North Bank Rogue, Wedderburn, 541/247-4438, open for lunch and dinner Wed.–Sat. and Sunday brunch, reservations required, dinner entrées $12–28), a pint-sized bistro with some of the best food on the southern Oregon coast. Everything here, from the bread to the salad dressing, is homemade by Patti, the good-natured proprietor. For lunch, if tuna is in season, try a pan bagna (a smashed tuna sandwich, $9) or a salad Niçoise ($14); dinner can be pasta if you want to keep the cost down, or truffled scallops with sherried oyster mushroom sauce if you're feeling more expansive. If you're not up for a meal here, stop by for a pastry to go—the muffins are excellent.

Seafood and Meat

The Nor'Wester (10 Harbor Way, 541/247-2333, open for dinner nightly) is located at the port of Gold Beach, so sometimes you get to watch boats unloading your dinner. Not surprisingly, the menu is dominated by seafood, although the waitstaff tout the New Zealand lamb chops. What is surprising are such occasional culinary flourishes as chinook salmon broiled under a flame, then covered with a glaze of sake, cayenne, ginger, and soy. Dinner prices top out above $40 for steak and lobster, but most entrées are in the $20 range. There are also lighter, less expensive dinner options.

A very good dinner house with ocean views (and corresponding prices) is **Spinner's Seafood, Steak and Chophouse** (29430 Ellensburg Ave., 541/247-5160, open for dinner nightly, main courses $20–30). The menu is wide-ranging and the dining room extremely pleasant. Look for fresh seafood, pasta, prime rib, and choice beef and chops. A children's menu is available.

Locals recommend the **Port Hole Café** (29975 Harbor Way, 541/247-7411, open 6 A.M.–9 P.M. daily), in the Cannery building at the port with bay and river views, for hearty portions of fish and chips, chowder, and homemade pies at decent prices.

Pick up some fresh seafood or the best canned tuna you'll ever taste at **Fishermen Direct Seafoods** (29975 Harbor Way, 541/247-9494).

PRACTICALITIES
Information

The **Gold Beach Visitor Center** (29692 Ellensburg Ave., 541/247-7526 or 800/525-2334, www.goldbeach.org) is open 9 A.M.–5 P.M. Monday–Friday and 10 A.M.–4 P.M. Saturday–Sunday. Its website is excellent and informative, and staff will send you a good, comprehensive information folder upon request.

The **Gold Beach Ranger District** (29279 Ellensburg Ave., Gold Beach, 541/247-3600, open 7:30 A.M.–5 P.M. Mon.–Fri.) offers a free packet on camping and recreation in the district.

Services

The **post office** (541/247-7610) is at the port on Harbor Way. A modern building houses the **public library** (29775 Colvin St., 541/247-7246, 10 A.M.–8 P.M. Mon.– Thurs., 10 A.M.–5 P.M. Fri.–Sat.), one block east of the highway in the north end of town.

Curry General Hospital (94220 4th St., Gold Beach, 541/247-6621) is the only hospital in the county.

For your banking and walk-up teller needs, go to the **Sterling Savings Bank** (29804 Ellensburg Ave., 541/247-0478).

Getting There and Around

Curry County's **Coastal Express** buses (800/921-2871) run up and down the south coast weekdays only between North Bend and the California border, including local service in Gold Beach.

SOUTH COAST

Brookings-Harbor and Vicinity

There are people who don't like Brookings, and if you form your judgment by simply driving down U.S. 101, it's easy to join that crowd. But something as simple as turning off into Harris Beach State Park can begin to change your view. To really fall for the area, it may take a drive up the Chetco River. A couple of miles inland, the fog that frequently drenches the coastline here during the summer months burns away. There are ample hiking opportunities upriver, especially in the Kalmiopsis Wilderness Area.

During winter Brookings (pop. 5,725) and its unincorporated bigger neighbor, Harbor (pop. 8,775), enjoy mild temperatures. Enough 60–70°F days occur during January and February in this south coast "banana belt" town that more than 50 species of flowering plants thrive here—along with retirees, outdoor sports lovers, and beachcombers. With two gorgeous state parks virtually part of the city and world-class salmon and steelhead fishing nearby, only the lavish winter rainfall, averaging over 73 inches a year, can cool the ardor of local outdoor enthusiasts. In the springtime, the area south of town is lush with lilies—it's the Easter lily capital of the world.

Brookings and Harbor sit on a coastal plain overlooking the Pacific six miles north of the California border, split by U.S. 101 (Chetco Avenue) and the Chetco River. Flowing out of the Klamath Mountains east of town, the Chetco drains part of the nearby Siskiyou National Forest and the Kalmiopsis Wilderness, extensive tracts encompassing some of the wildest country in the Lower 48 and renowned for their rare flowers and trees. This area enjoys strict federal protection, safeguarding the northernmost stand of giant redwoods as well as the coveted Port Orford cedar (whose strong but pliable lumber can fetch over $10,000 for a single tree). The Kalmiopsis Wilderness is named for a unique shrub, the *Kalmiopsis leachiana*, one of the oldest members of the heath family (Ericaceae) that grows nowhere else on earth.

But you don't have to trek miles into the backcountry to enjoy the natural beauty of Brookings and vicinity. Just make your way past the somewhat drab main drag to Samuel Boardman State Park north of town, where 11 of the most scenic miles of the Oregon coast await you. Or head down to the harbor to embark on a boating expedition, amid some of the safest offshore navigation conditions in the region. In short, Brookings is the perfect place to launch an adventure by land or by sea.

SIGHTS

Camellias bloom at Christmas, and the flowering plums add color the next month. Daffodils, grown commercially on the coastal plain south of Brookings, bloom in late January and into February. Magnolia shrubs, some early azaleas, and rhododendrons also bloom in late winter.

Harris Beach State Park

At the northern limits of Brookings, across from the State Information Center on U.S. 101, Harris Beach State Park makes up for all the ugly architecture you'll find on Chetco Avenue. One look at the 24 miles of rock and tide visible from the parking-lot promontory should quell any misgivings.

Harris Beach was named after the Scottish pioneer George Harris, who settled here in the late 1880s to raise sheep and cattle. Besides stunning views, this state park offers many incoming travelers from California their first chance to actually walk on the beach in Oregon. You can begin directly west of the park's campground, where a sandy beach strewn with boulders often becomes flooded with intertidal life and driftwood. The early morning hours, as the waves crash through a small tunnel in a massive rock onto the shoreline, are the best time to look for sponges, umbrella crabs, solitary corals, and sea stars.

Offshore, Bird Island (also called Goat Island) is the largest island along the Oregon coast and the state's largest seabird rookery.

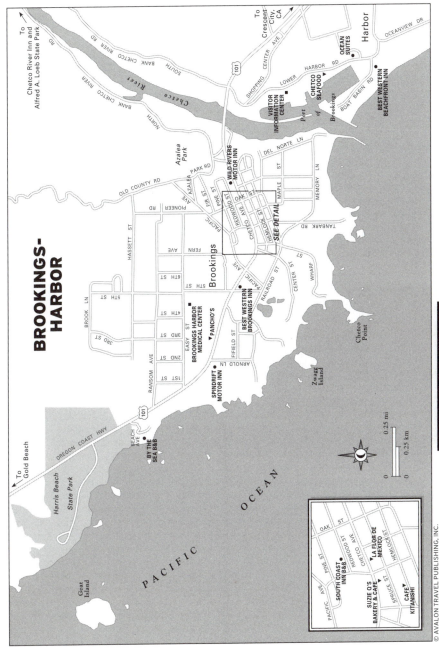

BROOKINGS-HARBOR

To Crescent City, CA

Harbor

OCEANVIEW DR

OCEAN SUITES

LOWER HARBOR RD

CHETCO SEAFOOD

BEST WESTERN BEACHFRONT INN

BOAT BASIN RD

Port of Brookings

SHOPPING CENTER AVE

VISITOR INFORMATION CENTER

To Chetco River Inn and Alfred A. Loeb State Park

NORTH BANK CHETCO RIVER RD

SOUTH BANK CHETCO RIVER RD

Chetco River

Azalea Park

OLD COUNTY RD

AZALEA PARK RD

DEL NORTE LN

WILD RIVERS MOTOR INN

FIR ST

PINE ST

REDWOOD ST

OAK ST

HEMLOCK ST

MAPLE ST

MEMORY LN

PINE ST

PACIFIC AVE

PIONEER RD

HASSETT ST

FERN AVE

CHETCO AVE

TANBARK RD

Brookings

SEE DETAIL

6TH ST

5TH ST

4TH ST

3RD ST

2ND ST

1ST ST

BROOK LN

RANSOM AVE

5TH ST

RAILROAD ST

CENTER ST

WHARF ST

PACIFIC AVE

FIFIELD ST

EASY ST

BROOKINGS HARBOR MEDICAL CENTER

PANCHO'S

BEST WESTERN BROOKINGS INN

Chetco Point

ARNOLD LN

SPINDRIFT MOTOR INN

Zwagg Island

BEACH AVE

BY THE SEA B&B

OREGON COAST HWY

101

To Gold Beach

Harris Beach State Park

PACIFIC OCEAN

Goat Island

0.25 mi

0.25 km

0

0

N

SOUTH COAST

BROOKINGS-HARBOR

Detail

OAK ST

PINE ST

PACIFIC AVE

REDWOOD ST

CHETCO AVE

SPRUCE ST

HEMLOCK ST

LA FLOR DE MEXICO

SOUTH COAST INN B&B

SUZIE Q'S BAKERY & CAFE

CAFE KITANISHI

© AVALON TRAVEL PUBLISHING, INC.

This outpost of Oregon Islands National Wildlife Sanctuary dispatches squadrons of cormorants, pelicans, tufted puffins, and other waterfowl, which divebomb the incoming waves for food.

In addition to beachcombing, you can picnic at tables above the parking lot, loll about in the shallow waters of nearby Harris Creek, or cast the surf for perch.

Mill Beach is the southernmost part of the Harris Beach area. Locals prefer the beach access from downtown, which is easy to miss. To get there, drive toward the ocean on Center Street in downtown Brookings, make a right at the plywood mill, and stop next to a small ballpark. An unimproved road leads to a hillock from which trails take you down to a beach full of driftwood. Residents say that Japanese fishing floats occasionally roll up onto the beach after a storm.

Chetco Valley
Historical Society Museum

The Chetco Valley Historical Society Museum (5461 Museum Rd., Brookings, 541/469-6651, open 1–5 P.M. Fri.–Sun. Memorial Day–Labor Day, $3 donation suggested), in the red-and-white Blake House, sits on a hill overlooking U.S. 101 two miles south of the Chetco River. The structure dates to 1857 and was used as a stagecoach waystation and trading post before Lincoln was president.

Even if you are not one for museums, several exhibits here stand apart from the traditional collections of pioneer wedding dresses, Indian baskets, and spinning wheels. These include a small trunk that came around Cape Horn in 1706 and an Indian dugout canoe. Should these fail to inspire, a mysterious iron casting of a woman's face might do the trick, especially in light of the speculation that this relic was left by an early undocumented landing on the Oregon coast, perhaps by Sir Francis Drake. Drake has been commonly suggested because of the mask's likeness to Queen Elizabeth.

Oregon's largest Monterey cypress tree is located on the hill near the museum. The 99-foot-tall tree has a trunk circumference of more than 27 feet and has been home to a pair of owls for years.

◖ Samuel H. Boardman
State Scenic Corridor

The stretch of highway from Brookings to Port Orford is known as the "fabulous 50 miles." Some consider the section of coastline just north of Brookings to be the most scenic in Oregon—and one of the most dramatic meetings of rock and tide in the world. The offshore rock formations and winding roadbed hundreds of feet above the surf invite comparison to Europe's Amalfi Drive. The fabulous 50 sobriquet is perhaps most apt in the first dozen miles north of Brookings, encompassed by Samuel H. Boardman State Scenic Corridor. You'll want to have a camera close at hand and a loose schedule when you make this drive, because you'll find it hard not to pull over again and again, as each photo opportunity seems to outdazzle the last. Of the 11 named viewpoints that have been cut into the highway's shoulder here, the following are especially recommended (all viewpoints are marked by signs on the west side of U.S. 101 and are listed from north to south).

Near the north end of Boardman Park, a short walk down the hillside trail leads you to the **Arch Rocks** viewpoint, where an immense boomerang-shaped basalt archway juts out of the water about a quarter mile offshore. This site has picnic tables within view of the monolith.

A few miles south, the sign for **Natural Bridges Cove** seems to front just a forested parking lot. However, the paved walkway at the south end of the lot leads to a spectacular overlook. Below, several rock archways frame an azure cove. This feature was created by the collapse of the entrance and exit of a sea cave. A steep, winding trail through giant ferns and towering Sitka spruce and Douglas fir takes you down for a closer look. Thimbleberry (a sweet but seedy raspberry) is plentiful in late spring. Here as in similar forests on the south coast, it's important to stay on the trail. The rainforest-like biome is exceptionally fragile, and the soil erodes easily when the delicate vegetation is damaged.

© PAUL LEVY

Don't be surprised if you have the whole beach to yourself, especially at some of the coves that make up the Samuel H. Boardman State Scenic Corridor.

Thomas Creek Bridge, the highest bridge in Oregon (345 feet above the water) as well as the highest north of San Francisco, has been used as a silent star in many TV commercials. A parking lot at the south end of the bridge marks a trailhead down. Do not take the path you see closest to the bridge; it's too steep. At the south end of the lot, the true trail eventually leads down to a view of the bridge on one side and miles of coast on the other. The offshore rock formations are especially interesting. From here hikers can access the Indian Sands Trail, ending up in pine-rimmed dunes and a sandstone bluff high above the sea.

House Rock was the site of a World War II air-raid sentry tower that sits hundreds of feet above whitecaps pounding the rock-strewn beaches. To the north, you'll see one of the highest cliffs on the coast, Cape Sebastian. A steep, circuitous trail lined with salal goes down to the water. The path begins behind the Samuel Boardman monument on the west end of the parking lot. The sign to the highest viewpoint in Boardman Park is easy to miss, but look for the turnout that precedes House Rock, called Cape Ferrelo (for Cabrillo's navigator, who sailed up much of the West Coast in 1543).

Carpenterville Road

The current roadbed of U.S. 101 was laid in southern Oregon in 1961. The previous coastal route still exists along Carpenterville Road, which can be picked up near Harris Beach (inquire at the state Welcome Center located nearby). It comes out near the Pistol River, where it descends in a series of switchbacks. Its highest point is 1,700 feet above sea level at Burnt Hill. Views of the Siskiyous to the east and the Pacific panoramas to the west make the sometimes-rough road worth the effort. In very clear weather, it's possible to look back toward the southeast at Mount Shasta between the ridgelines. This route is best appreciated going south, and it makes a great 20-mile **bike ride,** with a long climb to 1,700 feet above sea level.

Alfred A. Loeb State Park

Eight miles northeast of Brookings on North

Bank Chetco River Road along the Chetco River, Loeb State Park preserves 320 acres of old-growth myrtlewood, the state's largest grove. Many of the aromatic trees here are well more than 200 years old.

The 0.25-mile Riverview Trail passes numerous big trees to connect Loeb Park with the **Redwood Nature Trail.** This trail winds 1.2 miles through the northernmost stands of naturally occurring *Sequoia sempervirens.* This is Oregon's largest redwood grove and contains the state's largest specimens. Within the grove are several trees more than 500 years old, measuring 5–8 feet in diameter, towering more than 300 feet above the forest floor. One tree here has a 33-foot girth and is estimated to exceed 800 years in age. When the south coast is foggy and cold on summer mornings, it's often warm and dry in upriver locations such as this one, inviting the possibility of swimming in the Chetco River.

The Kalmiopsis Wilderness

The lure of untrammeled wilderness attracts intrepid hikers to the Kalmiopsis, despite the summer's blazing heat and winter's torrential rains. In addition to enjoying the isolation of Oregon's largest (179,655 acres) and probably least-visited wilderness, they come to take in the pink rhododendron-like blooms of *Kalmiopsis leachiana* (in June) and other rare flowers. The area is also home to such economically valued species as Port Orford cedar and *Cannabis sativa*. The illicit weed is a leading cash crop in this part of the state, and its vigilant protection by growers should inspire extra care for those hiking here during the late fall harvest season. The potential for violence associated with the lucrative mushroom harvest here also mandates a measure of caution.

In any case, the Forest Service prohibits plant collection *of any kind* to preserve the region's special botanical populations. These include the insect-eating Darlingtonia plant and the Brewer's weeping spruce. The forest canopy is composed largely of the more common Douglas fir, canyon live oak, madrone, and chinquapin. Stark peaks top this red-rock

forest, whose understory is choked with blueberry, manzanita, and dense chaparral.

Many of this wilderness's rare species survived the glacial epoch because the glaciers from that era left the area untouched. This, combined with the fact that the area was an ancient offshore island, has enabled the region's singular ecosystem to maintain its integrity through the millennia. You'd think that federal protection, remoteness, and climatic extremes would ensure a sanguine outlook for this ice-age forest, but an active debate still rages over the validity of some logging claims.

In summer 2002, the so-called **Biscuit Fire** raged out of control for weeks, ravaging nearly half a million acres of southwestern Oregon, engulfing most of the Siskiyou National Forest and virtually all of the Kalmiopsis Wilderness. This inferno, the nation's largest wildfire of 2002 and the biggest in Oregon for more than a century, destroyed extensive habitat of the endangered northern spotted owl, whose population U.S. Forest Service biologists predict may drop by 20 percent. It will likely be decades before the forest returns to normal. The good news, however, is that flora of the region is well adapted to periodic fires; many of the old-growth trees survived the blaze, and within a few months green sprouts and new growth of many species were reappearing amid the ashes.

Even if you don't have the slightest intention of hiking the Kalmiopsis, the scenic drive through the **Chetco Valley** is worth it. From Brookings, turn off U.S. 101 at the north end of the Chetco River Bridge, follow County Roads 784 and 1376 along the Chetco River for six miles, and then turn right and follow County Road 1909 to its end. Driving distance from Brookings is 31 miles.

Bombsite Trail

Brookings takes a peculiar pride in having been bombed by the Japanese during World War II. In 1942, two incendiary bombs were dropped about 16 miles east of town on the slopes of Mount Emily. Although they were intended to start a fire, conditions were wet and the small fire that resulted was easily controlled. A sort of mutual respect eventually developed between the Japanese pilot who dropped the bomb and the town of Brookings. The pilot was a guest of honor at one Azalea Festival, and his family later presented the town with his samurai sword, which he wore during the bombing and throughout the war. The sword is now on exhibit at the local library (420 Alder St.).

The Mount Emily Bombsite Trail commemorates the bombing. It's a two-mile stretch with redwoods near the beginning and fire-dependent species such as knobcone pine and manzanita along the way. To reach the trail, head eight miles east up South Bank Road and turn right onto Mount Emily Road. At the fork, turn onto Wheeler Creek Road and follow the signs.

SPORTS AND RECREATION
Fishing
Fishing on the Chetco was once one of southern Oregon's best-kept secrets, but word has gotten out about the river's October run of huge chinook and its superlative influx of

winter steelhead. If river traffic becomes too heavy, the late-summer ocean salmon season out of Brookings may be the best in the Northwest. Boatless anglers can try their luck at the public fishing pier at the harbor and on the south jetty at the mouth of the Chetco. Chinook season generally runs mid-May to mid-September, but that's subject to change, so check the regulations.

Various fishing trips for salmon ($75 for 5–6 hours), tuna ($125 for 12 hours), and bottom fish ($60 for 5–6 hours) can be arranged through **Sporthaven Marina** (16374 Lower Harbor Rd., Brookings, 541/469-3301). In addition to fishing charters, **Tidewind Sportfishing** (16368 Lower Harbor Rd., 541/469-0337) offers **whale-watching** excursions in season.

In the fall and winter, look upriver. Pick up literature on fishing and a Siskiyou National Forest map at the ranger station in town. In addition to offering printed matter about Siskiyou and Kalmiopsis trails for hikers, the rangers can tell you where to find some good fishing

SOUTH COAST

© BILL MCRAE

The Brookings-Harbor area is an active fishing port.

holes on the nearby Chetco River, noted for its good fall salmon runs and winter steelhead.

Vulcan Lake Hike

A good introduction to the Kalmiopsis Wilderness Areas is along the one-mile trail to Vulcan Lake at the foot of Vulcan Peak, which is the major jumping-off point for trails into the wilderness. The trail begins at Forest Road 1909 and takes off up the mountains past Pollywog Butte and Red Mountain Prairie. The open patches in the Douglas fir reveal a kaleidoscope of Pacific Ocean views and panoramas of the Chetco Valley and the Big Craggies. For the botanist in search of rare plants, however, the real show is on the trail. No matter how expert you might consider yourself, bring along a good plant guide to help you identify the many exotic species here. On the final leg of the hike, sadler oak, manzanita, Jeffrey pine, white pine, and azalea precede the sharp descent to the lake. Despite steep spots, the walk from County Road 1909 to Vulcan Lake is not difficult.

If you backtrack from the lake to Spur 260 on the trail, you can make the steep ascent over talus slopes and brush to Vulcan Peak. At the top, from an old lookout, a view of Kalmiopsis treetops and the coast awaits. Before going, check with the Forest Service in Brookings to see if the road to Vulcan Lake trailhead is open, because weather-related closures occasionally occur.

To reach the trailhead from Brookings, turn east off U.S. 101 at the north end of the Chetco River Bridge, follow County Roads 784 and 1376 along the Chetco River for six miles, and then turn right and follow County Road 1909 to its end. Driving distance from Brookings is 31 miles. Hikers should watch out for the three shiny leaves of poison oak, as well as for rattlesnakes, which are numerous here. Black bears also populate the area, but their lack of contact with humans makes them more shy than their Cascade counterparts.

Camping

Harris Beach State Park (1655 U.S. 101, 541/469-2021 or 800/452-5687, $17–21), two miles north of town, is open all year, but reservations are definitely necessary from Memorial Day through Labor Day. With a total of 155 spaces, there are 149 paved sites (50 electricity only, 36 full), some with shade, six yurts, and a special camping area for hikers and bicyclists. Picnic tables and fire grills are provided. Flush toilets, electricity, piped-in water, sewer hookups, sanitary service, showers, firewood, laundry, and a playground are available. Whale-watching is particularly good here in January and May, and the birding is good year-round.

The 320-acre **Alfred A. Loeb State Park** (541/469-2021, sites $12–16 depending on season, cabins $35 year-round) is nine miles northeast of Brookings on North Bank Chetco River Road. There are 53 sites with electrical hookups for trailers/motor homes (50 feet maximum), a special campground for bicyclists and hikers, and some cabins. Electricity, piped water, and picnic tables are provided; flush toilets and firewood are available. The campground is located in a fragrant, secluded myrtlewood grove on the east bank of the Chetco River. From here, the Riverview Trail takes hikers to the Siskiyou National Forest's Redwood Nature Trail, where nature lovers will marvel at 800-year-old redwood beauties.

Beyond Loeb State Park is the more primitive **Little Redwood Campground** (mid-May–Sept., $10). To get there, go 0.5 mile south of Brookings on U.S. 101 to County Road 784, then go northeast for seven miles. At Forest Service Road 376, turn northeast and drive six miles to the campground. Contact **Chetco Ranger District** (539 Chetco Ave., 541/412-6000, www.fs.fed.us/r6/rogue-siskiyou) for information. Little Redwood is located on the main access route to the Kalmiopsis Wilderness, 20 miles away, and is a good spot for fishing during the winter steelhead run.

The Forest Service rents several cabins and fire lookouts. Contact the **Chetco Ranger District** (539 Chetco Ave., 541/412-6000, www.fs.fed.us/r6/rogue-siskiyou) for information about renting Packer's Cabin, Ludlum House, or the Quail Prairie lookout.

Surfing and Boogie Boarding

The best surfing is usually found at **Sporthaven Beach,** at the north end of the jetty in Harbor. Reach it by driving to the end of Boat Basin Road to the RV park. There's plenty of parking at the very end of the road. Even if the surf is not spectacular (it's usually best in the winter), it's a pretty mellow place for beginners, and, as a fringe benefit, it can be a good spot to see whales during their springtime or December migrations.

Boogie boarders tend to favor **Harris Beach State Park.** From fall to spring, the waves are big and dangerous and the water is cold. If you know what you're doing, come on in!

Rent gear for surfing or boogie boarding from the friendly folks at **Escape Hatch** (649 Railroad St., 541/469-2914, closed Sundays).

For some more mellow fun in the sun, cruise down Easy Street, east off U.S. 101, to Bud Cross City Park for some tennis or a dip in the outdoor pool.

Golf

All the press about Bandon Dunes has obscured the development of another great course, **Salmon Run Golf and Wilderness Preserve** (99040 South Bank Chetco River Rd., 541/469-4888, greens fees $29 for nine holes, $49 for 18 holes, excluding cart). This beautiful new 18-hole public links—not far from the Kalmiopsis Wilderness—was designed with environmentally sensitive imperatives, so numerous wildlife sightings may be enjoyed here long into the future. Whether it's the chance to see salmon (usually after the first rains in November) and steelhead spawning (January), black bears, elk, and wild turkeys, or just the opportunity to play a first-rate course, golfers shouldn't overlook this one. Beginner and intermediate players may find the executive nine-hole course ideal. This par-34 course within a course is located on the back nine holes and measures 1,310 yards. Your Oregon coastal golf pilgrimage can begin here, then hit Bandon Dunes, Sandpines (Florence), and Salishan (near Lincoln City).

ENTERTAINMENT AND EVENTS

The **Beachcomber's Festival** (800/535-9469), held in late March at the Azalea Middle School (505 Pacific Ave.), features exhibits, demonstrations, and slide shows, as well as an art competition for the best works wrought from indigenous materials such as driftwood, agates, and other beachcomber treasures. To get there, follow Pacific Avenue east of the highway.

Brookings' big event is the **Azalea Festival** (541/469-3181 or 800/535-9469), an unforgettable floral fantasia that takes place each Memorial Day weekend. Among the activities are a parade, flower display, crafts fair, 5K run, seafood luncheon, and beef barbecue. Much of the activity revolves around Azalea Park. This Works Progress Administration–built enclave features 20-foot-high azaleas (several hundred years old) and hand-hewn myrtlewood picnic tables. Wild cherry and crabapple blooms, wild strawberry blossoms, and purple and red violets round out the bouquet. Butterflies, bees, and birds all seem to concur with locals that this array smells sweetest around graduation time in mid-June. To get there, take Pacific Avenue east of the highway, and turn onto Azalea Park Road.

Like several other Oregon coast towns, Brookings puts its windy weather to good use with its annual **Southern Oregon Kite Festival** (541/469-2218), held over two days in mid-July. Individuals and teams display their aerial skills at the port of Brookings-Harbor.

Azalea Park is also home to **Nature's Coastal Holiday Light Show** in December, with more than 75,000 lights. The city park is located on the south end of town. The Brookings-Harbor Garden Club and Chamber of Commerce offer garden tours of this park and other gardens. Call the chamber (541/469-3181) for more information on tours and garden-related events.

ACCOMMODATIONS

Rooms in Brookings are generally rather expensive; there are more budget lodging 29

BROOKINGS: FROM BOX FACTORY TO RETIREMENT HAVEN

What is now the shopping hub of rural Curry County started out as a factory town for the Brookings Box Company in 1913. Owner J. L. Brookings hired the architect Bernard Maybeck (famous for designing the Palace of Fine Arts in San Francisco) to lay out the streets and design housing and community buildings for his mill workers. Maybeck drew up extensive plans for a model company town, but most of them were never realized; his central vision was eventually gutted when the state highway was laid through, rather than around, the town. Examples of Maybeck's craftsmanship can still be seen around Brookings, notably in the 1917 Craftsman-style residence (now the South Coast Inn B&B) he drew up for lumber baron William Ward.

In the years that followed, the lumber industry was augmented with fishing, horticulture, and tourism. Omitting, for the moment, the possibility that the offshore waters here were visited by Juan Cabrillo (in 1542) and the English explorer Sir Francis Drake (in 1579), the local event with the greatest historical significance was the Japanese aerial bombing in 1942. On September 9 of that year, a Japanese incendiary bomb scorched the treetops of Mt. Emily, southeast of town, in one of only two documented wartime air bombing missions against the U.S. mainland (the other occurred three weeks later, near Port Orford). The resulting fires were quickly doused by the damp conditions, and no significant harm was done.

Ironically, this episode had two positive outgrowths of enduring significance. First, it sounded the death knell for a secessionist movement by southern Oregonians and northern Californians. During the 1930s, these people wanted to break off from the Union to set up the self-sufficient agrarian state of Jefferson. Second, the bombing encouraged the local lily industry to expand in an effort to make up for the cutoff of Japanese flowers. Today, the area produces 90 percent of the world's Easter lily crop.

Twenty years after the bomb attack, the Japanese pilot Nobuo Fujita accepted an invitation to return to Brookings during the town's Azalea Festival. He brought with him the 400-year-old samurai sword he had carried on his missions during the war and presented it to the people of Brookings as a token of reconciliation. It still hangs on display in the Brookings city library. Fujita returned again in 1992, as the guest of honor for the opening of a new Forest Service trail to the bombsite, on the 50th anniversary of the attack. At age 80, he hiked the new trail and planted a redwood seedling in the bomb crater as a token of peace.

Since the late 1980s, Brookings' greatest growth industry has been as a haven for retirees, and that population has been booming in recent years.

miles north in Gold Beach. It's also harder to find pet-friendly lodgings here than in most other coast towns.

$50-100

Just north of the Chetco River Bridge, **Wild Rivers Motor Inn** (437 Chetco Ave., 541/469-5361, www.wildriversmotorlodge.com, doubles from $60) is the most attractive roadside budget motel in town. Rooms come with refrigerators and microwaves.

The **Spindrift Motor Inn** (1215 Chetco Ave., 541/469-5345 or 800/292-1171, doubles from $55) is a good value. However, its ambience is strictly roadside budget, and it is a bit of a walk to the beach.

The highway-side **Best Western Brookings Inn** (1143 U.S. 101, 541/469-2173 or 800/822-9087, doubles from $85) may be about a mile from the ocean, but it's family-friendly with a pool and whirlpool tub, a comfy myrtlewood-paneled lounge, and a decent on-site restaurant.

At the southern edge of the Brookings-Harbor stretch of U.S. 101, the **Harbor Inn Motel**

(15991 U.S. 101 S., 541/469-3194 or 800/469-8444, $82) is not a bad place to land. It's nothing fancy, but it's pretty quiet and permits pets. If you head west from the stoplight at the motel, it's about a mile to the port of Harbor.

$100 and Up

The nicest places to stay in the Brookings area are bed-and-breakfast inns, and they aren't that much more expensive than the run-of-the-mill local motel rooms.

A coastal gem one block north of the highway, the [**South Coast Inn B&B** (516 Redwood St., Brookings, 541/469-5557 or 800/525-9273, www.southcoastinn.com, doubles $99–159) is a 1917 Craftsman building and was once the home of lumber baron William W ard. Designed by famed architect Bernard Maybeck and situated in the heart of old Brookings just blocks away from the beach and shopping, this 4,000-square-foot B&B offers four rooms, a guest cottage, and an apartment. All rooms have TVs with VCR (and access to the inn's video library), private bath, and other amenities. An indoor spa with a sauna and hot tub and an included breakfast featuring a health-conscious menu are additional enticements to book space early. Ask the friendly innkeepers about other Maybeck structures in town.

Head upstream to find a really great B&B, the [**Chetco River Inn** (21202 High Prairie Rd., 541/251-0087 or 800/327-2688, www.chetcoriverinn.com, doubles $125–145), an intimate inn surrounded by water on three sides. Eighteen miles inland from the coast, the half-hour drive to the inn takes you to the periphery of the Kalmiopsis; once there you feel as if you're in your own private forest. Its location near prime fishing river frontage makes this place especially popular during steelhead season. Swimming holes abound close by, and the absence of city lights makes for good stargazing. The welcome mat here is laid out in the form of thick oriental carpets on floors of green and black marble. Tasteful antiques also decorate this reasonably priced first-class lodging. The five rooms plus cottage can easily accommodate up to 14 people in separate beds, or six couples. Children are welcome; cottages are suggested for their comfort. Smoking is limited to outdoors only. No pets are allowed.

For a B&B that's close to the ocean, **By the Sea B&B** (1545 Beach Ave., 541/469-4692 or 877/469-4692, www.brookingsbythesea.com, doubles $150) offers a choice of two rooms or the lodge room, which features fishing and hunting decor. A full breakfast is served upstairs in the dining room. Enjoy breakfast and breathtaking ocean views from the stained-glass-topped windows. The house is filled with antiques and the smell of homemade bread. A deluxe continental breakfast is also available, with seasonal fruits and homemade breads, if you prefer to eat in private. On the upper veranda, a spa and a wood-burning fire pot is available for guest use.

The best conventional hotels are in Harbor. Here, **Best Western Beachfront Inn** (16008 Boat Basin Rd., Harbor, 541/469-7779 or 800/468-4081, doubles from $149) is the nicer of the town's two Best Westerns. It's off the main highway, offering a window on a colorful port. All units feature private decks, microwaves, and refrigerators. Kitchenettes as well as suites with ocean-view hot tubs and an indoor pool are available. Pets are permitted on a very limited basis; call the hotel direct to plead your case.

Perhaps the best value in Brookings lodgings is [**Ocean Suites** (16045 Lower Harbor Rd., 541/469-4004, www.oceansuitesmotel.com, doubles from $99), at the Harbor end of town, which also has weekly rates ($550). These really are suites: each has a full kitchen and living room. No pets are allowed.

Vacation Rentals

For vacation home rentals, **Coastal Country Rentals** (15957 U.S. 101 S., 541/469-9568, www.coastalcountryrentals.com) and **Premier Properties Brokerage and Property Management** (1025 Chetco Ave., Ste. 3, 541/469-7400 or 800/221-8175, www.aaa oregonrealestate.com) can provide you with a list of available homes.

Cottage rentals are also available at **Whaleshead Beach Resort** (19921 Whaleshead Rd., 541/469-7446 or 800/943-4325, www.whalesheadresort.com) by the night or by the week. This sprawling development is on a bluff north of town, just across the highway from Whaleshead Beach, a beautiful spot in Boardman State Park.

FOOD

Brookings has a profusion of family-friendly, though somewhat mediocre, restaurants that serve large portions at a good value. For slightly more distinctive fare, check out the following places.

Breakfast *Wonderful quiche!*

Suzie Q's Bakery and Cafe (613 Chetco Ave., 541/412-7444, open for breakfast and lunch daily, dinner Thurs.–Sat., dinner entrées around $20) is a cheery spot with delicious morning pastries, artisan bread, and good breakfasts. There's a more romantic bistro-style ambience at dinner, but baked goods are really the forte here.

Breakfast is also good at family-friendly **Mattie's Pancake House** (15975 U.S. 101 S., 541/469-7311).

Mexican

At the north end of town, **La Flor de Mexico** (541 Chetco Ave., 541/469-4102, open for lunch and dinner daily) has a lunchtime buffet and good Mexican dinners. Another longtime Brookings favorite, Rubio's, has reopened in its old location with a new name: **Pancho's** (1136 Chetco Ave., 541/469-4919). Look for homemade salsa and chiles rellenos here.

Seafood

In Harbor, **Chetco Seafood** (16182 Lower Harbor Rd., 541/469-9251) is the best place in town to buy fish, either to cook yourself or to eat onsite. It's owned by anglers, and you'll always find the freshest stuff here. The fish and chips in beer batter are as good as any on the coast.

A coastal town is certainly a safe place to eat sushi. In Brookings, find it at **Cafe Kitanishi**

(632 Hemlock St., 541/469-7864, open for lunch Tues.–Sat., dinner Thurs.–Sat.), which also serves bento boxes to go and has an espresso bar with Internet access.

Casual Fare

Wild River Pizza (16279 U.S. 101, Harbor, 541/469-7454, open for lunch and dinner daily) is part of the Wild River Brewing family, with pizza-brewpubs in Cave Junction and Grants Pass. The crispy crust pizza is the best you'll find in the area. While the food is good and inexpensive, this large restaurant tends to fill up with families enjoying the video games and pool tables on weekends. In other words, go elsewhere for an intimate Saturday night dinner. Look for it on the east side of the highway about a mile south of the Brookings-Harbor Bridge at the four-way stoplight.

For lighter fare for those heading out to explore, try **The Tea Room** (434 Redwood St. #4, 541/469-7240) for sandwiches, soups, salads, and baked goods; fill your to-go mugs with a nice cuppa the hot stuff. This place is worth seeing just for its humongous collection of teapots.

PRACTICALITIES
Visitor Information

Pull off the highway and talk to the friendly folks at the **Oregon Welcome Center** just north of town (1650 U.S. 101, Brookings, 541/469-4117, open 9 A.M.–5 P.M. Mon.–Sat., Apr.–Oct.). It offers brochures about the coast and the rest of the state. For additional information pertinent to Brookings and environs, the **Brookings-Harbor Chamber of Commerce** (16330 Lower Harbor Rd., Brookings, 541/469-3181 or 800/535-9469, www.brookingsor.com) is located down at the harbor.

Recreational information, including forest and trail maps for the Siskiyou National Forest and the Kalmiopsis Wilderness, is available at the **Chetco Ranger Station** (539 Chetco Ave., Brookings, 541/412-6000, open 7:30 A.M.–4:30 P.M. Mon.–Fri.).

Wondering about **offshore weather conditions?** The Coast Guard hotline (541/469-2242) has the answers.

Services

Brookings-Harbor Medical Center (585 5th St., 541/469-7401) is the largest medical facility in town. The **post office** (711 Spruce St., Brookings 97415, 800/275-8777) is downtown, one block south of U.S. 101. For laundry, the **Old Wash House** (corner of Shopping Center Ave. and Grodendorst Lane, 541/469-3975) is clean and convenient.

For banking and a walk-up ATM, try **Evergreen Federal** (850 Chetco Ave.).

Getting There and Around

It's tough to get to Brookings using public transportation. Curry County's **Coastal Express** buses (800/921-2871) run up and down the south coast weekdays only between North Bend and the California border, including local service in Brookings. **Porter Stage Lines** (541/269-7183) also runs along the southern Oregon coast, then turns inland at Florence and goes to Eugene, Bend, and Ontario.

BACKGROUND

The Land

The Oregon coast we know today encompasses nearly 400 miles of beaches, rainforest, dunes, high-rise headlands, rocky sea stacks and islands, and tidal pools showcasing marine worlds in miniature. The narrow coastal plateau is hemmed in by the Klamath Mountains in the state's southern quarter and by the Coast Range beginning near Coos Bay in the north, which together form a palisade between the sea and the state's interior. Neither range is particularly high; the tallest peaks in each of these cordilleras barely top 4,000 feet. More than a dozen major rivers and scores of smaller streams cut through these mountain barriers to the sea. The valleys that the rivers follow through the mountains are the same routes traversed now by the east-west highways that link the coast with the rest of the state.

Tectonics

Timeless as it may appear to the modern observer, the Oregon coast hasn't always been where or as we see it today. Titanic forces shaped—and continue to affect—this coastal region and indeed the entire Pacific Northwest. The giant tectonic plates that make up the earth's crust slide under one another as they collide. In Pacific Northwest coastal regions, this takes place when the Juan de Fuca plate's marine layer is subducted, or pushed under, the

© BILL MCRAE

continental North American plate. The stress of this collision heaved up the Klamath Mountains some 225 million years ago and created the Coast Range 20–50 million years ago. This subduction is ongoing, and the resulting geologic pressure that builds from it is released periodically in earthquakes, large and small.

With virtually every part of the coastline possessing seismic potential that hasn't been released in many years, the pressure along the fault lines is increasing. Scientists have unearthed discontinuities in rock strata and tree rings on the north Oregon coast, indicating that Tillamook County has experienced major tremors every few hundred years. They estimate that the next one could come within our lifetimes and be of significant magnitude. In coastal areas, one of the greatest dangers associated with earthquakes is the possibility of **tsunamis.**

The ocean waves produced by seismic activity can be enormous and devastating. Ever since a tsunami unleashed by Alaska's Good Friday quake in 1964 (measured at 14.2 feet high at the mouth of the Umpqua River) resulted in four casualties in Beverly Beach and more than $1 million in damage, local authorities have made seismic preparedness a priority.

Along the coast today, warning sirens stand ready. Visitors will also see blue evacuation signs pointing the way to higher ground and escape routes, acknowledging the imminent danger of a 30-foot wave that could strike within minutes of an offshore tremblor.

Ice and Fire

At the height of the most recent major glaciation, sea level of the world's oceans was some 300–500 feet lower than it is now. North America and Asia were connected by a land bridge across the Bering Strait. The Oregon seashore lay miles west of where it is now, and the Columbia Gorge extended out past present-day Astoria.

As the glaciers melted, the sea rose. When that glacial epoch's final meltdown 12,000 years ago unleashed water dammed up by thick ice, great rivers were spawned and existing channels were enlarged. A particularly large inundation was the Missoula Flood, which began with an ice dam breaking up in present-day Montana. Before it subsided, it carved out the contours of what are now the Columbia River Gorge and the Willamette Valley. Other glacial floodwaters found their outlet westward to the sea, flushing out silt-ridden estuaries in the process. Pacific wave action eventually washed this debris back up onto the land, creating beaches and sand dunes.

Like the rest of the state, the Oregon coast also shows off distinct remnants of Oregon's volcanic past. The offshore waters are scattered with 1,477 volcanic islets. These rocky outcrops, as well as many of the headlands that separate the beaches, are made of erosion-resistant basalt, an extremely durable igneous material that has endured long after wind and waves have eroded the softer surrounding earth.

The Beach: Contours and Character

For most Oregon visitors who travel west of the Coast Range, life is a beach. Despite Pacific temperatures cold enough to render swimming an at-your-own-risk activity, the cliffside ocean vistas, wildlife, beachcombing, and other attractions make the coast the state's number-one regional destination.

With rare exceptions, all beaches in Oregon below mean high tide are owned by the public. This is thanks largely to Governor Oswald West, who in 1913 pushed through legislation defining Oregon's ocean beaches as public highways (which they in fact were before real roads were built) and thus off-limits to private encroachment. Later, Oregon's Beach Bills of 1967 and 1972 were written to further guarantee public access to the state's gem of a coastline. In recent years, however, certain sections of this publicly owned paradise have increasingly become exclusive bailiwicks of the wealthy, with gated communities cutting off access to the beaches.

Black sand, high in iron and other metals, is common on the coast, particularly south of Coos Bay. There was also enough gold in the black sands to spur a flurry of gold-mining activity on the south coast 140 years ago. Scientists have known for decades of the placer deposits of heavy minerals washed ashore on prehistoric beaches thousands of years ago when ocean levels were much lower. These beach sands now lie submerged. These days, mining companies are eyeing the continental shelf off the south coast for possible exploitation of ilmenite, magnetite, chromite, zircon, garnet, gold, and platinum. Despite a study indicating a significant presence of precious metals in the sands offshore from the Rogue River and Cape Blanco, incipient prospecting ventures were abandoned.

Speaking of sand, the central Oregon coast has about 32,000 acres of shimmering white **dunes,** the largest oceanfront collection in North America and the highest in the world. Some hills top out at more than 500 feet high. Oregon's Sahara is located along a 40-mile stretch between Coos Bay and Florence. Buffeted by winds, the dunes are continually on the move; in some places, highways are in danger of being engulfed by the shifting sands.

CLIMATE

Oregon's location equidistant from the equator and the North Pole subjects the state to weather from both tropical and polar air flows. This makes for a pattern of changeability in which calm often alternates with storm. Although it's difficult to predict daily weather patterns in western Oregon, there are definite seasonal climatic shifts here. In winter, arctic and tropical air masses collide over the Pacific, producing much of the state's rain. During summer, the clashes are much less frequent. At that time, Oregon weather is most affected by Pacific Ocean temperatures and air pressure differences between inland and coastal areas.

Oregon's coastal weather can best be summed up as wet and mild. The coast as a whole receives roughly 70 inches of rain yearly on average. Most of that falls from late fall to mid-spring, whereas May through September are generally fairly dry.

Lincoln City and vicinity tend to record the highest amounts of rain, with nearly 100 inches per year, while towns both north and south are

generally less wet by comparison. Coastbound travelers should bear in mind that inland from the coastal plateau, the Coast and Klamath ranges receive substantially more precipitation because as moisture-laden westerlies blow in from the Pacific, they slam into the mountain slopes and are pushed upward. As the clouds climb higher, they drop their moisture in the form of rain or snow because rising air cools, and cooler air can't hold as much moisture as warm air. As a consequence, precipitation averages 150 inches a year over the coastal mountains (in the winter of 1996–1997, Laurel Mountain, in the Coast Range near Lincoln City, was drenched with 204 inches, Oregon's record). Anyone driving through the Coast Range sees evidence of the siege mentality that sets in with each winter monsoon season. Giant satellite-TV dishes and stacks of covered firewood are common lawn ornaments here in the rainiest part of the state.

The moderating influence of the Pacific Ocean gives the coastal region an unusually mild climate for a state so far north. Coastal temperatures are fairly constant throughout the year, and extremes are rare. With infrequent freezes and rarely recorded snowfall, Old Man Winter definitely pulls his punches here. In fact, Coos Bay, for example, is often touted as having one of the mildest (in terms of absence of extremes) year-round climates in the United States. Even in winter, daytime highs along the coast tend to reach the mid-50s Fahrenheit, and nighttime lows generally drop into the 40s. Spring, summer, and fall see highs in the 60s and into the 70s, with overnight lows staying in the mid-40s to mid-50s. Summer highs above 90°F are unusual, although the mercury in south coast locations such as Brookings and Bandon has topped 100°F on rare occasions. Midwinter and spring dry spells with 60°F-plus temperatures commonly occur.

Any time of year, the coast can be very windy; particularly in winter and spring, you may encounter proper gales scouring the beach. Although that can make for terrific kite-flying, picnics aren't quite so much fun at those times. In winter, the winds typically blow from the south and southwest, whereas the gentler summer winds usually come from the northeast.

Flora and Fauna

FLORA

The state of Oregon has long been associated in the public mind with such sobriquets as the Emerald Empire and the Chlorophyll Commonwealth. Although giant conifers and a profuse understory of greenery do in fact predominate, this ecosystem represents only the most visible part of the Oregon coast's bountiful botany. In addition to Brookings' Azalea Festival and Florence's Rhododendron Festival, coast-bound travelers come to take in such horticultural highlights as the insect-eating Darlingtonia plant, Oregon myrtle trees, and some remaining stands of ancient old-growth forest. Serious botanists might search out the pine mushroom, exclusive to the Oregon dunes and Japan, or probe the Kalmiopsis Wilderness near the south coast, habitat to many rare plants.

Coos Bay marks the boundary between the Mediterranean beach floras found south into California and the subarctic species growing north from there into Washington and British Columbia.

Trees

Sandwiched between the mountains and the sea, the mixed-conifer ecosystem of western Oregon's wet lowlands, comprising primarily fir, western hemlock, Sitka spruce, and cedar, is the most productive belt of evergreens in the world. The conifers are broken up by pockets of alder, oak, vine maple, bigleaf maple, and myrtle trees. With its dense understory of rhododendron, thimbleberry, salmonberry, blackberry, and salal interspersed among the ferns and mosses that carpet the forest floor, this woodland carries up to 1,000 tons of plant matter per hectare and sometimes more. Because of the construction industry's penchant for Douglas fir *(Pseudotsuga menziesii),* which they replant assiduously, this tree predominates.

Oregon schoolchildren learn to distinguish between fir, spruce, and hemlock by a mnemonic device: The needles of a fir are flat, flexible, and friendly. Spruce needles are square, stiff, and will stick you. Hemlock needles have a hammocklike configuration, and the crown of the tree is curved like it's tipping its hat. *Trees to Know in Oregon,* published by the Oregon State University Extension Service in Corvallis, is an excellent aid to tree identification, as well as a compendium of useful facts.

The Oregon myrtle, *(Umbellularia californica),* the only tree in its genus, is native only to the Holy Land, southern Oregon, and northern California (where it's more commonly known as California laurel or California bay). The hard, yellowish wood of the aromatic myrtle tree is so dense that when green it sinks in water. It is prized by woodworkers and especially woodturners for its distinctive coloring and grain. The value of myrtlewood, in fact, reached a peak during the Depression, when North Bend issued myrtlewood scrip, in the form of coins ranging from $0.50 to $10, after the only bank in town failed.

Among these coastal forests, several extraordinary individual trees have managed to survive the ax and chainsaw, and the region boasts such record specimens as the 329-foot-high, 11.5-foot-diameter Doerner fir in the Coast Range outside Coquille, rated the nation's largest Douglas fir by the American Forestry Association based on height, diameter, and crown size. An exceptionally large, though perhaps not the world's largest, Sitka spruce grows off U.S. 26 near Cannon Beach, and the world's largest Monterey cypress is found in Brookings.

Dune, Beach, and Bog

Apart from the spectacular springtime fireworks of rhododendron and azalea blossoms, the Oregon coast doesn't show off its wildflowers as boldly as other parts of the state, such as Steens Mountain, the Cascades, and the Wallowas. The flowering plants of beach, dunes, and headlands tend to be more subtle but are nevertheless varied and worth seeking out. Among some of the species found only along the Oregon coast are beach bursage, yellow sand verbena, beach evening primrose, seashore bluegrass, dune tansy, and silvery phacelia. The best time for wildflowers is usually June and July. An excellent guide for those interested in coastal wildflowers is *Introduction to Shore Wildflowers of California, Oregon, and Washington,* published by the University of California Press.

Many coastal travelers will notice **European beachgrass** *(Ammophila arenaria)* covering the sand wherever they go. Originally planted in the 1930s to inhibit dune growth, the thick, rapidly spreading grass worked too well, solidifying into a ridge behind the shoreline, blocking the windblown sand from replenishing the rest of the beach and suppressing native plants. Populations of formerly common natives such as beach morning glory, yellow abronia, gray beach pea, and American dune-grass are now much diminished. The endangered pink sand verbena—once abundant along the coast from British Columbia to northern California—is now restricted to a few locations along the central and southern Oregon coast. Herbicides, burning, and tilling have been employed in recent years to remove European beachgrass and restore the dune ecosystem to a more natural state, but progress against the pernicious weed is slow and difficult.

Freshwater wetlands and bogs, created where water is trapped by the sprawling sand dunes along the central coast, provide habitats for some unusual species. Best known among these is the cobra lily *(Darlingtonia californica),* which can be viewed up close at Darlingtonia State Natural Site just north of Florence. Also called Darlingtonia or pitcher plant, this carnivorous bog dweller survives on hapless insects lured into its specialized chamber. For more information, see *Darlingtonia Botanical Gardens* in the *Florence and Vicinity* section of the *Central Coast* chapter.

Coastal salt marshes, occurring in the upper intertidal zones of coastal bays and estuaries, have been dramatically reduced because of land reclamation projects such as drainage, diking, and other human disturbances. The halophytes (salt-loving plants) that thrive in this specialized environment include pickleweed, saltgrass, fleshy jaumea, salt marsh dodder, arrow-grass, sand spurrey, and seaside plantain. For an excellent introduction to this complex ecosystem, visit the South Slough National Estuarine Research Reserve, south of Coos Bay. Bandon Marsh National Wildlife Refuge protects the largest remaining tract of salt marsh within the Coquille River estuary. Major habitats include undisturbed salt marsh, mudflat, and Sitka spruce and alder riparian communities, which provide resting and feeding areas for migratory waterfowl, shore and wading birds, and raptors.

Mushrooms

Autumn, particularly from the first rains until the onset of frosts, is the season for those who covet chanterelle, matsutake, and morel mushrooms. The Coast Range from September to November is the prime picking area for chanterelles—a fluted orange or yellow mushroom in the tall second-growth Douglas fir forests. If you plan to sell what you find, you need to purchase a permit from the National Forest Service for a nominal fee. Of course, you should be absolutely certain of any wild mushroom's identity before you eat it.

In recent years, fungus fever reached epidemic proportions, largely because of a matsutake mushroom shortage in Japan, where it is prized for medicinal and spiritual qualities and enjoyed as a soup garnish. In the mid-1990s, for example, matsutakes fetched up to $500 per pound in Japan, a price that precipitated violence in northern Klamath County forests and other areas saturated with pickers during the fall harvest. This mycological harvest, along with the cutting of ferns (maidenhair ferns command an especially high price from florists), beargrass, and other ornamental greenery, helps many residents of forest communities make ends meet.

FAUNA

The animal kingdom is well represented by a great diversity and abundance of creatures along the coast, in the air, on the land, under the water, and in between. Opportunities for

© MARK MORRIS

Inspecting tidepools is a favorite activity on the Oregon coast.

wildlife viewing abound all along the coast, but standout areas include the state's six coastal national wildlife refuges: Oregon Islands, Cape Meares, and Three Arch Rocks protect important habitat for seabirds, seals, and sea lions among coastal rocks, reefs, islands, and several headland areas, while Nestucca Bay, Siletz Bay, and Bandon Marsh national wildlife refuges preserve estuarine habitats of salt marsh, wetlands, and woods rich in waterfowl, raptors, fish, and other fauna. *The Audubon Guide to the National Wildlife Refuges: Alaska and the Northwest* is an excellent reference book to have along on your explorations.

Tidepools

For most visitors, the most fascinating coastal ecosystems in Oregon are the rocky tidepools. These Technicolor windows offer an up-close look at one of the richest—and harshest—environments, the intertidal zone, where pummeling surf, unflinching sun, and the cycle of tides demand tenacity and special adaptation of its inhabitants.

Marine biologists subdivide this natural blender where surf meets bedrock into three main habitat layers, based on their position relative to tide levels. The **high intertidal zone,** inundated only during the highest tides, is home to creatures that can move, such as crabs, or are well adapted to tolerate daily desiccation, such as acorn barnacles, finger limpets, chitons, and green algae. The turbulent **mid-intertidal zone** is covered and uncovered by the tides, usually twice each day. In the upper portion of this zone, California mussels and goose barnacles may thickly blanket the rocks, while ochre sea stars and green sea anemones are common lower down, along with sea lettuce, sea palms, snails, sponges, and whelks. Below that, the **low intertidal zone** is only exposed during the lowest tides. Because it is covered by water most of the time, this zone has the greatest diversity of organisms in the tidal area. Residents include many of the organisms found in the higher zones, as well as sculpins, abalone, and purple sea urchins.

Standout destinations for exploring tidepools

include Cape Arago, Cape Perpetua, the Marine Gardens at Devil's Punchbowl, and beaches south and north of Gold Beach—among many other spots. Tidepool explorers should be mindful that, although the plants and animals in the tidepools are well adapted to withstand the elements, they and their ecosystem are fragile, and they're sensitive to human interference. Avoid stepping on mussels, anemones, and barnacles, and take nothing from the tidepools. In the Oregon Islands National Wildlife Refuge and other specially protected areas, removal or harassment of any living organism may be treated as a misdemeanor punishable by fines.

Birds

One of the most immediately noticeable forms of wildlife at the coast are the birds of sea, shore, and estuary. The abundance and variety of species you may encounter are a large part of the reason that Oregon is rapidly gaining a reputation as one of the best bird-watching states. Seasonal variance in populations is often dramatic, so timing is important.

The **Oregon Islands National Wildlife Refuge,** which comprises all the 1,400-plus offshore islands, reefs, and rocks from Tillamook Head to the California border, is a haven for the largest concentration of nesting seabirds along the west coast of the United States, thanks to the abundance of protected nesting habitat. During the April–August breeding season, seabirds that can be seen here include common murres, pigeon guillemots, rare tufted puffins, Brandt's and pelagic cormorants, and black oystercatchers, along with the ubiquitous western gulls. June to October, you may spy brown pelicans skimming the waves. Aleutian Canada geese use Table and Haystack rocks during March and early April.

In terms of sheer numbers and variety, the coast's mudflats at low tide and the tidal estuaries also make excellent bird-watching environments. Species to look for on the flats and shorelines include Pacific golden plovers, pectoral, and Baird's sandpipers. The **western snowy plover,** listed as threatened under the Endangered Species Act, gets special protec-

© PAUL LEVY

Remember to bring binoculars on a trip to the Oregon coast – it's prime bird-watching territory.

tion at the state's nine nesting sites in Curry, Coos, Douglas, and Lane counties. The small shorebird, which resembles a sandpiper, nests on open sandy beaches above the high-tide line and is sensitive to disturbance from human foot traffic, vehicles, and unleashed dogs. During the nesting season, mid-March–mid-September, coast visitors may encounter areas posted or roped off to protect snowy plover nests.

Resident and migratory birds commonly spotted on the estuaries and lakes of the coast include common loon, western and horned grebes, great blue heron, American widgeon, greater scaup, common goldeneye, bufflehead, and red-breasted merganser.

Seals, Sea Lions, and Otters

Pacific harbor seals, California sea lions, and Steller sea lions are frequently sighted in Oregon waters. California sea lions are the animals you might have seen in circuses. These 1,000-pound mammals are characterized by their large size and small earflaps, which seals lack. Unlike seals, they can point their rear flippers forward to give them better mobility on land. Without the dense underfur that covers seals, sea lions tend to prefer warmer waters.

Steller sea lions can be seen at the Sea Lion Caves north of Florence. They also breed on reefs off Gold Beach and Port Orford. They are the largest sea lion species, with males sometimes weighing more than a ton. Their coats tend to be more gray than the black-coated California sea lion's. They also differ from their California counterparts in that they are comfortable in colder water.

Look for Pacific harbor seals in bays and estuaries up and down the coast, sometimes miles inland. They're nonmigratory, have no earflaps, and can be distinguished from sea lions because they're much smaller (150–300 pounds) and have mottled fur that ranges in color from pale cream to rusty brown.

Another marine mammal that was once common on the Oregon coast, and along the entire Pacific coast from Japan to Mexico, is the **sea otter.** Two centuries of ruthless hunting by Russian, European, and American fur

traders, though, nearly eradicated the species. By the time Oregon's last known sea otter was killed, in 1906, the otters had disappeared from British Columbia to central California. Today, the only sea otters living in Oregon are those in the Oregon Zoo and the Oregon Coast Aquarium, but an organization called the Elakha Alliance is working to restore wild otters to their natural habitat. You can learn about and support their important work at www.ecotrust .org/community/elakha.html.

Gray Whales

Few sights along the Oregon coast (or any coast, for that matter) elicit more excitement than that of a surfacing whale. The most common large whale seen from shore along the west coast of North America is the gray whale *(Eschrichtius robustus)*. These behemoths can reach 45 feet in length and weigh 35 tons. The sight of a mammal as big as a Greyhound bus breaking water has a way of emptying the mind of mundane concerns. Wreathed in seaweed and sporting barnacles and other parasites on its back, a California gray whale might look more like the hull of an old ship but for its expressive eyes.

After decades of hunting brought them to the brink of extinction, gray whales gained full protection in 1946 by the International Whaling Commission. In the ensuing years, the population has recovered dramatically. When the gray whale was delisted from the Endangered Species List in 1994, the population was estimated at 23,000, which is thought to be close to the pre-whaling population. Gray whales continue to enjoy protection worldwide, apart from a quota of 176 whales harvested each year along the Siberian coast.

Some gray whales are found off the Oregon coast all year, including an estimated 200–400 during summer, although they're most visible and numerous when migrating populations pass through Oregon waters on their way south December–February and northward early March–April. This annual journey from the rich feeding grounds of the Bering and Chukchi seas of Alaska to the calving grounds of Mexico amounts to some 10,000 miles, the longest migration of any mammal.

Grays feed primarily on bottom-dwelling, shrimp-like amphipods, scooping up huge mouthfuls from which they filter out water and sediment through the fringe of baleen inside their mouths. After fattening up in the rich waters of the arctic during the summer and fall, gray whales begin their migration south. In early December, pregnant females are the first to begin showing up along the Oregon coast, followed by mature adults of both sexes and then by juveniles. Their numbers peak usually during the first week of January, when as many as 30 per hour may pass a given point. By mid-February, most of the whales will have moved on toward their breeding and calving lagoons on the west coast of Baja California.

Early March–April, the juveniles, adult males, and females without calves begin returning northward past the Oregon coast. Mothers and their new calves are the last to leave Mexico and move more slowly, passing Oregon late April–June. During the spring migration, the whales may pass within just a few hundred yards of coastal headlands, making this a particularly exciting time for whale-watching from many vantage points along the coast. Researchers speculate that gray whales stay close to shore as a way to help them navigate.

Land Mammals

Many of the most frequently sighted animals in coastal Oregon are small scavengers, which are frequently encountered in woodsier campgrounds, parks, and picnic areas: raccoons, skunks, Townsend's chipmunks, Douglas squirrels, and opossums.

Black-tailed deer are commonly spotted in woods and meadows all along the coast, and a herd of their larger cousins, the majestic Roosevelt elk, can be seen at the Dean Creek Elk Viewing Area near Reedsport.

On streams and brooks, observant hikers may spot the handiwork of **beavers**—lodges and dams built of branches and twigs—if not the camera-shy builders themselves. The state's animal mascot is widespread, most commonly sighted in second-growth forests near marshes after sunset. Fall is a good time to spot beavers as they gather food for winter.

Although **black bears** proliferate in remote mountain forests of Oregon (the state's Department of Fish and Wildlife estimates that 14,000–19,000 black bears roam the western Cascades and the Coast Range), chances are slim that you'll sight one. Black bears shy away from people except when provoked by the scent of food, when cornered or surprised, or upon human intrusion into territory near their cubs.

A little-known oddity of the coast, from southern British Columbia to northern California, is the **mountain beaver** *(Aplodontia rufa),* known locally as "boomers." This most primitive species of living rodents is not actually a beaver but resembles (and is roughly the size of) a grayish-brown guinea pig. Although the animal was first reported by Lewis and Clark, and it's still fairly populous, most people have never heard of the boomer, let alone seen one. They thrive in dense understory vegetation such as coniferous forests and coastal scrub. These herbivores eat all types of succulent vegetation, including plants that are inedible to other species such as nettle, bracken fern, and salal. Their predilection for Douglas fir seedlings has made them the scourge of the timber industry.

Another rodent common along the coast is the **nutria,** introduced to Oregon in the 1930s from South America to be farmed for its fur (and meat). After numerous escapes, this furry pest established a niche in the woodlands of the Coast Range. About two feet long and similar in appearance to a true beaver (minus the flat tail), voracious nutrias damage many crop plants in Oregon. Furthermore, they may cause erosion by digging into streambeds or the levees that protect lowlands from floods. Currently, a year-round open season encourages hunting and trapping of this varmint to reduce its numbers.

Other Land Creatures

You won't have to look for long in the coast

© MARK MORRIS

the banana slug, ubiquitous denizen of the forest floor

woodlands or underbrush before you encounter Oregon's best-known invertebrates— **banana slugs**—and lots of them. In few places on earth do these snails-out-of-shells grow as large and in such numbers. The reason is western Oregon's climate: moister than mist but drier than drizzle. This balance and calcium-poor soil enables the native banana slug and the more common European black slug to thrive as the bane of Oregon gardeners. When these 3- to 10-inch squirts of slime are not eating plants, you'll see them moving along at a snail's pace on some sidewalk or forest trail. The eight species of nonnative slugs that have established themselves in the Northwest tend to prey on crops and gardens. Native species generally confine themselves to forests and eat indigenous plants.

Another distinctive but rarely sighted resident of coastal forests is the **Pacific giant salamander** *(Dicamptodon tenebrus),* the largest terrestrial salamander found in the United States and Canada. This stout, mottled brown or blackish amphibian can reach lengths of 13–14 inches from nose to tail. They may be found around cold streams and mountain lakes in damp forests and around stagnant pools in the Kalmiopsis. They have been known to climb in shrubs and small trees. Among the few salamanders capable of vocalizing, Pacific giants may produce a sharp, low-pitched, dog-like yelp when agitated. Their powerful jaws can inflict a painful bite and make them a formidable predator of just about anything they can catch, including insects, slugs, snails, frogs, snakes, and rodents.

Salmon and Steelhead

In recent decades, dwindling Pacific salmon and steelhead stocks have prompted restrictions on commercial and recreational fishing in order to restore threatened and endangered species throughout the Northwest. The following paragraphs envision a time when conservation measures have helped restore better health to this ecosystem. Encouraging signs of progress have been seen in some recent years, with some rebounding runs, but the jury is certainly still out on the long-term prognosis for many anadromous fish populations. For more information about fish populations and fishing restrictions, visit the **Oregon Department of Fish and Wildlife**'s website (www.dfw.state.or.us).

Spring and fall are prime times to savor the splendor (as well as the flavor) of the Pacific salmon. During these seasons, some of Oregon's rivers and streams become choked with spawning fish returning to the site of their conception, where they mate and die. As with the eruptions of Old Faithful geyser and the return of the swallows to Capistrano, this poignant dance of death affords a look at one of Mother Nature's time clocks.

The salmon's life cycle begins and ends in a freshwater stream. After an upriver journey from the sea of sometimes hundreds of miles, the spawning female deposits 3,000–7,000 eggs in hollows (called redds) she has scooped out of the coarse sand or gravel, where the male fertilizes them. These adult salmon die soon after mating, and their bodies then deteriorate to become part of the food source for young fish.

Within three to four months, the eggs hatch into alevin, tiny immature fish with their yolk sacs still attached. As the alevin exhausts the nutrients in its yolk sac, it enters the fry stage and begins to resemble a very small salmon. The length they remain as fry differs among various species. Chinook fry, for example, immediately start heading for saltwater, whereas coho or silver salmon will remain in their home stream for one to three years before moving downstream.

The salmon are in the smolt stage when they start to enter saltwater. The five- to seven-inch smolt will spend some time in the estuary area of the river or stream, while it feeds and adjusts to the saltwater.

When it finally enters the ocean, the salmon is considered an adult. Each species varies in the number of years it remains away from its natal stream, foraging sometimes thousands of miles throughout the Pacific. Chinook can spend as many as seven years away from its nesting (and ultimately its resting) place; most other species remain in the salt for two to four years. Theories about how the salmon's miraculous homing instinct works range from electromagnetic impulses in the earth to celestial objects, but one thing has been established with certainty—"the nose knows." When salmon's olfactory orifices were stuffed with cotton and petroleum jelly, they were unable to find their spawning streams. The current belief is that young salmon imprint the odor of their birth stream, enabling them to find their way home years later.

The salmon's traditional predators, such as the sea lion, northern pike minnow, harbor seal, black bear, Caspian tern, and herring gull, pale in comparison to the threats posed by modern civilization. Everything from pesticides to sewage to nuclear waste has polluted Oregon waters, and until recent mitigation efforts were enacted, dams and hydroelectric turbines threatened to block Oregon's all-important Columbia River spawning route.

History

The First Peoples

No one knows when the first inhabitants took up residence on the Oregon coast, but ongoing research periodically turns up ever-older evidence. In 2002, archaeologists began excavating a site at Indian Sands, in Samuel H. Boardman State Park north of Brookings, which yielded artifacts dating back more than 12,000 years, making it the oldest known site of human activity yet found on the coast. Prior to that discovery, the dig site at Tahkenitch Landing, in the Oregon Dunes near Gardiner, had been the earliest known coastal habitation, dated at 9000–8630 B.C. It seems likely that further digs will uncover even older human artifacts, though scientists speculate that the oldest sites lie underwater, dating to a time when sea level was significantly lower.

A popular theory concerning the origins of Native Americans maintains that their ancestors came over from Asia on a land-ice bridge spanning what is now the Bering Strait. Along with archaeological evidence, shipwrecks of Asian craft on the Pacific Coast also support the theory that Native Americans had Eastern Hemisphere contact. This contention has been further substantiated by facial features and dental patterns common to both peoples, as well as isolated correspondences in ritual, music, and dialect.

Despite common ancestry, the tribes on the rain-soaked coast and in the Willamette Valley lived quite differently than those on the drier eastern flank of the Cascade Mountains. Tribes west of the Cascades enjoyed abundant salmon, shellfish, berries, and game. Great broad rivers facilitated travel, and thick stands of the finest softwood timber in the world ensured that there was never a dearth of building materials. A mild climate with plentiful food and resources allowed the wet-siders the leisure time to evolve a startlingly complex culture. This was perhaps best evidenced in their artistic endeavors, theatrical pursuits, and ceremonial gatherings such as the traditional potlatch, where the divesting of one's material wealth was seen as a status symbol. Dentalium and abalone shells, woodpecker feathers, obsidian blades, and hides were especially coveted. Later on, Hudson's Bay blankets were added to this list.

After contact with traders, Chinook—a patois of Indian tongues with some French and English thrown in—became the common language among the diverse tribes that gathered in the Columbia Gorge during the summer solstice. At these powwows, the coast and valley dwellers came into contact with their poorer cousins east of the Cascades.

By the time the white explorers and settlers came here, Indian culture was a patchwork of languages and cultural traits as diverse as the topography. Most native coastal communities typically included a dozen or more small bands linked by a common dialect. These bands or villages consisted of an extended family in one or two houses or a larger grouping under a headman. The linguistic and lifestyle divisions between native communities were reinforced by mountains, an ocean too rough for canoes, and other geographic barriers.

Early Explorers

In 1542, the Spanish explorer Juan Rodríguez Cabrillo sailed into what are now southern Oregon waters. Although partisans in California may dispute it, there's tantalizingly compelling evidence that the English privateer Francis Drake spent the summer of 1579 at Whale Cove (see the sidebar *Drake's Lost Harbor?*) and named the land New Albion, claiming it in the name of Queen Elizabeth. Other voyagers of note included Spain's Sebastián Vizcaíno and Martin de Aguilar (1603) and Don Bruno de Heceta (1775), and England's James Cook and John Meares during the late 1770s, as well as George Vancouver (1792). Robert Gray's 1792 voyage 13 miles up the Columbia River estuary was the first American incursion into the area. A succession of Spanish, English, American, and Russian explorers followed in search of whales, sea otter and beaver pelts, and hides for the tallow trade.

A major impetus for exploring this coast was the quest for the Northwest Passage—a sea route connecting the Pacific with the Atlantic. Although the Northwest Passage turned out to be a myth, the fur trade became a basis of commerce and contention between European, Asian, and eventually American governments. The pattern was repeated inland when the English beaver brigades eventually moved down from Canada to set up headquarters on the Columbia near present-day Portland.

Dispatched by President Thomas Jefferson to explore the lands of the Louisiana Purchase and beyond, the first American overland excursion into Oregon was made by the Corps of Discovery, which crossed the continent 1804–1806. Led by Meriwether Lewis and William Clark, the expedition trekked to the mouth of the Columbia in fall 1805 and spent a wet and miserable winter camped south of the river and explored as far south as Cannon Beach. Lewis and Clark's trailblazing dramatically accelerated interest in the Oregon Territory, and by 1811 John Jacob Astor's Pacific Fur Company had established the settlement of Astoria, just north of the Corps of Discovery's campsite.

Rogue River Wars

In the 1850s, a short-lived gold-mining boom in the Rogue River Valley and south coast beaches drew settlers to southern Oregon. Another gold rush, however, had the greatest implications for development of the region. In 1849, the influx of prospectors into California's Sierra Nevada occasioned a housing boom in San Francisco, port of entry to the goldfields. The demand for Coast Range timber and foodstuffs from Oregon's inland agricultural valleys caused downriver Pacific ports such as Astoria and Newport to flourish. As a result, the coastline of California's friendly neighbor to the north was able to develop the necessary economic base for it to prosper and endure.

Like the tragic story played out all across the continent, however, the coming of white settlers to Oregon meant the usurpation of tribal homelands, exposure to European diseases such as smallpox and diphtheria, and the passing of a way of life. Violent conflicts ensued on a large scale with the influx of settlers and government land giveaways, and the mining activity in southern Oregon and on the coast incited the Rogue Indian Wars, when the native peoples along the south coast began to fight back. The conflict lasted for six years, during which more than 2,000 Indians died.

The hostilities compelled the federal government to send in troops and to eventually set up treaties with Oregon's first inhabitants. In the aftermath of the Rogue Indian Wars in the 1850s, the Chetco, Coquille, Coos, Umpqua, Siuslaw, Alsea, Yaquina, Nestucca, and Tillamook peoples were grouped together with the Rogue River tribes and forced to live on the 1.1-million-acre Siletz Reservation, which reached from Cape Lookout in Tillamook County to near the mouth of the Umpqua River. The culture and heritage of many indigenous peoples were lost forever. More tragic than the watering down of cultural distinctiveness was the huge mortality rate resulting from natives being forcibly removed to the reservation. Of the approximately 3,240 natives moved to the reservation in 1857, disease, starvation, and exposure would reduce their number to 1,015 in 1880; by 1900, only 430 coastal Indians survived on the reservation.

Over the years, whatever wealth the Siletz tribes had left was stripped as a result of the

White Star Packing Company label, Astoria, 1885

COURTESY OF THE OREGON STATE ARCHIVES

United States not honoring a multitude of treaties. The final indignity came in 1951 with the termination of the Siletz Reservation. The divestiture of tribal status meant the loss of health services, educational support, tax exemptions, and other benefits. Predictably, this last in a long line of forced transitions brought about alcoholism and despair in many native peoples. In 1977, Senator Mark Hatfield and Congressman Les AuCoin helped push a bill through Congress for tribal restoration. This has resulted in the tribe getting the wherewithal to flourish economically in everything from logging and construction projects to gaming establishments. The casino endeavor has been accompanied by an interest in the old ways and a renewed sense of pride in native identity.

Industry, Exploitation, and Development

The exploitation of Oregon's fishing resources has been an enduring aspect of life in the region for thousands of years. Salmon has always been the most valued species, from prehistory up to modern times. Native Americans on both sides of the Cascades depended on it, and commercial anglers have viewed it as a mainstay for more than a century. Canning technology and fishing methods first perfected in Alaska made their way to Oregon in the 1860s, in time to meet the demands of emerging domestic and foreign markets. Canneries crowded the shores of the Columbia at Astoria and all of the other major rivers down the coast and exported thousands of tons of fish yearly until the dwindling supplies finally closed them down.

Logging of coastal and inland forests supplied the sawmills that were established at every port, supplying the building booms of the Northwest and beyond. A brisk coastal trade developed, as steamships plied Oregon ports on busy routes between San Francisco and Seattle. Before roads were built through the coastal ranges, transportation between coastal communities and the inland valleys was by river, and sternwheelers moved goods and passengers up and down the Siletz, Yaquina, Umpqua, and other navigable rivers. Popular tourist areas developed in Newport, Seaside, and other towns.

In the latter half of the 19th century, rail lines began to connect the coast to the interior, but it took the development of reliable roads to bring the coast out of its isolation. In 1919, Oregon voters approved construction of a north-south coastal route, first called the Roosevelt Military Highway and later the Oregon Coast Highway. The road was completed in 1932, and the last of a dozen magnificent bridges, designed by Oregon's master bridgebuilder Conde McCullough, was finished in 1936, finally opening up the entire coast to auto travel.

Recreation

The outdoor appeal of the Oregon coast is unmatched, and the beaches are only the beginning. Hikes through ancient rainforests, excellent fishing for salmon and steelhead, crabbing and clamming in bays and estuaries, white-water jetboat rides, hiking, cycle-touring, surfing, whale-watching, and birding are all on the agenda. Following is an overview of recreational opportunities along the coast; you'll find many additional suggestions and details in individual destination chapters.

BEACHCOMBING

Among the first things a newcomer to the Oregon coast notices are the huge piles of driftwood on the beach. Closer inspection usually reveals other treasures. Beachcombers particularly value agates and Japanese glass fishing floats. The volume and variety of flotsam and jetsam here come courtesy of the region's unique geography. Much of the driftwood, for instance, originates from logging operations located upriver on the many waterways that empty into the Pacific. In addition, storms,

© PAUL LEVY

Starfish are commonly seen in coastal tidepools or washed up on the beach.

floods, rockslides, and erosion uproot many trees that eventually wash up on shore. In addition to driftwood and floats, shells, coral, sand dollars, sea stars, and other seaborne trophies can be best culled from the intertidal zone on south coast beaches. Although you may not always come across a perfectly polished agate or a message in a bottle, you'll probably find beachcombing on the Oregon coast its own reward.

Japanese fishing floats are swept into Oregon waters when the Kuroshio current crosses the Pacific and takes a southerly turn. These balls of green and blue glass sometimes require more than a decade to reach the Oregon coast after breaking free from fishnets thousands of miles across the sea. Although glass floats are rather rare these days, having largely been replaced by plastic and foam, March is the best time to look for them, especially after two-day storms from the northwest, west-southwest, or due west. In Lincoln City, hand-blown glass floats are planted on the beaches from October through May—if you find one of these beauties, it's yours to keep! December–April is the best sea-

son to find agates, jaspers, petrified wood, and a variety of fossils. At that time, the gravel bars covered by sand in summer are exposed.

On the southern coast, the Coos Bay sandspit, Bandon's beachfront, the beaches on the western side of Humbug Mountain, and the isolated shorelines of Boardman State Park are choice treasure-hunting spots. Tenmile Creek south of Yachats and Agate Beach north of Newport are the central coast's best places to look. The more settled and accessible north coast has slimmer pickings because of the larger population of resident beachcombers and the higher visitor influx; the best beachcombing is on the Nehalem, Netarts, and Nestucca sandspits.

Consult a **tide chart** any time you anticipate an extended beachcombing excursion (or any other activity on or near the sea). Half a dozen people perish here yearly from being washed off a beach, jetty, or outcropping. Local newspapers usually include tide predictions, and tide charts are available from visitors centers, chambers of commerce, and shops. Online, you can get free tide charts for over 40 coastal locations at www.saltwatertides.com. It's also wise to anticipate weather changes, so bring layers.

FISHING

Since the first people arrived on these shores 12,000 years or more ago, Oregon's rich coastal waters have provided sustenance and sport. The king of fish here, economically as well as recreationally speaking, is the salmon. The once-abundant fish was a self-replenishing gold mine that enriched the state and fueled the development of coastal towns like Astoria and Gold Beach.

In the modern era, Oregon salmon fisheries grew into a megabusiness, until stocks dramatically declined in the 1990s. The many factors are complex and fraught with political tension. In the early days, fish wheels and nets depleted rivers once so choked with spawning fish that a pioneer pitchfork stuck haphazardly into the water would often yield a salmon. Dam construction and pollution joined overfishing to further reduce the catch. Watersheds have been compromised by clearcuts, which increases erosion that clogs spawning streams with silt and mud and reduces shaded riparian environments for the cold water–loving salmon. Cattle grazing has also affected spawning areas with collapsed stream banks and polluted water.

Despite the habitat degradation and other pressures, there have been several good years since 2000. In 1997, returning Oregon coastal coho salmon numbered an alarmingly low 22,000 fish, which triggered a listing as threatened under the Endangered Species Act. Commercial and sportfishing for coho were shut down. Coastal coho returns recovered in the early 2000s and peaked at more than 200,000 in 2002. But since 2003, coho returns have declined. Additionally, most of the returning fish are from hatcheries, with negative implications for the long-term health of the species.

Runs of spring and fall chinook, coho, and steelhead draw thousands of anglers to the coast each year. Fleets of charter boats operate out of all the navigable ports on the coast, and there are countless opportunities for do-it-yourselfers from boats, banks, jetties, and piers.

Past salmon shortfalls have spawned alternative ocean fisheries. Bottom fishing for black ling cod and rockfish, together with the harvest of such long-ignored species as hake, whiting, and pollock, have increased in proportion to the decline of salmon, flounder, albacore tuna, smelt, and halibut. Growing out of the pollock fishery has been the development of a successful surimi (artificial crab) industry, supplying Asian and U.S. markets. Be that as it may, the aggressive harvest of the 55 species of rockfish that are marketed as red snapper brought about catch limits in 2000, giving another signal that fisheries are in transition.

Where and When to Go

Salmon are targeted offshore, as well as in freshwater. For up-to-date information on exactly where, when, and how you can fish—which is subject to frequent change—get a copy of the **Oregon Department of Fish and Wildlife**'s regulations (2501 SW 1st Ave., Portland, 503/872-5268, www.dfw.state.or.us), available at sporting goods stores and many other outlets; better yet, check the website for the most current information.

In addition to chinook and coho salmon and steelhead in scores of coastal rivers, the Kilchis and Miami rivers near Tillamook see Oregon's only runs of chum salmon, in autumn; this is a catch-and-release fishery only. Another catch-and-release-only species is wild sea-run cutthroat trout, which return to the Alsea River and Yaquina Bay, among other waterways, in summer. Sturgeon are popular gamefish (weighing into the hundreds of pounds) in the larger rivers, particularly the Columbia and the Umpqua.

Bottom fishing for rockfish and other species is pretty much a year-round activity—depending on the weather. Warm ocean currents bring albacore tuna in August and September, and halibut are usually available in summer, although the season is variable and is set yearly by the Pacific Fishery Management Council.

Charters and Guides

Major charter-fishing centers on the coast include Astoria, Hammond, Warrenton, Garibaldi, Depoe Bay, Newport, Winchester Bay, Charleston, Gold Beach, Bandon, and Brookings. Charter rates vary a bit, but typical prices up and down the coast are $120 for a half day (5–6 hours) of bottom fishing; $175 for a full eight-hour day of salmon or bottom fishing; $225 for 12 hours of tuna fishing; and $185 for a 10-hour halibut charter. Guide and charter services are listed in each destination chapter. Chambers of commerce in each town can also provide extensive listings.

Crabbing and Clamming

Egalitarian ventures that require a minimum of gear, crabbing and clamming are popular ways to land a delicious meal. The Oregon Department of Fish and Wildlife's *Sport Fishing Regulations* booklet has details, or check its website (www.dfw.state.or.us) for more information. Crabbing requires a license ($6.50 resident, $16.50 out of state, $9 for a three-day nonresident license) that's available just about anyplace that rents traps or sells fishing gear.

Crabbing just requires a trap, ring, or pot, and some bait (veteran crabbers recommend raw poultry—chicken or turkey backs and necks). Opinions vary about the best time to crab, but many agree that an incoming tide yields the best catches. Just drop your trap in a likely spot, with a tethered float marking the spot, and haul it up 15–30 minutes later—hopefully full of legal-sized male Dungeness crabs. A handy item to have is a crab caliper, a gauge that measures the minimum-sized crabs you can keep. Bait shops and marinas can instruct you on how to catch dinner. Boats and crab pots are usually available to rent at these places. If boats are unavailable, many harbors have public piers. Some of the best crabbing spots are the estuaries of the Coos, Siuslaw, Yaquina, Tillamook, Netarts, and Nehalem rivers. Bays and estuaries are open for Dungeness crab year-round; the ocean is open year-round except August 15–November 30.

A spade or small pitchfork—and a bucket to carry away your take—are all you need to dig clams on beaches and mudflats. Large gaper clams, cockles, soft-shells, and littlenecks are the most common clams found in tidewater areas, while prized razor clams are found on north coast beaches. With the exception of the summer closure for razor clams north of Tillamook Head, the season on shellfish is year-round in Oregon. Low tides, particularly morning minus tides during spring and summer, are the best times for clamming. Mussels are also available for harvest from rocky intertidal areas. Note that all oyster beds are privately owned. Check the *Sport Fishing Regulations* for catch limits, and before harvesting always inquire locally or contact the **Recreational Shellfish Hot Line** (503/986-4728) to get current information on shellfish toxins and quarantines.

HIKING

Opportunities for hiking abound on the coast, from short loops suitable for just about anyone to the magnificent Coast Trail running the entire length of the coast, and a myriad of choices in between. Wherever you choose your outing, here are some suggestions to help keep the environment as natural as possible:

- Stay on the trails so you do not increase the rate of erosion or destroy such fragile vegetation as dune and wetland wildflowers.

- Use established campsites, and avoid digging tent trenches or cutting vegetation.

- In wilderness areas, camp several hundred feet from water sources. Bring a tool to dig a latrine, and make it at least six inches deep.

- If you pack it in, pack it out. Leave nothing but footprints.

- Avoid feeding wild animals so you don't inhibit their natural instinct to fend for themselves.

The Oregon Coast Trail

For 362 miles, from the Columbia River to the California border, the Oregon Coast Trail hugs the beaches and headlands, leading hikers into intimate contact with some of the most beautiful landscapes anywhere. Most of the trail runs through public lands, although some portions traverse easements on private parcels, and the trail follows the highway and city streets in several places. The only coastal long-distance treks separated from U.S. 101 are the 30 miles between Seaside and Manzanita and Bandon and Port Orford. A free trail map and directory are available from the **Oregon state parks information center** (800/551-6949, www.oregonstate parks.org). This pamphlet makes it clear where the trail crosses open beaches, forested headlands, the shoulder of the Coast Highway, and even city streets in some towns. Be sure to bring water, particularly on northerly sections of the trail, because much of the trek here is on beachfront away from a potable supply.

CAMPING AND RV PARKS

Oregon lodging prices are, for the most part, significantly lower than those of neighboring California and Washington. Nonetheless, coastal resort areas can put a strain on the pocketbook. Fortunately, state park and national forest campgrounds proliferate in these areas, offering low-cost overnight lodgings in attractive settings. As if by design, the highest percentage of Oregon's 200 state parks surround the high-ticket areas, with sites usually priced around $12–20 per night. Most of these have restrooms, showers, fire rings, piped water, and other basic amenities. National Forest campgrounds usually cost less but offer more primitive facilities; many of them are chosen for their proximity to swimming holes and/or scenic appeal.

If creature comforts are a priority, privately owned RV parks and campgrounds are often equipped with every amenity you can ask for, from laundry facilities to game rooms to cable hookups.

Camping in State Parks

Despite charging the highest camping fees in the West, the coast's state parks are still the most heavily used (per state park acre) in the country—a tribute to their excellence.

Prices for camping at state parks May 1–September 30 average the following rates: electrical hookup sites $21; tent sites $17; primitive/overflow sites $9; hiker-biker sites $4–6; yurts $29–42. During the discounted Discovery Season, October 1–April 30, prices average as follows: electrical hookup sites $17; tent sites $13; hiker-biker sites $4; yurts $27–42. The extra vehicle charge during any season is $7.

Yurts are available for rent at most state park campgrounds. Yurts are canvas-walled, wood-floored, and equipped with fold-up beds, heaters, and lamps; they sleep five people, but pets are not permitted inside.

Most of Oregon's coastal state park campgrounds accept campsite reservations, but a few are first-come, first served. The state has a central information phone, 800/551-6949, and a reservation line, 800/452-5687. (Go to www .oregonstateparks.org to look up specific rates or to get information.) You can also make reservations for any of these options online with a Visa or MasterCard through **ReserveAmerica** (800/452-5687, www.reserveamerica.com). Reservations may be made from two days up to nine months in advance. In addition to the campsite fee, which ranges $7–21 per night, a $6 processing fee is charged. Telephone hours are 8 A.M.–7 P.M. Monday–Friday.

If you need to cancel your reservation three days or more before your scheduled arrival, call **Reservations Northwest** (800/452-5687 statewide, 503/731-3411 in Portland). Two or fewer days before your trip, call the park directly to cancel your reservation. Phone numbers for all parks are found on each individual park's website (www.oregonstateparks.org). Cancellation service fees and requirements for special facilities, such as yurts and cabins, may vary. Your $6 reservation fee is nonrefundable, and a $3 cancellation fee will be charged if you cancel in the last two days. If you reserve through ReserveAmerica, the cancellation policy differs; see its website for details.

Camping in National Forests

The U.S. Forest Service maintains campsites, trails, and day-use areas in both the Siuslaw and Siskiyou National Forests. The Siuslaw National Forest encompasses more than 630,000 acres and is situated within the Oregon Coast Range. It's one of only two national forests located in the Lower 48 to include beachfront area. The Siskiyou National Forest is located in the Klamath Mountains and the coast ranges of southwestern Oregon, with a small segment of the forest extending into northern California and the Siskiyous. It includes 1,163,484 acres within its boundaries, 69,234 acres of which are owned or privately managed by other agencies. Within the boundaries of these two national forests, there are hundreds of choices. Refer to the **Forest Service** website (www.fs.fed.us.gov/recreation) or the specific destination chapters in this guide for listings.

Campsites generally include a table, a fire grate, and a tent or trailer space. Electric hook-ups are not available, although most campgrounds have water and vault or flush toilets. Most overnight sites require a user fee. You may camp a maximum of 14 days out of every 30 in the forest. Fees are $10–15 for campsites and $5–7 for an extra vehicle. Campsites can be reserved online with a Visa or Master-Card through ReserveAmerica (800/452-5687, www.reserveamerica.com).

It's important to note that National Forest passholders who plan to use specialized facilities (such as camping, trailhead, parking, boat launch, ramps, swimming sites, etc.) in the national forest still have to pay for an overnight campsite.

RVs

The Oregon coast is a summer haven for RVers, with activities in each coastal town designed to appeal to this perennial visitor. RV sites in private parks and state parks are abundant but can fill up as early as April with travelers fleeing the hot winds of the California desert for the balmy climes of the coast. Many RV grounds are open year-round, but some are seasonal, responding to the level of visitors.

Along the coast, many service stations, truck stops, campgrounds, and RV parks provide RV sanitary dump stations. Local chambers of commerce and visitors centers can provide information on activities for seniors, RV-friendly sites, and other services.

USER FEES AND PASSES

In recent years, numerous state and federal parks, national recreation areas, trails, picnic areas, and other facilities have begun charging day-use fees, which are separate from overnight camping fees (the exception to this is camping at rustic campsites in national forests, which is covered by the Northwest Forest Pass). At sites that charge fees, the day-use fee is currently $3 per vehicle at state parks, $5 per vehicle at federal sites. Visitors can pay for day use at individual sites, or, if you're planning to visit several coastal parks or hike the trails on federal lands, you can save money by purchasing one of the passes described here.

Oregon Pacific Coast Passport

The best deal if you plan to visit many state and federal sites, this pass covers entrance, day-use, and vehicle parking fees at all state and federal fee sites along the entire Oregon portion of U.S. 101. It does not cover the cost of camping at state parks, which is a separate fee. This pass was created to alleviate some of the confusion caused by having to buy different passes at the various federal (Forest Service, National Park Service, Bureau of Land Management or BLM) and state (Oregon Parks and Recreation Department) fee sites along the U.S. 101 corridor.

As of 2003, more than 15 coastal sites managed by the National Park Service, U.S. Forest Service, BLM, and Oregon state parks are covered by the passport, including Fort Stevens State Park, Ecola State Park, Nehalem Bay State Park, Cape Lookout State Park, Fogarty Creek State Recreation Area, Heceta Head Lighthouse Viewpoint, Honeyman State Park, Shore Acres State Park, Fort Clatsop National Memorial, Oregon Dunes National Recreation Area, Sutton Recreation Area, Cape Perpetua Scenic Area, Sand Lake Recreation Area, Drift Creek Falls Trail, Yaquina Head Outstanding Natural Area, and Hebo Lake.

Two basic passports are available, depending on your needs and preferences. An Annual Passport, valid for the calendar year, is $35. A Five-Day Passport is $10. Passports may be purchased at welcome centers, ranger stations, national forest headquarters, national memorials, and state park offices. Call 800/551-6949 to purchase by credit card or for directions to a convenient location.

State Park Passes

Another option, valid only at Oregon state parks, is to buy a one-year ($25) or two-year ($40) pass. They're available from state park offices, by phone (800/551-6949), and from G.I. Joe's sporting goods stores and other vendors. See the Oregon State Parks website (www.oregonstateparks.org/dayuse_permit.php) for more details and a complete list of vendors.

Northwest Forest Pass

In response to major reductions in timber harvests and cutbacks in federal money, a revenue shortfall has made it hard to keep up trails and campgrounds at a time when the region's population has put more demand on these facilities. The Northwest Forest Pass ($30, valid for one year) is a vehicle-parking pass for the use of many improved trailheads, picnic areas, boat launches, and interpretive sites in the national forests of Oregon and Washington. Funds generated from pass sales go directly to maintaining and improving the trails, land, and facilities. You will see Northwest Forest Pass Required signs posted at participating sites. Passes are available at kiosks or dispensed by machine. Passes are also available at many local vendors (such as G.I. Joe's, park stores, and chambers of commerce), as well as by phone (800/270-7504). You can also order them online at www.fs.fed.us/r6/feedemo; you can also check this website to find out if a pass is required before you head out. (If you don't want to buy a $30 pass, you can pay a $5 daily parking fee at these sites.)

The Northwest Forest Pass is good all over the Northwest, eliminating the need to purchase a separate pass with each entrance to another national forest. This pass covers most national park and forest service sites in Oregon and Washington but is not valid for campground fees (with the exception of rustic campsites), concessionaire-operated sites, and Sno-Parks.

Golden Eagle Passport Program

Honored at all Forest Service, National Park Service, Bureau of Land Management, Bureau of Reclamation, U.S. Fish and Wildlife Services, and U.S. Army Corp of Engineers sites charging entrance or day use fees. Anybody can buy one, and a pass is good for all occupants in a vehicle. Get additional details or purchase these $65 super passes from the National Forest Foundation (877/465-2727, www.natlforests.org).

WHALE-WATCHING

Whale-watching charters of various kinds are offered along the coast from December into the early spring. By land or by sea, early morning hours are best because winds can whip up whitecaps later in the day, obscuring the signs of surfacing whales. Remember to bring your binoculars and sunglasses. If you go by boat, dress warmly, take precautions against seasickness, and expect to get wet if you go out on deck.

You don't need to be on a boat or plane to successfully whale-watch, however. Coastal headlands and beaches provide excellent vantage points from which to spy the gray whales on their 10,000-mile round-trip between Baja and the Arctic, the longest migratory movement by land or sea of any mammal. It's possible to spot whales here year-round because several hundred have taken up permanent or semi-permanent residence in Oregon waters, but whales are far more numerous (and your chances of sighting them far better) during their twice-yearly migrations. The southward migration along the Oregon coast lasts until early February, although their numbers usually peak around the last week in December. Whales migrating northward can be sighted off Oregon March–May, with numbers usually peaking in late March.

By Land

Just about any coastal location with a view of the sea holds the potential for a whale sighting, but some spots are definitely better than others. Offshore reefs supporting the proliferation of amphipods, the food of the gray whale, are conducive to sightings. Combine the latter with a promontory such as Cape Perpetua or Yaquina Head and you increase your chances even more.

Whale Watching Spoken Here (http://whalespoken.org) is an organization of enthusiastic, trained volunteers who staff 28 prime whale-watching sites in Oregon (plus one in northern California and one in southern Washington) during key weeks of the gray whale migrations. In coordination with the Oregon Parks and Recreation Department, these folks provide information and assist in spotting whales 10 A.M.–1 P.M. December 26–Janurary 2 and through the week of spring break in late March. Get more information from its website.

These sites, marked by Whale Watching Spoken Here signs during Whale Watch Weeks, are among the best vantage points any time of year. From north to south, with their nearest town, they are:

- Ecola State Park
- Neahkahnie Mountain Historic Marker Turnout (Cannon Beach)
- Cape Meares State Scenic Viewpoint (Three Capes Loop)
- Cape Lookout State Park (Three Capes Loop)
- Inn at Spanish Head (Lincoln City)
- Boiler Bay State Scenic Viewpoint (Depoe Bay)
- Depoe Bay Sea Wall
- The Whale Watching Center (Depoe Bay)
- Rocky Creek State Scenic Viewpoint (Depoe Bay)
- Cape Foulweather (Depoe Bay)
- Devil's Punchbowl State Natural Area (Otter Rock)
- Yaquina Head Lighthouse (Newport)
- Don A. Davis City Kiosk (Nye Beach, Newport)
- Yaquina Bay State Recreation Site (Newport)
- Devil's Churn Viewpoint (Yachats)
- Cape Perpetua Overlook (Yachats)
- Cape Perpetua Interpretive Center (Yachats)
- Cook's Chasm Turnout (Yachats)
- Sea Lion Caves Turnout (north of Florence)
- Umpqua Lighthouse (Winchester Bay)
- Shore Acres State Park (Charleston)
- Face Rock Wayside State Scenic Viewpoint (Bandon)
- Cape Blanco Lighthouse
- Battle Rock Wayfinding Point (Port Orford)
- Cape Sebastian
- Cape Ferrelo
- Harris Beach State Park (Brookings)

By Sea

Depoe Bay and Newport are the centers for whale-watching, attracting the majority of the state's whale-watching visitors. Other major ports are Charleston, Winchester Bay, and Garibaldi, but you'll find whale-watching charters operating out of just about all the ports along the coast. Rates range $15–50 per person for a two- to three-hour tour. See each destination for specific charter companies and details.

BICYCLING

In the wake of the oil shocks of the 1970s, the Oregon legislature allocated 1 percent of the state highways budget to encourage energy-saving bicycling by developing bike lanes and special parks and campgrounds with bicycle and foot access specifically in mind.

Although not for everybody, biking part or all of the Oregon coast is the surest way to get on intimate terms with this spectacular region. Before going, get a free copy of the extremely useful **The Oregon Coast Bike Route** Map from the Department of Transportation (Salem, OR 97310, www.odot .state.or.us) or from coastal information centers and chambers of commerce. This brochure features strip maps of the route, noting services from Astoria to the California border. With information on campsites, hostels, bike-repair facilities, elevation changes, temperatures, and wind speed, this pamphlet does everything but map the ruts in the road. Because the prevailing winds in summer are from the northwest, most people cycle south on U.S. 101 to take advantage of a steady tailwind. You'll also be riding on the ocean side of the road with better views, easier access to turnouts, and generally wider bike lanes and shoulders. The entire 370-mile (or 380 miles, including the optional Three Capes Loop) trip involves nearly 16,000 feet of elevation change. Most cyclists cover the distance in 6–8 days, pedaling an average of 50–65 miles daily.

If you want to cycle the full length of the coast, fly into Portland and ride to Astoria. (Go ahead and unpack your bike and take it on the MAX train if you don't want to ride from the airport into town.) It's a little harder to figure out how to end your trip, as public transportation is rather limited on the southern Oregon coast. Consider riding about 25 miles into California, where you'll find Greyhound service in Crescent City.

On Oregon's roads and highways, bicyclists have the right of way, which means that cars and trucks are not supposed to run you off the road. Most drivers will give you a wide berth and slow down if necessary in tight spots, but remember that there are also motorists whose concepts of etiquette vis-à-vis bikers were formulated elsewhere. Play it safe: Always wear a helmet and bright or reflective clothing, keep as close to the shoulder of the road as you safely can, and use a light if you must ride at night.

Cycle Tours

Several companies offer preplanned group bicycle trips, with everything from the bicycle to the meals and lodging included. **Cyling Escapes** (714/267-4591, www.cycling escapes.com) runs a weeklong trip from Astoria to Crescent City for about $1,825. **Bicycle Adventures** (206/786-0989 or 800/443-6060, www.bicycleadventures.com) offers several coast packages at costs ranging $200–340 per day (budget tours feature more modest accommodations and restaurants). **Hidden Trails** (604/323-1141 or 888/9-TRAILS, www.bcranches .com/outdoor/bike/index.htm) offers a fully supported, 10-day tour for about $2,600.

ENTERTAINMENT AND EVENTS

It seems there's some kind of festival or other event happening just about every week somewhere on the coast. Celebrations revolving around cultural or historical heritage, food and wine, crafts, kites, sandcastles, windsurfing, the arts—you name it, and there's probably a festival dedicated to it—and more sprout up every year. Most are concentrated during summer, when the choices can be overwhelming.

SHOPPING

The lack of sales tax in Oregon is a boon to visitors. They can revel in the shopping opportunities on the coast, which include a profusion of shops selling local art, collectibles and antiques, handmade items, as well as the requisite T-shirts and trinkets.

If it's mall-type shopping you live for, the **Seaside Factory Outlets** center (1111 N. Roosevelt Dr., www.seasideoutlets.com) has 30 big-name manufacturers with designer labels and national brands. With products (of all quality levels) at about 20–50 percent below regular retail price, the center is also home to one of the best wine shops on the Oregon Coast, featuring more than 850 labels, plus 309 imported and domestic beers. Lincoln City is home to another outlet mall, **Factory Stores at Lincoln City** (1500 S.E. East Devil's Lake Rd., www.shoplincoln city.com), with similar offerings.

For unique arts and crafts, the coastal resort areas are overflowing with the work of local and nationally known potters, woodworkers, painters, jewelers, and glass artisans. These homemade items often go for quite a bit less than would be charged in out-of-state markets for work of comparable quality. While these arts cottage industries don't have the bottom line of timber and agriculture, they are one of the more visible and appreciated forms of economic activity.

Seasonally, farm stands, farmers markets, and U-pick options dot the routes to the coast. Oregon berries (so quick to ripen that their unparalleled sweetness is more likely to be appreciated in jams and ice cream than in the supermarket) and other indigenous treats can be bought direct from the farmer here. Oregon coast stores also purvey locally made food products, which make excellent gifts. You'll come across Oregon jams, smoked fish, hazelnuts, wines, cheese, sweets, and similar products.

ESSENTIALS

Accommodations and Food

ACCOMMODATIONS

Coastal accommodations run the gamut from campgrounds and humble fishing lodges to bona fide five-star resorts. In between are a kaleidoscopic range including condominiums rented as guest rooms, bed-and-breakfasts, vacation rentals, a lighthouse keeper's quarters, yurts, a paddlewheeler, and a plethora of conventional motels.

Regardless of the lodging, you'll generally pay more for direct access to the beach or for an ocean view. If you're willing to walk a block or two, or settle for a view of mountains or forests, you'll probably save a few dollars.

Finally, keep in mind that a hotel reservation at many lodgings *does not* guarantee exactly what you reserved. Regardless of how far in advance you reserve or even if you give your credit card number, all you are really guaranteed is a room. Especially during peak season, this may translate to the whole family piling onto a king-size bed for a dubious night's rest, sleeping in a foul-smelling smoker's den, or perhaps bedding down in a dingy closet-sized cell instead of the suite you requested. Nonsmoking rooms, bed configuration, and preferred room styles are often given out to confirmed-reservation guests on a first-come, first-served basis. To avoid problems, clarify your room type and the check-in time when you make

© JUDY JEWELL

the reservation, and schedule an early check-in time (most hotels have midafternoon vacancies available) that may be followed up by an afternoon activity.

Although there's no sales tax in Oregon, note that you will find local lodging taxes—ranging 8–12 percent, depending on the locale—added to your bill.

Cutting Costs

Prices up and down the coast peak during summer, a flexible term that generally means Memorial Day to Labor Day. In summer, as well as during spring break, many destinations fill up, and you'll need to reserve well in advance if you don't want to sleep in your car. Many lodgings drop their rates a bit during spring and fall shoulder seasons. In winter, euphemistically called the storm-watching season, room rates can drop still further, sometimes approaching 50 percent less, with special weekend-getaway packages quite common. This can be a wonderful time for a stay at the coast, when the crowds are long gone and the sea and sky are at their most dramatic. When making a reservation, it pays to ask (or check the lodging's website) about specials and discounts.

The cost-conscious traveler should also keep in mind that there is no shortage of large condos and vacation homes that rent out to large parties who can split costs.

Paying More

As noted above, lodging prices along the coast peak in the summer, when rather unexceptional motel rooms go for close to $100. If your budget can tolerate it, this is a good time to investigate some of the slightly more expensive B&Bs and lodges. The difference in quality between a $95 highway-side motel and a $130 B&B room can be astounding and can make for a far more memorable and enjoyable trip.

Bed-and-Breakfasts

This European-style lodging provides a homey alternative to the typical motel room. The Oregon coast leads the country in bed-and-breakfast establishments per capita, but the

idea seems to be catching on elsewhere. And why not? Whether they offer a glass of sherry by a crackling fire to warm up beachgoers or a huge picture window on a Pacific storm, these retreats can impart that extra-special personal touch to the best the coast has to offer.

If an early-1900s Victorian or an old farmhouse doesn't give a bed-and-breakfast an extra measure of warmth, the camaraderie of the guests and the host family usually will. Most bed-and-breakfasts restrict kids, pets, and smoking. Offsetting any potential intrusions on privacy is an included full or continental breakfast. In Oregon, it has become customary to see homemade jams and breads, as well as a complimentary glass of local wine for a nightcap.

Vacation Rentals

B&Bs can add to a romantic weekend on the coast, but these establishments don't make sense all the time for everyone. This book also lists property rental agencies and realty companies in certain locations whose properties afford more privacy. Deals are plentiful, thanks to the volume of vacation homes that often sit idle or can accommodate large enough parties to offset a high nightly rate.

FOOD AND DRINK

Visiting gourmets can tell you why many people will happily drive two hours from Portland for a meal at any number of coastal restaurants: Inventive chefs, fully exploiting the freshest regional ingredients—wild chanterelles, fiddlehead ferns, marionberries, locally made cheeses, Oregon wines, and, of course, seafood—mean that limited notions of clam chowder and greasy fish and chips are long out of date. Not that there aren't plenty of eateries along the coast where everything but your salad—if you can get one—has been battered and deep-fried. It's just that now there are plenty of exciting alternatives. The coast seems to attract restaurateurs who want to dispel the old myths about the region being a culinary backwater, and here they can start with unbeatable raw materials to work their craft on, especially when it comes to seafood. The

giant inflated crab, on the roof of Manzanita Seafood restaurant

fish, oysters, crab, and clams here are as fresh as they can be. At many restaurants, it's a very short trip from the boat to the plate, with a short detour through the kitchen.

Not so long ago, coffee on the coast meant a thin, vengeful, and bitter brew that tasted like bilgewater. How things have changed! Now, it seems as if every bait shop and gas station has a neon Espresso sign glowing warmly in its window, and latte addicts no longer have to suffer through withdrawals as they drive U.S. 101.

Tipping

Tipping for food service is customary but discretionary. As elsewhere in Oregon, the suggested rate of recompense for acceptable service is 15–20 percent. Diners in larger parties (usually six or more) may find that a restaurant enforces a mandatory tipping policy as part of the bill.

Coastal Cuisine

What will newcomers to the Oregon coast notice most on their plates? The coast boasts such delicacies as Dungeness crab, razor clams, Yaquina Bay oysters, and bay shrimp, as well as world-famous salmon.

Let's start with the bay shrimp as an appetizer. Although a hasty visual appraisal of an Oregon shrimp cocktail might prompt an unfavorable comparison to the larger Gulf prawns, these savory morsels prove that good things come in small packages. Expect them to be in season during August. Another coveted crustacean is the Dungeness crab. West Coast chefs haven't yet mastered the succulence of Maryland-style crab cakes, but the Dungeness tastes richer in a cocktail than the less meaty Atlantic blue crab. The firm texture of Dungeness in peak season (March or October) has been compared to that of Maine lobster.

Speaking of which, those used to *Homarus americanus* from the East Coast will be disappointed by the oversized crayfish passed off as lobster on some menus. Freshwater crawdads here are another distant cousin. Among nonambulatory shellfish, Oregon's Yaquina Bay oysters are considered gourmet fare. If you

© ELIZABETH OPENSHAW

© JUDY JEWELL

There's plenty of ambiance and fresh fish when you eat at dockside restaurants.

want them fresh, avoid the summer months and wait until the weather is cooler. Razor clams are another indigenous shellfish—an acquired taste for many. Once you get past their rubbery consistency, however, you might enjoy this local favorite. Local mussels and albacore tuna near the end of July are also worth a try.

When it comes to fresh fish, you'll notice a variance in price based on how the salmon was caught. Troll-caught salmon (usually chinook and coho in Oregon) are landed in the ocean by hook and line, one at a time. This method permits better handling than netted salmon, which are caught in large groups as they come upriver from the ocean to spawn. Thus, you'll pay more for troll-caught salmon, but you can taste the difference. Currently, as efforts are undertaken to restore the species in the Northwest, most grocery-store salmon and some in restaurants comes from Alaska or fish farms in Chile. There are limited stocks of Oregon-caught salmon available, however, and it pays to be sensitive to nuances of harvest and preparation.

Spring chinook salmon (Apr.–May) from the Rogue River estuary is a can't-miss item for almost everyone. Although red snapper would normally also merit such an assessment, this is not always the case in Oregon, largely because of a case of mistaken identity. In contrast to the red snapper found on Southern and Eastern menus, this Pacific version is a bottom fish. The brown widow rockfish and dozens of other bottom fish species that receive the "red snapper" designation out here have a similar consistency but a fishier taste than their East Coast counterpart.

Despite the many delicacies available on the Oregon coast, it *is* still possible to have a bad meal in the region. In fact, the quality of the cuisine in some smaller towns is a source of self-deprecating humor for the locals. As many Yankees will tell you, there is no shortage of bland New England–style clam chowder on the Oregon coast. And some of the freshest fish can be had at even the most basic chowder house along the coast, although it may be fried to a crisp.

Still, it's easy to dine well at an affordable price; the region abounds in places with genuine ambience and home cooking at a good value.

Alcohol

As more and more wineries and wine outlets are popping up along the coast, a glass of an Oregon pinot gris makes a perfect complement to any seafood meal.

Please note Oregon's liquor laws: Liquor is sold by the bottle in state liquor stores, which are open Monday through Saturday. Beer and wine are sold in grocery stores and retail outlets. Liquor is sold by the drink in licensed establishments 7 A.M.–2:30 A.M. The minimum drinking age throughout the state is 21.

Information and Services

INFORMATION
Visitor Information and Maps

The **Oregon Coast Visitors Association** (137 NE 1st St., P.O. Box 74, Newport, OR 97365, 541/574-2679, 888/OCVA-101 or 888/628-2101, www.visittheoregoncoast.com) is a good clearinghouse of information for the entire coast, including events listings, weather, and links to all coastal chambers of commerce. The best sources of detailed, current information for the coast are the individual chambers of commerce in each town. Most do an excellent job of helping travelers with their questions, and all have websites.

The **Oregon Tourism Commission** (775 Summer St. N.E., Salem, OR 97310, 800/547-7842, www.traveloregon.com) is another good resource, producing several useful free maps and pamphlets on the coast and offering extensive listings of lodgings and activities.

Other useful contacts are the **Oregon Parks and Recreation Department** (1115 Commercial St. N.E., Salem, OR 97301, 503/378-6305 or 800/551-6949, www.oregonstateparks.org), the **U.S. Bureau of Land Management** (333 SW 1st Ave., Portland, OR 97204, 503/808-6002, www.or.blm.gov), and the **U.S. Forest Service** (333 SW 1st Ave., Portland, OR 503/808-2971, www.fs.fed.us/r6/). All offer free information and maps on the specific recreation areas and preserves under their respective auspices.

For members only, **AAA Oregon/Idaho** (600 SW Market St., Portland, OR 97201, 503/222-6734 or 800/452-1643, www.aaaorid.com) provides free, high-quality, detailed maps of each coastal county. Its *Oregon Coast Tour Map* is particularly good.

© MARK MORRIS

Signs up and down the coast point the way to safer ground in the event of a tsunami warning.

Travelers with Disabilities

The following numbers will serve outdoors enthusiasts who have disabilities, with specific information on their many options in Oregon: the U.S. Forest Service (503/872-2750) provides information on the **Golden Access Passport** and on specific accessibility features of each area; those visiting areas managed by the Bureau of Land Management (503/375-5646) can also use the Golden Access Passport;

the U.S. Fish and Wildlife Service (503/231-6214) can answer site-specific questions about accessibility; and the Oregon Department of Fish and Wildlife (503/872-5263) puts out a useful guide, called *Access Oregon,* which lists accessible recreation areas.

Publications

For big-city publications, both the Portland *Oregonian* and the *Eugene Register Guard* are available on the coast.

Even though regional monthlies such as *Northwest Travel* and *Sunset* magazines do not have a strictly Oregon focus, there are usually several destination pieces about the state in each edition. Sold throughout the state, *Oregon Coast* magazine (P.O. Box 18000, Florence, OR 97439-1030) is an excellent bimonthly about life on Oregon's western edge.

The alternative newspaper *Hipfish,* published in Astoria, is one of the liveliest community-based monthlies in the state. Frequent coverage of environmental issues is interspersed with cultural listings, reviews, and commentary. It's distributed free at selected locales on the coast.

MONEY AND COMMUNICATION
Money

Oregon has no state sales tax, which makes purchases at the coast all the more attractive, particularly to out-of-state visitors. Major credit cards are widely accepted at shops, lodgings, restaurants, and other establishments, but not everywhere. Acceptability of personal checks varies; it's worth asking beforehand. Traveler's checks in U.S. currency, issued by major firms such as American Express, are generally accepted with official picture ID.

The larger towns on the coast have at least one bank with an automated teller machine (ATM); these are noted in individual desti-

nation chapters. Many of the coast's small towns and villages, however, have no banking services. Larger grocery stores, such as Fred Meyer, Safeway, Ray's, and Clark's, with numerous coastal locations, usually have an ATM or offer cash back with a purchase.

Mail

Most post offices open around 7–9 A.M. and close around 5–6 P.M. Sometimes drugstores or card shops have a postal substation open on weekends and holidays when the government operations are closed. If it happens to be Sunday and the post office is closed, you can also get stamps from grocery stores and hotels, with little or no markup. Oregon also has many FedEx, UPS, and other private shipping companies operating across the state to complement government services.

Telephone

Coastal Oregon has two area codes: **503** for Astoria to Neskowin and **541** for the rest of the coast. Note that you must dial the area code, even for local calls. For long-distance calls within the state, dial 1 before the correct area code and then the seven-digit telephone number. For directory assistance, dial 1, followed by the appropriate area code for the locale you are searching, and then 555-1212.

Cell phone users should be aware that service in some coastal areas and in the coast ranges can be spotty, particularly along the south coast.

Internet Access

Wireless Internet service is widely available along the Oregon coast; it's relatively easy to find a hotel or coffee shop where you can fire up your laptop and check your email. Internet cafés, providing access by the hour, seem to come and go; see specific destination chapters for details.

Health and Safety

EMERGENCY SERVICES AND HEALTHCARE

Throughout Oregon, dial **911** for medical, police, or fire emergencies. You may always dial 0 to get the operator. In this book, look for contact information on additional local services in each destination's Practicalities or Information and Services section.

There are hospital facilities in Gold Beach, Bandon, Coos Bay, Florence, Newport, Seaside, and Astoria with 24-hour emergency rooms. See each destination chapter for details.

Oregon's larger cities maintain switchboard referral services, as well as hospital-sponsored free advice lines. Medical costs are high here, as in the rest of the United States. Emergency-room care is the most expensive.

COASTAL HAZARDS

Whether you're merely admiring its natural beauty or braving its waves, the Oregon coast holds potential dangers. Children are especially at risk because they can be easily distracted by tidepools and sandcastle construction, and they may not be aware of tidal changes, changing weather, or other natural dangers. For both adults and children, a little common sense goes a long way.

Hypothermia

The cold temperatures of Oregon's coastal waters (as low as 40–45°F) make swimming and other water sports potentially dangerous any time of year. Even in the hottest days of summer, sea temperature doesn't exceed 62°F. Hypothermia—a condition that sets in when the core temperature of the body drops to 95°F or below—is a danger visitors should be aware of. Hikers and others engaging in outdoor activities away from the water can be at risk as well, particularly when the weather is cool and windy.

One of the first signs of hypothermia is a diminished ability to think and act rationally. Speech can become slurred, and uncontrollable shivering usually takes place. Stumbling,

memory lapses, and drowsiness also tend to characterize those afflicted. Unless the body temperature can be raised several degrees by a knowledgeable helper, cardiac arrhythmia and/or arrest may occur. A wet human body loses heat 23 times faster than a dry one, so getting out of the water and being sheltered from the wind and rain in a dry, warm environment is essential for survival. This might mean placing the victim into a prewarmed sleeping bag, which can be prepared by having another person strip and climb into the bag with the endangered person. Ideally, a groundcloth should be used to insulate the sleeping bag from cold surface temperatures. Internal heat can be generated by feeding the victim high-carbohydrate snacks and hot liquids. Placing wrapped heated objects against the victim's body is also a good way to restore body heat. Be careful, however, not to raise body heat too quickly, which could also cause cardiac problems. If body temperature doesn't drop below 90°F, chances for complete recovery are good; with body temperatures between 80–90°F, victims are more likely to suffer lasting damage. Most victims won't survive a body temperature below 80°F.

Measures you can take to prevent hypothermia include avoiding the cold water of the Pacific, eating a nutritious diet, avoiding overexertion followed by exposure to wet and cold, and dressing warmly in layers of wool and polypropylene. Wool insulates even when wet, and because polypro wicks moisture away from your skin, it makes a good first layer. Gore-Tex and its counterparts, such as Helly-Tech or other new breathable fabrics, make for more comfortable raingear than nylon because they don't become cumbersome and hot. Finally, wear a hat: More radiated heat leaves from the head than from any other part of the body.

Why Not to Swim

Hypothermia aside, casual waders and swimmers alike are at risk of being swept off by riptides or undertows, which occur when one layer of water flows against the direction of the surface water. These powerful, usually localized, currents can be found just about anyplace along the coast and would be a challenge even to swimmers of Olympic ability. What every swimmer must know is that when caught in a riptide, one should swim with or across the current, not against it, which will only exhaust you; rather, try to swim parallel to shore, edging closer and closer to shore until it's possible to come in or call for help.

Floating debris is another concern for swimmers and waders. Storms can churn up inland riverbanks, yielding huge floating logs, which are then carried into shore along the backs of waves. These heavy objects can slam into swimmers or pin them down, so give these potential killers a wide berth.

Sharks

"No, dude, that's a porpoise." That's what one Oregon coast surfer said a moment before the great white shark bit his foot. Although shark attacks are rare in Oregon, with only three recorded between 2000 and 2006, they do occasionally occur.

The most common areas for an attack are places where rivers enter the ocean. Some of these places, such as Florence's South Jetty, are also popular surfing spots. Anyone who goes into the ocean should seriously consider taking some precautions.

Because sharks can detect minute amounts of blood, don't go into the water if you're bleeding—this includes menstruating. Stay near other surfers, and don't go too far out from shore. Avoid areas where anglers have been using bait, or where birds are circling. Also, know that sharks are most active at twilight and after dark, and that they tend to hang out near steep drop-offs. Some experts note that shiny jewelry could resemble fish scales to a shark and that they could be attracted to brightly colored clothing (your rental wet suit will almost certainly be black, making you resemble, above all else, a seal).

If you see a shark, or something you can't quite identify, swim quickly and calmly to shore. If you are attacked by a shark, fight. Try to punch it on the nose, eye, or gills, using your board if possible. Do not play dead! Alert other surfers if they don't hear your screams, and as soon as it lets go, swim to shore immediately.

Boating

Life jackets or vests are strongly advised for anyone aboard a watercraft. In 2003, a tragic fishing accident on Tillamook Bay yielded stark proof that life vests save lives. A 35-foot charter boat capsized while crossing the bar in rough conditions. Eleven people—none wearing life vests—were lost. In addition to keeping a person afloat and face-up, whether or not he or she can swim, the vests provide some insulation from the frigid water, thus decreasing the risk of hypothermia and injury.

State law requires that all children age 12 and younger must wear a Coast Guard–approved personal flotation device (PFD)/life vest while on an open deck or cockpit of sailboats or motorized and nonmotorized vessels (such as canoes, kayaks, rafts). Life vests are a smart idea for small children any time they're near the water.

Dangerous Terrain

Part of the appeal of the coast is its rugged terrain and raw natural state—two features that can also make it a dangerous place to explore. High cliffs, undesignated trails, rocky outcroppings, tidepools, and pocket beaches often lure intrepid hikers bent on getting that perfect view or photo opportunity. These are the same folks who are rescued from clifftops, stranded by a changing tide, or worse. In other words, stay on designated paths, avoid unfenced cliff edges, check your tide tables, and follow signage. The worst damage is often done to the environment, when hikers trample a native species habitat or disturb organisms living in tidal areas. Please stay on paths and avoid climbing on rocks that may be home to living things.

Sneaker Waves

Many a visitor to Oregon's coast has been the victim of the potentially deadly "sneaker wave."

Not as uncommon as one might imagine, these treacherous out-of-nowhere waves have a habit of cropping up when you least expect them. Most prevalent during the stormiest times of the year, sneaker waves are powerful enough to knock an angler from his or her perch or sweep an unsuspecting beachcomber out to sea. Unfortunately, small children are most vulnerable, so constant supervision is a must.

Even the unexpected large breaker can have the same effect as the rogue wave. So, be mindful of the everyday risks of strolling the beach or admiring the vista. Pocket beaches rimmed with cliffs are especially hazardous, as are rocky areas. A flat, gradually sloping sand beach is usually safer, but not without some risk.

Tsunamis

Many people think that tsunami is Japanese for tidal wave. Not so. Tsunami is a Japanese term for harbor wave. But a tsunami is not just one wave; it is a series of waves that are the direct result of seismic activity, such as earthquakes or marine quakes. A tsunami may begin in the middle of the ocean as a two-foot wave heading for shore at several hundred miles per hour—by this definition, it may sound like a great opportunity to put your surfing skills to the test—but once it reaches land or harbor, it can strike with devastating force.

As a tsunami draws closer to the shore, driven by the force of the quake, it takes in preceding waters and builds into a series of waves traveling as fast as 500 miles per hour and reaching as high as 100 feet. Waves of this size would submerge whole towns; smaller ones would cause major property damage and threaten the lives of those in its path.

Along the coast, you will see blue-and-white tsunami evacuation signs, which warn locals and visitors of impending danger and direct them to higher, safer ground. Visitors should also be aware of the global alarm system, which sounds off when tsunami danger is high. To be fully prepared, one must be attuned to any news of seismic activity in the area or in the Pacific Rim. Also note that any dramatic change in water levels (which are not part of the normal tidal activity) may be nature's own early warning that a tsunami may be minutes away.

Getting There and Around

BY AIR

Of the dozen airports on the coast, only North Bend's Southwest Oregon Regional Airport has regularly scheduled commercial service. **Horizon Air** (800/547-9308, www.horizonair.com), the commuter-league farm club of Alaska Airlines, connects Seattle and Portland with directs flights to and from North Bend. Flights to and from other Horizon destinations (in Alaska, Washington, California, Idaho, and beyond) are routed through these hubs. Horizon operates commuter prop planes with 10–40 seats. If you are sensitive to loud noises and pressure change, you may want to ask for earplugs when you check in for your boarding pass.

Newport Municipal Airport, North Bend, and other coastal and inland airports (including Eugene, Medford, Portland, Corvallis, and Grants Pass) are also served by **Sky Taxi** (503/365-0200), a charter service that flies twin-prop Cessnas for up to five passengers.

BY BUS

Greyhound has abandoned most of its coastal routes, making for a patchwork quilt of mass-transit providers on the western edge of the state. Add a dearth of city buses and only two airports serving Oregon's shoreline, and you can understand why it's especially difficult to see this area if you're not traveling by car. In most coastal towns, a local supermarket or convenience store usually acts as the bus stop.

Greyhound (800/229-9424, www.greyhound.com) does still operate a coast route twice daily between Eugene and Coos Bay, via Florence and points in between.

For the north coast, **Amtrak Thruway Motorcoach Service** buses (800/USA-RAIL or 800/872-7245, www.amtrak.com) run a daily coastal loop: Astoria-Warrenton-Gearhart-Seaside-Cannon Beach-Portland's Union Station and back to Astoria.

To get to and from the central coast, **Valley Retriever** (541/265-2253) buses connect Newport with Corvallis Monday–Saturday.

Porter Stage Lines (541/269-7183) runs along the southern Oregon coast, then turns inland at Florence and goes to Eugene, Bend, and Ontario.

Local north coast service in Clatsop County is provided by the Sunset Empire Transportation District, better known as **The Bus** (503/861-RIDE or 800/776-6406, www.ride-thebus.org), which provides reasonably frequent transportation around Astoria and along the coast from Warrenton (including Fort Stevens State Park and Fort Clatsop) to Cannon Beach. It operates Monday–Saturday.

On weekdays, **Lincoln County Transit** (541/265-4900, www.co.lincoln.or.us/transit) runs buses four times daily between Lincoln City and Yachats, with numerous stops en route. On the south coast, **Coastal Express** buses (541/469-6822) run up and down the south coast between North Bend and Brookings, weekdays only.

You'll find additional details on local bus transport in respective destination chapters.

BY CAR
Ever since the "Daddy Train" linking Portland to Seaside shut down in the 1930s, the automobile has been the vehicle of choice for getting to and around the coast.

Routes to the Coast
From the I-5 corridor, where most of the state's population is concentrated, 10 main routes will get you to the coast. All are two-lane highways for all or part of the journey through rural hinterlands and the coastal mountains.

From Portland, **U.S. 30** runs north through St. Helens and follows the bottomlands along the south bank of the Columbia River to Asto-

ria, 98 miles to the northwest. If you're coming down from the north on I-5, cross the Columbia from Longview, Washington, to Rainier, Oregon, and continue west on U.S. 30 from there.

Busy **U.S. 26** runs west, then angles northwest, from Portland, through agricultural Washington County and then into the woods of the Clatsop State Forest before joining U.S. 101 between Cannon Beach and Seaside. About 25 miles west of Portland, **Highway 6** branches off from U.S. 26 and follows a roller-coaster course alongside the Wilson River to Tillamook.

A third route from Portland starts with **Highway 99W** and a dozen maddening stop-and-go miles through the strip development of Tigard. After Newburg you emerge into a lovely countryside of vineyards and hazelnut orchards around Dundee. Pick up **Highway 18** for the second half of the trip, which runs past Oregon's number-one attraction, the Spirit Mountain Casino in Grand Ronde, before you hit the Coast Highway just north of Lincoln City and another Indian-owned casino, Chinook Winds. Note that the casinos attract more than three million visitors per year, which helps make Highway 18 one of the most dangerous roads to drive in the state.

From Salem, **Highway 22** runs 26 miles to the west and connects with Highway 18 about midway to the coast.

Farther south, **U.S. 20** curves down from Albany through Corvallis and on to Philomath. From there you can continue 46 miles to Newport or veer southwest on **Highway 34** for a winding 59 miles through a remote section of the Siuslaw National Forest to Waldport.

Highway 126, from Eugene to Florence, is one of the more direct routes, zipping through the flatlands and foothills before throwing you a few curves on the way to the burg of Mapleton, and then hugging the Siuslaw River the last dozen miles.

Near Curtin, south of Cottage Grove, leave I-5 for a brief detour on Highway 99 before catching **Highway 38.** This scenic two-lane road—Oregon's "foremost motorcycle road," according to Harley-Davidson—follows the valley of the mighty Umpqua River to Reedsport, about a 57-mile trip. If you're coming from the south on I-5, cut off onto **Highway 138** at Sutherlin to save some miles on this route.

Highway 42 shadows the Coquille River through farm country for much of its course from Roseburg to Coos Bay. Recent improvements to this highway make it possible to get there in less than two hours, but it's a longish 87 miles. Motorists should be aware that this thoroughfare carries more truck traffic than any other interior-to-coast road in Oregon. But weekenders will encounter few trucks and light traffic to impede the enjoyment of the waysides, wineries, and historic buildings. If the southern coast is your destination, branch off on **Highway 42S** at Coquille; from there it's 17 miles to Bandon.

South of Roseburg, if you're partial to pavement, there's no good direct route to the coast. The only option is **U.S. 199** from Grants Pass, skirting the remote eastern edge of the Kalmiopsis Wilderness before dropping into northern California. The highway runs through the awesome giants of Redwoods National Park before hitting the Coast Highway near Crescent City, California. From there, it's 22 miles north up to Brookings. All told, count on about two hours to travel this roundabout, albeit beautiful, 100-mile route.

Driving the Oregon Coast Highway (U.S. 101)

The Main Street of the Oregon coast, this 363-mile National Scenic Byway has been designated an "All-American Road," one of 20 in the country selected for their archaeological, cultural, historic, natural, recreational, and scenic importance.

As such, it's a route to be savored, not hurried through—and that's just as well, because sustained high-speed travel is not among the highway's many qualities. Maximum posted speed on U.S. 101 is 55 miles per hour; actual average speed is usually 50 mph or less. Along the way, several beach loops and inland routes are often less traveled and offer some outstanding scenery in their own right.

U.S. 101 is a two-lane road most of the way, with occasional passing lanes and four lanes along the main drags of the larger coastal cities. You can count on heavy traffic during summer and holidays, and chances are you'll spend at least a little time getting to know the rear end of a slow-moving log truck or a lumbering Winnebago. Relax. Be prepared to modify your schedule to accommodate inevitable slowdowns and enjoy the breathtaking scenery surrounding the road.

The automobile may be the first transportation choice for most visitors to the coast, but it's not the only vehicle on the road. Especially in summer, be mindful of bicyclists sharing the shoulder. Hills and dips, tight turns, and foliage can often obscure them from view until the last moment. And always beware of cars whose drivers are paying more attention to the view than to the road. Another consideration for drivers is the fact that the road signs found throughout the state are sometimes less than explicit. Whether it's a turn signpost 50 yards after the fact or directional markers hidden by shrubbery, Oregon seems to have more than its share of unwanted surprises for motorists.

In winter, heavy rain and wind are possible dangers, and you may encounter thick fog just about any time of year.

The Oregon Department of Transportation advises on **road conditions** by phone (800/977-ODOT in Oregon, 503/588-2941 out of state) and via its excellent and comprehensive TripCheck website (www.tripcheck.com).

Fuel

Gas is readily available on the Coast Highway, but motorists heading to the coast via some of the 10 main routes through the coast ranges should be aware that there are long stretches without a drop, so be sure to fill up beforehand. Out-of-state visitors will soon learn that Oregon is one of the few states that does not allow motorists to pump their own gas. This, combined with the gas tax levied to help pay for Oregon's roads, helps give the state some of the highest gas prices in the country.

Car Rentals

Car rental agencies are not unheard of on the coast, but most visitors drive their own vehicles or rent cars at a big-city airport. Renting a car is pain-free, as long as you plan ahead and have a credit card. The rental chains (Avis, Alamo, Budget, Dollar, Enterprise, National, and Thrifty) have outlets in the main population centers and airports (such as Portland, Medford, and Eugene). Astoria has the most car rental agencies on the coast but still far fewer than in larger cities elsewhere. For other locations, check the individual destination chapters in this guide or log on to www.american-car.net/car-rental/OR for a statewide directory of car rental agencies.

You can flip through the Yellow Pages and try to save some bucks with an independent operator, but consider that the larger chains have more service centers set up to assist you in case you break down in a backwater. Although it costs a bit more, we think it's wise to buy the car rental insurance. Members of AAA can call 503/222-6734 to receive guidebooks, maps, and tow, repair, and insurance services applicable to car rental.

RESOURCES

Suggested Reading

NATURAL HISTORY

Alt, David, and Donald W. Hyndman. *Roadside Geology of Oregon.* Missoula, MT: Mountain Press Publishing Company, 2003. Part of the fine Roadside Geology Series, the coast chapters describe, in layman's language, the geologic forces that shaped the region.

Evanich, Joseph E., Jr. *Birder's Guide to Oregon.* Portland, OR: Audubon Society of Portland, 2003. A good all-around guide to the state's birdlife, with a useful breakdown of specific coastal locations and details on what species to watch for and when.

Paulson, Dennis. *Shorebirds of the Pacific Northwest.* Seattle, WA: University of Washington Press, 2003. For the specialist rather than the generalist, there is no better book than this richly detailed guide for distinguishing an avocet from a stilt, a plover from a curlew, and identifying any of the dozens of other species found near the water's edge.

Pojar, Jim, and Andy MacKinnon (eds.). *Plants of the Pacific Northwest Coast: Washington, Oregon, British Columbia, and Alaska.* Edmonton, Alberta: Lone Pine Publishing, 2003. A highly regarded guide, illustrated with excellent photos, to the flora of the entire Northwest region.

Sept, J. Duane. *The Beachcomber's Guide to Seashore Life in the Pacific Northwest.* Vancouver, British Columbia: Harbour Publishing Company Limited, 2003. This ideal guide for the casual and curious observer aids in understanding the intertidal zone and in identifying more than 270 species encountered there, including crabs, clams, and other mollusks, seaweeds, sea stars, sea anemones, and more.

Yuskavitch, James A. *Oregon Wildlife Viewing Guide.* Helena, MT: Falcon Publishing Company, 1994. Not limited to the coast, this highly regarded resource covers 87 wildlife-viewing areas statewide, with detailed regional maps and tips on successful wildlife watching.

HISTORY

Beckham, Steven Dow, and Robert M. Reynolds (photographer). *Lewis & Clark from the Rockies to the Pacific.* Portland, OR: Graphic Arts Center Publishing Co., 2002. Focusing on the second half of the expedition's outward-bound journey, this gorgeously illustrated and insightful book covers Lewis and Clark's trying months spent camped in the rainy woodlands of the north Oregon coast.

Friedman, Ralph. *In Search of Western Oregon.* Caldwell, ID: Caxton Press, 1991. A fascinating read, packed with anecdotes, folklore, historical details, and more, all told in Friedman's engaging style.

Gibbs, James A. *Shipwrecks of the Pacific Coast* Portland, OR: Binford and Mort, 1989. Endlessly fascinating and frequently heartbreaking reading from a master of Northwest maritime lore. This book covers all known shipwrecks off the coasts of Oregon, Washington, and California.

Hadlow, Robert W. *Elegant Arches, Soaring Spans: C.B. McCullough Oregon's Master Bridge Builder.* Corvallis, OR: Oregon State University Press, 2003. Driving U.S. 101 along the Oregon coast wouldn't be the same without the dozen beautiful bridges designed by McCullough between the two world wars, and which he called "jeweled clasps in a wonderful string of pearls."

O'Donnell, Terence. *Cannon Beach: A Place by the Sea.* Portland, OR: Oregon Historical Society, 1996. A highly personal historical evocation of life in Cannon Beach and environs.

SPORTS AND RECREATION

Henderson, Bonnie. *Exploring the Wild Oregon Coast.* Seattle, WA: Mountaineers Books, 1994. Primarily a hiking guide, covering several lesser-known but rewarding hikes, and enriched with an abundance of information on flora and fauna.

Ostertag, Rhonda, and George Ostertag. *75 Hikes in the Oregon's Coast Range and Siskiyous* Seattle, WA: Mountaineers Books, 2003. A well-chosen selection of hikes along the length of the coastal ranges covers a broad variety of terrain and difficulty levels. Detailed trail descriptions and maps make this guide particularly useful.

Stienstra, Tom. *Moon Oregon Camping.* Emeryville, CA: Avalon Travel Publishing, 2006. Details more than 700 campgrounds across the state, with an excellent selection on the coast. Rich with tips on gear, safety, and other topics.

Sullivan, William. *100 Hikes Travel Guide: Oregon Coast and Coast Range.* Eugene, OR: Navillus Press, 2002. Hikes and tips from Oregon's best chronicler of hiking trails.

DESCRIPTION AND TRAVEL

Irving, Stephanie (ed.). *Best Places Destinations: Oregon Coast.* Seattle, WA: Sasquatch Books, 2003. Highly selective but reliable recommendations on where to stay and eat and what to see and do.

Nelson, Sharlene, and Ted Nelson (contributor). *Umbrella Guide to Oregon Lighthouses.* Kenmore, WA: Epicenter Press, 2003. Tells the stories of 11 Oregon coast lighthouses, as well as beacons on the Columbia and Willamette rivers. A good reference for anyone curious about these romantic aids to navigation.

Oberrecht, Kenn. *Driving the Pacific Coast Oregon and Washington: Scenic Driving Tours along Coastal Highways.* Guilford, CT: Globe Pequot Press, 2000. Compact and practical guide covers recreation, shopping, camping, dining, and lodging—with an emphasis on budget options—along U.S. 101, with interesting bits of history thrown into the mix.

Oberrecht, Kenn. *Oregon Coastal Access Guide: A Mile-By-Mile Guide to Scenic and Recreational Attractions.* Corvallis, OR: Oregon State University Press, 2003. Meticulously researched and informative guide to major sights, natural features, and recreational opportunities. Contains no restaurant or lodging info, but is an eminently useful resource for travelers nonetheless.

Internet Resources

PARKS AND PUBLIC LANDS

Oregon State Parks
www.oregonstateparks.org

Descriptions, maps, contact information, and more details on all Oregon state parks.

ReserveAmerica
www.reserveamerica.com

The central site for reserving campgrounds in the national forests and Oregon Dunes National Recreation Area.

Siskiyou National Forest
www.fs.fed.us/r6/siskiyou

Details on recreation, camping, and resources in the national forest.

Siuslaw National Forest
www.fs.fed.us/r6/siuslaw

Details on recreation, camping, and resources in the national forest and the Oregon Dunes National Recreation Area.

U.S. Bureau of Land Management
www.or.blm.gov

The BLM manages numerous recreational sites along the coast and the coastal mountains, including the Dean Creek Elk Viewing Area, Yaquina Head Outstanding Natural Area, and Cape Blanco Lighthouse.

RECREATION

Oregon Department of Fish and Wildlife
www.dfw.state.or.us

Complete details on fishing and hunting seasons, licenses, regulations, and more. Includes useful species-identification charts.

Oregon State Marine Board
www.boatoregon.com

Extensive information on boating safety, ramps and other facilities, bar conditions, and more.

Surf Forecasts
www.magicseaweed.com

User-driven surf forecasting service includes forecasts, graphs, and charts designed specifically for surfers.

Surfrider Foundation
www.surfrider.org

A nonprofit organization working to preserve oceans, waves, and beaches, including beach access.

Tide Predictions
www.saltwatertides.com

Current and future tide-prediction charts for three dozen coastal Oregon locations.

Whale Watching Spoken Here
http://whalespoken.org

Volunteer organization assists visitors with spotting whales at 29 sites from southern Washington to northern California.

INFORMATION AND TRAVEL SERVICES

AAA Oregon/Idaho
www.aaaorid.com

For members only, this site provides travel planning and booking services, plus detailed maps of each coastal county. Its *Oregon Coast Tour Map* is particularly good.

Oregon Coast Visitors Association
www.visittheoregoncoast.com

A good clearinghouse of information for the entire coast, including events listings, weather, and links to all coastal chambers of commerce.

Oregon Tourism Commission
www.traveloregon.com

A good statewide resource for useful free maps and pamphlets and extensive listings of lodgings and activities.

TRANSPORTATION

Amtrak
www.amtrak.com

Operates train service between Portland and Astoria, as well as bus service between Portland and other north coast towns.

Greyhound
www.greyhound.com

Operates a coast route twice daily between Portland and Brookings.

Oregon Department of Transportation Road Conditions
www.tripcheck.com

Displays current road conditions and advisories.

CHAMBERS OF COMMERCE AND VISITORS CENTERS

Astoria-Warrenton Area Chamber
www.oldoregon.com

Bandon Chamber of Commerce
www.bandon.com

Bay Area Chamber of Commerce
www.oregonsbayareachamber.com

Brookings/Harbor Chamber of Commerce
www.brookingsor.com

Cannon Beach Chamber of Commerce
www.cannonbeach.org

Depoe Bay Chamber of Commerce
www.depoebaychamber.org

Florence Area Chamber of Commerce
www.florencechamber.com

Garibaldi Chamber of Commerce
www.garibaldichamber.com

Gold Beach Promotion Committee
www.goldbeach.org

Greater Newport Chamber of Commerce
www.newportchamber.org

Lincoln City Chamber of Commerce
www.oregoncoast.org

Nehalem Bay Area Chamber of Commerce
www.nehalembaychamber.com

Port Orford Chamber of Commerce
www.portorfordoregon.com

Reedsport/Winchester Bay Chamber of Commerce
www.reedsportcc.org

Rockaway Beach Chamber of Commerce
www.rockawaybeach.net

Seaside Oregon Visitor Bureau
www.seasidechamber.com

Tillamook Chamber of Commerce
www.tillamookchamber.org

Waldport Chamber of Commerce
www.waldport-chamber.com

Yachats Area Chamber of Commerce
www.yachats.org

Index

MUSEUMS

SURFING

T

www.moon.com

For helpful advice on planning a trip, visit www.moon.com for the **TRAVEL PLANNER** and get access to useful travel strategies and valuable information about great places to visit. When you travel with Moon, expect an experience that is uncommon and truly unique.

HANDBOOKS | METRO | OUTDOORS | LIVING ABROAD

MAP SYMBOLS

≡≡≡ Expressway	◖ Highlight	✗ Airfield	⚓ Golf Course
⋯⋯ Primary Road	○ City/Town	✈ Airport	🅿 Parking Area
─── Secondary Road	◉ State Capital	▲ Mountain	▰ Archaeological Site
⋯⋯ Unpaved Road	◉ National Capital	✛ Unique Natural Feature	⚑ Church
------- Trail	★ Point of Interest		⛽ Gas Station
⋯⋯⋯ Ferry	• Accommodation	⚐ Waterfall	Glacier
⋯⋯⋯ Railroad	▼ Restaurant/Bar	▲ Park	Mangrove
≡≡≡ Pedestrian Walkway	■ Other Location	▣ Trailhead	Reef
⊞⊞⊞ Stairs	Λ Campground	⛷ Skiing Area	Swamp

CONVERSION TABLES

$°C = (°F - 32) / 1.8$
$°F = (°C \times 1.8) + 32$
1 inch = 2.54 centimeters (cm)
1 foot = 0.304 meters (m)
1 yard = 0.914 meters
1 mile = 1.6093 kilometers (km)
1 km = 0.6214 miles
1 fathom = 1.8288 m
1 chain = 20.1168 m
1 furlong = 201.168 m
1 acre = 0.4047 hectares
1 sq km = 100 hectares
1 sq mile = 2.59 square km
1 ounce = 28.35 grams
1 pound = 0.4536 kilograms
1 short ton = 0.90718 metric ton
1 short ton = 2,000 pounds
1 long ton = 1.016 metric tons
1 long ton = 2,240 pounds
1 metric ton = 1,000 kilograms
1 quart = 0.94635 liters
1 US gallon = 3.7854 liters
1 Imperial gallon = 4.5459 liters
1 nautical mile = 1.852 km

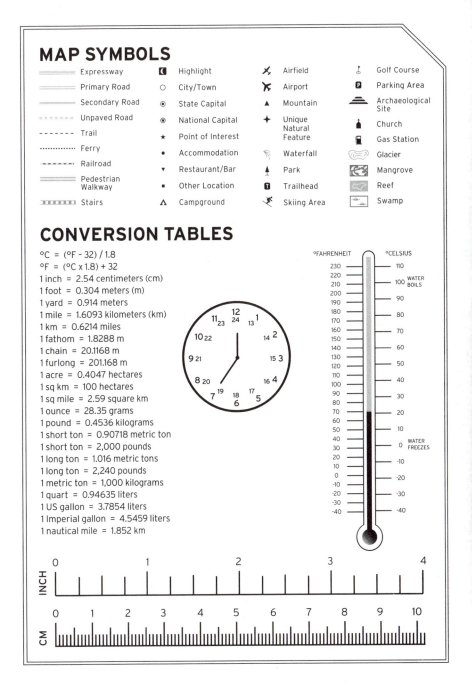

MOON COASTAL OREGON

Avalon Travel Publishing
An Imprint of
Avalon Publishing Group, Inc.

AVALON
publishing group incorporated

1400 65th Street, Suite 250
Emeryville, CA 94608, USA
www.moon.com

Editor: Elizabeth McCue
Series Manager: Kathryn Ettinger
Acquisitions Manager: Rebecca K. Browning
Copy Editor: Valerie Sellers Blanton
Graphics Coordinator: Stefano Boni
Cover Designer: Stefano Boni
Production Coordinator: Darren Alessi
Map Editor: Albert Angulo
Cartographers: Kat Bennett, Mike Morgenfeld
Cartography Director: Mike Morgenfeld
Indexer: Judy Hunt

ISBN-10: 1-56691-926-6
ISBN-13: 978-1-56691-926-5
ISSN: 1546-136X

Printing History
1st Edition – 2004
2nd Edition – May 2007
5 4 3 2 1

Text © 2007 by Elizabeth and Mark Morris.
Maps © 2007 by Avalon Travel Publishing, Inc.
All rights reserved.

Some photos and illustrations are used by permission
and are the property of the original copyright
owners.

Front cover photo: Bandon Beach © Marc Muench
Title page photo: Coquille River Lighthouse
        © Michael McClure

Printed in the United States by Malloy, Inc.

Moon Handbooks and the Moon logo are the property
of Avalon Travel Publishing, an imprint of Avalon
Publishing Group, Inc. All other marks and logos
depicted are the property of the original owners.
All rights reserved. No part of this book may be
translated or reproduced in any form, except brief
extracts by a reviewer for the purpose of a review,
without written permission of the copyright owner.

Although every effort was made to ensure that
the information was correct at the time of going
to press, the author and publisher do not assume
and hereby disclaim any liability to any party for any
loss or damage caused by errors, omissions, or any
potential travel disruption due to labor or financial
difficulty, whether such errors or omissions result
from negligence, accident, or any other cause.

KEEPING CURRENT

If you have a favorite gem you'd like to see included in the next edition, or see anything
that needs updating, clarification, or correction, please drop us a line. Send your
comments via email to feedback@moon.com, or use the address above.